The New History of England

General Editors
A.G. Dickens and Norman Gash

The New History of England

* In preparation; all other
titles published

Government and Community

England 1450 – 1509

J. R. Lander

Edward Arnold

A division of Hodder & Stoughton

LONDON   MELBOURNE   AUCKLAND

© 1980 J. R. Lander

First published in Great Britain 1980
Reprinted 1983, 1988

British Library Cataloguing in Publication Data

Lander, Jack Robert
   Government and community. — (New history of England; no.1)
   1. Great Britain — History — Wars of the Roses, 1455—1485
   2. Great Britain — History — Tudors, 1485—1603
   I. Title   II. Series
   942.04   DA250

ISBN 0—7131—6152—3 Pbk

Printed and bound in Great Britain for Edward Arnold, the
educational, academic and medical publishing division of Hodder and
Stoughton Limited, 41 Bedford Square, London WC1B 3DQ by
Athenaeum Press Ltd, Newcastle upon Tyne.

Contents

Preface

Any informed reader of this book will immediately perceive my immense debts to other scholars, in particular to the works of Mrs M. Bowker, Professor S.B. Chrimes, Dr P. Heath, Dr C. Ross, Dr R.L. Storey and Dr B.P. Wolffe, to name only a few though the list could be much extended. I should also like to thank Dr J.G. Rowe for his valuable comments on the chapter on religious life. Professor A.G. Dickens read the entire typescript and I owe him a debt of gratitude for many helpful comments and suggestions which have much improved the book. Finally I should like to thank Mrs R. Lemon and Miss M.P. Forani, secretaries of the Department of History of the University of Western Ontario, for their painstaking work upon the typescript.

J.R. Lander
London, Ontario, March 1978

Introduction

That historians have become constant revisionists is a truism, even a cliché, but the extent and timing of revision for various periods has varied immensely. For decades the fifteenth was a badly neglected century. Up to the late 1940s scholars were more attracted, on the one side, to the twelfth and thirteenth centuries with their magnificent Latin chronicles and their absorbing problems of the origins of English institutions and, on the other, to the sixteenth and seventeenth centuries with their growing volume of revealing state papers, intimate letters and personal diaries and their great themes of religious and constitutional development. By contrast the fifteenth century, especially the late fifteenth century, seemed devoid of significant developments. Its masses of administrative records were, and still are, distinctly unalluring and were little studied. Its mostly jejeune chronicles depicted an age given over to senseless bloodshed and violence, a kind of unfortunate hiatus between ages of far greater achievement. For the common reader the century became the domain of the historical novelist and the romancer. Although numerous specialized articles were published, none of this mass of writing produced major reinterpretations.[1] In their general interpretations professional historians were generally content tacitly to accept the melancholy verdict of William Stubbs who asserted 'the most enthusiastic admirer of medieval life must grant that all that was good and great in it was languishing even to death' and that it was 'a worn-out, helpless age that calls for pity without sympathy and yet balances weariness with something like regrets'.

Practically everything was condemned. Constitutional historians lamented the failure of the fabled Lancastrian constitutional experiment and the supposed rise of bastard feudalism dominated by a violent and thuggish aristocracy, with deleterious consequences for the state of public order. Literary critics rightly condemned the age's long-winded prose and post-Chaucerian courtly poetry, though excepting from their condemnation its lyric poetry and Malory's

---

[1] See J.R. Lander, *Crown and Nobility, 1450 – 1509* (1976), pp. 1 – 2.

1

Morte d' Arthur. Ecclesiastical historians trounced the laxity and decay of the church and art critics were distinctly cool in their reactions to the Perpendicular though some architects, like G.F. Bodley as early as 1876, were much more discerning. The only bright spot was the contention of the pioneer economic historian, Thorold Rogers, that the fifteenth century was a golden age for the peasant, the labourer and the artisan.

Since the late 1940s, however, a younger generation of historians has possessed the fortitude to devote its years to the perusal of the century's dreary records — and with notable results. This book is an attempt to incorporate their findings, which constitute, in effect, a very considerable revision of the social, governmental, administrative and ecclesiastical background. Against this new background it is now possible to some extent, as in the second part of the book, to reassess and to analyse more critically the attitudes and statements of the chroniclers. It is thus possible to produce a more convincing narrative of political events than formerly, though still a narrative that is often uncertain and dark from enormous gaps in the information available. In particular, the limited nature of the sources, their lack of intimate, personal information leaves the thoughts of statesmen almost impenetrably obscure. The unfortunate historian is thrown back upon the dubious expedient of deducing their motives from their actions — a hit and miss process both inevitable and unsatisfactory.

Modern research has completely vindicated Thorold Rogers's claim that the fifteenth century was a golden age for the masses, though, of course, by twentieth-century standards their level of existence was still extremely low. The major writers, with the exception of Malory, remain deservedly unread, but late Perpendicular architecture has come into is own again and social historians recognize the fifteenth century as the first great period of English domestic architecture, an epoch of rising amenity and standards of comfort. The endowment of colleges and chantries made it one of the great centuries of religious benefaction. The faithful of all classes lavished immense sums of money upon the reconstruction and decoration of their parish churches. The years from about 1480 to the Reformation were years of the great rebuilding of English urban and village churches — surely an indication that the majority of people were well enough content with the state of the church. Though some of them were almost completely absorbed in politics and secular administration, a number of bishops were more conscientious than they have often been given credit for. In several areas the standards of the parish clergy showed a marked improvement. Many more were university graduates at the end than at the beginning of the century and the proliferation of endowed, and other, grammar schools, uneven though it was geographically, gave the rest, as it gave contemporary laymen, wider opportunities to achieve an improved standard of education.

Nearly forty years ago V.H. Galbraith wrote: 'In the middle ages the members of the ruling class were in general men of arrested intellectual development who looked to those below them in the social scale for the intelligence necessary to order and govern society.'[2] His opinions at the time roused little protest. Indeed, it was generally accepted that the nobility ranked among the most brutal and selfish members of medieval society. Even allowing for the unlikely possibility that this was true of earlier centuries, it was certainly untrue of the fifteenth. Writers today exhibit more commonsense than to condemn an entire social class in such a terrifying wholesale manner. Some members of the aristocracy like John, duke of Norfolk (died 1461) and Lord Egremont (died 1460) were certainly disreputable thugs by any standards. On the other hand their contemporary, Humphrey Stafford, duke of Buckingham (died 1460) was a responsible statesman, always anxious to reconcile conflicting factions, and Anthony, Earl Ryvers (died 1483) was a cultivated patron of Caxton. His translation of *The Dictes and Sayings of the Philosophers* was the first book to be printed in England. At the same time he was a shrewd estate manager, while his reputation for uprightness and piety was so high that, after his execution by Richard III, the Carmelite friars of Doncaster preserved and venerated his hair shirt like a relic.

Nowhere, perhaps, has modern opinion changed so much as in its estimation of the nobility. Turbulent they certainly were, prone to quarrelling among themselves and acutely jealous of their local spheres of interest. Even so, the government of the realm was very much a matter of cooperation between the crown and the nobility through their networks of local affinities which were one of the principal methods of social control—those networks of bastard feudalism which historians for so long so little understood and so much abused. Evil they could be if they got out of hand, but in the absence of a police force, a standing army and a bureaucracy, and the lack of money to pay for such things, bastard feudalism was an essential part of contemporary government.

Nor did the nobility rush like the Gadarene swine into the Wars of the Roses. With estates scattered in many parts of the country they, above all people, had too much to lose from civil war. Their quarrels and their local violence towards each other did not easily burst through into treason against the king. Throughout the 1450s Richard, duke of York, conspicuously failed to attract the support of

[2] V.H. Galbraith, 'A New Life of Richard II', *History* XXXI (1941 – 2), p 227.

his fellow peers. The so-called 'Yorkist party' of that decade is a modern myth. Only the series of crises between 1459 and 1461 at last forced the peerage to take sides to the extent that about four fifths of them fought in the battles of those years. They never took the same risks again. During the later dynastic crises the majority remained cautiously aloof.

The fifteenth century was a somewhat confused age. As we have seen, standards in many ways were rising. People's expectations may also have been rising but they remained curiously conservative in their attitude to government. Judging from their increasing desire to sit in parliament, shown by their partial takeover of the borough representation, the gentry were taking an increasing interest in the government of the country. Yet there was little or no innovation in the forms of administration. Indeed, in one way that interest was distinctly restrictive. The political nation instinctively clung to traditional mores, that is government by the rich, by the small aristocratic and gentry class, no more than two or three per cent of the population, who dominated local affairs. Local government was the domain of the local men of property.

Although the commons, in parliament and elsewhere, ceaselessly complained of disorder and clamoured for 'good governance', they saw the solution to the problem rather negatively in the better working of existing custom rather than in terms of any extension of central control. The statutes of Henry VII's reign in particular seem to show a distinct reluctance to allow any long-term extension of royal power. Many of them were to remain in force for only a limited period and even the famous act of 1504 against retaining was to last only for the king's lifetime. This attitude became persistent and enduring in the English political nation — the attitude of local resistance to central control which became so prominent in the opposition to the early Stuarts and which finally triumphed after 1688.

Against this deeper knowledge of the social background, politics, in the second part of the book, can be more realistically assessed. Most important from this point of view have been Dr B.P. Wolffe's discoveries about Yorkist and early Tudor government finance. Financial attitudes and realities reinforced restrictive attitudes towards government. The period 1450 to 1509 was one of financial retreat for the monarchy. Since the mid-fourteenth century the expansion of English cloth manufacture had drastically reduced the amount of raw wool available for export and with it the yield of the customs revenues. Equally distressing, by 1450 the English had become adamantly and successfully resistant to personal taxation. By this time, the system of personal taxation, the fifteenth and tenth, was hopelessly antiquated, its rigid assessments unchanged for more than a century and totally inadequate. The adage, 'the king should live of his own', had become almost a dogma. Faced with such an attitude, the insecure Yorkists and Henry VII could do no other than let sleeping dogs lie. It would have been politically too dangerous to attempt to reform the taxation system so they were forced to exist mainly on the profits of the crown lands and the diminished customs revenues. Even this failed to satisfy the Commons. By 1509 they strongly resented Henry VII's exploitation of 'his own' as excessively harsh, too much directed towards the production of cash revenue from the crown lands and feudal rights and too little directed towards the dispensing of patronage for their benefit.

Edward IV and Henry VII, careful as they were in financial matters, both died with the unsavoury reputation of avaricious tyrants. Yet the niggling attitude of their subjects had limited them at every turn. Lack of money prevented any extension of central power, even if they ever thought in such terms. It also forced them into comparative isolation. As the French campaigns of 1475 and 1489 showed, the pecuniary demands of an expensive foreign policy produced extremely dangerous domestic tensions. They learned the lesson that they could not afford any kind of foreign policy which had to be financed from the proceeds of taxation. Adverse criticism of their supposedly squalid diplomatic manoeuvres has, therefore, been largely misdirected and based upon misunderstanding. Their weakness was not so much the result of indecision or temperamental avarice as the result of the attitudes of their subjects.

When I first began to write this book it was intended to cover the years from 1461 onwards. It soon became apparent, however, that some account of the tumultuous politics of the 1450s was necessary for any understanding of the Yorkist period. Some readers may consider the allocation of space between various topics unbalanced and eccentric. Both the quality of source materials and the amount of information available from modern researches, however, vary immensely from subject to subject and from decade to decade of the period under review. It therefore seemed better in the end to allow the material to dictate the length of particular essays or chapters rather than to aspire to any kind of artificial unity. A writer almost inevitably laments restrictions of space and in this volume such restrictions have ruled out the discussion of many interesting topics, especially the development of music, sculpture, the minor arts and lyric poetry.

I Government and Society

1 Economic Life

I

The economic life of fifteenth-century England has always been a dark pool of obscurity and historians have so far failed to produce a convincing consensus of opinion upon its tendencies. Wide-sweeping generalizations about countrywide depression and slump popular a generation or so ago have now given place to conceptions of more diversified regional economies with dissimilar economic developments. Fifteenth-century England was indeed much more regionalized than it is today. In the 1530s the antiquary, John Leland, could write of his tour of Lancashire as if it were a visit to a wild, foreign land and even in the early seventeenth century, according to Henry Spelman, Norfolk was 'an island' set apart from the nation at large. In addition to the vast agricultural and social differences between the pastoral areas of the north and west and the wide grain-producing plains of the Midlands, geography and geology could produce different agrarian and social conditions a few miles distant within the same county. Southern Warwickshire, south of the River Avon, known to contemporaries as the Felden, was manorial with a preponderance of grain crops; in the northern part, the Wealden, a far greater proportion of the land was devoted to cattle and sheep-rearing.

England was still overwhelmingly an agrarian country for nine tenths of the people lived more or less directly from the land. Probably no greater proportion of the population lived in towns than in Anglo-Saxon times and much writing about industry, particularly the cloth industry, has unfortunately conveyed a totally exaggerated impression of its proportionate economic importance. By 1500 England's one major industry possibly employed 30,000 people, or about 1.3 per cent of the population, full time. Although the industry, as a supplement to peasant agriculture particularly in pastoral regions, provided part-time work for a great many more people, it was still insignificant as compared with the contribution of agriculture to the national economy.

9

In such an economy the harvest was the harsh, fundamental fact of life, the vital autumnal event which predicted a rude plenty or hunger, acute deprivation, even starvation and disease for the coming year. In a 'normal' decade about one harvest in every four would be, in some degree, deficient, one in six really bad. We still know all too little about the Yorkist period in general, but from 1480 Dr W.G. Hoskins's work has produced really vital evidence. Edward IV's reign ended in dearth, with three bad harvests in a row, 1481 to 1483. There was only one really good harvest for the next six years, that of 1485, the rest being merely average. The 1490s were a golden decade. Five out of ten of the harvests proved plentiful. Only one was deficient. Unfortunately four bad years (1500 – 1503) followed upon the golden decade, but from 1504 onwards the harvests once more varied from average to abundant.

These harvest fluctuations produced price fluctuations so violent as to be almost inconceivable even in these days when inflation is the perennial topic of discussion. The year 1482 saw a leap of 74.7 per cent[1] in the price of wheat, and the failure of the grain harvest generally appears to have driven up other food prices whether or not it was accompanied (as it often was) by cattle murrain and sheep rot. Such fluctuations were appalling for a population one third of which lived below the poverty line, another third close upon it, spending, perhaps, even in good years as much as eighty or ninety per cent of their incomes on food alone. For families of this kind, with no reserves of either food or money, poor harvests meant the pangs of starvation and the prospect of death—and death as the consequence of malnutrition must, over the years, have carried off more of the poor than death in the battles of the Wars of the Roses and the brief continental military campaigns of the times.

The early fourteenth century had been a turning point in English economic development. The great famine of 1315 – 17, followed by lean years in the early 1320s, hit a population already in excess of the numbers which the country could support—a Malthusian demographic crisis in which agrarian output per head had become insufficient to sustain an adequate level of nutrition. It is possible that some regions and some estates never fully recovered from this catastrophe. Then the Black Death of 1349 and subsequent, and only slightly less lethal, outbreaks of bubonic and other types of plague resulted in a decline in population from about 3.75 to about 2.1 millions by the end of the century. No one would deny the physical and spiritual horrors of the plague years, but in the end the epidemics were a blessing in disguise for the surviving population. The excessive

[1] Calculated by Dr Hoskins on a thirty-one year moving average, that is more or less a human generation at this period. Fluctuations from year to year could be even more violent.

subdivision of tenements beyond the point where they were economically viable ceased. Former landless families were able to obtain farms. If rates in the building trades may be regarded as typical, real wages doubled between the Black Death and the battle of Agincourt (1415) and remained at the same high level until about 1510 when they began that massive decline which marked the sixteenth century. As Thorold Rogers claimed, the fifteenth century was a comparatively golden age for the artisan and the labourer. This is not to say that poverty was not ever present. It always is in underdeveloped agrarian economies where the demand for labour fluctuates violently with the seasons and a large proportion of the population is, perforce, underemployed. Professor Hoskins has calculated that probably one third of the population in the early Tudor towns were more or less destitute and it is most likely that his conclusions apply equally well to the fifteenth century. Many towns spent considerable weekly sums upon poor relief. As early as 1473 parliament passed a statute against that notorious Tudor horror, the sturdy beggar, and the town authorities of Romney in Kent in the last quarter of the century passed repressive local legislation against vagabonds and vagrants, generally migrants from the countryside.

II

On the other hand, historians have often claimed that the decline in population produced nightmarish conditions of decline for the landlord class. Apparent evidence of economic decay littered the countryside for a century and a half after the Black Death. Marginal land passed out of cultivation, reverting to waste and scrub, abandoned farm buildings fell into ruin, towns complained of numerous unoccupied tenements. The assertion of universal decline is, however, extremely dubious for, as remarked earlier, England was a land of varying regions — regions which experienced diverse economic development.

Landlords certainly experienced more difficult conditions. Owing to the difficulties and high expenses of administration, large-scale direct administration of their estates — demesne farming — could yield good profits only in days of low wages and high prices. By the end of the fourteenth century most great landlords had switched from direct exploitation to a system of leases. This did not, however, mean, as some historians have misleadingly claimed, that they became mere *rentiers* completely devoid of any active interest in the estates which

they possessed. By modern standards corruption was universal at all
levels of society and any landlord who did not take an active interest in
his estates would soon have found his income declining. Landlords
became estate managers, many of them, indeed, vigilant enough to
achieve the dubious reputation of grasping, avaricious exploiters, no
less harsh than their more notorious Tudor successors.

For some estates bulky evidence in the way of surviving accounts
exists—but mere bulk does not always mean comprehensiveness. Our
knowledge is, on the whole, poor and deceptive for lay estates.[2] By the
end of the fourteenth century on many estates trusted servants of a
lord's central administration rather than the local manorial officials
were collecting the very valuable 'casualties' (that is irregular sources
of income) such as entry fines, wood sales and the profits of mining,
quarrying and brick-making. Often these officials then paid them
directly into the lord's coffers, so that they were not recorded even in
the accounts of the receiver general.

Such limitations must be borne in mind in the following discussion
of particular estates. The rents of some estates, particularly in the
corn-growing districts of the Midlands and East Anglia, were acutely
depressed during the first half of the fifteenth century. The monastic
houses of Leicestershire and Ramsey Abbey in Huntingdonshire
suffered a severe decline in their incomes, but there is insufficient
evidence from the later part of the century to enable us to say whether
or not they recovered. The Whitchurch lands of the Talbot earls of
Shrewsbury in northern Shropshire—a compact estate of about
32,000 acres of mixed farm land—showed a marked decline in
income. Copyhold rents remained remarkably stable during most of
the century, with a modest increase of about eight per cent during the
1460s and the 1470s. Demesne rents, however, dropped about 36 per
cent between 1400 and 1437 and thereafter remained stable. The
greatest fall, however, took place in the seigneurial revenues, the
profits of lordship, of the three courts baron and one court leet, and of
the farms of mills and tolls, which fell by 75 per cent in the course of
the century—a catastrophic decline which may have been due to the
estates' proximity to Wales and the Marches where seigneurial control
weakened far more than anywhere else in the course of the century.[3]

The same may be true of the Welsh estates of the duchy of
York—though the York estates elsewhere in England seem to have
been badly run. The Yorkist administration failed completely to
cream off higher rents from the developing cloth industry of Bisley,
part of the advancing cloth district known as Stroudwater, in

---

[2] It is possible, though unproven, that such strictures may not apply to ecclesiastical estates.

[3] See below, chapter 2, p. 46.

Gloucestershire. In the 1450s the tenants of Longford's Mill, then a fulling mill and still a well-known cloth factory today, paid the duke an annual rent of £15 4s. ½d. and sublet for 66s. 8d. From the early fifteenth century to the reign of Henry VIII income from the manor of Bisley remained more or less static and its accounts were a complete farce: tenants' names recur unchanged for a century and more, even after 1461 when the manor became part of the royal estates and Edward IV was making a determined effort to tighten up the entire administration of the royal demesne. The Yorkist estate accounts are too fragmentary to yield firm conclusions. However the gross value of all the lands stood at £8,800 or more,[4] but their net value, or the cash income after the deduction of administrative espenses was no more than £4,500.[5] Leakage of revenue seems to have been extraordinarily high—about 19 or 20 per cent on the returns—so that the income available may have been no more than £3,500.

The Percy earls of Northumberland were also unfortunate. If they had not increased their properties their agrarian income would have shrunk by a quarter between 1416 and 1460. Most of the loss, however, occurred before 1437 when, owing to the treason of Earl Henry Percy I, the estates, confiscated under an act of attainder, had been dispersed among several holders and were only returned to the family in piecemeal fashion. A lack of administrative continuity had probably contributed to the decline. Although later rents remained remarkably stable, there may have been a considerable increase in the rate of entry fines between the mid-fifteenth century and 1510 – 20. Even so, during the first four decades of the sixteenth century the Percy rent roll fell behind the rising prices of the times.

Other lords seems to have been more fortunate. Experience in the duchy of Lancaster was mixed. Unfortunately figures for the whole vast complex of these estates do not exist; some, however, showed a considerably higher yield, others declined.[5] The Greys of Ruthyn, always vigilant estate managers, fortunate that there was no minority in the family for over a century, fortunate also that the continuity of their administration was never broken by the political hazards of attainder and forfeiture, maintained a remarkably consistent income from their thirty-four manors over the whole century, with a rise of about five per cent in gross income in the two decades after 1467.

In the southwest in Devon the estates of Tavistock Abbey were more buoyant than in former times. Between 1451 and the dissolution Tavistock was prosperous enough to rebuild on a very extensive scale

---

[4] Excluding Irish lands and certain hereditary annuities to which the dukes were entitled at the Exchequer. English monetary figures in the text are given in pounds, shillings and pence sterling.

[5] See below, chapter 3.

and, very unusually, after 1492 to enlarge the numbers of the community. Cornwall presents contrasting experiences. The manors of the duchy of Cornwall on the western side and in the central areas of the country showed a ten per cent decline in income between 1400 and 1460 and then seem to have stabilized for the rest of the century. On the eastern side growing output of tin in the Stannaries, the rapid advance of local textile manufacture and the prosperity of the western ports stimulated a sharp increase in the demand for food and, therefore, for land. By 1460 the eastern manors of the duchy were showing unmistakable signs of prosperity with revenues from 15 to 40 per cent higher than those of 1400 — a buoyancy which continued under the Yorkists. In addition to rising trade and population these increases in revenue must also have been due in part to a firm and determined ducal administration, for the revenues of other manors which had been granted out between 1369 and 1459 had been allowed to stagnate. Then in 1459 their assession fines were drastically increased (by 11 − 15 per cent).

To turn to southeastern England, to Kent, the income of Christchurch Priory, Canterbury, reached a record figure of over £4,000 in 1411. Although this figure declined by some 22 per cent by 1469 and although the monks were from time to time in debt, there was obviously no real shortage of money: there was enough to meet the immense cost of rebuilding the nave of the cathedral (1391 − 1411) and at the end of the century to rebuild the great central tower, Bell Harry (1490 − 97), not to mention the expenditure of £1,500 between 1449 and 1472 on the reclamation of Appledore Marsh. The titular abbot, the archbishop, fared considerably better. His net income from land rose by about 32 per cent between 1391 and 1432 and by about another 15 per cent between 1422 and 1535. Although it sagged slightly in the 1440s, there was no disaster. The archbishop let his manorial demesnes to a wide variety of tenants, substantial gentry and townsmen some of them but mostly well-to-do peasants, on leases which allowed for adequate maintenance and strict tenant control. His rent roll began to rise again after about 1480 owing to an increase in the number of tenants on the manors nearer to London, a more intensive exploitation of rich arable and marshland in east and north Kent and possibly more effective administration.

The agrarian situation was, therefore, extremely complex and it is unwise to press any theory of universal depression too far. Depression for the landlord class there certainly was in some regions and on some estates, but exceptions were too numerous for us to accept a universal canvas of darkness and gloom, and the worst of the depression, or stagnation, seems to have been over by the 1480s or the 1490s with the resumption of a slight rise in population and prices, both gathering in

momentum by the second decade of the sixteenth century.[6] The move
by great landlords out of direct demesne farming had not *ipso facto*
meant a loss of income. Techniques of estate management greatly
improved during the late fourteenth and the fifteenth centuries and,
moreover, the new tenants were men who, unlike the great absentee
landlords themselves, had an intimate knowledge of their local
conditions and local markets. With this knowledge and with much
lower administrative expenses, they could pay their landlords substantial rents while making good profits for themselves at the same
time. Something of a rise in productivity may also have helped the
process. The post-Black Death decline in population by reducing the
amount of land under cereal crops had left more available for animal
production (fifteenth-century Englishmen had a great reputation as
meat-eaters), thus producing more of the perennially scarce
farmyard manures for the cultivated acres.

III

One of the main problems of the late fifteenth century is that of
enclosures. Owing to the increasing demands of the expanding
English cloth industry exports of raw wool were constantly falling.
After 1440 exports rarely reached an average of more than 9,000 sacks
and they declined to an average of less than 5,000 in the 1530s.
Impressive as increased exports of cloth were (in spite of considerable
fluctuations they increased about four-fold in the course of the
century), total production probably rose even more than the figures
would indicate. The lower ranks of the population, more prosperous
after the Black Death than for decades earlier and spending a smaller
proportion of their income on food, were able to spend more on
textiles. It is even possible that the domestic consumption of cloth
doubled.

[6] The question of population is controversial. Numbers probably stabilized in the 1430s and
slowly increased from the 1460s. There is, however, some debate as to whether the increase
became really significant before *c.* 1510. As to prices, taking the average of 1451 – 75 as a base
of 100, real wages would read:

1480s	88
1490s	99
1500s	95 +
1510s	90 +
1520s	66 +

Source: tables in E.H. Phelps-Brown and S.A. Hopkins, 'Seven Centuries of the Prices of
Consumables, Compared with Builders' Wage Rates', *Economica*, new series XXIII (1956),
reprinted in *Essays in Economic History*, ed. E.M. Carus-Wilson, II (1962).

Traditionally historians have maintained that, cereal prices being depressed, landlords found it far more profitable to switch to wool production. Although sheep were subject to various epidemic diseases, particularly murrain, sheep-rearing suffered far less violent fluctuations from the vagaries of the weather than cereal production. Wool could be produced with a minimum of labour — far less than that required for grain crops — and long-term prices remained steady as compared with the violent seasonal fluctuations of cereals.

Consequently landlords turned to enclosures, depopulating whole villages for the sake of these profit-making activities — a depopulation especially prominent in the counties of the central Midlands where, in the absence of navigable rivers, the cost of transporting grain over the district's heavy clay roads was prohibitive in proportion to its value — a factor which did not apply to wool. The cost of transport for wool in comparison with its value was only about one tenth that of wheat. The Warwickshire antiquary John Rous (died 1491) stated that he presented a petition against enclosures as early as the parliament of 1459 and in his *Historia Regum Anglie* he left a list of fifty-eight depopulated places in his native county alone and bitterly denounced the greed of the landlords who made the changes. Rous's Warwickshire list is now known to be incomplete for at least seventy-five Warwickshire villages were depopulated between about 1450 and 1520.

Recently, however, the whole traditional concept has been attacked. Rous in his denunciations never referred specifically to sheep as the cause of depopulation, only to greed. Nor did the chancellor, John Russell, bishop of Lincoln, who, in a draft sermon prepared for parliament in 1483, denounced the sloth and negligence of landlords which led to ruin and decay, though it is possible that he was referring only to cities and boroughs.

It is true that many landlords — the Berkeleys, the Howards, the Greys of Ruthyn, the Hungerfords, the Stonors, Sir John Fastolf and the abbots of Gloucester, Dorchester, Oseney and Winchcombe among others — retained their sheep flocks long after they had abandoned demesne farming. It is, however, dubious that they did so for the sake of higher profits. In spite of increased production of cloth both for export and for the domestic market, and in spite of periodic complaints about shortages of wool and high prices, there does not appear to have been a shortage of wool in general. It is far more likely that a shortage in some grades coincided with a glut in others. By the middle of the century the prices of the highest grade wools, those of Shropshire and the Cotswold area for example, the wool very much in demand both for the highest grades of English cloth and for the looms of Italy and Flanders, were higher than they had been in the mid-fourteenth century. The prices of the inferior grades were on the contrary low—low enough to make sheep farming considerably less profitable than arable. Sir Thomas More's notorious jibe that a shepherd and his dog alone could tend a thousand sheep was wildly exaggerated. The overhead expenses of running a large demesne flock were far, far greater than that. The lower grade wools probably produced only about half the profits of land in arable.

Peasants, however, continued to keep considerable flocks. They may even have increased them. Peasants, after all, were not cost accountants and, like peasants in underdeveloped countries today, probably counted their wealth in visible flocks and herds rather than in nice calculations of profit and loss. Some landlords in the period of low population and a scarce tenantry probably allowed their tenants to go in for sheep-rearing and maintained their own flocks as an alternative to seeing marginal land revert to waste—a couple of sheep per acre at least prevented the deterioration of land into scrub. They would vastly have preferred corn-growing tenants. Consequently few deserted villages were the direct result of calculated, brutal evictions of wretched, innocent peasant tenants. Some evictions there certainly were—in villages already deserted by all but a few people where the landlord could benefit neither from a full complement of tenants nor from the advantages of a complete sheep-run.

Accusations of landlord greed, tyranny and evictions seem to date from the second decade of the sixteenth century and stem from a complete misapprehension of the economic process involved. By then rising population had brought in its wake a stimulated demand for farms, which landless people could not find, and landlords who had earlier, in many cases, turned to sheep-runs *faute de mieux* found themselves pilloried by public opinion and by government commissions as ruthless, stony hearted depopulators and oppressors of the poor.

IV

The tenth or so of the population who were urban dwellers lived in towns which were, by continental standards, minute. As in Thomas Hardy's Casterbridge a butterfly could easily have fluttered from one end of the high street to the other. English market towns varied in population from a mere two or three hundred people to about a thousand, or even two thousand if they were county towns or the site of a cathedral or some other great church. Perhaps twenty provincial towns had as many as three thousand people. At the top of the scale there were a few giants, by English though not by European standards, like York with 7,000 – 8,000, Coventry with perhaps 8,500, Bristol with 9,500 – 10,000, and Norwich, the second city in the realm, probably topped the 10,000 mark.[7] In the second quarter of the sixteenth century the antiquary John Leland called Uppingham the best 'town' in Rutland. It had about three hundred inhabitants. Oakham, though its population was little more than five hundred could even be described as 'a great town'. Only London, perhaps, with 50,000 – 60,000 inhabitants could bear comparison with the great cities of Europe.

The local role of the towns, of course, differed immensely. Battle in Sussex more or less existed to serve the needs of a considerable monastery. Durham, with probably about 2,000 inhabitants out of a total county population of 24,000 – a good deal less than half the size of the county's port, Newcastle-upon-Tyne – had no powerful mercantile patriciate, no specialized industry or specialized trade. It was a market town and an administrative town, with a high proportion of the city properties held by clerics – a professional hierarchy of ecclesiastical administrators and lawyers serving the bishop and the monastery. High Wycombe was the leading corn market of the Chilterns with a substantial trade in grain with the London area. New developments were taking place in Wycombe – the substitution of the shop for the market stall. Its periodical fair was declining because (it was said) the burgesses chose to keep 'their shops and their stalls at home' rather than move them to temporary sites. Coventry was a prosperous centre for weaving and dyeing, ribbon- and nail-making.

Unless they were ports or cloth making centres, however, most towns were minute market centres for villages within a radius of about six to twelve miles – small places still surrounded by their common fields, the use and regulation of which were a prime source of altercation between the authorities and the citizens. Agriculture was still very much part of urban life. Oakham's thirty-four tradesmen, plying twenty different crafts, were all, with one possible exception, part-time farmers. Their neighbours in the town were two yeomen, thirty-three husbandmen and seventy-five labourers and servants. Agriculture remained the mainstay of the town and overshadowed all else. Even in Coventry, one of the urban giants, the town bull was an important object of concern and in Norwich, another of the giants, the citizens were required to shut up shop and go out into the fields at harvest time.

By this time these rural preoccupations strangely combined in

---

[7] It should be stressed that these figures are somewhat conjectural.

many places with an atmosphere of decay and an ambiance of highly expensive civic dignity and pageantry. In 1483, John Russell, bishop of Lincoln, the chancellor, in the draft sermon already mentioned, demanded:

> That there be all way ordained officers to oversee and not to permit any owner to abuse the possession of his own thing, *Ne civitas defloretur ruinis*, lest that by the several sloth and negligence of the landlords, cities and towns should fall to extreme decay and ruin. If this law be not so well accepted in this land as liberty, it is light to see what is growen thereof, by the decay of well nigh all the cities and boroughs of the same.

Statesmen were much given to propounding fantastic, generally authoritarian, remedies for economic problems which they misunderstood, usually attributing decay and malfunction to vicious individual delinquencies rather than to long-term trends of which they had little or no conception.

Bishop Russell's observations — unlike his suggested remedy — were by no means wide of the mark. Though cloth towns like Coventry, Exeter, Salisbury, Totnes, Tiverton, Lavenham and Lewes were extremely prosperous, probably most of the older and greater towns were declining. Some like Winchester and Lincoln were extremely decayed. So were Gloucester, Chester, Great Yarmouth and York. In 1452 a petition from Winchester claimed that 997 houses stood empty, seventeen parish churches stood unused and because of the burden of taxation and urban expenses upon the remaining inhabitants 'many notable persons have withdrawn from the city.' *Gregory's Chronicle* notes that after anti-alien riots in London in 1455 – 6 the Lombards took 'great old mansions' in Winchester — with further loss to the city for, after the landlords had repaired them, the Lombards, after all, decided not to move. Lincoln's export trade in raw wool had declined. The River Witham had silted up. As early as 1428 seventeen of its forty-six parishes were described as having no more than ten inhabitants each and by 1509 only nine churches were still functioning. With suburbs and back streets abandoned, only the main street, the Bail and the Close continued to be occupied until modern times. The government cut the fee-farm of Bristol by nearly 60 per cent in 1486 and by 1518 800 households were 'desolate, vacant and decayed'.

Hull presents more doubtful features. Like Lincoln it had once flourished on the export of raw wool — the wool of Lincolnshire and Yorkshire now absorbed by the domestic cloth industries of York and Beverley and newer centres like Halifax and Wakefield. Then in about 1450 its export trade in cloth to the Baltic area had been stifled by the Hanseatic League. By 1460 its foreign trade was less than a quarter of its value half a century earlier. A port's export trade, as

mirrored in customs accounts, is not, however, an infallible index of
the prosperity of its inhabitants. It may well be that a good deal of the
export trade had been that of York merchants who had merely used
Hull's storage and quay facilities; and the prosperity of the
inhabitants may well have been maintained by a coasting trade in
bulky goods which provided far more local employment than the
former exports of wool and cloth.

V

The economic decay of many towns most probably affected their
government. Declining population, declining prosperity and
declining municipal revenues with all their attendant consequences
resulted in increasing reluctance on the part of members of the town
oligarchies to take offices which were time consuming and expensive
burdens. In 1501 the Scottish poet, William Dunbar, wrote of the
mayor of London as the 'exempler, loode-star and guye [guide]' of the
city and the description aptly applied to mayors in general. The
mayor of London was obliged to keep a large official household and
only a man of considerable wealth could afford the honour—or the
burden—of election. A provincial mayor's term of office was only
proportionately less costly. The citizens expected the mayor of
Coventry to keep open house during the twelve days of Christmas. It
was also extremely arduous. We know in detail from *Ricart, the
Mayor of Bristowe, is Kalendar*, begun in 1471, the burdens which
such an existence entailed.

The mayor and his brethren, the bailiffs and the aldermen, had to
carry out in person regulatory duties which in these days would be
performed by full-time paid officials. The mayor of Bristol was bound
to hold a court each weekday from eight to eleven a.m. and, except on
Saturdays and the eves of festivals, again from two to five in the
afternoon. Twice a week he (personally) and his ale-taster were
required to check the measures of the brewers and the quality of their
various concoctions. He was responsible for maintaining sufficient
supplies of grain and firewood and for seeing that coal merchants did
not give short weight—all this, besides keeping the peace of the town,
chastising evil doers, defending and keeping all widows and orphans,
doing everyone right, poor as well as rich, and maintaining the
franchises and free customs of the town and all its 'laudable
ordinances'. In a litigious age these last requirements alone could
involve an appalling amount of work, worry and strain. The mayor of
Bristol certainly earned his salary of £20 a year (paid quarterly), with

twelve yards of 'scarlet' valued at £8, eight marks for his fur, five for his wine and five for his minstrels. Even at this provincial level magnificence was as much a part of the ethos of authority as it was in the royal court itself.[8] In any considerable town only the rich could afford public office and the probable neglect of their own affairs which its time-consuming duties entailed—and even they often tried to avoid it. In 1491 Leicester passed an ordinance prohibiting burgesses from refusing the chamberlainship. Sixty years later it became necessary to extend the provision to the office of the mayor, and by acts of 1499 and 1500 suitors who absented themselves from the Portmanmote at Christmas and Whitsuntide were to be fined.

The councils—in some cities there were two, sometimes with a total membership of over fifty—and offices in religious, merchant and craft gilds absorbed a considerable number of men. Few people of any standing could avoid these honours or burdens, which was how they were regarded depending upon the individual temperament and point of view. The city government and the gilds were often very closely connected. In Coventry there was a definite kind of civic *cursus honorum*, through office in the Corpus Christi Gild to the mayoralty, followed by office in the Holy Trinity Gild.

Though the office-holding circle was reasonably wide, both the cost of office and a general hierarchical social feeling excluded even the lesser freemen, not to mention the unenfranchised, from the making of decisions. In many places the popular assembly of burgesses had some vague rights of approval, but more and more 'the assent of the whole community' (a vague enough phrase in any case) had come to be taken for granted or obtained from a limited number of specially invited or elected people (often the origin of the second, lower, and numerically greater town council). At Leicester, for example, in 1466, the unenfranchised were specifically forbidden from attending the common hall meetings. By 1489 even the mass of burgesses, contemptuously described in an act of parliament as 'being of little substance and haveour, and of no sadness, discretion, wisdom ne reason', were also excluded except for forty-eight of the 'most wise and sad' commoners, chosen by the mayor and the existing council of the four and twenty on the ground that such rabble had swamped the more discreet and well disposed burgesses in such assemblies. The four and twenty were a self-perpetuating body who, alone, could elect to vacancies in their own ranks. The same act also applied to Northampton. So from this time forth Leicester and Northampton, like a good many other towns, became completely closed corporations.

[8] See below, chapter 2, p. 49.

Appeals to higher authorities supplemented legislation in attempts to discipline Demos. Popular accusations of corruption against the authorities seem to have been very frequent in Coventry and Nottingham, particularly upon the contentious subject of the administration of the common lands. Coventry's quarrelsome affairs not infrequently called for royal intervention and in May 1512 the recorder of Nottingham wrote a letter of advice to the governing body of the town about the nefarious ambitions of certain commons of the town who 'confederate themselves together ... to make alderman and other officers at their pleasure'. The recorder wrote that 'if that should be suffered it should be contrary to all good politic order and rule, and in conclusion to the destruction of the town'. He therefore advised them to send some wise person to 'the Treasurer'[9] who, knowing of the situation, had advised the recorder to write to them. Everybody must combine to enforce a salutary discipline upon such miscreant wretches 'for if ye shall suffer the commons to rule farewell all good order'—much the same reasoning that had been advanced in the Leicester and Northampton act of parliament of 1489. The letter added darkly: 'In any wise beware of calling any common hall at the request of any one of them that make this confederacy. I doubt not but that divers of you remember the saying of Mr Treasurer of the inconveniences that had ensued upon the calling of the commons together in London and other cities and boroughs.' Mr Treasurer duly promised his assistance for the punishment of the subversives.

Even the oligarchy more and more resented the high costs of office. The Black Death and subsequent plagues had produced extensive urban depopulation. Though the years 1380 to 1430 had seen something of a general economic recovery of the towns, the late fifteenth century once again saw the beginning of a prolonged decline in some of the older centres, which worsened in the 1520s and continued until about 1560 – 70, forming an impoverished hiatus between the great days of the medieval town and the beginnings of the more modern seventeenth-century development. The older and greater towns had developed an exceptionally high level of civic and associated religious expenditure. To go through the Coventry *cursus honorum* cost a good deal of money. Therefore some of the rich, as in the impoverished city of Winchester, developed a tendency to move out of the towns and live more cheaply in the countryside. In 1480 the city authorities of Lincoln complained of the same type of exodus. The expense of office-holding 'causeth many men that have been brought up in this city by prenticehood, service or otherwise to avoid

[9] Sir Thomas Lovell, treasurer of the royal household and constable of Nottingham Castle.

and go forth thereof, and to inhabit them in other places: and there is neither craftsman ne sojourner that will come to abide or dwell here, for fear of the said office, and thus this city desolates and falleth in great decay.' A level of expenditure which had been tolerable in earlier days of higher population and greater prosperity became over-burdensome as civic and religious ritual and pageantry became very much overblown — almost a way of life in itself. The Reformation in the towns became an economic as well as an ecclesiastical turning point. By destroying the great religious gilds, with their expensive civic as well as religious ceremonial, it vastly reduced the expense of urban life.

New industrial settlements, like Castle Combe, Stroudwater, Halifax and Wakefield, never became boroughs. Lavenham had over a thousand inhabitants. By 1515 its cloth manufacture had thriven to the point where there were only twelve richer communities in the whole realm. Even so, such towns as Lavenham remained numerically small as compared with the older, major centres. Legally Lavenham remained a village governed through a manorial court. Apart from its size the reason may have lain in a kind of legal inertia or fossilization, though the development of new forms of incorporation in some of the older boroughs may tell against any theory of this kind. Perhaps in some places, as in Stroudwater, the new industrial settle-ment was too scattered, too little concentrated, to form a genuine urban nucleus. A complete dependence upon one single industry may have told against the development of more formalized and sophis-ticated urban constitutions, whether in towns inhabited by numerous small clothiers as in the north of England or dominated by two or three great families like the Springs at Lavenham. Or they may, indeed, have learned their lesson from contemplation of the vast expense of life in the older boroughs. As Miss E.M. Carus-Wilson once wrote,[10] by this time 'the relative advantages and disadvantages of doing business in borough or manor were very different from what they had once been. The feudal society was in dissolution; villeinage had all but disappeared; the borough with its battlemented walls was becoming as much an anachronism as the baronial castle; its liberties had become privileges for the few, and its economy was more rigidly regimented and more heavily taxed than that of the manor had ever been. The ancient proverb 'City air maketh free' could have had little meaning for an Englishman of the late fifteenth century, least of all for an aspiring captain of industry.'

[10] *The Cambridge Economic History of Europe* II (1952), ed. M. Postan and E.E. Rich, p. 422.

VI

The late fifteenth century was a prosperous time for the minority of the population engaged in industry and trade. Although the cloth trade was overwhelmingly important — together with the rapidly declining exports of wool it accounted for nine tenths of England's export trade — industrial innovations, both in cloth and other trades, were marginal. In 1435 we hear of the first recorded use of a gig-mill,[11] at Castle Combe. Such machines must have become widespread during the next decade for a statute in 1463 prohibited their use owing to 'great deceits'. However, this was merely a finishing process and there were no changes in the basic methods of production, the distaff, the spinning wheel and the traditional wide loom. In iron-smelting there is some evidence of coppicing and the increasing use of young and small trees instead of dead wood. There was a blast furnace at Newbridge, in the Weald, in 1496 — an iron works sponsored by the crown for the manufacture of armaments for the Scottish war — and in 1509 cast-iron guns were successfully made in England for the first time. Progress, however, was slow and as late as 1542 there were only nine blast furnaces in the whole of Sussex for Henry VIII had reversed his father's policy and had placed his largest orders for arms abroad. In 1495 there was a paper mill near Hertford but it had probably closed by 1509. It was not until the later sixteenth century that the English paper industry really flourished. Coal began to be used in the smelting of tin and Newcastle-upon-Tyne was exporting coal to Germany and the Low Countries. In 1486 a water-powered pump for a coal mine was mentioned at Finchale near Durham — the first known example and a great advance, for the lives of medieval coal pits had been short because of the lack of anti-flooding techniques. Of minor industries Coventry produced nails, Sheffield was already famous for cutlery and Derbyshire and Nottinghamshire produced alabaster figures and altars in considerable quantities both for the domestic market and for export. Yet all those activities were still marginal: nothing could yet compare with the great traditional industry, cloth produced under the putting-out, or domestic system, predominantly in the rural areas.

From the mid-fourteenth century the cloth industry had come to absorb more and more of the country's wool crop. At this period labour generally counted for about half the cost of production. Therefore each sack made up at home must have been twice as valuable as the export of a sack of raw wool. Even so we do not know

---

[11] A machine for raising the nap on cloth instead of a hand process, both using teasels.

the full value of the export trade. The customs figures certainly give no true indication for the customs officials were not expert valuers and more or less had to take the word of the merchants concerned. Moreover, the figures may be affected in one direction by a stricter administration of the customs system from the mid-1470s onwards and in the other direction by the undervaluation of 'long cloths'[12] until 1536.

Nevertheless even the unsatisfactory figures which we do command reveal an astonishingly rapid growth. For more than a decade before 1460 the export trade had been depressed. Between 1462 and 1465, owing to political difficulties,[13] average annual exports totalled only 25,000 cloths. By 1476 − 9 they had risen to 51,889, the next three years saw a jump to 62,586. By 1506 − 8 they had risen to 90,000 (an increase of 61 per cent for Henry VII's reign) and continued to rise fairly steadily until the 1540s.

Exports and imports of miscellaneous merchandise show a similar prosperous trend, from depression in the late 1450s and early 1460s to rapid expansion in the second half of the Yorkist period and further expansion under Henry VII.[14] Imports of wine, which had slumped disastrously after the loss of Gascony in 1453, also recovered although the annual fluctuations were very marked. Between 1453 and 1465 they dropped to just over 40 per cent of their earlier values, by 1479 − 83 they had recovered to 78 per cent and by 1506 − 9 to 90 per cent.

Both Edward IV and Henry VII were interested in trade but hardly in the manner of modern governments. Like many of the nobility and gentry of those times they traded on their own account and Edward, in particular, through some of his courtiers and councillors, had very strong connections with prominent London merchants; both have been correctly described as 'merchant kings'. As early as 1463 Edward IV was interested in the profits of the cloth trade, possibly first attracted to it as a means of paying off the arrears of wages of the dissatisfied and politically dangerous Calais garrison. In May 1464 he commissioned an Italian factor, James de Sanderico, to export as many as 8,000 cloths and soon after Sanderico had exported 3,000 of them valued at £6,589. Edward more or less dominated the export

[12] That is, cloths in excess of the standard size of 24 yards long by one and a half to 2 yards wide.

[13] See below, p. 26 − 7.

[14]

	Value in the £
1456 − 9	59,089
1462 − 5	57,449
1476 − 9	120,223
1479 − 82	179,340
1506 − 9	358,503

trade in tin during his reign and in February 1470 twenty-five ships in the port of London were carrying some of the king's merchandise. Henry VII, on a single occasion alone imported a cargo of alum worth over £14,000.

Although the navigation acts of 1463, 1485 – 6 and 1489, restricting the carrying of certain goods wherever possible to English ships, were most probably inspired by sectional interests, both kings were interested in shipping. In 1474 at Bristol Edward IV offered rewards to any of the townsmen who would build ships and Henry VII offered bounties for the building of large vessels. Edward IV built up a navy of sixteen ships, some of which were used to convoy trading fleets, particularly the wool fleets to Calais. After 1488 Henry VII let the number fall to only five, though he built the first English dry dock at Portsmouth in order to ensure better maintenance. Both kings hired out their ships to merchants from time to time.

Both reigns produced what, at first sight, appear to be impressive programmes of commercial legislation. Nearly half the statutes passed during the Yorkist period deal with commerce and industry. The parliament of 1463 – 5, in particular, produced eleven more or less protective and restrictive statutes, ranging from a navigation act stating that all native merchants were to ship their goods in English bottoms whenever they were available, to specifications for the manufacture of woollen cloth, and for ten years it prohibited the importation of a wondrous variety of articles — cloth, laces, silk ribbons and fringes, saddles, stirrups, dripping-pans, gloves, tennis balls and curtain rings among others. Henry VII's reign saw about fifty statutes, often dealing with equally trivial matters or equally concerned with similar sectional interests.

Henry VII seems to have shown no particular interest in enforcing commercial legislation except where it concerned the customs revenues. Though both Edward and Henry were clearly interested in industry and trade and were, to some extent, responsive to their subjects' demands, it may be doubted whether either of them had any consistent economic programme: there were few statutes which had no predecessors of similar content in earlier reigns, for example, a restrictive navigation act in 1449. Direct government action probably contributed little to the impressive increase in trade already noted. Economic measures always took second place to politics, often serving a non-economic end — the paramount consideration of dynastic security. Commercial considerations always, in the last resort, gave way to the pragmatic, occasionally even irrational, demands of foreign policy and diplomacy.

In 1461 trade had been in the doldrums for more than a decade, owing to a combination of piracy, Anglo-French hostility and suspicions, and the bullionist and protectionist policies of Duke Philip the Good of Burgundy (1419 – 67). Neither Burgundian nor English subjects backed up their respective governments with a united front on these matters. Flanders and Brabant strongly demanded the exclusion of English cloth which competed with their own declining industries while other provinces of the Low Countries, interested in exporting a miscellany of general merchandise, wanted free trade with England. In England the Merchant Adventurers called for free access to the cloth markets of the Netherlands while many people suspected that the Staplers, anxious to boost their declining wool exports, secretly encouraged Duke Philip to ban the import of English cloth into his territories in the hope, thereby, of increasing their own diminishing sales. However, after mutual embargoes from 1463 onwards, in November 1467 as part of Edward IV's anti-French foreign policy, free trade was restored between England and Burgundy, with the result that exports of cloth by native English merchants from London almost doubled in the last three years of the decade.[15]

Political considerations in the Netherlands became even more prominent under Henry VII, so much so that violent fluctuations in the exports of both wool and cloth can possibly be explained to some extent by diplomatic factors. Edward IV's sister Margaret, the formidable dowager duchess of Burgundy, and the Emperor Maximilian strongly supported the pretender, Perkin Warbeck. By 1493, Henry VII, both fearful and exasperated, chose a policy of economic sanctions against the Low Countries, forbade any merchants at all, either English or foreign, to trade there and instead commanded them, like the Staplers, to conduct their affairs from Calais, except by special licence under the great seal. The government of the Low Countries retaliated and trade remained under an embargo for over two and a half years. The embargo ended in 1496 in the treaty which Sir Francis Bacon named the *Intercursus Magnus*, though the two governments were still haggling about details as late as 1499. English merchants were allowed to sell their goods freely everywhere except in Flanders (later included in 1502) without paying any tolls or customs beyond those customary during the last fifty years, and the treaty also included a number of definite rules on commercial procedures. In 1503 Henry, more alarmed probably than he need have been by Imperial support for the Yorkist claimant, Edmund de la Pole, again imposed an embargo. Negotiations dragged on until 1506 when the *Intercursus Malus* was negotiated. Under this new treaty the English

---

[15] The devaluation of the pound sterling in the recoinage of 1464 – 5 also encouraged exports. English goods became 25 per cent cheaper abroad.

were allowed freely to import their cloth free of any duty and in other ways also it was more favourable to English merchants. The treaty was never ratified, however, and matters more or less reverted to the position of 1496.

Thus, Henry, on two occasions, was prepared, for long periods, to sacrifice commercial prosperity upon the altars of dynastic security, though, in the end, the English did obtain more or less open access to and advantageous customs in their most vital market area.

Similarly relationships with the Hanseatic League exhibit a mixture of commercial rivalry and considerable concessions dictated by political need. An intense chauvinism dominated the emotions of certain sections of the English commercial classes, and it was nowhere greater than in the attitude of the Merchant Adventurers towards the Hanseatic League. In the last two decades of the Lancastrian era Hanseatic pressure had increasingly deprived English merchants of direct access to the Baltic, Scandinavia and north Germany. It was also forcing them out of the Icelandic trade. At the same time the Hansards had maintained a highly privileged status in England, including a much resented exemption from the customs duty of poundage which English merchants had to pay. English merchants clamoured for the abolition of such conspicuous alien privileges and demanded that Edward IV impose a poll tax upon foreign merchants.

During his earlier years the Hansards, through almost incessant, if somewhat intermittent, negotiations, obtained a series of temporary renewals of their privileges. From 1467 — 8 increasing pressure was brought to bear upon the Hansards, but the government badly mis-handled the situation and Anglo-Hanseatic trade came almost to a standstill.

In 1471 the king was indebted to the Hansards for providing ships for his return to England and by 1473 he needed a settlement with them to leave him a free hand to make his warlike preparations against France. The resultant Treaty of Utrecht in 1474 confirmed the Hansards in all their ancient privileges in England while giving the English only general assurances of reciprocity in the territories of the League — distinctly vague promises which the League never imple-mented.

Henry VII was no more successful than Edward IV had been in dealing with the League. Insecure as he was at the beginning of his reign, he could not afford to offend so powerful an interest and in 1486 he confirmed the Treaty of Utrecht without any success in enforcing the reciprocity clauses. In 1493 he forced the Hanseatics in London, like everybody else, to obey his embargo upon trade with the Netherlands and even restricted some of their preferential customs rates. Even so Henry, in the end, almost completely yielded to the

Hanseatic position and in 1504 conceded them the privileges of 1474. Once again the Hansards had defeated the English. The cause may lie in a combination of political and economic considerations. Henry may, even as late as 1504, have desired to give the Hansards no excuse for assisting the pretender, Edmund de la Pole, earl of Suffolk. If this is true the sacrifice of English commercial interests was out of all proportion to the feeble threat which, by this time, was all that the de la Pole interest represented. On the other hand if the Merchant Adventurers detested the Hansards their activities were certainly beneficial to other English interests. They were indispensable importers of forest products, especially potash, the essential mordant[16] for dyeing with woad, and their exports of cloth supported many an English producer: Hanseatic exports shot up after the Treaty of Utrecht to reach an average of well above 13,500 cloths between 1479 and 1482 and the expansion continued later.

Other trade areas, though less important, still deserve mention. The Treaty of Pécquigny in 1475 freed Anglo-French trade from restrictions, which, together with the economic recovery of France after the end of the Hundred Years War, led to a very considerable expansion of commerce. In six years cloth exports to France rose from 1,000 to about 6,000 pieces. Bristol's cloth exports alone had more than doubled by Henry VII's accession.

In 1466 a commercial treaty with Spain and later the Treaty of Medina del Campo in 1489 were highly favourable to the English. In 1478 there was a new treaty with Burgundy and between 1486 and 1498 new treaties with Brittany, Denmark, Portugal and France. Government-sponsored efforts to break into Mediterranean trade proved only partially successful. At the beginning of the period the Venetians held a monopoly on imports of eastern spices and luxury goods and the much favoured sweet wines of Crete and Greece and a monopoly of the export of wool and cloth on the return journey. When the English tried to break into the trade, the Venetians, in retaliation, imposed extra taxes. Then in December 1490 Henry VII concluded a treaty with Florence which designated Pisa as the Italian staple for English wool. He also restricted exports to Venice and, moreover, restricted them to English ships. In the event, however, hopes of a considerable English trade were frustrated when the Pisan revolt against Florence in 1494 badly upset the local commercial system.

[16] A substance used for fixing colours in the process of dyeing.

VII

Two final, notable points emerge from this survey. With the exception of the Hanseatic sector, Englishmen themselves took over a growing share of all this expanding trade. It is also highly probable, though we cannot be certain, that a growing share was also carried in English ships. For the first time we can discern the independent ship-owner with his fleet as distinct from a merchant holding a share in a ship with five or six others or owning a ship or two freighted with the goods of other traders as well as his own. Now a class of rich, specialized ship-owners had appeared, possessing fleets of ten or more vessels, fully occupied with their building and management. William Canynges the youngest (died 1474) of Bristol was just such a specialist. In his early career a merchant, later, according to William Worcester, he employed a hundred workmen, masons and carpenters in his shipyard and for eight years kept eight hundred men engaged on his fleet of ten ships. Yet another Bristol owner, Thomas Strange, possessed about twelve ships. Moreover, a certain proportion of English ships had considerably increased in size. In 1400 they had rarely been larger than 100 tons. Even at the end of the century these small ships still predominated in the merchant marine as they were the most useful and economically viable type, yet, again according to William Worcester,[17] if four of Canynges' ships were under 200 tons, one was 400, one 500 and the *Mary and John* a huge vessel of 900. With a fleet close upon 3,000 tons Canynges controlled perhaps a quarter of Bristol's shipping and with two voyages a year, if the freight paid on wine is at all an accurate guide, could have taken in over £10,000 in twelve moths, though it is quite impossible to say how much of this would have been profit.

The other notable feature was the growing predominance of London in the cloth export trade. The exports of Bristol reached a peak in the 1490s those of Exeter a few years later, Southampton's about 1522, and all thereafter declined in competition with those of London[18] which, allowing for considerable annual fluctuations, rose steadily from the 1480s. Moreover, with the Hanseatic exclusion of English merchants from the Baltic area, English exports increasingly composed of undyed, unfinished cloths became more and more concentrated upon that narrow London — Antwerp axis which became so prominent, and so dangerous, a feature of the Tudor economy.

---

[17] Worcester's figures have been attacked but Miss E.M. Carus-Wilson was very much inclined to accept them. *Medieval Merchant Ventures* (1954), p. 89.

[18] Export from other ports were comparatively negligible.

All in all the turn of the century showed a prosperous land. Artisans and peasants, owing to a favourable balance between numbers of people and agrarian resources, enjoyed comparatively high standards of living. Landlords, even those whose estates had earlier been depressed, were beginning to benefit from slowly rising rent rolls. If most of the older boroughs were in decay, others and newer industrial centres flourished through rising domestic demand and increasing exports of cloth. The prospects for the future seemed fair indeed.

Yet new trends, though people at the time were, of course, unaware of them, already bore the seeds of long-term disaster. The fifteenth century has been described as 'the golden age of bacteria'. Judging from the evidence of wills, mostly from East Anglia, frequent outbreaks of bubonic plague and other forms of epidemic disease combined to keep population levels depressed during most of the century. Marriage and child replacement rates declined during major epidemics but rapidly recovered thereafter. Recurrent outbreaks, however, wiped out these recoveries and frustrated any advance in the numbers of the population. Contrary to popular belief, bubonic plague was quite as much a rural as an urban killer. Moreover, certain unhealthy rural areas such as parts of the archdeaconry of Sudbury in Norfolk and certain areas in the brecklands of Suffolk and the fens of Cambridgeshire — possibly because they harboured a large and varied rodent population, the carriers of certain types of both epidemic and endemic disease — showed a persistently high mortality over the years.

The 1420s and the 1430s seem to have experienced particularly high levels of mortality from plague. Although plague died down during the two following decades, this decline was unaccompanied, as far as we can see, by any upturn in demographic trends. The 1460s saw renewed outbreaks and the 1470s proved a disastrous decade, with outbreaks of a 'bloody flux' in 1472 and the so-called 'French pox'[19] of 1475 as well as plague. Yet paradoxically enough (explanations are obscure and no more than hypotheses at best), in East Anglia, Hertfordshire and Kent the number of marriages increased, replacement rates within the family for the first time during the century showed an upward trend and people may have been living longer. Then the virulence of plague seems to have died down after a great outbreak in 1479 – 80. The sweating sickness (probably a form of virulent influenza) introduced into the country in 1483, though it terrified everybody by its sudden appearance and the swiftness with which it killed its victims, seems to have been far less widespread geographically than bubonic plague had ever been.

[19] Possibly intestinal dysentery and some form of venereal disease.

The decade after 1480 may well have been a demographic turning point in England, marking the beginning of the general increase in population that was advancing rapidly by the second or third decade of the sixteenth century—an advance which once again progressively outstripped the country's resources and led to that rapid decline of living standards for which the Tudor period is now so notorious.

2 The Government of the Realm

I

The government of any country at any time is always an extremely complex matter, far from easy to analyse in simple, precise terms. With institutions always numerous, diverse and to some extent over-lapping, government in practice rarely works with the neatness and ease which some political scientists attribute to it. Attempts to analyse it in mainly theoretical terms all too often conceal the complicated realities and practical defects which human elements inflict upon its workings. Therefore, to take account of such inconvenient factors this chapter must be to some extent descriptive rather than analytical in the hope of depicting the rich diversity of fifteenth-century life rather than imposing upon it an artificial theoretical structure.

II

Although fifteenth-century Englishmen accepted a monarchical form of government without question, the lack of theoretical writing on the subject and their grudging attitude towards it must come as something of a surprise to students more familiar with perennial Tudor adulation of the 'mighty prince'. No startling new theory of the constitution appeared, perhaps because a people almost obsessively preoccupied with questions of property, inheritance and law regarded their kings as little more than the protectors of these ancient liberties and privileges — protectors whose powers they somewhat grudgingly regarded — and therefore wrote of their authority in terms resembling the prudent exhortations of a catechism rather than in the persuasive appeals of political philosophy.

In a sermon delivered at the opening of parliament, in May 1468, the chancellor, Robert Stillington, bishop of Bath and Wells, took

33

advantage of the occasion to define the scope of government. Stating 'justice' to be 'the foundation, well and root' of all prosperity, he claimed it to be found when 'every person should perform his office in which he is put according to his estate or degree' and when the king provided 'an outward peace for the defence and surety of the realm.' Edward Hall's famous and influential *Chronicle*, first published in 1548, in an imaginary speech attributed to Archbishop Arundel (1354 − 1414) at the beginning of the fifteenth century, expressed the desirable results of such activity − 'that the noble men shall triumph, the rich men shall live without fear, the poor and needy persons shall not be oppressed nor confounded' − a definition almost exactly that of Edward Gibbon some two centuries later. It is therefore obvious that in the minds of the political nation the scope of government was both limited and negative, restricted externally to the defence of the realm, internally to the protection of existing rights under the law, so that, free from disorders, each man might live at the level regarded from time immemorial as appropriate to his status. A people eternally jealous of hierarchy based upon property rights, while craving the orderly conditions necessary for their enjoyment and eternally bewailing their absence, viewed with an intense, wary suspicion the monarchical authority essential for the achievement of even these limited ideals. As Chief Justice Finieux (1488(?) − 1527) wrote, 'the prince's prerogative and the subject's *privileges* are solid felicities together and but empty notions asunder. That people is beyond precedent free and beyond comparison happy who restrain not the sovereign's power so far as to do them harm, as he hath none left to do them good.' The machinery of English government could operate only under firm royal authority. At the same time that authority faced restrictions upon its activities at almost every turn.

Formalized departments, the royal household, the Signet and Privy Seal offices, the Chancery, the Exchequer, the courts of King's Bench, Common Pleas, the assizes and lesser jurisdictions, the justices of the peace and the sheriff's offices, naturally hold a prominent place in all descriptions of government. Perhaps, indeed, a misleadingly prominent place, for their staffs, by modern standards, were exceedingly small and, in the absence of a police force, their powers of enforcement were appallingly limited, quite inadequate, alone and unaided, to meet even the restricted aims of the government of the day. Under Edward IV and Henry VII the total bureaucracy could hardly have exceeded 1,500 men. The politically significant (as distinct from the menial) section of the royal household consisted of some 250 to 300 knights, esquires, yeomen and pages. The Exchequer accounted for perhaps 100, the Chancery 150, the law courts possibly about the same. There were probably about 30 or 40 auditors and receivers of crown lands, 80 or 90 customs officials and the crown, over the whole country, disposed of about 700 or 800 offices, mostly keeperships of castles and forests and the stewardships of manors—some of them, by this time, sinecures and most of them concerned more with the exploitation of royal property rights and largely used for political patronage than with the effective enforcement of specific government policies.

The formal institutions of government were almost exclusively financial[1] and legal. It is essential to stress the limitations and comparative inefficiency of the organs of the central government to avoid thinking of them in unrealistically modern terms. As a secretariat the Chancery was efficient enough, issuing charters, patents and letters close at the royal command, and writs against payments to subjects. Indeed it could hardly have been otherwise. The same may be said of the Privy Seal and Signet offices. The Exchequer, though a pertinacious collector of royal debts, niggling to the point of wasting valuable time upon hopeless, decades-old cases, was completely lacking in drive in the matter of estate management and the royal estates were one of the main sources of revenue.

III

Superficially at least there existed a most impressive hierarchy of law courts. At the lowest local level the manorial courts, besides deciding upon the agricultural arrangements for the year, possessed civil jurisdiction over debts worth less than 40s., over contracts and conventions made within the power of the manorial lord, actions over freehold land under writs of right up to the point of their removal to the royal courts for the grand assize,[2] jurisdiction over the customary tenures of the lordship, and on the criminal side over cattle wounding, damage to crops by animals, assaults not leading to bloodshed, trespass and the damaging of timber where the king's peace was not concerned. The limits of this type of jurisdiction were comparatively narrow but the great majority of all cases, being petty matters, were most probably heard in such local courts.

The ancient jurisdiction of the hundred was more or less obsolete by this time and in 1461 a statute finally abolished the jurisdictional powers of the sheriffs on account of the notoriously corrupt indict-

---

[1] For financial institutions see below, chapter 3.
[2] By this time, more or less obsolete.

ments made in their twice yearly tourns or law days by dishonest jurors, men 'of no conscience, nor freehold and little good — servants, menials': a reform long overdue for such complaints had been heard at least as early as 1376. In future, under a ruinous penalty of £40, the sheriffs were to hand over indictments to the justices of the peace for trial. Oddly enough, however, franchises (that is, similar courts which had fallen into private hands) were exempted, thus forming the basis of the court leets under which many prosperous, but non-incorporate, towns, even cities, were later administered.

The justices of the peace, appointed from among the local gentry in each shire, with a few nobles to back them with prestige and additional power and a small stiffening of royal councillors and professional judges, had to a very great extent taken over the former functions of the hundred and shire courts. They were competent enough to do so for most country gentry had some knowledge of the law. Legal knowledge was essential for the defence and preservation of their own estates. Meeting in quarter sessions, among other multifarious and ever widening powers, they could hear cases concerning land, debts and contracts. They exercised jurisdiction for the keeping of the peace, including powers to bind any person to keep it, could arrest people on suspicion, hear all manner of felonies and trespasses including robbery, maiming and homicide (though here the more difficult cases were generally reserved for the assize justices). They could deliver gaols (that is try suspected criminals imprisoned waiting for trial) and possessed wide powers over economic and moral offences. They could raise the counties against those who attacked their neighbours with bands of men-at-arms and archers and in such cases they could command the sheriff's cooperation by demanding that he call out the shire levies. They could enter all private franchises and their sessions by this time had become the basis of criminal jurisdiction. About nine tenths of the cases finally heard in the King's Bench originated in indictments begun before the justices of the peace.

Over and above these local commissions the justices of assize, organized in six circuits, visited rather more than seventy assize towns twice a year, generally in February and late July or August.[3] The commissions appointed to each circuit generally consisted of three men, a judge from one of the central courts, a sergeant-at-law from the small group of the most eminent lawyers of the day (from whose ranks the judges themselves were ultimately selected) and a local

[3] They went to the more remote areas of the north only once a year. The counties palatine of Chester and Durham did not fall within the system and in the Isle of Ely and Lancashire the justices of the bishop and the duke of Lancaster appear to have enjoyed concurrent jurisdictions.

man. The assizes were, therefore, in the hands of some of the best legal minds available. The justices of assize exercised both civil and criminal jurisdiction, of much the same nature as that of the justices of the peace. Also, when in the neighbourhood, they were entitled to sit on the commission of the peace. Their 'charge', as it was called, or speech to the grand jury, was one of the principal methods of making the government's views on various matters known in the countryside. Edward IV widely used such charges but, according to tradition, after his time they were then abandoned, only to be revived in 1595.

Edward IV also relied to an unusual degree upon specially appointed commissions of oyer and terminer.[4] The Chancery issued no less than seventy such commissions in the course of his reign. This type of commission was perhaps the most useful and flexible part of the entire common law system. As many as twenty or thirty men might be appointed to a commission which could investigate offences from a single felony to all those committed in half a dozen named counties or even, occasionally, over the whole country. To give it power and prestige a prominent nobleman headed the commission (several might be found upon it if difficult cases were involved) and one or two of the royal judges gave expert professional assistance. As few as two members could hold the pleas. Therefore a large commission could divide itself into panels, working simultaneously in different places. Henry VII used the system rather less, possibly choosing to rely more upon the justices of the peace and quarter sessions.

The courts of Common Pleas and King's Bench completed the pyramid of the common law courts, Common Pleas being devoted to civil, King's Bench to both civil and criminal matters,[5] though King's Bench possessed the power of correcting errors in other courts. Common Pleas was by far the busier of the two. During the first two terms of the year 1466 it dealt with 13,452 cases as against only 1,601 in King's Bench.

The chancellor possessed jurisdiction in equity and Chancery as a court saw a great leap forward during the Yorkist period. Until the late 1450s its principal officials, the master of the rolls and the twelve masters in Chancery, had been no more than higher clerical officers, few of them possessing more than a first degree. From 1467 the chancellors themselves were mostly civil lawyers. In 1472 a doctor of civil law, John Morton, was, for the first time, appointed master of the rolls and by 1483 at least seven, and probably nine, of the masters were trained lawyers, no less than four of them being doctors or licentiates in civil or canon law. At the same time the number of petitions

---

[4] That is, to hear and determine.
[5] See below, p. 336.

for justice handed in to the chancellor rose from about 130 a year in the Lancastrian period to an average of 553 after 1475. The Chancery changed from being an administrative department with a mere fringe of judicial business to one of the major central courts of the realm, though still much smaller than Common Pleas or King's Bench.

A growing, but small total[6] proportion of cases came from the land-owning classes in matters of trusts and uses. It was, however, the mercantile community, both native and alien, which presented a far greater number of petitions in matters concerning contracts and debt and, in particular, cases in which the Chancery clerks, by the use of skilful technicalities, could enable merchants to avoid the full rigours of the usury laws. Jurisdiction over disorders and riots also added con-siderably to the Chancery's judicial business.

In the more remote parts of the kingdom the Council in the Marches of Wales and the Council in the North,[7] although they had a somewhat intermittent existence, brought increased discipline and the prospect of better standards of public order. At the centre the 'Council in Star Chamber', especially under Henry VII, was much occupied with ostensible cases of riot. These emanated largely from the petitions of individuals, especially about the possession of land and, in spite of appearances, they were in essence civil cases. A prolonged reading of the bills presented can give a totally exaggerated impression of disorder for to get the court to hear complaints petitioners indulged in the legal fiction of riots on the part of their opponents—legal fictions which led in Star Chamber bills to incredible accounts of hundreds, even thousands, of rioters armed to the teeth attacking inoffensive innocents and wantonly damaging their properties. At the same time the court was developing new conceptions of crime in areas where the judges of the King's Bench were remarkably somnolent—conspiracy, forgery, defamation and perjury.

In 1483 Richard III appointed a second clerk of the council for 'the custody, registration and expedition of bills, requests and supplica-tions of poor persons'. Councillors specially appointed came to act as a tribunal and in the end this Court of Requests (though the term itself did not come into use until about the end of the second decade of the sixteenth century) covered essentially private litigation, treated as questions of equity and conscience, and so resembled a kind of poor man's Chancery; its swiftness of procedure soon attracted litigants who were anything but poor. Like those of the Chancery the court's judges were usually skilled civil lawyers and it therefore dealt with

[6] See below, p. 39.
[7] See below, chapter 8, pp. 298–9.

mercantile cases and matrimonial disputes which would earlier have gone to ecclesiastical courts.

Finally, the royal council itself retained a wide supervisory and residual jurisdiction and it especially dealt with, or arbitrated upon, the disputes of the nobility — one of the principal ways of maintaining social peace in the countryside.[8]

IV

In spite of this proliferation of courts flaws and incompetence throughout pervaded the enforcement of the law. Notwithstanding a diminished population land-hunger among aristocracy, gentry and yeomanry alike remained persistent and tenacious, litigation for the possession of land incessant. Few families or institutions went for more than a few years without a legal case of some kind over estates or franchise rights. The Second Anonymous Croyland Continuator thought it worthy of approving comment that Prior Wysbech (died 1476) had kept the convent free of lawsuits during the entire seven years of his term of office. Once embarked upon, a suit was a dilatory process. Common law procedures, devised largely to protect defendants, subjected litigants to atrocious delays. The simplest case could rarely be settled in less than a year and a half, cases lasting three or four were quite usual and twenty years and more by no means unknown. The common lawyers, to a great extent fossilized in anti-quated attitudes, only grudgingly recognized entails. Trusts and uses, by means of which more and more of the richer families regulated their estates, the common law did not recognize at all until 1536. Only the Chancery dealt with them in equity jurisdiction. No statutes of limitation had been passed since Edward I's day and in real actions the term of legal memory stretched as far back as 1189. Since then the descent of many manors, in both memory and record, had become so tangled that titles to many properties existed in a state of appalling confusion. The illegitimate revival of ancient claims to property could bring disaster even upon those long in possession of their estates. Incautious buyers could find their titles to land challenged by subse-quent revelations of dower interests, confusion between bond and free tenures, conflicting entails and older, deliberately concealed conveyances. Bad titles could prove as disastrous to landowners as bad debts to merchants. When even the hard-headed Sir John Fastolf

[8] See below, pp. 54, 178, 181, 217.

(died 1459) incautiously bought property in the East Anglian villages of Tichwell, Beighton and Bradwell for £1,230, ten years of litigation followed, costing another £1,085 in legal costs and bribery before he obtained undisputed possession of his purchases.

Robert Burton's (1576 – 1640) remark in *The Anatomy of Melancholy* that 'a man who owns a house must needs own a houseful of evidences' was as true for the fifteenth century as for his own day. In the complete absence of any system of land registration, ancient deeds, genealogical trees, records and the memories of neighbours as to the descents of manors formed the essential, if inadequate, basis of land ownership.

Moreover, the forms of legal procedure in cases concerning land still bore thick traces of the violent nature of their immemorial origins in self-help, and in this period the procedures very often spilled over into actual violence. A man considering that he had a sound title to land was, in law, permitted to enter it himself and to take possession, but a series of statutes of forcible entry passed between 1378 and 1429 hemmed in these original rights with ever greater restrictions, so much so that they made it virtually impossible for the aggrieved party to enter without himself falling foul of the law. The right to take possession of one's own was still almost universal but restrictions had diminished that right in practice to a more or less ceremonial demon-stration. Although the statutes may have reduced the extent of violence involved in comparison with earlier times, tradition in a highly emotional, excitable, universally armed generation was still far too strong to eradicate it completely. Readers of *The Paston Letters* are well aware that attacks upon the Paston family properties were often based upon some semblance of revived antiquated titles and that opponents' entries which, on the face of things, could have been quite legal often degenerated into illegal riots and even, at times, minor sieges; though as in later Star Chamber cases around the turn of the century, we need to view very sceptically indeed some of the more lurid details of these events, as exaggerated or possibly even as fictions blatantly invented to meet the technicalities of the law of riot.

Owing to their early publication[9] and easy accessibility, *The Paston Letters* have exerted an entirely disproportionate influence upon discussions of fifteenth-century England. Both historians and general readers have all too credulously accepted the *ex parte* statements of various members of the Paston family at their face value, without taking into sufficient account (as in some cases it is possible to do) the very different stories given by their opponents. In a society where

[9] Partly published by James Fenn in two volumes in 1787, two further volumes were published in 1789 and a fifth by Fenn's nephew Serjeant Frere in 1823.

perjury flourished like the green bay tree at all levels, it is always dangerous to accept particular accounts of violence at their face value.

On the criminal side the execution of English law had always been unduly feeble. From the lowest to the highest, the courts came to grief upon the adamantine rock of reluctant juries who refused to convict their neighbours and the absence of anything like a police force to execute their verdicts. Indignant judges in vain denounced juries who refused to convict their neighbours and quite well known offenders could appear in the courts with little risk of conviction and punishment. The *Rex* section of the King's Bench plea rolls indicates that only habitual criminals like highway robbers were ever convicted. This lamentable state of affairs may seem surprising if we recall perennial contemporary lamentations about disorder and 'lack of governance', but it was nothing new. Earlier records amply reveal that only a very small proportion of indicted suspects had ever been convicted. Even so, during Henry VI's personal rule the number of royal pardons for specified crimes like murder and rape increased to between twenty and thirty a year and numerous other offenders had taken advantage of general pardons. Between 1446 and 1448, 172 persons appeared in the King's Bench flourishing such pardons in cases of murder, theft, burglary, rape, abduction, assault and violent entry into property. The failure of the legal system to bring people to trial was appalling. One woman charged with the murder of her husband had escaped, had been declared an outlaw and had survived for twelve years. A certain John Scotland had lived in outlawry for as long a period as twenty-two years, plying his trade in London all the time. Even Edward IV, who personally devoted a good deal of time and attention to judicial matters was hardly less free with the issue of pardons.

The case of Rogers Kinaston vividly reveals the weakness of the entire system of enforcement. In 1467 Lord Strange complained to the royal council that Kinaston, who was his mother's second husband, had wrongfully detained from him certain family estates and in the ensuing quarrel about them had refused to abide by the award of arbitrators. Kinaston then refused to obey commands under the royal signet to appear before the council and later had nearly beaten to death a king's messenger bearing a summons under the privy seal; but to escape the consequences of his rashness and violence Kinaston fled to the high parts of Wales, there consorted with outlaws and robbers and became an outlaw himself. Nothing could more vividly illustrate the lack of coercive power at the disposal of the government and the courts. It must, however, be said that such feeble execution of justice was by no means unique to this country.

Standards were certainly no higher in France and Germany and England was certainly not a chaotic exception to an orderly continent.

V

As the coercive powers at the command of the government were so exiguous, it had no alternative but to rely on the powerful to bolster up the throne in times of crisis and in more normal periods to carry out the functions of local government and the maintenance of order which would nowadays be performed by public authorities. Contemporaries were acutely aware of these harsh facts of life. Sir John Fortescue wrote: 'The might of the land *after* the might of the great lords thereof standeth most in the king's officers' (my emphasis). Judge and royal councillor though he was, he had no illusions whatever about the superior powers of great men. Sir John Fastolf's secretary, William Worcester, averred that it was a prime duty of the nobility and gentry to 'maintain' the justices and other royal officials in carrying out their duties. In a draft sermon written for parliament in 1483 Bishop John Russell described the nobility as firm rocks in an unstable sea, maintaining that 'the politic rule of every realm standeth in them.' Edmund Dudley praised the ideal of a king abounding in virtue 'that with the nobles of his realm may reign gloriously' and in two different works William Caxton described government as a cooperative effort between the crown and the nobility.

The greater nobility consisted of between fifty and sixty men who received individual writs of summons to parliament. The lesser nobility, traditionally known in England as the gentry, made up about two or two and a half per cent of the population. In the county of Rutland, for example, one family in about fifty-seven claimed the status of 'gentlemen', though some of them could have been little more than well-to-do peasants. They were much thinner on the ground than is often supposed. In the same county only one village out of every four or five supported a resident gentry family and, most probably, the proportion was much the same elsewhere. Romantic impressions of English life tend to convey a picture of every village with its benevolent, if somewhat dictatorial, squire. In fact the amount of land owned by the church limited such possibilities and many of the larger landowners were, of course, absentees. It was not until after vast transfers of landed property in the sixteenth and early seventeenth centuries resulted in a great increase in the number of gentry families that anything like the romantic conception emerged.[10]

Although the peerage more and more regarded themselves as a class apart, other men did not necessarily share their increasing snobbery. The popular mind still regarded rich non-titled men as noble. *The Arrivall of Edward IV* uses the phrase 'all the lords, noblemen and other'. A description of the creation of Prince Henry as duke of York in 1494, having tabled a number of earls by name, runs on 'and the substance of all the barons of the realm, all in their robes; and in like wise the judges, the master of the rolls, the mayor of London and his brethren the aldermen and great press of knights and esquires and other nobles'; and Polydore Vergil more than once included untitled men in lists of nobles.

The method of recruiting the peerage may partly explain the persistence of this attitude. Across the centuries the idea of 'old nobility' seems to have become an almost indestructible myth for baronial families died out in the male line, on average, about every third or fourth generation, their ranks being constantly replenished by new members drawn from a pool of armigerous agrarian plutocrats whose wealth and way of life differed little, if at all, from those of the baronial ranks to which they successfully aspired. Anyone sufficiently rich and giving adequate service to the crown might ultimately expect to be rewarded with a peerage, and although the nobility continued to be militarily significant, the kind of service by this time required was predominently civilian rather than military.

Strengthening the peerage with loyal adherents had become a major means of buying support in periods of tension and crisis — a method deliberately employed from the days of Edward III to those of Henry VIII. In the troubled years of 1447 – 50 there had been no less than fifteen new creations. Immediately upon his accession in 1461 Edward IV created seven new barons, and had created another six by 1470 and the same decade witnessed a dukedom, a marquessate and eight new earldoms. The recipients of these honours were already rich men in their own right; nevertheless Edward in some cases deliberately built up their estates and powers to enhance their local influence. Henry VII, deeply distrusting a class which had given him absolutely minimal support in his bid for the throne, refrained from such practices but his son, Henry VIII, deliberately revived them to cope with the strain caused by the break with Rome, creating no less than eighteen new peers between 1529 and 1547.

Such men were intensely jealous of their local influence. In 1453

---

[10] For Kent a list of gentry *c.* Henry VII gives 187 names. A. Everitt estimates about 1,000 families in the early seventeenth century. *Archeologia Cantiana* XI, pp. 394 – 7. A. Everitt, *The County Community of Kent and the Great Rebellion* (1966), pp. 240 – 44.

the duke of Norfolk wrote that he intended to hold 'the principal rule and governance' in that shire no matter who grudged his dominance. The earl of Warwick detested Lord Herbert, partly owing to their conflict for supremacy in south Wales, and he equally detested Sir John Fogge, the treasurer of the household, partly for leading something of a revolt of Kentish squires against his jurisdiction as constable of Dover. In 1475 Godfrey Greene advised Sir William Plumpton against 'labouring' the king or the duke of Gloucester to bring pressure to bear upon the earl of Northumberland to reappoint him deputy keeper of Knaresborough Castle, for the earl (its keeper by royal patent) would 'have no deputy but such as shall please him, and can thank him for the gift thereof, and no man else ... and so the labour shall be fair answered, and turn to none effect, but hurt.' Greene gave this advice in spite of his knowledge that only the previous year Henry Percy, earl of Northumberland, had become Gloucester's retainer but, in fact, the indenture of agreement between them makes it amply clear that this was merely a formal method of defining their spheres of territorial influence. Nor would Lord Hastings use his influence to get Plumpton appointed to the commission of the peace for fear that it should cause a 'jealousy' between him and Northumberland. It was always necessary both for the central government and for other magnates to be careful to respect the local influence of territorial magnates and, if possible, to leave them undisturbed in their hereditary territories.

About one third of the local gentry took an active part in the government of their shires, holding local offices and sitting on commissions, culminating in the commission of the peace and in the much coveted election to be knight of the shire in parliament. As a group they are difficult to classify. Men were differently described as esquires or gentlemen in different documents. Others advanced to knighthood in due course. A few would eventually become peers. This governing group, something of a *corps d'élite*, were not necessarily the richest members of their social class though their incomes were generally above average, and lesser men sat on the minor commissions like sewers (dealing with water courses and drainage). Again, some of the middling men more or less confined their activities to their own sections of the shire. Others like Sir John Fogge, Sir John Scotte and Sir Richard Haute in Kent, all three of them closely connected with the royal court, rode the length and breadth of the shire in the course of their many governmental missions.

Intimately connected by service, and in many cases by blood, such men (and many below them in the social scale) were by no means always servile to aristocratic interests. There had to be give and take, accommodation on both sides of the relationship and their survival power was conspicuous indeed. The Pastons, it is true, thought it expedient to remain in the service of the dukes of Norfolk through years of injustice and oppression on the part of their employers. On the other hand in 1469 Edward IV told Sir William Brandon that although Brandon could twist the duke of Suffolk round his fingers he would be ill-advised to try that particular game on the king and in 1478 Lord Strange told Sir William Stonor that he would not be 'over-mastered' by any of his 'feed men'. One source states that in 1460 a northern mob lynched Warwick's father, the earl of Salisbury, because they 'loved him not' and in 1471 the Percy earl of Northumberland may have been powerless to join Edward IV because so many of the northern gentry were of a different mind. Perhaps his influence then was still weak because he had only recently been released after several years of imprisonment. Yet even in April 1489 events do not suggest a strong and powerful authority: then his retinue stood by when a mob attacked and assassinated him at Topcliffe while he was attempting to explain the royal need for taxation.

The activities of the Stafford dukes of Buckingham are also instructive. Polydore Vergil states that the army which Duke Henry led against Richard III in 1483 consisted of Welshmen 'whom he, as a sore and hard dealing man, had brought into the field against their wills, and without any lust to fight for him' and, when in flight, his hiding place is said to have been revealed by a disgruntled tenant. By 1520 his son, Duke Edward, had made himself so unpopular by his policy of screwing up traditional rents that he needed an escort of three or four hundred armed men to make a progress through his Welsh and Marcher estates.

On the other hand, Lord Hastings in 1471 through the influence of his friends and dependents could raise 3,000 men for the king and in the 1470s his 73 retainers — 2 peers, 7 knights, 45 esquires and 19 gentlemen — although some of them quarrelled with each other, must have carried his influence very strongly indeed into the Midland counties of Leicestershire, Warwickshire, Derbyshire and Staffordshire and to only a lesser extent into Lincolnshire and Yorkshire. In February 1484 John Howard, seven months earlier created duke of Norfolk, promised Richard III 1,000 men. His note books list the names of several hundreds of them and the estates from which they came, including the contingents of two knights and three or four gentlemen. Howard expected his tenants and officials to make their contributions. His auditor, John Knight, promised to provide seven soldiers at his own expense.

Yet by this time the interchange of liveries and offices among the powerful had become so indiscriminate that their binding force of

loyalty may well be doubted. After the revolution of 1461 the duke of
Norfolk, Anne, duchess of Buckingham, John Lord Lovell, Sir Henry
Stafford and the Wydevilles (not yet connected by marriage with the
king) rushed to bestow estate offices and annuities upon Hastings. It
was well to have so influential a friend at court but the political effects
of so many conflicting interests may well have cancelled each other
out.

In counties where there was no dominant peer, men could be independent and restive and general conditions perhaps more turbulent
than where aristocratic spheres of interest were firm and well defined.
Kent was notorious for its turbulence even apart from the famous
occasions of 1381, 1450, 1461, 1471 and 1483 when its men were
among the first to take up arms. During the middle years of the
century a noteable decline in public order occurred in Wales and the
Marches owing to the absenteeism of great magnate landlords
(including the king) who allowed the cancellation of many of the
sessions of the Marcher courts in return for collective fines and left
their duties to be performed by corrupt Welsh deputies mainly drawn
from the ranks of the local squirearchy.

VI

Both nobles and gentry were turbulent: the respectable were as prone
to violence as the rabble, but their turbulence made less difference to
their social and political existence that might be supposed. Members
of the London Mercer's Company were known to draw their knives on
each other at the company's meetings. The statutes of more than one
Oxford and Cambridge college specified homicide as a reasonable
cause for the deprivation of a fellowship. Landed families after
accusing each other of a variety of crimes from forcible entry to
mayhem were soon on good terms again and even arranging
marriages between their members. At the height of a prolonged and
violent quarrel between their families in 1472, John Paston the
Youngest, meeting the duchess of Norfolk in Norwich, twitted her on
her pregnancy in coarsely jovial terms which, pondering upon later,
he thought might have been altogether too familiar for the lady's
taste.

At the political level the personnel of government, both central and
local, showed a remarkable continuity over revolutions. Bishops,
though occasionally imprisoned for brief periods, were never, judges
rarely, disturbed in office. Twenty-five of Edward IV's councillors

continued on the council of Richard III. Sixteen of Richard's served Henry VII in the same capacity. Eleven served all three. Even offenders notorious enough to be attainted could expect to make their peace after a time with a new regime, with restoration of estates and honours and appointment to prominent offices. The same tolerance applied at the local level. In Kent in 1471 most of the thirty lesser, rather fringe, gentry involved in the Bastard of Fauconberg's rebellion were fined, but escaped any more stringent penalties. So it was with the more prominent men of the Cinque Ports also involved in the rebellion. Such men were too prominent, too useful in their local communities, for the government to turn them out of office for long as a punishment for one political miscalculation. Both Edward IV and Henry VII would have agreed with Machiavelli's dictum that a prince brought in by revolution should not rely exclusively upon his former supporters. In any case, however, honest administrative talent being as scarce as it was, they were more or less forced to ignore a certain amount of political (and criminal) aberration in their governing class, and it was respectable enough to change sides as long as one did not do it too often.

So government was a function of property — government by the few, by the rich and to a great extent for the rich. The justices of the peace may have been mere officials in the sense that the government appointed them, but to insist too much upon this fact is to mistake the shadow for the substance. The government had no choice but to appoint prominent local men and once appointed they relied for their powers of social discipline upon their tenants, friends and dependants. Contemporaries not only accepted such time-hallowed arrangements, they vehemently demanded them, cleaving to the belief that richer men were more honest men. Statute after statute imposed property qualifications for office-holding and for jury service. In 1439 – 40 a common petition resulting in a statute forbade the appointment of justices of the peace with incomes of less than £20 a year from land, alleging that among the excessive numbers recently appointed in many counties 'some be of small substance by whom the people will not be governed or ruled and some for their great necessity do great extortion and oppression upon the people.' The government itself shared the prejudices of the Commons. The 1475 Ordinances for the Duchy of Lancaster laid down that the stewards should call all the homagers and *especially the gentlemen* to every leet and great court, for if presentations were made only by the poorer homagers they would not dare to present defaulters.[11] The ordinances also instructed the sheriff of the county palatine of Lancaster 'to empanel

[11] cf. above, p. 35 – 6, for allegations of corrupt presentations by poor jurors in the sherrifs' tourns.

knights and esquires and the most sufficient men of lifelode' to inquests both for the king and between party and party. Edward IV again in 1478, in the preamble to an act of parliament degrading George Neville from the dukedom of Bedford on account of poverty, expressed the same views with emphatic clarity: 'Oft times it is seen that when any lord is called to high estate and have not lifelode to support the same dignity, it induces great poverty, and causes oft times great extortion, embracery and maintenance to be had, to the great trouble of all such countries, where such estate shall hap to inherit.'

Although at the highest levels of administration kings thought that lesser men had more inducements to be faithful than aristocrats, in such matters most men in the fifteenth century held essentially the same opinions as the later humanists. Fickleness and lust for change, as well as a low morality, were the great faults of the mob. Great men were more stable. 'Nobility is virtue and ancient riches.' The aristocrat was wealthy enough to serve only for honour, not for gain — an aspiration rarely achieved in practice, however, before the nineteenth century. The poor man or the *nouveau riche* without pride of ancestry or a tradition of government service was unlikely to possess the primary virtue of devotion to the prince or to the public weal. There was, after all, more than mere snobbery in the various sixteenth-century schemes for 'saving the aristocracy'.

Action, of course, did not equal these admirable theories. Most men, in fact, employed maxims of impeccable morality as sticks with which to beat their opponents rather than as guides to their own conduct. Even in the courts they wanted not perfect justice but channels to further their own, often nefarious, designs. Accusations of corruption flew like missiles at all levels of society. Conscience-stricken kings and noblemen instructed their executors to make restitution for ill-gotten gains accumulated during their lifetime and, after the deaths of Edward IV, Richard III and Henry VII, private people brought against them, one and all, accusations of oppression, perversion of justice and disinheritance.

VII

The court, the royal household, was the nodal point of political life. The splendour of the ducal court of Burgundy was as famed and envied as that of Versailles two centuries later. When even men who looked over their accounts with the keenest eye for detail indulged in orgies of conspicuous waste, splendour was an indispensable attribute of royalty. His people expected a king to be magnificent. If he was to maintain his prestige he had to spend lavishly on rich clothes, furs, jewels, hangings and tapestries for his palaces, vessels and vestments for his chapel, horses of great price. Three people, Margaret of Anjou, Edward IV and Henry VII, who could hardly have been more divergent in character, all spent lavishly on jewels at times when they were financially very straitened indeed. Behind his back the French jeered at Louis XI's shabby old felt hat with a cheap lead figure of the Blessed Virgin stuck in it and in 1471 the populace of London derided the spectacle when his supporters brought Henry VI out in procession in an over-familiar old blue gown, 'as though he had no more to change with'. Edward IV made no such parsimonious errors. In 1467 the splendid formality of the English court very much impressed the Bohemian traveller, Leo of Rozmital. The following year the king spent £1,000 on silks for his sister Margaret's wedding and in his later years he was something of a trend setter in male fashions. When the great Flemish nobleman, Louis of Gruthuyse, paid a visit in 1472, he was housed in three chambers 'richly hanged with cloths of arras and with beds of estate' and the infant Prince of Wales (only two years old) was already being ceremoniously carried in formal processions in 'robes of estate'. Though splendid, the household (and the separate household of the queen) was economically run, costing considerably less than those of both Henry VI and Henry VII. Henry VII equally believed in the virtues of magnificence and, although he was notoriously avaricious in the gathering-in of money, he was in no way parsimonious about spending it.

Two hundred and fifty to three hundred gentlemen and clerics (or thereabouts) formed the ceremonial as distinct from the menial staff of the household. The knights and esquires for the body, sewers (servers), ushers, gentlemen and pages attached to the chamber and the hall equalled in numbers the members of parliament and the justices of the peace — the very men, in fact, from whose ranks they were largely drawn. On the most intimate terms with the king, he used them on all kinds of confidential tasks, both diplomatic and domestic. A succession of chaplains became proctors at the Roman Curia. Sir William Parre (controller of the household, 1471 – 6) became something of an expert in northern and Scottish affairs. The chamberlain, Lord Hastings, in the 1470s handled French and Burgundian affairs and organized a kind of secret service. Edward's relations with some of his staff were so close that in 1479 he could add a personal postscript to a letter to John Harcourte, one of the ushers of the Chamber, rebuking him for slowness in providing money for the sergeant of the Catery from the royal lands under his control.

Nor should the military significance of the household men be underestimated. They made a vital contribution to the troops recruited on Edward's return from exile in 1471. In the 1470s they played a major role in organizing the defence of Calais, provided 50 out of 192 contingent leaders in the French campaign of 1475 and took a considerable part in the expeditions against Scotland towards the end of the reign. Perhaps because of his deep, perennial distrust of the nobility, Henry VII relied to an even greater extent upon the military capacities of his household men.

One of their most important functions was to keep the king informed of conditions and opinion in various parts of the country. Doing stints of duty, turn and turn about, three months at court, three months in their own districts, they brought back valuable information to the king. Here at this point this 'intimate' affinity to some extent merged[12] with the wider affinity of seven or eight hundred royal officials spread over the land, mainly on the royal estates. Edward IV had a natural capacity for detail. According to the Croyland Chronicler he could remember the names and estates of nearly all the private gentlemen in the kingdom. A selection of this important group, apparently so familiar to the king, provided the wider affinity of local office-holders. Again, according to the same well-informed writer, Edward in his later years took care 'to distribute the most trustworthy of his servants throughout all parts of the kingdom, as keepers of castles, forests, manors and parks' so that 'no attempt whatever could be made in any part of the kingdom by any person, however shrewd he might be, but what he was immediately charged with the same to his face.' This greater royal affinity, the only countrywide network of bastard feudalism, provided to some extent a counterpoise to the more localized, limited networks of even the greatest of the magnates, but, important as it was, it could have been no more than a precautionary check upon their activities: a widespread tale-bearing, rumour-gathering network for the whole realm was certainly a useful asset, but it hardly provided the means of keeping the great bullies completely in check.

Competition to break into the charmed circle of the household was intense for it paved the way to considerable financial rewards and the exercise of invaluable royal maintenance in the perennial local disputes of landed families. John and Margaret Paston, who were adept at placing their sons in influential clerical and noble households, chose the royal court as the heir's, John Paston's, potential contribution to the augmentation of the family influence; but in spite of warnings from John Waynflete, a more worldly

---

[12] In so far as they held many local offices between them.

acquaintance, with a parvenu and provincial lack of sophistication they kept the unfortunate young man too short of money to make the necessary dashing impression.

If the expenses of life at court were considerable, so were the pickings for the successful. Before the Industrial Revolution service to the state was one of the principal avenues, if not the principal avenue, to a fortune or to a modest competence, depending upon rank and the type of employment involved. Apart from the gains of the peers discussed elsewhere, members of the royal affinity — both those of the court itself and of the wider affinity — could add enormously to their incomes. Sir John Fogge, the treasurer of the household from 1460 to 1469, already rich in his own right, quickly obtained a fee of £80 a year as a royal councillor. Then, his appointment to the office of keeper of the writs of the Court of Common Pleas brought in, according to contemporary estimates, at least one hundred marks a year in fees over and above its nominal salary of ten marks. In addition Edward IV granted Fogge at least three other offices, seven manors,[13] tenements in London, the custody of other estates, two wardships with right of marriage of the heirs, the gold- and silver-bearing mines of Devon and Cornwall for twelve years, rights of appointment to two ecclesiastical benefices and in 1472, together with James and Nicholas Goldwell, he was allowed to enjoy the temporalities of the bishopric of Norwich during a vacancy — and the bishopric of Norwich was worth over £900 a year.

Sir Thomas Montgomery, a Knight of the Body during the whole of Edward's reign, began life as a poorly endowed younger son. He early deserted the Lancastrian cause, fought with the Yorkists at Towton and from 1461 counted as one of the king's most trusted supporters. Edward gave him annuities and offices worth nearly £100 a year (an underestimate for the value of some of them is unknown), four wardships and extensive grants of land. By the end of 1483 the royal service had certainly brought him wealth, for in addition to the gains which he had received from Edward, Richard III bought his support with a life grant of estates worth the enormous sum of £412 a year — the income of many a peer. He had travelled very far from the young squire who, thirty-three years earlier, had alleged that he had very little to live on apart from £23 a year from the royal gift.

At a lower level in the outer affinity, a successful administrative career brought Sir John Popham of South Chalfont (died 1463) an annuity of 20 marks from the duke of York, 100 from the Exchequer and he received another six as constable of Southampton — a total of £84 to add to the £40 a year which his own estates produced.

---

[13] Although granted in fee, some of these may not have been permanent acquisitions as they were granted from the estates of the attainted.

VIII

Successful kings were always hardworking. They had to be in order to survive at all. Both Edward IV and Henry VII took their jobs very seriously indeed. In the Yorkist period the increase in the amount of business transacted under the royal signet and sign manual was especially noteworthy. Although Edward occasionally authorized documents the contents of which he had not sufficiently mastered, he personally signed every exemption from the acts of resumption during his reign. Henry VII's personal attention to financial matters has long been notorious. Yet, in spite of their very considerable personal industry, both kings needed a central coordinating body, a council, to relieve them from the enormous burden of work which was rather above the mere routine, to decide questions of middling importance and to advise them on major affairs. Unfortunately we can only dimly realize these councils for their principal records have disappeared, leaving us only a fairly wide range of indirect and circumstantial evidence from which to reconstruct their composition and activities.

A total of 124 names of councillors has survived from Edward IV's reign, 227 from that of Henry VII. Some of these, probably about one fifth, received the title only to add to their dignity on embassies or other diplomatic missions. Of the rest, the balance of various groups was traditional and normal enough by this time. About one quarter or more were nobles. Under Edward IV at least 44 per cent of the peers summoned to parliament also sat at some time in the council chamber. In spite of traditions to the contrary neither king ever wished to exclude the aristocracy from his council. It would, in fact, have been high political folly to exclude interested, powerful men whose influence was vital in both local government and defence. Rather more were ecclesiastics, principally bishops, with half as many lesser men and two or three abbots. Apart from a few who it is almost impossible to classify, the rest were lay officials of various kinds, sometimes, but erroneously, described as middle class. Most of them came from the gentry, or minor aristocracy, and their employment was due less to any preference on the king's part for men of lower social standing than to the gradual, but by this time cumulative, rise of educated laymen, anxious, even eager, in view of the financial rewards and influence involved, to assume arduous burdens at this highest of all levels.

The working council at any given moment never had a well-defined, nominated membership. Even the most important councillors were away from the king's side for long periods — on embassies, on special missions in the countryside, on the royal estates and the like. Some members accompanied Edward and Henry in their progresses through various parts of the country while others remained at Westminster to transact business there. The council at Westminster kept up regular contact with the king, referring important matters to him for decision. Thus the council was a fluctuating group, its members present at the king's will. Although various groups existed, advocating rival policies, and even showing considerable personal animosities, it was always the king who had the last word, who ultimately decided major matters, possibly even many minor matters, for many questions which the council discussed were put into effect by orders under the sign manual and the signet.

From time to time we catch glimpses of inner, perhaps confidential, groups. In 1469, judging from denunciations issued by Clarence, Warwick and Archbishop Neville and various other sources, the Herberts, the Wydevilles, Sir John Fogge, the earl of Essex (the king's uncle by marriage) and his family connections, Sir Humphrey Stafford of Southwick, Lord Audley, Sir John Howard and Lord Hastings, were especially influential. After the Treaty of Pécguigny in 1475 Louis XI of France, who was generally well-informed, chose Lord Hastings, Howard (by this time a lord), Sir Thomas Montgomery, Bishop Rotheram, the chancellor, and Dr John Morton, the master of the rolls, as councillors powerful enough to be given considerable pensions. Later Henry VII had an exceptional regard for John Morton whom he promoted to the archbishopric of Canterbury and in 1497 a Milanese ambassador described Sir Reynold Bray as the only one who could 'do anything' with the king; later in the year another Milanese envoy reported that Bray, Lord Daubeney, the chamberlain, and Sir Thomas Lovel, the treasurer of the household, all had French pensions and 'as these leading satraps are very rich the provision has to be very large.'

Judicial proceedings of their very nature leave records: it is essential for successful litigants to preserve the verdicts. Decisions needing immediate administrative action also leave evidence in the form of orders and advice and a good deal of scattered material of this kind is fortunately extant, telling us of the lesser matters decided at council meetings. On the other hand the almost complete loss of any conciliar minutes and memoranda, such as those which still exist for the earlier Lancastrian period, means that we are most in the dark about political decisions at the highest level. The extant conciliar records, for example, never mention that the events leading to the duke of Clarence's attainder and mysterious execution in 1478 were to some extent played out in the council. We know of this only from the pages of a well-informed chronicler.

Nevertheless, sufficient evidence remains to show that the council dealt with almost every conceivable matter. Besides the administration of justice and arbitration, particularly where the quarrels of the powerful were concerned, they discussed petitions for grants from individuals, interfered in the affairs of towns and cities, dealt with the administration of the royal lands and the customs, diplomacy and foreign affairs, the reform of the royal household, the summoning of parliament and the defence of Calais. The council was, indeed, the central coordinating body essential to every system of government.

IX

To turn to parliament. At this time the House of Lords consisted of two archbishops, 19 bishops, 27 abbots and priors and between 50 and 60 lay peers entitled to receive personal writs of summons. For various reasons, however, absence abroad on royal business and minorities to name only two, only about 45 writs or less were issued to lay peers for individual parliaments. In theory, therefore, a small majority of ecclesiastics dominated the sessions of the Lords. The writs of summons are, however, a deceptive guide to the composition of the working assembly, for although a peerage was highly valued many peers regarded attendance in parliament as a tiresome obligation rather than as a position from which to exercise political influence. After 1461 evidence is too thin to allow firmly based conclusions but, if earlier habits remained unchanged, the House of Lords was generally a much smaller body than the writs alone would indicate. The higher ranks of the lay peerage were reasonably conscientious in their attendance, the mere barons far less so. Their attendance had sometimes fallen as low as one out of three. The bishops came fairly regularly, the abbots and priors were the most delinquent of all, generally leaving the working assembly with a secular majority. In normal times the Lords could often have been no more than an ample session of the royal council reinforced by a small number of other peers. In most periods of crisis the barons turned up in greater force. They may well have done so more from instincts of self-preservation than from any passion to dominate events but, once again, the verdict remains in the limbo of hypothesis. The government, in fact, always desiring the solidarity of the peerage behind them, ardently wished for the greatest possible attendance. In 1454 Richard of York, dismayed by the thin attendance of the previous session and wishing to force the greatest possible appearance of approval for his plans, for the first and only known occasion in English history imposed very stiff fines for non-attendance. In 1459 the Lancastrians must have been particularly gratified that the Coventry Parliament, which attainted the Yorkists, was one of the best attended in the entire fifteenth century.

The House of Commons was not a democratic assembly representing counted heads or numbers of people. It was a 'community of communities' reflecting organic social and governmental units through the media of their more prominent and worthy members. Thirty-six counties each returned two members, the city of London 4 and 105 boroughs returned two each. Four more boroughs were added to the list between 1462 and 1468 thus giving a total membership of 293.[14] Representation over the country was, however, most uneven. Wiltshire alone returned 34 borough members, more than the whole of England north of the Wash.

County elections took place in the shire court. A statute of 1429 had restricted the franchise to residents with an annual income of 40s. from freehold land. The statute, following three notoriously turbulent elections, probably aimed to reduce the danger of disorders at shire elections and expressed a current feeling that gentry MPs — knights of the shire was, after all, their official title — should be elected by gentry and by the 'common suitors' of the court rather than by some unidentifiable rabble. Yet the framers of the statute, wishing for a more select group of voters and restricting them to the better men of the shire, had not, by the standards of the day, imposed an unduly high qualification. It was after all only two fifths of the £5 a year which Sir John Fortescue regarded as a fair living for a yeoman and it was considerably below the property qualification demanded for service on several types of jury.

In the boroughs the electorate had developed in a traditional, haphazard way. A statute of 1445 had laid down that the 'citizens and burgesses' should elect. In practice the phrase concealed a wide variety of local customs and often down right evasion. In some cities like Gloucester and Coventry, which possessed county status, the 40s. freehold prevailed. Elsewhere there was a bewildering variety of franchises varying from the wide to the very restricted — householders paying scot and lot, freemen, freeholders, burgage tenants, members of the corporation only.

The London Letter Books often state, according to the law, that the parliamentary elections had taken place 'in pleno hustengo et commune consilio'. The Journals, the rough memoranda books from which the more formal Letter Books were later concocted, however, more honestly state that the common council elected the four

---

[14] Much Wenlock, enfranchised in 1467, was abnormal in that it was given only one member.

members. At most the hustings were limited to formal approval and the authorities blatantly falsified the formal record. The Leicester records allow an opportunity for checking the official election returns. In 1478 the election indenture stated that the election took place in a full county court at Leicester but the Hall Book shows that the Commons chose Piers Curteis and the mayor and his brethren John Wigston. At Norwich there was a fairly wide electorate in the town's common assembly. At Cambridge, as at Leicester, the mayor and his brethren chose one member, the commonalty the other. At Hull all freemen took part in an election of members first nominated by the mayor and aldermen. At Lynn a complex formula for indirect election resulted in a final choice by the aldermen and common council. The later the franchise was defined, however, the more restricted it tended to be. All in all, hierarchic social feeling, probably a widespread indifference, and the economic depression of many towns during the fifteenth century ensured that the borough franchise should be far from democratic, that the local *potentiores* chose the candidates either from among their own ranks or from those of outsiders.

We can do no more than hazard an informed guess at the total size of the electorate. Professor B. Wilkinson has suggested no more than about 10,000 for the whole country,[15] but this appears to be an unduly conservative estimate. Even a county as small as Huntingdon could muster rather more than five hundred electors. There may, therefore, have been a possible minimum county electorate of about 18,000. At Shrewsbury where the franchise was restricted to the aldermen and council, in fourteen elections between 1460 and 1492 there was an average attendance of 47 out of a possible 72. Using this and other scraps of information we may possibly suggest a borough electorate of not more than 10,000, giving a combined total of around 30,000.

In fact, whatever its size, whatever its composition was, did the electorate count for much? These two questions seem to be very much interrelated. In boroughs with a franchise restricted to the aldermen and common council the extent of the electorate was obviously precise enough. Equally obviously such was not the case in boroughs with a wide franchise or in the counties and cities with county status. The complete absence of anything resembling electoral registration left the sheriff, the returning officer, face to face with a somewhat haphazard crowd with no well defined national issues upon which to choose, for there were no national 'party' programmes put forward at the hustings as there are today. As Sir Goronwy Edwards remarked, a

[15] B. Wilkinson, *Constitutional History of England in the Fifteenth Century* (1964), p. 292.

fifteenth-century election was no more than 'the sense of the meeting' and it was decided upon mainly local and personal grounds. Moreover, it occurred in a general assembly, the shire court, which normally met for other purposes every three or four weeks. In this assembly at election time the famous 1429 statute empowered the sheriff to examine any elector on oath as to his property qualification, but it did not make such an examination mandatory. In this rather vaguely constituted multitude an election usually took the form of ascertaining a 'general majority', that is by voices, by a show of hands, by a view, and only in the last resort, if there happened to be a very close contest, by the more precise method of the poll. It was not until the seventeenth century that the polled majority finally drove out the general majority. Such haphazard methods, in practice, obviously could not restrict the vote to the genuine 40s. freeholder. All and sundry who happened to be there were quite likely to take part.

We possess some little information about the social groups from which these electors came. In the polled Huntingdonshire election of 1450 out of a total of 424 or 430 people, knights made up about one per cent, esquires 6, gentlemen another 8, leaving about 65 per cent, as far as we can see, plain, genuine 40s. freeholders.

The majority of elections were not, however, contested, though there is some evidence that contests became a little more frequent towards the end of the fifteenth century. Though the evidence is exceedingly scanty, most recognized authorities more or less agree that the same attitude prevailed as in better documented Elizabethan days: powerful people who mattered very much disliked contested elections as productive of 'faction' or 'distraction'. On the other hand people were most anxious that elections should be fairly conducted in accordance with traditional local customs.

Long-established convention demanded that prominent local men should represent the counties in parliament. A statute of 1445 directed that such members should be 'notable knights of the same shires for which they shall be chosen, or otherwise such notable esquires, gentlemen of birth, of the same shires as be able to be knights, and no man shall be such knight as standeth in the degree of yeoman and under.' In other words resident members of the upper classes were to monopolize the shire representation. *The Paston Letters* report that in 1455 a section of the Norfolk gentry were intensely opposed to Sir John Howard, who had the duke of Norfolk's backing for election to the county, on the ground that he had 'no lifelode — nor conversement'[16] in the shire.

County representation had not only become the preserve of the

---

[16] That is, friends or acquaintances?

gentry: they were so anxious to sit in parliament that, in defiance of the law, they had conducted a considerable invasion of the borough seats. Their desire was also the reason for the creation of new parliamentary boroughs, some of them like Gatton (which first returned members in 1450), Maldon, Reigate and Dunwich, rotten boroughs from the first moment of their existence.

According to the statute of 1445 cities and boroughs should have been represented only by prominent members of their own communities. As early as the 1320s, however, there were a few examples of gentlemen sitting for boroughs. By the 1420s a switch to non-resident members from among the ranks of the gentry had already reached considerable proportions. The tendency continued to grow throughout the rest of the fifteenth century, the most rapid period of change coming during the 1440s. The boroughs often evaded the law by technicalities. A common device was to admit prospective members to the freedom of the borough just before election, sometimes even afterwards. Nevertheless, the election of outsiders continued to develop in complete defiance of the law.

The more prosperous boroughs valued representation and wished to perserve their independence. In 1448 Shrewsbury declared that only residents should be elected. Ten years later Cambridge followed suit and in 1474 Ipswich passed a resolution against outside interference. Wealthy merchants from great cities remained prominent among the parliamentary burgesses. John Bagot, who served as city bailiff and sheriff, and illicitly traded with Scandinavia, represented Bristol in 1467 – 8 and 1472 – 5. Another Bristol mayor (1461) and MP (1459, 1460), Phillip Meede was connected by marriage with the aristocratic Berkeleys. John Forster, MP in 1489 – 90, who also held office as bailiff, sheriff and mayor, was rich enough to endow the still existing Forster's Almshouses and the Chapel of the Three Kings of Cologne. The greater towns, jealous of their position, generally continued to elect wealthy burgesses of this type.

The smaller towns often far from desiring representation, tolerated, or even encouraged non-residence. As late as 1453 the charter issued to New Woodstock contained the proviso that 'the mayor and commonalty shall not be compelled to choose any burgesses for the borough to come to the king's parliaments' and in 1462 the charter of Ludlow for the first time permitted representation by non-residents. While men of limited education and only local horizons in the smaller boroughs seem to have had little active interest in the policy-making activities of the central government, in an age of urban economic stagnation combined with rising expenses in urban office-holding they were exceedingly anxious to cut costs. And the costs of representation could be quite considerable. The parliament of 1467 − 8 lasting 56 days would have cost a borough over £11 in wages for two members at 2*s*. each per day, plus the same rate for the days spent in travelling to the meeting of parliament and back home again. Gentry members usually paid their own expenses.

Medium sized boroughs might return one resident and one non-resident. In 1478 Canterbury sent to Westminster Roger Brent, ex-mayor and alderman, and Richard Haute of Ightham, the heir of a local landowner connected with the Wydevilles. It was generally in the smaller boroughs that 'carpet-baggers' took over completely. In 1478 Lostwithial was represented by Thomas Kebill, a Leicestershire justice of the peace and Thomas Powtrell, later a justice in Derbyshire.

'Carpet-baggers', in fact, were touting themselves round such boroughs. Outsiders seem to have canvassed many of the numerous small boroughs of Surrey, Sussex and Wiltshire very freely indeed. There was frequent interchange of constituencies between those seeking election and prospective candidates were prepared to go to widely separated areas of the country. By the time of Edward IV, Richard Leuknore sat in turn for Bramber, East Grinstead, Horsham and Shoreham, Nicholas Gaynesford for Bletchingley, Guildford, Southwark and the county of Surrey. The Tymperleys, father and son, between them sat for the towns of Bramber, Gatton, Ipswich, Reigate, Steyning and Yarmouth. The Jenney family represented Dunwich, Norwich, Tavistock and the county of Suffolk. In 1472 John Paston wrote to his brother: 'If ye miss to be burgess of Maldon and my Lord Chamberlain will, ye may be in another place; there be a dozen towns in England that choose no burgess, which ought to do, and ye may be set in for one of those towns and ye be friended.' The impetus to borough creation came from the squire and the landlord class and the creation of a pocket borough was obviously a matter of no great difficulty.

Up to 1485 there were always about forty genuine merchants in the Commons and in the middle of the century a few merchants took a leaf out of the gentry's book and sought election in small and unimportant boroughs not their own. There was then a gap until 1491 when the tendency returned again in a small way. In the Yorkist parliaments for which something like full returns have survived (those of 1467 − 8, 1472 − 5 and 1478[17]) there were among the Commons two gentlemen to every townsman whereas the townsmen, if the law had been observed, should have outnumbered the gentry by three to one. Under Edward IV only 56 per cent of the boroughs sent even one resident member to parliament.

[17] 1478 was the last parliament with anything like full returns until 1491 − 2 and even that is exceptional.

By the late 1460s even knights were anxious to sit for boroughs if they could not obtain one of the much coveted county seats. The first to do so was Sir John Fogge, the treasurer of the royal household, who sat for Canterbury in 1467 − 8 and his close acquaintance Sir John Scotte, the controller, sat for the distant northern borough of Appelby in 1472 − 5. In 1472 Sir John Paston would have liked the county seat in Norfolk but in the end he apparently had to be content with a borough (unknown), and in 1489 Thomas FitzWilliam, the recorder of London and speaker, was originally returned for the city, but resigned that seat on being elected for Lincolnshire a few days later. Although knights from boroughs were still exceptional by this time they made up between 9 and 13 percent of the entire knightly contingent in the House. To such men election to parliament, especially for the county, was one of the crowning stages of a well-recognized *cursus honorum* — the recognition and the privilege of social eminence.

In view of this increasing gentry grip upon the Commons one might well ask the question to what degree, if any, was parliament packed? In the shires freedom of election seems to have been a jealously guarded aspiration. Aristocratic influence cannot be dismissed as an insignificant factor in elections, though it was only one of many influences. After all, considering the generally thin personal attendance of the baronage in the House of Lords and considering the general absence of 'party politics', it seems unlikely that members of the peerage would have shown any intense interest in packing parliament or in borough-mongering. Yet, as we have seen, borough-mongering was already well established in political life but the impulse to it, as later in the sixteenth century, more probably came from the gentry or minor aristocracy who wanted a seat in parliament. Certainly, peers from time to time, particularly in the disturbed middle years of the century, tried to influence elections and they may well have thought it desirable to seat some of their members in the Commons during times of crisis. The younger branch of the Nevilles did so in the north between 1450 and 1475. As comparative *arrivistes* in the northern power structure they may have done so as a means of asserting their interests against their more firmly established rivals, the Percies, who seem to have shown no interest whatsoever in the matter.

Even those magnates who chose to interfere could hardly dominate elections. Influence through skilful management was essential and, so far as the limited evidence available goes, it seems that most of them did not proceed even to these comparatively modest lengths. Although John Paston wrote in 1472 that Lord Hastings could put a man in parliament if he so wished, an investigation of the parliamentary careers of his retainers hardly demonstrates a strong urge to push them into seats. Only 7 (possibly 10) out of 90 of them sat in the Commons, at the most three per cent of the known members of parliament, far too few to form anything like a voting 'bloc'. Even if a number of other peers acted in a similarly modest way, the proportion of the total membership of the House which they influenced could hardly have destroyed the independence of the Commons. On the whole the evidence is too thin to decide whether they wanted to seat their followers or whether they acted to oblige members of their affinities, but the latter was probably nearer the truth.

It was almost certainly otherwise with the 'Westminster element', members of the royal household and the central government departments — members of the royal affinity in the wider sense — who sought seats in parliament, for the king may possibly have pressed them to do so. Such people generally filled about 30 per cent of the shire and 17 per cent of the borough seats. In the parliament of 1478, called for the attainder of the duke of Clarence, the figures rose to 40 and 23 per cent — 17 per cent of the whole House, as high a proportion as in the middle years of Elizabeth I.

If packing there was, it undoubtedly occurred within this group. Members of the household grabbed borough as well as the more prestigious county seats. They especially invaded six distinctly over-represented counties with an exceptionally large number of small boroughs — Dorset, Somerset, Wiltshire, Surrey, Sussex and Cornwall — though they also extended their activities to the royal duchies of Lancaster and Cornwall[18] and to the four nothernmost counties. In the shires named, at least 8 per cent of the borough returns were tampered with, either by the Chancery or locally. Sometimes erasures and alterations in returns were no more than the legitimate correction of mistakes and there was nothing sinister about them. Most cases, however, were those of the complete 'carpet-bagger' class, and Professor J. S. Roskell considers that in these counties in particular the sheriff conducted negotiations with the boroughs for the election of minor household retainers and that quite possibly he received a list of recommended candidates with the writs of summons sent down from Westminster. On occasion interference was even more blatant. In 1467 the election indentures for Bodmin and Liskeard were written in advance in what appears to be a Chancery hand including the name of one of the burgesses; the other was added, presumably later, in a much cruder local script.

Such men very well knew what the king expected of them. In 1450 a petition after a disorderly election in the county of Huntingdon stated

---

[18] Which had wide estates outside the county itself.

that the electors discreetly considering it 'behovefull to your royal estate and considering the safeguard of your most gracious person ... that gentlemen of this your most noble household named in your chekir roll should be most like the expedience and [illegible] to execute and assent to the said aids for you our sovereign lord' had chosen two esquiries of the household, Robert Stonham and John Styvacle. A solid government front bench obviously expedited the grant of taxation and other matters of royal policy.

X

Taxation could be obtained only by means of a parliamentary grant, technically, at least, initiated by the Commons. Laws could be made, changed or repealed only by statutes and statutes too could be made only through parliament. By this time contemporaries were definite enough in their notions of what the assembly was. One of its original and most important functions, the administration of justice, had fallen to minimal proportions and in a parliamentary sermon of 1442 the bishop of Bath and Wells declared that its chief function was 'prudent ordaining'. In 1449 the archbishop of Canterbury said that parliament was summoned so that the king could hold colloquy and treaty concerning the government of the realm upon matters which could not be disposed of outside the assembly. In 1482 Sergeant Catesby, in a case argued before all the justices, apparently assuming that everybody would accept his statement as self-evident, remarked that any legislation which the Commons passed was binding upon all the king's subjects 'because every man is privy and party to the parliament, for the Commons have one or two for each community to bind or unbind the whole community'. Such remarks became commonplace under Henry VII; but perhaps the most succint definition was that of Bishop Russell in 1483: parliament was 'the place of wordly policy'.

'The place of wordly policy' or not, there were different opinions about its utility. The gentry, with their strong desire to sit in such assemblies, may well have regarded them with some enthusiasm. On the other hand, we have no evidence of any ideological commitment on their part. Except at times when dangerous dynastic issues were involved (and at such times the Commons were remarkably passive), they seem to have concentrated upon the passing of private and local petitions, commercial legislation generally inspired by some lobby or other and demands for better public order and the more upright conduct of officials. As long as government was, by current standards, effective, the Commons tended to be docile. What roused them were excessive disorder and suspicions of royal extravagance which would result in demands for taxation to make up a financial deficit. Both Edward IV and Henry VII succeeded in 'living of their own'. Edward IV made vigorous attempts to improve the state of public order. There is so far, except for the passing of additional statutes, no comparable evidence for Henry VII, though, on the other hand, there seem to have been no complaints of failure during his reign.

Possibly the Commons did not always effectively represent the views of their constituents. In 1472 – 5 and in 1489, for example, they voted war taxation, the collection of which proved to be a dreadful fiasco. It is perhaps more surprising, in view of the blacklash which so swiftly followed his death, that they did not complain about Henry VII's extortionate administration of the royal lands and his notorious perversions of justice in numerous individual cases, but after all there were only two parliaments in the last sixteen years of his reign.

The negligent attitude of the peers towards parliament shows a profound indifference and kings seem to have been far from enthusiastic about meeting the representatives of the communities. The main pretext for taxation had vanished with the end of the Hundred Years War in 1453. After 1461 the Commons were grudging indeed with their grants—an attitude which Edward and Henry, both insecure upon their thrones, reluctantly accepted, for the alternative lay in the development of perilous discontents. Although most important legislation was increasingly based upon bills drafted by the judges and other royal councillors, neither Edward nor Henry thought that new legislation was sufficiently important to call for frequent or regular sessions. During the personal rule of Henry VI parliament met, on average, for 49 days a year. Under the Yorkists the figure fell to just over 24. Under Henry VII it declined yet further to just over 18. Such average figures, however, conceal the cumulative extent of the decline. From 1495 to the end of his reign Henry summoned only two parliaments, lasting a total of 123 days—an average of a mere 9 days over 15 years. Henry wanted as few parliaments as possible. The act of 1504, authorizing him to reverse attainders at will, he in part justified on the ground that he was not minded '*for the ease of his subjects*, without great necessity and urgent causes, of long time to call and summon a new parliament' (my emphasis). Nor did he ever call another before his death. Whether the Commons appreciated this royal consideration or not is another matter.

No observer at the time of Henry's death in 1509 would have

predicted a vigorous future development for the English parliament. Although, as a result of the gentry invasion of the borough seats, the House of Commons bore a closer resemblance to that of the early Stuarts than to the parliament of Edward I, the experience of at least six decades of financial recalcitrance had severely limited its utility to the monarchy. The protection of individual liberties still lay more in the common law than in parliament and as long as the monarchy's policy of 'living of its own' remained viable that monarchy could well manage without parliament unless it chose to embark upon an expensive foreign war. Only the unforseen financial stringency and the religious divisions of the sixteenth century would bring parliament into its own again.

3 Royal Finance

I

As we have seen earlier the functions of English government in the later middle ages were distinctly limited — limited externally to defence and internally to ensuring that public order did not fall below a certain, but somewhat indefinite, standard, which most people regarded as tolerable. As there were no grandiose projects of public development and, at the local level, the major part of the internal task of maintaining order fell upon the rich as a function of their property-holding, folk regarded the royal need as equally limited and they saw little necessity for any large government expenditure in normal times. Therefore they did not expect the government to call upon them to pay its recurrent expenses. Englishmen in the fifteenth century took for granted Seneca's concise dictum, 'To the king belongs authority, to the subject property', and firmly held the view that except in times of war their property should not finance the exercise of the royal power. The highest of all authorities, St Thomas Aquinas, supported these ingrained conventions, maintaining that God appointed rulers not to seek their own gain but to prosper the general welfare. After rhetorically asking whether the taxation of Christian subjects was legitimate at all, the great doctor, quoting Ezekiel — 'To the King shall be given a certain possession in Israel and princes shall no more prey upon my people' — laid it down that rulers were appointed a 'pension' which should suffice for their needs and which removed any excuse for the spoliation of their subjects. Taxation was therefore justifiable only in special cases, principally defence, though the saint admitted that these special circumstances could include insufficient revenue for the upkeep of a suitably dignified court. An English extremist like Adam of Usk (writing in the 1420s) even claimed that God had cast his righteous judgement in the defeat of Sir John Arundel's naval expedition of 1379 because it had been impiously financed from the proceeds of taxation; in a later section of his chronicle he sanctimoniously hoped that Henry V would not share the

fate of tyrants like Caesar, Asshur, Alexander, Hector, Cyrus and
Maccabeus in divine retribution for the enormous sums of money he
had wrung from wretched victims of all classes to pay for his French
war.

Sir John Fortescue, the century's best known publicist, in *The
Governance of England*, written in its final form probably in the
1470s, expressed in much more moderate language the platitudes
about government current in the mid-century—platitudes reinforced, particularly on matters financial, by bitter experience in the
last two decades of Lancastrian rule. He divided the royal expenses
into ordinary and extraordinary charges, the ordinary charges being
the expenses of the royal household, the wages and fees of the king's
great officers, his courts and his 'counsel', the expenses of the Marches
against Scotland, and the king's 'works', the maintenance of the royal
castles and other buildings. Sir John regarded these charges as
necessarily great but, at the same time, as reasonably constant and
therefore requiring no more than a fixed, predictable revenue—the
equivalent of Ezekiel's possession in Israel, though he did not,
himself, use this particular phrase.

A monarch, careful of his income, watchful of his household
expenditure and, above all, ever on guard against courtiers and
officials eager to dilapidate his properties and revenues for their own
benefit, should need to demand assistance from his subjects only to
meet extraordinary, unpredictable charges which no ruler could
reasonably expect to foresee. The greatest of these was the defence of
the realm. The remainder of Fortescue's list makes somewhat curious
reading. It is, perhaps, a reflection of the disorders which he had lived
through under Henry VI that, although he included the expenses of
the law courts among the ordinary charges, he classed as abnormal
expenditure the considerable cost of sending special commissions and
judges to various parts of the country 'to repress and punish rioters
and risers', and even the personal journeys of the king himself for the
same purpose. Extraordinary charges also included the cost of
sending and receiving ambassadors and all the valuable gifts and
large *douceurs* which custom demanded should be given upon such
occasions. The northern European courts had not yet adopted the
new Italian practice of maintaining resident ambassadors abroad.
Embassies were still *ad hoc* affairs coming and going to meet the needs
of particular occasions and they were always expensive. But, in fact,
Fortescue's attitude was rather out of date by this time for diplomatic
activity had become so frequent and intensive that, like the maintenance of justice, it was really one of the continual, normal features of
government. The other main charges of extraordinary expenditure
were those expenses, such as the purchase of splendid jewels, which

contributed a suitable magnificence to the royal state.

Since the days of Blackstone (1723 – 80) English historians, rein-forcing their views by comparison with continental practices, have described medieval kingship as being, from time immemorial, a form of endowed monarchy, with a parallel division of revenue (like expenditure) into ordinary and extraordinary: its ordinary revenues, or endowment, consisted of feudal dues, the profits of justice and the royal estates (or crown lands), reinforced from the end of the thirteenth century by the profits of the customs system, while extra-ordinary revenues were the proceeds of direct taxation.

Recently, however, Dr B. P. Wolffe has vigorously challenged this whole conception of the sources of the English medieval royal revenue and, in particular, the financial importance of the royal endowment in land, maintaining that, at least from the time of the Norman Conquest until the later fourteenth century, the kings of England had never looked upon their estates as a major source of revenue and the amount of cash which they produced had, in fact, been astonishingly small.[1] The major function of the crown lands lay in maintenance for members of the royal family and in the provision of political patronage rather than in the generation of revenue. The exigencies of patronage reduced them to a condition of. perpetual flux, now replenished by the feudal law of escheat, by forfeitures for disloyalty to the king which, by the early fourteenth century had developed into forfeitures for the crime of treason; now reduced in extent and value as the king endowed members of his own family with land, made gifts for the good of his soul to the church, rewarded supporters with per-petual grants, which varied from single manors to estates broad enough for the endowment of a baron or an earl, or made leases at low reserved rents which left the recipients to enjoy the bulk of the income from a manor. Consequently, the monarchy depended for its revenues mainly upon taxation and the fourteenth century showed an astonishing, if somewhat premature, exploitation of the national wealth, notably through immensely high export taxes on wool and to a somewhat lesser extent in the taxation of personal property.

Such exploitation did not pass without resistance. Over and above vehement objections to particular taxes, from the early fourteenth century kings and their advisers began to hear ominous murmers of the notorious maxim 'The king should live of his own.' When the

---

[1] For the following paragraphs see B. P. Wolffe, *The Crown Lands, 1461 – 1536* (1970), pp. 1 – 28, and *The Royal Demesne in English History: The Crown Estate in the Governance of the Realm from the Conquest to 1509* (1971), chapters 1 – 3. Chapters 6 and 7 of this latter book are revised reversions of articles published in the *English Historical Review* in 1956 and 1960. Both versions need to be used, however, as the earlier versions contain materials not included in the revisions and *vice-versa*.

phrase first appeared, critics of the monarchy used it in a much more restricted sense than it later, and usually, came to bear. It registered protests not against the general lines of royal financial policy, but merely against oppressive, arbitrary purveyance of men's goods for the use of the royal household and armies — an abuse of power regarded as so intolerable that in about 1330 his subjects threatened Edward III with deposition should it continue.

From the early thirteenth century, however, successive kings began, deliberately, to form new and more permanent complexes of estates which contributed a larger and more stable revenue to their coffers. By the early years of Richard II the Commons, impressed, perhaps over-impressed, by the current value of such inherited possessions, began to insist that the government could meet a greater proportion of its expenses from them and should therefore show a greater restraint in its demands for taxation. In 1385 they demanded that the king should increase his income and protect both his interests and their own by a resumption of the extravagant grants which he had recently made to some of his followers. From this time onwards the demand that 'the king should live of his own' became, for generations, an almost sacred cliché, at the same time changing its meaning to the sense that he should live on the known revenues of his hereditary rights and properties, particularly upon his endowment in land. The Commons adamantly asserted such views whenever they suspected the king of extravagance and mismanagement. They demanded such policies of Henry IV in 1404 and 1406 and Henry VI's reputation notably improved after he had yielded to parliamentary demands for an act of resumption in 1451. By 1450 a House of Commons whose members were more experienced than at any time thereafter until the reign of Queen Elizabeth I had become adamantly opposed to any realistic assessment for direct taxation,[2] and their resistance to royal demands upon their purses became so conspicuously successful that, by the 1460s, they had confined the government in a financial strait-jacket from which it finally struggled free only in the seventeenth century — a rigid system within which subjects forced their king 'to live of his own', to live in unadventurous existence upon the profits of the crown estates and the yield of the indirect taxation of foreign trade.

[2] A. R. Myers (ed.), *English Historical Documents* IV, 1327 – 1485 (1969), pp. 379 – 81.

II

Richard, duke of York, had supported the Commons' demands that the king should live of his own, had supported their demands for resumptions. His son, Edward IV, or at least Edward's advisers were well aware of the popularity which Henry VI had gained from giving way to these demands.[3] They had so fully observed the political and financial lessons of the 1450s that they immediately adopted as the official policy of the government what had begun in the demands of a disgusted House of Commons, so that the royal lands became one of the two substantial pillars of the royal endowment.

These lands consisted of a core of hereditary royal estates, the vast lands of the duchy of Lancaster, which had always been separately administered, the wide hereditary estates of the Yorkists themselves, lands which the king purchased from time to time, estates which came to him as the penalty of forfeiture for treason and escheats, estates which reverted to him as lord paramount of the feudal system of land-holding upon the death, without direct heirs, of his tenants-in-chief.

For the efficient exploitation of the system three things were necessary: to ensure that the acres of the crown lands were not diminished, that, if possible, they were increased; to see that they were efficiently run; and finally that the patronage as well as the cash which they provided should be used for the king's own benefit.

Acts of resumption — four under Edward IV (in 1461, 1465, 1467 and 1473), followed by another five under Henry VII (two in 1485 – 6, one in 1487 and two in 1495) — maintained and increased these estates. Numerous exceptions, some general, many in favour of particular persons, burdened all these acts. Some exceptions had to be granted for technical reasons to avoid hardship to office-holders or to avoid disturbing property settlements. Nor, of course, was a wholesale abolition of government patronage either feasible or desirable. At the same time Edward's interest in the operations of the acts was minute enough to prevent wholesale concessions at the demand of former grantees. Throughout his reign he personally signed every petition for exemption.

In spite of the hundreds of concessions and exemptions granted over the years the acts were very successful. The real gains came under Edward IV, so much so that by 1485 the monarchy possessed most of the land to which it could decently lay claim and Henry VII's acts seem mostly to have safeguarded — and only marginally extended — this Yorkist achievement.

[3] See below, chapter 6, pp. 189, 192.

To the considerable estates regained under the operation of the acts of resumption, forfeiture for treason added many more. Immense estates fell into the hands of the crown following acts of attainder for treason, particularly the wholesale act of 1461 which, apart from members of the Lancastrian royal family, condemned to forfeiture no less than one hundred and thirteen people. Although these gains were not in most cases permanent since the majority of attainders, particularly those of the great, were reversed, they were helpful as a temporary relief for the crown: supporters could be rewarded from them thus easing pressures upon the monarchy's more permanent assets.

Historians have often implied that in the long run the most significant potential source of increase was the king's position as lord paramount in the hierarchy of feudal tenures. On the death of any of his tenants-in-chief, their lands permanently escheated to the crown. No one has yet, however, produced convincing evidence for this period to show any significant increase from this source; and even, *a priori*, the theory seems to be somewhat unconvincing for few families were without collateral heirs sufficiently close to the main stock to lay reasonably convincing claims to inheritances, and to deny such claims to powerful families resulted in dangerous political resentment.[4] The development of what historians have come to call 'fiscal feudalism' was, therefore, seriously hampered by considerations of political expediency, even of political appeasement.

The augmentation of the crown lands was only part of the task. The other part was to ensure their efficient management. Edward IV, upon his accession, almost immediately began to introduce a new and vigorous policy. In 1461 he set up a new council, mostly composed of trained professional men, to supervise the estates of the duchy of Cornwall and in the following year he extended his attentions to other estates, appointing eight regional officers to be responsible for royal lands let to farm in groups of contiguous counties, to collect the farms and make new leases where appropriate. Although the yield of these particular estates showed no appreciable increase over the next few years (they produced no more than £2,000 in any one year), the arrangement was symptomatic of a new spirit, for this was the first time since the thirteenth century that such fee-farms had been supervised by special, salaried local officials.

This method, however, was no more than a minor amelioration of existing practices. No great improvement could be expected as long as overall supervision of the royal estates remained with the Exchequer, for its methods were totally unsuited to a system of

[4] See below, pp. 299 – 301.

vigorous estate administration. So overcentralized was it that its officers rarely, if ever, moved from their comfortable accommodation in Westminster. Their immobility denied them sufficient knowledge of the estates which they were supposed to supervise and thus left them quite incapable of imposing adequate local control in days when most men looked upon their appointment to official positions as a heaven-sent occasion for personal gain.

The Upper Exchequer, or Exchequer of Account, was an extremely conservative, extremely tenacious, and abominably slow enforcement or debt-collecting court. Clinging to inadequate, almost fossilized, techniques of control developed in an earlier, more primitive, less literate age, it had failed to adopt the up-to-date dynamic business methods more recently developed upon private estates — methods essential once the decison had been taken to exploit the royal estates for cash as well as for the distribution of patronage.

During the late fourteenth and early fifteenth centuries the techniques of private estate management had advanced so rapidly that they were not to be improved again before the development of scientific methods of surveying in the later sixteenth century. Early methods of estate supervision (those to which the Exchequer clung) had no greater aims than the mere checking of officials' accounts for the prevention of fraud and peculation. In the later part of the fourteenth century the development of the *valor*, and the practices whicy lay behind it, as an effective feature of private estate management, showed a leap forward to more modern techniques of rationalization and control. The *valor* was more or less a digest, made by a landowner's auditors, of all the estate accounts for one year, analysing very fully the character of the lord's income and the charges which it had to meet. The information which it provided could then serve as a guide to future exploitation. Advancing lay literacy, developing education with its production of the lay 'gentleman-bureaucrat' trained in the common law and in methods of accounting — some of them even in a 'business school' at Oxford — had made possible these more refined and efficient practices. This 'business school' was a kind of adjunct to the university run by grammar masters who taught the arts of formal letter-writing in Latin and French, conveyancing, the drafting of deeds and the holding of courts — more or less courses in estate administration. The owner of any considerable estate employed a corps of professionally educated, highly skilled officers, usually a surveyor, a receiver-general, assisted by other receivers and one or more auditors. Often minor, even middling, landowners themselves, these officials were no mere petty rent-collectors. Their employers expected receivers-general to be men of substance, 'of haviour of richesse', prosperous enough to put up substantial bonds and recognizances, backed by those of friends and acquaintances, to guarantee their honesty and good conduct. Nor did they work remote from their charges like the Exchequer officials. They rode far and wide, the length and breadth of the estates under their control, supervising, checking, advising, keeping the activities of the minor local officials under constant scrutiny. Many of them must have spent a great part of their working lives in the saddle. Particular families specialized in this kind of work, generation after generation—the Heton family employed by the Stafford dukes of Buckingham, the Leventhorpes in the duchy of Lancaster, the Luthingtons in the service of the earls of Warwick.

The most extensive system of estate management of this kind, and one of the most successful, in the later middle ages was the duchy of Lancaster. Its lands, scattered over most of the counties of England and Wales, had always been kept completely distinct from the crown lands administered by the Exchequer. It says a good deal for the conservative fecklessness of the three Lancastrian kings (not one of them seems to have had much financial sense) that they never attempted to introduce the incomparably more effective methods of their duchy into the management of their crown lands. The house of York itself had received its income from such a system as that which operated within the duchy of Lancaster, although their estates appear to have been considerably worse run. Edward IV and his advisers, therefore, probably took the estates of the duchy of York and the earldom of March as their example in applying the methods of private estate management to the crown lands and to those lands regained under the acts of resumption. Ill-run as these Yorkist estates had probably been, they yet provided a far better model than Exchequer methods.

Edward IV (or the council, to which a fair proportion of this work seems to have fallen) kept the royal lands firmly away from the treasurer and barons of the Exchequer, arranged them in convenient groups and placed them in the care of specially appointed professional officials. Auditors working locally, not Exchequer auditors sitting at Westminister, now went through their accounts. As early as 1461 Edward created a new unit covering lands in ten counties in Wales and the Marches. Cutting across in a new way the boundaries of traditional estates, it grouped conveniently together the local estates of his own earldom of March, some duchy of Lancaster lands, some crown lands and lands which were in the king's hands owing to the minority of Henry, duke of Buckingham. The king appointed John Milewater receiver-general and John Luthington, who had many years of service on the earl of Warwick's estates behind him, was to audit the accounts at Hereford. Likewise Richard Crofte, the receiver of a group of lands in Oxfordshire, presented his accounts for audit at Woodstock and Gervase Clifton, whose charge lay mainly in the northern Midlands, submitted his at Nottingham Castle.

Not all the crown lands were placed under this type of skilled professional control. Some, undoubtedly for political reasons, the king leased to private people for lump sums. Yet most of the larger estates which fell in were administered as part of the new decentralized system. By the last years of Edward IV's reign the six receivers of the lands forfeited by the duke of Clarence after his attainder in 1478 were making declarations of their accounts at the Exchequer, but all the rest of the king's receivers were accounting to the 'foreign' auditors as the new type of men were called. During Richard III's reign no receiver of royal lands made any appearance at the Exchequer at all.

The staff required was, for the times, large. Edward IV, apart from the duchy of Lancaster, made nearly one hundred separate appointments of receivers, surveyors and auditors to operate outside the Exchequer. Their high pay and their lavish expense accounts were commensurate with their expert training and their considerable responsibilities. John Luthington received 5s. a day as auditor of north Wales and Chester, John Milewater, as receiver-general of the group of estates in the ten counties, Wales and the Marches, fees and expenses totalling £60 a year, John Hayes £20 a year for collecting money and £34 for other duties. Such pay in many cases probably exceeded the profits of their own modest estates and their professional incomes alone were enough to place them among the two or three thousand most prosperous men in the realm. This decentralized system of estate management reported its doings and paid its revenues no longer to the Exchequer but to the Chamber — a department of the royal household — and possibly to a number of provincial treasuries. Gradually the Chamber absorbed more and more of all the king's revenues, not merely those from the crown lands. In 1461 a great loan of £11,000 from the city of London was paid there. By the early 1490s the Exchequer was handing over most of the income from the customs system and by the last years of Henry VII's reign the Chamber was receiving well over 90 per cent of the monarch's cash.

This being so it may well be asked why the king did not completely abolish the Exchequer, its action being so notoriously inefficient and so many of its functions being transferred elsewhere. In fact, although the king's coffers in his Chamber became his principal treasury, the Lower Exchequer, or Exchequer of Receipt, still performed useful routine functions which prevented the Chamber from becoming overloaded with detailed work. It provided, as in the past, for the routine expenses of various departments. The Upper Exchequer also performed useful auxiliary duties and therefore continued in existence. Although obsolete as a central estate and audit office, its authority as a court of law left it still useful as an enforcement branch, for initiating and deciding actions against defaulting officials (below the rank of receiver-general) whose defalcations or negligence the local auditors had revealed in their scrutiny of the accounts.

The earlier stages of these developments are shadowy, for unfortunately the Yorkist Chamber records have completely disappeared. We owe what knowledge we have to circumstantial evidence, mainly exemption orders to the Exchequer protecting the new estate staff from its interference. It was not until the reign of Richard III that government memoranda described the system in general terms. A set of instructions then issued for the honour of Tutbury showed the king's concern to appoint to offices expert professionals rather than local men, who would more easily yield to the temptation to feather their own nests. Another memorandum summarized and described the whole system, now comparatively matured, which Richard's brother had introduced in a series of experiments begun twenty years and more in the past.[5]

With Henry VII's accession the new system received a temporary setback. His complete inexperience in all forms of administration did not augur well for the royal financial affairs. The new Yorkist system had depended upon the king's own intense, personal application and direct action. Edward IV had frequently issued instructions to his estate officials under his signet or sign manual and by word of mouth. Newly arrived in England, insecure, threatened by rebellion, and with most things about government still to learn, Henry failed to grasp the significance of the Yorkist land experiment. For lack of royal attention the system fell into abeyance. The Exchequer moved in again, returning to Lancastrian financial methods. Then in 1487, the king in the preamble to a new act of resumption declared that he had been so occupied with his own preservation that he had not found time to appoint officials to manage his estates, so that they 'been greatly fallen into decay'. A rueful statement amply confirmed by the decline in their receipts: they had declined from £25,000 a year under Richard III to about £11,700 in the first year of Henry's reign.

From then onwards, undoubtedly under the influence of ex-Yorkist bureaucrats, Henry began the gradual restoration of the Chamber system, but, as in everything he did, he proceeded slowly, with a wary suspicion, at first cautiously exempting only individual receivers from the rigid procedures of the Exchequer and assigning foreign auditors to go through their accounts. He did not swiftly restore the Chamber to its paramount position. For several years the

[5] British Library, MS. Harley 433, 270 – 71, printed in J. Gairdner (ed.), *Letter and Papers Illustrative of the Reigns of Richard III and Henry VII* (Rolls Series, 2 vols, 1861 – 3) I, pp. 79 – 85, and Wolffe, *The Crown Lands*, pp. 131 – 7.

Chamber and the Exchequer existed side by side performing, in their different ways, similar functions. It was not until well into the 1490s, perhaps as late as 1497, by which time the Chamber had become the treasury for most of the other royal revenues as well as the profits of the crown lands, that the new system once again became supreme and the treasurer of the Chamber became the most important financial official in the kingdom. Sir John Heron, who held the office from 1492 to 1521, regularly attended the royal council for the discussion of financial matters and by 1506 he was called 'the general receiver of our lord the king'. By the mid-1490s the Chamber auditors were known as the 'general surveyors' and for the years between 1502 and 1506 books of summaries of 'declarations' of final account show the appearance of some forty receivers a year before the king and the conciliar committee, some of them several times a year for several charges. In addition these 'general surveyors' heard all the final accounts of a number of farmers of lands and a conciliar docket book reveals considerable financial specialization. Even so, however, the organization was still as informal as it had been in Yorkist days. Henry himself supervised it very closely, issuing detailed orders and personally inspecting the accounts of the treasurer of the Chamber. Until April 1503 he initialled every entry of a receipt himself; thereafter he was content to initial only each page.

No less was his concern for the advantages which he enjoyed as lord paramount of the feudal hierarchy. The king possessed potentially valuable rights over his tenants-in-chief. Although the feudal system had long since lost its original military significance (the feudal host had last been summoned in 1385), it survived as a system of financial exploitation. The heir of any tenant-in-chief had to sue out livery for his inheritance against a fee — a kind of succession duty. Any lands which he held of other lords fell in like manner under the king's control. If heirs were under the age of twenty-one they became royal wards. The king held their property until they were old enough to sue for livery and he controlled their marriages. Moreover, widows of the feudal classes might not remarry without the king's consent, often obtained only for a substantial fee.

Although foreign observers found this commercialized feudal system, with its deleterious effects upon family life, uniquely revolting, the English at this time resented it less that we might expect because if many lost by it many also profited. Lesser lords enjoyed the same rights over their own tenants so that the upper ranks of society were throughly steeped in the spirit of the system. Feudal families often handled their own affairs in accordance with its conventions even when they were uncomplicated by the existence of royal rights, so that a tangle of estates, wards and widows played something like the part of an investment system. Stephen Scrope, Sir John Fastolf's stepson, once bitterly remarked that in his childhood he had been bought and sold like an animal, but his horrible memories did not later prevent his telling an acquaintance, 'for very need I was fain to sell a little daughter I have', and complaining that the transaction had not brought in as much as it ought to have done. Margaret Paston, in her will, left 500 marks for purchasing land for her son, William, or to buy a well-endowed ward for him to marry, and in 1475 Thomas Stidolf, the king's attorney, on hearing of the death of a neighbour, rode all through the night to court to be first there with the news and to ask the king for the wardship to the heiress. Wardships were even bought and sold on the instalment system. The dangers of meddling with a royal widow are vividly illustrated by an incident in *The Paston Letters*. According to Sir John Paston, one hot August day in 1478:

> Young William Brandon is in ward and arrested for that he should have by force ravished and swived an old gentlewoman, and yet was not therewith eased, but swived her oldest daughter, and then would have swived the other sister both; wherefore men say foul of him, and that he would eat the hen and all her chickens; and some say that the king intendeth to sit upon him, and men say he is like to be hanged, for he hath wedded a widow.

The writer obviously considered this squalid rape of two obscure women and the attempted rape of a third by a young man of apparently insatiable lusts a less heinous offence than holy matrimony when holy matrimony involved tampering with the king's rights.

The enforcement of these feudal rights demanded eternal vigilance. The concealment of feudal tenures both by collusion between the families concerned and royal officials and by the creation of uses or trusts had become notorious during the fifteenth century. Governments had been well aware of such evasion, and general enquiries into feudal tenures had gone on more or less continuously under Henry VI. They were probably ineffective as no protests against them are known. Under Edward IV similar action was effective enough to be resented. By 1474 the Chancery had issued commissions of enquiry covering ten counties and three cities and more commissions followed. The Croyland Continuator stated emphatically that the king himself 'examined the rolls and registers of Chancery and exacted heavy fines from those whom he found to have intruded and taken possession of their estates without prosecuting their rights in the form required by law, and by way of return for the rents they had in the meantime received' and the Tudor chroniclers preserved a tradition of heavy fines levied during Edward IV's later years.

Henry VII continued in the same way, steadily issuing commissions, both general and particular, for the investigation of his rights, much to the distaste of his subjects who, in the parliament of 1495, showed their fear of increasing exploitation by refusing to approve the grant of a feudal aid which would have meant a countrywide investigation of tenures. Interest in these matters had now become so great that in the same year two sergeants-at-law, Robert Constable and Thomas Frowick, made the king's feudal prerogatives the subject of their readings (or lectures) at Lincoln's Inn and the Inner Temple. For a time Sir Reynold Bray was in charge of this aspect of the royal finances but after his death the king created the office of master of the wards for Sir John Hussey, who soon organized a network of local officers in every country to manage wards' estates. Even so, as we shall see, the results were disappointing.[6]

The other main source of royal revenue was the customs, introduced by Edward I in 1275. The principal duties levied in the late fifteenth century were the 'ancient custom' on wool, hides and woolfells, the custom on cloth, the subsidy of tunnage on wine, and the petty custom and poundage on general merchandise. The 'ancient custom', cloth custom and tunnage were *specific* duties, the petty custom and poundage *ad valorem.*

The export duties on wool were far higher than any others. The rates fixed by an act of parliament of 1465[7] were 33s. 4d. per sack of wool or 240 woodfells and 66s. 8d. per last of hides for denizens, but aliens paid at the much higher rate of 66s. 8d. and 73s. 4d. These sums amounted roughly to an *ad valorem* duty of 25 per cent for denizens and 33 per cent for aliens, and they rose to something like 41 per cent for aliens in 1471. If a denizen shipped in a carrack or a galley, in other words a foreign ship, generally Italian, he had to pay alien rates. The duties for cloth had not varied since 1347, standing at 1s. 2d. per cloth for denizens, 1s. for Hanseatics and 3s. 9d. for other aliens, at the most about two to three per cent in *ad valorem* terms. Other rate were 3s. per tun for wines, 6s. for sweet wines and 12d. in the pound on all other merchandise, imported or exported, with the exception of tin. On tin denizens paid 12d. in the pound, aliens 2s. Certain imported foodstuffs (corn, flour, fresh fish and cattle) were completely exempted together with exports of ale and victuals for Calais. The penalty for concealment was fixed at double the subsidy.

Legal theory about the customs was anomalous. Although theoretically regarded as part of the king's inheritance or 'livelode' they required a parliamentary grant—a grant which Edward IV did not

---

[6] See below, pp. 89–90.
[7] *Rotuli Parliamentorum* etc., ed. J. Strachey, (6 vols, 1767–77) v, pp. 508–10. Some of the rates were slightly varied from time to time in later acts.

obtain until this act of 1465, although he had collected them since the beginning of his reign.

During Edward's reign the average annual yield substantially increased, particularly during his later years. It must remain an open question whether this increase was due to expanding trade or to stricter administration—or both. A veil of uncertainty will always cover this problem for, owing to the very nature of the methods involved and the conditions under which the customs officials worked, it is much more difficult to detect corruption in this type of fiscal administration than in a system of direct taxation.

As with the crown lands, Edward IV made great efforts to tighten up the system. For some years his efforts were tentative rather than vigorous. In the 1460s a few, probably useless, acts of parliament were passed and from time to time the king issued commissions of enquiry into breaches of the staple laws. More vigorous action followed after the king's return from exile in 1471. A statute of 1472 increased the penalty for evading tunnage and poundage from payment of double the subsidy to forfeiture of the smuggled goods. The real remedy, however, lay less in more legislation than in stricter enforcement.

In 1473 a most comprehensive commission into all sorts of evasions was issued for Devon and Cornwall, authorizing among other things enquiries into the conduct of the customs officials as far back as the first day of the reign. From then onwards the periodic issue of such commissions was standard practice. In 1474 a really searching investigation began when commissions covering twenty-one counties and districts were issued ordering enquiries into evasions of the staple laws. If anything, the scope of enquiries widened rather than diminished. When commissioners were instructed in August 1480 to investigate the smuggling of wool in Sussex, they not only received the usual powers to examine merchants but in addition were given authority to examine sheep owners in the county as to the disposition of their wools during the previous five years. The king even invoked the help of Louis XI to prevent the smuggling of wool into Normandy.

Beginning with an experiment at Southampton and Poole in 1473, Edward imposed stricter methods of supervision upon the customs staff. By 1481, for the first time apparently since 1447, he had reintroduced officials called surveyors into twelve of the principal ports, giving them almost absolute authority over the existing staff. In 1480 the king, probably angered by revelations of widespread evasion, subjected London, by far the greatest port in the kingdom, to a double system of control, separately appointing William Western as surveyor of tunnage and poundage while leaving the other customs under the joint control of William Grimsby and Robert Fitzherbert. Edward IV was a hard-headed man of business, not given to paying out good money for nothing, and, as with the estate officials, their remarkably high pay attests the importance with which he looked upon the work of the new surveyors. John Taylour, who covered the southwestern region (the ports of Exeter, Dartmouth, Plymouth, Fowey and Bridgewater), received £20 a year and a moiety of all the forfeitures, William Weston 100 marks a year for himself and £10 for his clerk. One hundred marks a year equalled the income of one of the minority of the richer gentry and even the king's envoy at the papal court in Rome received only £120. William Weston was definitely among the more highly paid office-holders in the kingdom and many of the London merchants whom he met in the course of his work may well have envied his salary.

If resentment is any criterion of success, by the end of the 1470s this new, intensive supervision had begun to bite and to bite deeply. In July 1479 the Merchant Adventurers were vehemently lamenting 'upon the streytness of the Custumers' and the Croyland Continuator has left us his impression of the new system:

> Through all parts of the Kingdom he [the king] appointed inspectors of customs, men of remarkable shrewdness, but too hard upon the merchants according to the general report.

Once again, as with the crown lands, Henry VII was content to follow where Edward IV had led, continuing in the same courses and from time to time closing up loopholes in the system. From 1487, for example, merchants in the coasting trade who shipped goods from one English port to another were required to produce a certificate from the customer at the first port of call giving specifications of their merchandise and declaring that duties upon it had been paid, and in 1495 additional safeguards were introduced to ensure the payment of customs upon cloth exported. Basically, however, Henry in no way changed the system.

The last main source of income, though by this time of diminished importance, was direct taxation. Edward I had introduced the standard late-medieval tax upon personal property in 1275. Though at first immensely lucrative, within about four decades a combination of conventional evaluations and fraudulent assessment had reduced its yield by about two thirds. In 1334 a disillusioned government tacitly admitted failure, abandoned the established method of directly assessing individuals to the levy on each occasion the tax was granted and allocated lump sums to be raised by each county and borough. The system possessed the advantages of being politically inoffensive and cheap in its operation, the cost of collection being probably less than two per cent of the yield. Unfortunately, however, the yield thereupon became fixed at a figure merely derisory when

compared with that of forty years earlier and at a figure which hardly
began to tap the country's real wealth.

The tax was the fifteenth and tenth — one fifteenth of the value of
movable goods in the rural areas and one tenth in towns and on the
royal demesne — a capital levy rather than an income tax, producing
over the whole country about £37,000. Lancastrian governments had
been forced to make even further concessions. In 1433 parliament cut
the proceeds by 10.4 per cent and in 1446 by 15 per cent so that the
gross yield was reduced to about £31,000 and the net yield to about
£29,000. The pretext for reduction was relief for towns and districts
which had decayed since 1334, but in fact each county received an
exact percentual remission. The clergy taxed themselves separately in
their convocations, this time upon incomes and upon equally out-of-
date assessments, producing about £13,000 from the province of
Canterbury and £1,400 from York. The scandal of the facts was
notorious enough. As the Venetian envoy wrote home in 1497: 'This
tithe is not taken according to the real property of either the clergy or
the laity, but by an ancient assessment of the kingdom.'

Neither Edward IV nor Henry VII ever dared to make a frontal
attack upon these now venerable abuses. The advisers of both kings
recognized that they must, above all, be circumspect in their
demands for money. The very narrow basis of support which was all
they both at first enjoyed would never be widened if they made heavy
direct demands upon the purses of their subjects. Neither, therefore,
requested parliament to make a direct grant for two years after they
came to the throne — in Edward's case two years during which he was
in the most desperate financial straits for cash, living from hand to
mouth and forced to raise it by all kinds of shifts and contrivances. In
April 1463 he at last asked for a fifteenth and tenth and screwed up his
courage to the point of demanding that the Lancastrian cuts should
be restored. Even this modest triumph must have produced murmers
which scared the king for in the next session of parliament he gave way
and allowed the now customary remission of £6,000.

In 1497 Henry VII, in addition to two fifteenths and tenths of the
usual kind, also obtained a special grant equivalent in value to two
more, but now directly assessed by special royal commissioners upon
individuals instead of lump sums being allocated for collection by the
counties and the vills. It was still a tax with a traditional limited, set,
total yield but more realistically assessed. Somewhat similar was a
special tax levied in 1504. The assessment of these two taxes formed
something of a precedent for Henry VIII's taxation reforms introduced from 1513 onwards, but these were much more far-reaching in
that the grants set no upper limits upon the amounts to be collected.
They were open-ended subsidies with the assessors instructed to raise

as much as they possibly could. Henry VII's modifications were therefore no more than a somewhat timid effort at fairer assessment, with no real attempt to raise total yield.

Other experiments in taxation, it is true, there were. Earlier in the century the Lancastrian kings had made a number of attempts to levy an income tax. Edward again made such a demand in 1472 and Henry in 1489. On both occasions passive resistance to the levy was so great, and the results so unsuccessfully humiliating,[8] that neither of them ever felt inclined to repeat the effort. The English propertied classes had become so adamantly resistant to realistic levels of direct taxation that the insecure monarchy, successful though it was in introducing some other financial reforms, here found it wise to yield and to admit defeat.

Denied the assistance of their subjects through traditional, regular channels, both kings turned to somewhat dubiously unroyal methods to swell their purses. Both wisely accepted pensions from the king of France, more or less as bribes to end foreign campaigns. Both engaged in trade upon a considerable scale and Edward, even, was not above retailing wine to his own troops on campaign. At times they demanded a proportion of their wages and pensions from royal office-holders to meet emergencies, took forced loans for the same purposes, exacted 'benevolences', or more or less compulsory 'free' gifts from their subjects (not only from the rich but from people as far down the social scale as comparatively poor yeomen), revived obsolete military burdens such as distraint of knighthood, took stiff fees for the reversal of outlawries: in short they widely employed such dubious methods as Sir John Fortescue had condemned as 'exquisite means' — dubious, more or less lucrative, but generally politically irritating financial methods forced upon kings whose patrimony was somewhat too slender for comfort and whose subjects refused them their collective assistance.

III

It is easier to describe financial methods at this period than to assess their results. The Yorkist accounting system in the Chamber was extremely informal. Even such records as it produced have completely vanished. All that survive are orders to particular people, some scattered estate acounts, the customs accounts and, from the reign of Richard III, some valuations of estates and lists of offices.

[8] See below, pp. 287 – 8, 341 – 2.

From this circumstantial evidence Dr B. P. Wolffe, with infinitely minute labour and ingenuity, has produced some plausible estimates of income. For the reign of Henry VII we are in somewhat better case. Various financial notebooks and docket books survive which give better, but still, unfortunately, far from complete information. None of the surviving financial records were cast in the form of balance sheets from which it is possible to calculate exact levels of income and expenditure. At best, therefore, most figures calculated from these sources (except for the customs revenues and for the fifteenth and tenth) are no more than plausible estimates, which enable us to say that, at most, the results of all this new activity were respectable rather than spectacular.

When in 1433 the treasurer, Lord Cromwell, produced his famous estimates of the royal expenses, revenues and debts to persuade a reluctant House of Commons to vote taxes for the French war, it seems that the estimated gross figure of all revenues was about £54,000 a year, but the total net revenues had sunk as low as £36,000. It is true that the Lancastrians met a fair, though unknown, proportion of their expenses by assignments[9] upon local revenues, many of which sums were therefore most probably excluded from these estimates. Nevertheless, it is sufficiently evident that in 1433 the monarchy was abominably poor. It is true that a grant of two fifteenths and tenths a year could have rescued it from its difficulties, but these in the political temper of the times it was impossible to obtain. Even so matters grew far worse for between 1437 and 1449 royal resources were alienated to courtiers and supporters on the most extravagant scale. By 1450 the royal finances had sunk so low that many writers bitterly attacked the way his friends robbed the king and more than one saw fit to comment upon Henry VI's shabby personal appearance, itself a grave political disability in days when royal splendour was very much a factor in maintaining the prestige of government.

Nevertheless, with the resumptions of the early 1450s the royal finances did improve, though it is impossible to say how much. The accusation in *Davies' Chronicle* (the author was an ardent and none too truthful Yorkist partisan) that by 1460 the king was poorer than he had ever been, having given away all the manors and possessions of the crown, seems to echo merely the violent criticisms of a decade earlier. There had almost certainly been a modest improvement. Edward IV's position in 1461 was certainly better than that of Henry VI before the acts of resumption of 1449 – 51. Even so, the immediate prospects were bleak indeed. Edward could not avoid heavy expenditure during his earlier years to repress Lancastrian opponents and, for

---

[9] That is, warrants to a creditor to collect money from a local receiver, customs officers etc.

political reasons, he accepted responsibility for Henry VI's debts to the Calais garrison.

There could be no immediate solution to his financial problems. The reorganization of the royal estates took time before it increased the revenues and he could not impair what little support and authority he had by asking for direct taxation. Nor could he keep his principal creditors waiting too long for their money. The finances of his earlier years were a web of shreds and tatters. He lived from hand to mouth as best he could, borrowing here, there and everywhere. In June 1461, a week before his coronation, he obtained a loan of £11,000 from London and in the next six months he managed to borrow another £18,000 from various sources. Between 1461 and 1470 he seems to have borrowed at a rate of at least £19,000 a year, though the loans were very unevenly spread and the figures are by no means complete.

In addition to borrowing he was forced to run up considerable debts. It was not until 1466 − 7 that light at last began to shine through these lowering financial clouds. The treasurer of the royal household then for the first time had a surplus — as much as £650 and more — on the year's working account although the settlement of accounts from earlier days remained long in arrears. By the end of the 1460s Edward had at least made a breakthrough.

These favourable trends continued on the king's return from exile in 1471. After 1472 the level of loans registered was remarkably small compared with those of the previous decade and after 1475 they shrank to almost nothing. In 1472 Edward, while naturally taking the precaution that his creditors should properly prove their claims, began arrangements for paying off in twenty annual instalments all debts which he had contracted before the 1st December 1470. By 1476 he was able to improve on these arrangements, but at the same time he was forcing his creditors to accept compositions — the remission of a proportion of the debt in return for firm arrangements for the repayment of the rest. Gerard Caniziani agreed to accept £3,000 to liquidate the remains of a debt which at the end of 1471 had stood at over £14,390. Two years later London bargained for £7,000 and rights of appointment over certain city offices including that of coroner, on a debt of £12,933 9s. 8d., and a few months later many smaller creditors were accepting final compositions. By the end of the reign Edward's debt to the merchants of the Staple, which had stood at £32,861 in 1466, had been steadily reduced to no more than £2,616 0s. 10d. and with this powerful corporation, probably because it was so involved with the defence of Calais, Edward did not bargain.

Historians have usually trounced Edward for cheating his creditors in a uniquely shabby fashion, but in fact he was merely following the example of earlier kings.[10] Even so, his record was considerably better than that of his grandson, Henry VIII, who, on more than one occasion, demanded that parliament repudiate his debts completely and whose final debts remained unpaid for a quarter of a century after his death.

In his later years Edward was sufficiently affluent to lend quite considerable sums of money to merchants and to carry on a war against Scotland for nearly two years without calling on parliament for money — which he did only in 1483 when the Treaty of Arras between the Emperor Maximilian and Louis XI of France made additional war preparations imperative.

Henry VII likewise began his reign in difficulties, though unfortunately his borrowings have not been worked out in the same detail as those of Edward IV. In 1485 he owed the duke of Brittany 10,000 gold crowns and within a few weeks of his accession he borrowed well over £10,000. For the first five years of his reign (the period when the new Yorkist land system was in abeyance and the land revenues were shrinking), he depended upon short term loans to keep his head above water, though at the same time, to establish a reputation for fair dealing he paid off debts and redeemed (often for more than their intrinsic value) gems and other valuable objects which Richard III had pledged to various citizens. Once more with the passage of time the position reversed itself. During his last five years Henry lent over £87,000 to English and foreign merchants and he paid out over £220,000 to his continental allies.

As to the revenues which made possible this reversal of fortune, it is possible to attempt only the crudest of estimates. No figures can even be guessed for the income from the crown lands before the reign of Richard III. By that time the king was receiving between £22,000 and £25,000 a year,[11] and possibly another £4,643 from sheriffs' farms, fee farms of towns, payments by bailiffs of liberties, vacant temporalities of bishoprics, wards, marriages and various feudal incidents. In the later years of Edward IV the customs had produced an average of about £34,000, lay taxation just about £10,700 and clerical taxation just over £7,000 a year. The benevolence of 1475 had netted £21,656 8s. 4d. and, if that of 1482 – 3 yielded a similar sum, together they would have produced an average of somewhat over £2,000 a year for the entire reign. In addition Edward raised local taxation from the communities of Flint and Chester which averaged about 1,100 marks

[10] For discussion of this point see G. L. Harriss, 'Preference at the Medieval Exchequer', *BIHR* xxx (1957), 21.

[11] C. Ross, however, points out that over £13,000 a year must be deducted for the expenses of various members of the royal family, so that Edward IV's actual income from land may have been less than £10,000. *Edward IV* (1974), p. 381.

a year. Local revenues at Berwick and Calais (also spent locally,
however) produced about £9,000. All told, in about 1483 cash
revenues may have amounted to between about £90,000 and £93,000.
In addition both Edward and Richard made profits, now unknown,
from trading ventures, and from 1475 to 1483 Edward received a
pension of 50,000 crowns (£10,000 a year) from the king of France.

Between 1502 and 1505 (the years for which the most reliable
figures survive), Henry's *regular* revenue averaged £104,863 a year. If
certain *ad hoc* payments such as Catherine of Aragon's dowry and
arrears of the benevolence of 1491 are also included, the average for
the last nine years of the reign comes to rather more than £113,000.
This figures does not include direct taxation for none was levied
during these years.[12] The increase during the reign had accrued
mainly from the customs and the crown lands. The customs revenue
had increased by about a quarter and the land revenues, in the widest
possible sense of the term, by about two fifths. Once again, how much
the increased customs revenue was due to stricter administration it is
impossible to say. The land revenues, however, showed no greater
intrinsic profitability than the Yorkists had achieved. The increase
was simply due to further forfeitures for treason and to deaths in the
royal family which brought more estates into the pool.

Compared with the estimates for 1433, these figures appear to show
a mighty increase. In fact, however, a direct comparison between the
two sets of figures is certainly misleading. By the 1490s, at the latest,
the government had adopted more 'modern' methods of centralized
collection and centralized payment, abandoning the older practice of
assignment upon local source of revenue. More items therefore
appear in the centralized accounts than had been the case eighty years
earlier.

These cash results, though sound, were hardly spectacular. They
still fell considerably below the revenues of Edward III which, for a
brief period in the mid-1350s, had exceeded £157,000 a year. In spite
of all their strivings the later medieval kings never attained the income
of some of their forbears!

IV

Reform is so relative a concept that any analysis of improvements can

---

[12] Henry averaged about £12,000 – £13,000 a year over the whole reign from lay taxation,
possibly £9,000 a year from clerical taxation and the benevolence of 1491 brought in rather over
£48,000.

all too easily convey an exaggerated impression of achievement, particularly to people accustomed to the operations of sophisticated
modern bureaucracies. In spite of superficial appearances, the
reformed financial system was in the end neither popular, strong nor
wholly successful. Political conventions, dishonesty, resentment and
resistance flawed its operations at every turn.

Serious limitations were almost built in to the new system of estate
management. The king, no matter what his need or greed for money
may have been, still dared not exploit it with a single-minded concentration upon cash revenues. The offices, employment and rewards
which the royal estates provided for his supporters were at least as, if
not more, important than the money which they provided for his
coffers.[13] These two aspects of administration were complementary
and no discussion can realistically separate them.

Sir John Fortescue was fully aware of these interlocking problems,
though his recommendations about them were simple and one-sided
to the point of naiveté. By and large, reflecting the opinions which he
had heard so vehemently expressed in the Commons in the 1450s, he
looked upon the royal estates as an asset from which the maximum
cash yield was to be obtained to meet the current needs of government. He recommended that offices be rationed to the king's own
servants on the basis of one man one place — a point of view showing a
doctrinaire simplicity quite impracticable in the conditions of the
day.

William Worcester, the author of the *Boke of Noblesse*, the
spokesman of the dispossessed captians of the French wars, expressed
a totally different point of view. Worcester thought that the king
owed such a debt of gratitude to the men who had suffered grievous
losses from the fall of English rule in France that he should, if the
worst came to the worst, strip himself even of his treasure and jewels to
support them until better times when war in France could be resumed
again. Worcester, and the tiny minority for whom he spoke, pressed
these opinions to an extreme as absurd as it was dangerous, yet their
absurdities enclosed a kernel of hard reality. In spite of the new and
growing emphasis on money, the royal estates were still one of the
king's most important political assets and they had to be used as
such — as rulers as late as the early Stuarts found to their cost. Most
men not only voiced the fiercest objection to taxation, but in politics
they felt it far more blessed to receive than to give. They expected to
be rewarded for their services, even for their mere loyalty, according
to their status. The higher the rank the greater the gain demanded
almost as of right, and an eager, avaricious horde anxious for the

---

[13] Wolffe, *Crown Lands*, p. 53, thinks that the redisposal of offices was a more important
factor in Yorkist resumptions than financial considerations.

pickings of estate management constantly besieged the king and every considerable landowner. Before the Stonors rose in the world they fiercely competed for offices from the local religious houses. Afterwards they pestered the king. This type of gratification had risen to such absurd proportions that aristocrats gave each other offices on their respective estates and noblemen prominent about the court could expect to receive many profitable grants of this kind. Therefore the crown could never regard its lands exclusively as a profit-making enterprise. A nice balance had always to be held between financial and political considerations.

From this point of view, both the Yorkists and Henry VII were fortunate in having at their disposal the forfeited lands of those opponents whom they had attainted for treason. Though only a minority of the greater estates remained permanently in the hands of the crown, at least for a time they brought in both a cash income and, more importantly, provided a pool from which the king could make grants of land and offices, thus reducing pressure upon the crown lands themselves. The process was, perhaps, rather cynical for it soon became obvious that tenures thus granted were precarious. As the attainted made their peace, such lands and offices had to be surrendered to their original owners. Yet even with this assistance, the drain upon the royal lands was very great.

Such patronage may well have been better controlled than at any time in the past. From the days of Richard III there survive four separate lists of royal offices in England and Wales. It is doubtful whether any earlier kings had such comprehensive and precise information available to them and the wise distribution of this patronage was, according to the Croyland Continuator, a vital aid to political stability in Edward IV's later years. So it should have been, considering its immense cost. The Ricardian lists reveal at least eight hundred offices worth £13,000 a year. Out of this grand total as many as seven hundred derived their income from the crown lands, the farms and sheriffs' farms to a total of about £7,000 a year. Many were, in effect, valuable sinecures and, together with annuities and pensions granted from the same estates, they absorbed about £10,000 a year—£10,000 as compared with about £25,000 at the most in cash revenues. Much of this, of course, formed legitimate administrative expenses. Even so, the crown appointed many local officers more for the sake of their influence than for any professional competence—and many of them were painfully corrupt.

Even allowing for the effects of patronage, it is doubtful whether the crown could ever have exploited its estates to their productive limits. In spite of the general advance in administrative techniques and the activities of the travelling bureaucrats, the crown lands were probably too great in extent for them to be run effectively as a whole. The almost standard combination of patronage, immensely strong conservative resistance to change and the normal tendency to corruption among officials meant that the wider the estates the more intractable became the problems of supervision and control.

The record of the new estate administrators was patchy to say the least and in some parts corruption certainly flourished. After his death in 1475 Stephen Preston, who had been one of the most trusted officials of the royal household, trusted over the years with several important financial assignments, was found as keeper of the forest of South Pederton to have felled most of the standing timber and to have sold it for his own profit. If some lands showed greater profits, others registered a decline. Between 1467 – 7 and 1481 – 2, after a progress by the duchy of Lancaster council through the duchy estates in Cheshire and Lancashire, their receipts rose from £347 to £885 a year. A group of Yorkshire manors produced £117 a year from the beginning to the end of Edward's reign. And, as mentioned earlier, the duke of York and his royal successors completely failed as landlords to exploit the industrial development of the manor of Bisley.

Even though many men enjoyed a stake in the royal estates and their profits, they, or others, soon came to resent what they considered to be the crown's excessive exploitation of its lands for cash. The Commons not only grudged taxation, they wanted to have their cake and eat it and they more and more grudged the king his own. The extent to which Henry VII stressed financial gain in his relationships with his subjects had made him most unpopular by the end of his reign.

His eighteen-year-old son, whom Henry VII had kept totally inexperienced in government business, immediately gave way to aristocratic pressure. Richard Empson and Edmund Dudley, the two most notorious agents of his fiscal policies, were at once arrested and later condemned to death on trumped-up charges of treason. Then in October and November 1509, the royal council, in which nobles and lawyers rather than financial experts for the moment predominated, recommended the abolition of the 'bye courts' — the agents of Henry's financial policies. Their pretext alleged that these were not courts of record. Legally, they could neither 'charge nor discharge' any person coming before them. Such procedures, therefore, were abusive and vexatious to the king's subjects and their continued use might also result (through legal uncertainly) in the loss of royal rights in future.

The council, therefore, immediately subjected the general surveyors to the Exchequer. Whatever the legal and political tensions thus eased, the financial results were so immediately calamitous that the authority of the general surveyors was partially restored in 1512. Even so, there was no full renewal of that maximum drive for profit which had formely caused such intense resentment. Although the revenues recovered somewhat, they never again rose to their old level. By 1515 they were yielding little more than £25,000 a year as compared with £40,000 in 1509. As Dr B. P. Wolffe remarks: 'With the removal of the old king's personal drive and control the crown lands had thus become a rapidly wasting asset.'

Nor, in spite of the loud resentment which it produced, was royal exploitation of feudal rights conspicuously successful. Its problems baffled royal ingenuity for well over a hundred years. By the end of the fourteenth century most wealthy families had placed a good deal of their landed property in the hands of trustees to be held to their use, thus enabling them to devise real estate by will and to evade the feudal incidents of livery, wardship and marriage. Henry IV had tried to deal with the widespread evasion of his feudal rights due to such trusts and uses, but unsuccessfully. His failure, in parliament, followed by a number of adverse verdicts in the courts seems to have discouraged any further efforts by the crown so that by the middle of the century the right of the *cestuy que use* (or the man who benefited under the trust) to escape the incidents of tenure was so well established that the judges refused to take advantage of him even if the technicalities of the law failed him.

In spite of the immense resentment which both Edward IV and Henry VII drew upon themselves in their attempts to end this evasion of feudal rights, once again success eluded them. In 1492 the Office of Wards produced only £343. By 1507 its profits had risen to £6,163. Even this, however, was minute compared with the £83,085 which Charles I forced from the system in 1639. Less than half this vast increase could have resulted from sixteenth-century inflation. Probably many small estates escaped completely. The greater the estate the more difficult concealment was, but even some of the richest in the land were undoubtedly successful in evading a major part of their obligations. When the earl of Northumberland was assassinated in 1489, leaving an heir only eleven years old, three quarters of the family estates were found to be in the hands of trustees. In fact, a jungle law prevailed. Henry, probably deeply resentful of being so widely cheated, exacted scandalously high sums wherever he saw the chance — exactions which naturally aroused the indignation of the victimized who saw so many of their neighbours escaping. Henry harassed those of his feudal tenants whom he found to be individually vulnerable but his attempts to make a frontal attack upon his recalcitrant feudatories by legislation were humiliatingly feeble and unsuccessful. So the matter rested until, in 1529, Henry VIII was prepared to consider and, in 1540 after a long battle with the landed classes, both in parliament and in the law courts, to accept a compromise under which he granted feudal tenants the right at common law to make trusts and uses in return for the guarantee of his full feudal rights over *one third* of their estates. So great an attrition of its legal rights can hardly be called a triumph for endowed monarchy.

Although the customs revenues after 1509 showed no decline comparable with those from the crown lands, it is doubtful whether, in spite of all efforts for administrative improvements, the king had earlier received his just income.

In the first place the method of evaluation for the *ad valorem* petty custom and poundage was far from effective.[14] A parliamentary grant made in 1439 laid down that the goods of denizen merchants should be valued for poundage 'after that they cost at the first buying or achat, by the oaths of the same merchants denizens, or of their servants in their absence, or by their letters, which the same merchants have of their factors and in none otherwise'. Every subsequent grant, up to and including that made for life to Henry VIII in 1510, included an almost identical regulation. These grants are oddly silent about any method of valuing the goods of alien merchants but there is some evidence to suggest that it was the same as that used for Englishmen. In other words, the merchant could give more or less what value he pleased. In the absence of any expert check, such a method was an invitation to corruption. And the crown failed to devise an expert check. Only an experienced trader could adequately value merchandise and, although the government often appointed merchants as customs officials, it was suspiciously aware that they traded and cheated on their own account. The only remedy was almost as bad as the disease.

The government made no reform in rating until 1507, and even then only upon a very limited scale with a somewhat primitively arranged 'Book of Rates' issued by the royal council with the advice of the surveyor, controller and customers of London and the Merchant Adventurers of the city. Although many writers have assumed that the purpose of the book was a general increase in rates, this does not seem to have been the case. Its valuations, in fact, were mostly based upon those already current in the port of London and some of these, such as those for salt, pewter and woad, were as low as one seventh of the true value of the merchandise. It increased only the valuations of a few staple commodities. The book, therefore, probably aimed only at the more limited objective of securing greater order and uniformity in the collection of the London customs, and perhaps to check fraud

---

[14] For a full discussion of this disputed topic see H. S. Cobb, 'Books of Rates and the London Customs, 1507 – 1558', *The Guidhall Miscellany* VI (1971), pp. 2 – 3.

between customs officers and merchants by adding to the general statements of the parliamentary acts precise, if extremely low, valuations for wide ranges of goods.

Secondly, in spite of immense efforts and considerable expenditure, the drive against corruption was not conspicuously successful. Recent investigators of the customs system have asserted that, at this period, the dues on goods other than wool were too low to make evasion worthwhile and that wool itself was too bulky to be smuggled on any considerable scale. Therefore the enrolled customs accounts may be accepted as reasonably accurate.[15] Such an opinion strongly conflicts with the views of well-informed and intelligent contemporaries who, throughout the fifteenth century, were convinced that merchants, with the connivance of officials, practised evasion upon a wide scale. Investigations in particular ports strongly supported their opinions and successive governments were convinced that they were being extensively cheated.

Smuggling, in fact, was easy, owing to the lack of any effective system of checks and controls. The word 'port' was a technical term. During the fourteenth century it had come to be used not merely to denote a place for the anchorage of ships, but also in the sense of a delimited length of coastline based upon a privileged haven — a fiscal collection. These areas consisted of fifteen head ports where the customs officers lived, member ports controlled by their deputies and creeks more or less unsupervised where it was comparatively easy for the small ships of the day to sneak in and lade cargo undetected.

The customers (there were generally two in each port except for London which had a larger staff) were responsible for the evaluation of goods and the collection of dues and the controller was supposed to check their records or rolls. Against collusion between the customers and controller the crown had no safeguard except in the case of wools shipped to the Calais staple. There at Calais, the searcher collected the merchants' cockets[16] which listed the amount of wool in each shipment; he was also supposed to examine the wool and to retain the cockets for comparison, if required, with both the books and the counter-rolls of the port of origin. Even so the risk of detection was probably not great. In 1428 the Exchequer devised a scheme to tighten up the administration by sending down to each head port certain parchment books, known as port books, in which the local

[15] For the detailed arguments see P. Ramsey, 'Overseas Trade in Reign of Henry VII: The Evidence of Customs Accounts', *ECHR*, 2nd series VI (1953 – 4), pp. 173 – 82 especially p. 178 and E. M. Carus-Wilson and O. Coleman, *England's Export Trade, 1457 – 1547* (1963), pp. 21 – 7.

[16] A sealed document delivered to merchants as a certificate that their merchandise has been duly entered in the records and has paid customs duty.

officers were ordered to record the details of all transactions. So matters still stood in 1461.

An examination of one group of ports reveals both the vigour and the defects of the system. The southwest, though certainly not the one in which the volume of trade was the greatest, was probably the toughest of all the regions within the customs jurisdiction — long notorious for piracy, violence and smuggling. Edward IV began a successful drive against piracy in the 1470s and during the same decade Thomas Gale and Thomas Grayson, the customs collectors in Exeter and Bridgewater, themselves merchants and by no means above suspicion, presented more cases of smuggling and evasion in the Exchequer than the officials in any other provincial ports. In 1481 Edward appointed another merchant, John Taylour of Exeter, as surveyor for the whole region. The government had felt the need for action for some time and John Taylour, before his appointment to the surveyorship, had brought himself to the government's notice through his activities as a common informer. In December 1475 the government took such a serious view of the corruptions of the southwest that, after deliberation in the Exchequer, the barons directed a privy seal to Roger Keyes, the chancellor of Exeter Catherdal; at the same time they sent him a 'roll of paper', signed by no less a person that the king's own secretary, William Hatteclyff, giving details of the 'great deceits' perpetrated in Topsham and Dartmouth during the previous year and more, and ordering him to conduct an investigation on the basis of the information sent to him. He was to interrogate the masters and owners of all vessels belonging to these ports, the masters of all foreign ships named in the paper roll and any others named to him by John Taylour. He was also to examine several named merchants. Keyes did his job thoroughly, sending in a report giving details of sixty-nine sailings during the time in question — from which it appears that abuses in Topsham and Dartmouth had indeed been extensive.

Rather less than two years later Taylour was also involved in another notorious incident. Early in September 1477 a ship called the *Anne of Ottermouth* had taken on board at Exeter a cargo of cloth and tin worth 50 marks, on only part of which had export duties been paid. Hearing of this, Taylour.had pursued the *Anne* from Exeter to Brixham where he seized her on the eve of the Feast of the Exaltation of the Holy Cross as she lay in the bay waiting for a fair wind for Brittany. He examined the ship on the eve of the Feast and the following morning again went on board with a force of men drummed up apparently from the riff-raff of the town. Finding only one man and a child on board he courageously demanded to see the customs' cocket. This was alleged to be on shore with Phillip Atwyll, an Exter merchant who was part-owner of the cargo. Leaving a guard on the ship, Taylour went back into Brixham to hear mass, taking the additional precaution of carrying away the ship's helm with him. The ship's company were also at divine service and there the master, John Baker, 'moved' Taylour three or four times, but Taylour proved adamant as a rock and swore that he would take the ship to either Dartmouth or Topsham. Taylour, who seems to have been as devout as he was vigorous, then in the north aisle of the parish church, with somewhat unconscious irony in the circumstances, knelt to make his devotions before the image of Our Lady of Pity. While their persecutor was immersed deep in prayer, the mariners, on the instructions of the ship's master, quietly departed one by one and at last, the unsuspecting Taylour still being deep in prayer, the master himself made off out of church with the helm. Taylour must have prayed long and deep (according to his own account at least) for it was only when the men whom he had left on the *Anne* angrily burst in upon him accusing him of double-crossing them that he realized what had happened. Tearing down to the waterfront, they found that Baker had weighed one of his anchors, in his frantic hurry had cut the cable of the other, and had already hoisted his sails. After a vigorous exchange of missiles Taylour's riff-raff attempted to board the ship from two boats. Then Taylour, hanging on to the stern, argued with Baker until, in the end, he agreed on oath to take the *Anne* to Topsham and allowed three of Taylour's men on board. He soon broke his oath, put them ashore between Brixham and Topsham and sailed off to Brittany. On her return from Brittany the *Anne* was arrested under a royal commission and Phillip Atwyll was also taken into custody. Atwyll escaped and, brandishing a pole-axe, threatened that Taylour would not have long to live if ever he came near him.

It was this same John Taylour who, rather less than three years later, Edward appointed surveyor of the customs in the southwestern ports and shortly afterwards he combined the post with that of ulnager.[17] Taylour's whole career is interesting. He was a merchant of Exeter who had also been in the service of the duke of Clarence. Edward IV afterwards made him a yeoman of the Chamber and employed him in the administration of part of Clarence's forfeited estates. Later, under Henry VII, he went into exile, was attainted and plotted from abroad for a Yorkist restoration. In the 1470s he and his family were deeply involved in the violent and squalid politico-personal disputes of the city of Exeter, where the Taylour and the Atwyll families were at daggers drawn. It is more than likely that personal spite moved Taylour in his pursuit of Atwyll and in 1482 the

---

[17] Ulnage was the duty paid on all manufactured cloth, whether for home consumption or export.

Atwylls were charged with forging a 'bill', alleged to have been found by a jury of Exeter citizens, accusing Taylour of concealing a valuable forfeiture of cloth which he had seized in Topsham instead of surrendering half to the king as he was required to do under the terms of his patent of office. By modern standards a quarrelsome maverick like John Taylour was hardly the incorruptible civil servant and there can be no doubt that many local agents of Yorkist and early Tudor administration were decidedly shady characters.

Smuggling was by no means confined to the lesser traders of the provincial ports. Brazen smugglers were to be found among the richest mercantile societies of London, the Mercers and the Merchant Adventurers. At a general meeting of the Mercers Court held on 30 July 1479 (their records and those of the Adventurers were, at this time, kept together), some discussion took place upon the 'streytnes' of the London customs officials in putting men to their oaths 'and such great inconveniences'. Previous consultation with 'Master Essex', the king's remembrancer of the Exchequer, one of the king's council, had produced only some unsatisfactorily trite remarks about adjustment in standards of behaviour on both sides. So matters stood until, at another meeting on 4 September, the presiding officer reported that the king had been 'strangely informed' that London merchants had been 'embezzling his subsidy' and through the mayor and alderman had issued a stern warning against such malpractices. The Mercers and Adventurers then agreed upon a common form for the future submission of their customs declarations. Though at this point the minutes remain tantalizingly obscure, the Mercers and the Adventurers were obviously very worried indeed for they decided that, in order to avoid proceedings in the Exchequer, a deputation should wait upon the chief baron, Master Whaytes, and Master Essex to seek their advice. Early in November the minutes at last reveal what the trouble was: 'divers persons' were already in serious trouble at the Exchequer and the Exchequer was threatening action against others. The crisis now appeared sombre enough for five alderman and ten fellows to be sent to seek a personal interview with the king, who was reasonably polite but non-committal.

The fellowship debated whether to see the matter through in common or let each man, so mysteriously concerned, take his chance individually. In the end they decided upon the former course of action, a 'general labour', though there may have been some demurrers against the decision, and still agitated, resolved to send two men to a meeting of the royal council.

The language of the minute book is cautious and guarded in the extreme. All that we can tell from it thus far is that these merchants were most upset about something to do with 'the subsidy', that at successive meetings they had grown more and more disturbed and agitated about it. They had disreputable reason enough for the evasions of their mealy-mouthed minutes. The clue lies in the reference to the Exchequer and the Exchequer records reveal that something like a customs drive had been going on in the port of London which had begun with a large-scale raid on all shipping lying at the wharves in May 1478. At all events, between June 1478 and the end of 1479, sixteen Mercers and Adventurers (among a good many others) had been prosecuted in the Exchequer for smuggling. One unfortunate Mercer, John Marshall, had no less than fourteen cases brought against him, quite apart from cases of the same kind in other ports.

It is true that most of these cases involved goods of only small value but in one concerning Richard Bell the custom officers had seized. at All Saints, Barking, Brabant cloth worth 500 marks. The Mercers' Acts indicate that the Exchequer was contemplating more prosecutions and it may well be that this threat of further revelations accounted for the merchants' acute anxiety and had prompted their decision for collective action.

At all events, as a result of the 'general labour', the king demanded a collective fine of £2,000, which the merchants impudently countered with an offer of £200, which they shortly afterwards increased to 500 marks. At this point the royal council agreed to defer consideration of the matter but the Exchequer, obviously taking no chances, insisted that those already prosecuted should appear in court so that a date might be fixed for hearings the following term. The Mercers' minutes so far had been so cautiously worded that this was the first time that they had ever mentioned the prosecutions.

The merchants now began to lobby in quite a big way. They appealed for help to the marquess of Dorset, Lord Hastings and other 'gentles' and even to the queen herself. They thought it would be a good thing to keep up pressure on Lord Hastings during the Christmas festivities when he might be able to catch the king in a particularly good humour and persuaded him to see the merchants representatives again. Early in the New Year (1480) they again waited upon the Marquess, Earl Ryvers and Lord Hastings, but the fellowship had evidently been rather less than discreet in their conversation for Hastings sharply told them not to brag so much about the doings of their influential friends. A few days afterwards, at the queen's intercession, the king reduced his demands by 500 marks and gave them the choice either of paying 2,500 marks (£1,666 13s. 4d.) or of facing continued individual prosecutions in the Exchequer. They reaffirmed their wish to pay a collective fine, set about raising the money by a levy on the fellowship while at the same time pressing the king for a further reduction. They wanted to pay £1,000 at the most. Finally the king agreed to accept 1,500 marks (£1,366 6s. 8d.) and to issue a pardon. The merchants then, to avoid the risk of more unwelcome investigations into their doings by the king and council, decided to discipline any of their members who, in future, tried to bilk the customs. Offenders were to be fined 100 marks for a first offence, £100 for a second and expelled from the Mercers Company if they offended a third time, with a recommendation to the mayor and alderman that such persistent offenders be dismissed from the franchises and liberties of the city.

Difficulties in the customs system continued apparently unabated. Under Henry VII the Exchequer court dealt with 1,140 smuggling cases. Between 1486 and 1488 Henry dismissed twenty officials for absence from their posts, illegally engaging in trade on their own account and embezzlement. Towards the end of his reign the informal notebooks of John Heron and Edmund Dudley, which record some of the cases in which the king himself was specially interested, reveal among others that John Paul de Byles forfeited 1,300 quintals of alum; divers merchants of Boston and Hull were fined £521 13s. 1d. for concealments; Sir John Hussey and William Hussey, both royal servants, had wool confiscated; two London merchants forfeited wool and five others owed £113 13s. 4d. in fines for smuggling the same commodity. The famous Thomas Spring of Lavenham smuggled in alum without the necessary licence and paid a heavy fine. Other cases involved the smuggling of cloth, madder, wine and silk.

As to officials, during the same short period, William Grene, the customer of Lynn, bought a pardon for 100 marks, Jasper Fifilol and his sureties in Poole forfeited £200, Henry Uvedall, the controller in Poole and Weymouth (had there been collusion between him and Fifilol?), 300 marks and Simon Digby, the weigher of wool in Hull, 100 marks. In 1509 the London surveyor, John Myllys, was dismissed after only three years in office for 'manifold misdemeanours'. These offences, however, pale into insignificance before the note, 'Robert Fitzherbert, late customer of London, hath deceived the king in his customs for which he is indebted to the sum or £4000.' Even the highly trusted Sir Reynold Bray, the under-treasurer of England, one of whose jobs it was to check the customs accounts, cheated. After his death the king forced his executors to enter into indentures to pay 800 marks (another 400 being pardoned) 'for a forfeiture of wools ... being at Calais'.[18]

All in all, in spite the scepticism of some historians on the subject,

[18] The sums involved in these last two cases may have been recognizances for enforcing payment rather than fines.

and the difficulties which must always surround it, both Edward IV and Henry VII were wholly convinced that they were being cheated of their just dues.

Finally, in the matter of direct taxation, defects were even more glaring then in the administration of the royal demesne, the feudal incidents and the customs. In those spheres, at least, the Yorkists and Henry VII had introduced improvements great enough to incur their subjects' resentment. By contrast, their failure with direct taxation was almost startling. Edward met resistance even in the collection of the ludicrously obsolete and low fifteenth and tenth and both he and Henry VII each found the results of their single experiment with an income tax a scandalous rebuff to their pride and power.

Between 1472 and 1475 Edward found his experiences in collecting an income tax to pay for his French campaign bitterly humiliating, both in parliament and in the countryside. In November 1472 he induced the Lords to grant him one tenth of their incomes from land, annuities and offices and the Commons separately granted a similar tax from non-aristocratic revenues. Both houses, however, surrounded their grants whith the most galling restrictions. The Lords instructed the collectors of their grant to pay the proceeds to the archbishop of Canterbury, the bishop of Ely, the prior to St John of Jerusalem in England and John Sutton, Lord Dudley, who in turn were to commit them to the dean and chapter of St Paul's Cathedral to hold until such time as they authorized release to the king. The Commons also appointed special collectors and ordered their collectors to place the proceeds in special provincial repositories — local castles, towns, houses of religion and other suitable places — again until they authorized its use. Either the Lords and Commons bitterly grudged the money or they doubted the sincerity of the king's war policy — possibly both!

Five months later, in April 1473, the Lords relented and allowed their taxes to be paid into the Exchequer, having it seems cynically underassessed themselves on the most staggeringly impudent scale. The parallel story of the Common's grant proved to be a woeful tale of delay following upon delay, shifty expedient upon shifty expedient, turning into evasion, dishonesty and outright theft. First, by April 1473, no certificates of assessment had come in from the collectors and the Commons alleged (though they were, in fact, mistaken) that as no records existed for any previous tax of this kind, it was impossible to estimate what the tax would yield. So as the king's need for money was urgent, the Commons granted (in addition to the income tax) a standard fifteenth and tenth on the value of moveable property — also be withheld in the local repositories until the proclamation of the army musters. Over a year later, in June 1474, the government revealed that the combined sums for both taxes would not meet the expected war expenses. To make up the deficit the Commons therefore granted a further tax, cynically shifting the burden on to the normally exempt religious order of St John of Jerusalem in England and on to that part of the population usually regarded as too poor to pay taxes.[19]

So things dragged on until the parliament roll of the following year (1475) reveals the deplorable results of this wretched tissue of distrust and evasion. Some of the taxation commissioners had not delivered the money which they had collected and were now dead, others had refused to deliver to the receivers at the appointed local repositories and had converted the money to their own use. Some of the 'governors' of the repositories themselves had yielded to temptation and had embezzled the funds and 'some persons ... with strong hand have taken parcel of the said tenth out of the place where it was put to be kept.'

Over two years after the first war grant had been made, no money at all had reached the king apart from the meagre proceeds of the Lords' tenth. Everything was still in a welter of confusion. The Commons at last, however, relented, released to the king what money had been collected and again substituted one and three quarters — fifteenths and tenths for the last experimental grant which they had made few months earlier.

In the end, Edward, through parliament, had raised nearly the equivalent of four normal fifteenths and tenths — almost as much as Henry V had raised in a similar period — but with infinitely more trouble than Henry V had ever encountered and against far greater resistance to payment. Even so, money for his campaign was so short that he had resort to a benevolence.

Though detailed contemporary accounts are lacking, Henry VII had no better fortune in raising money for foreign war or even for the defence of the realm. In 1489 Henry, to finance a campaign in Brittany, again induced parliament to vote an income tax, on this occasion also combined with a tax on moveable property and a graduated tax. He was even less successful than Edward IV had been. The Exchequer had estimated that it would bring in £25,000 from the clergy and £75,000 from the laity. Laymen so successfully resisted that parliament itself estimated that they paid no more than £27,000 and even this may have been an exaggeration. The next parliament, it is true voted two traditional fifteenths and tenths to make up the

[19] H.L. Gray, 'The First Benevolence', in *Facts and Factors in Economic History Presented to J. F. Gay*, ed. A. E. Cole, A. L. Dunham and N.S.B. Gras (1932), pp. 104 – 77, claims that this was an attempt to shift the burden of taxation on to those with a good deal of moveable property who normally contributed little to the fifteenth and tenth. I do not, however, find his arguments convincing.

deficit, but two years later, proposing to invade France, Henry, by experience a sadder and a wiser man, ignored parliament and raised £50,000 by a benevolence. Even so, his subjects had not shown the end of their resistance to taxation. When parliament in 1496 – 7 voted money for war with Scotland, basically a defensive war, the men of Cornwall rose in revolt rather than pay taxes for the defence of what they regarded as an outlandish part of the realm which was no concern of theirs.

Benevolences, though imposed without the consent of parliament, were not totally arbitrary royal actions. Neither Edward nor Henry ever called for direct taxation without the excuse of war or defence. Nor did they do so in the case of benevolences. It was a long-recognized obligation of every subject to put himself and his property at the king's disposal in time of emergency. Yet the resort to the benevolence was, after all, the dismal confession of failure of the elaborate, traditional methods of taxation – a bizarre combination of financial progress and institutional atavism. In a crude way it was a general tax tapping sources of new wealth ignored by the fifteenth and tenth, but tapping it by a reversion to a more primitive personal form of government, more or less to the tedious expedients of thirteenth-century kings before they had hit upon the labour-saving device of centralizing money grants in parliament. The king appointed commissioners for various districts to take from his subjects sums in proportion to their visible wealth and in 1475 Edward IV travelled about the country demanding with enormous personal trouble, in face-to-face interviews, donations from his subjects. Though immensely troublesome, such levies were politically less explosive than parliamentary taxation. The author of the *Great Chronicle of London* remarked of the benevolance of 1491 (with some considerable exaggeration about the sums of money involved):

> Then the King visited many counties, and the commissioners the residue, in calling the people before them and in such wise exhorted them, that the King's grace was well contented with the loving demeanour of his subjects. And so he had good cause for by this way he levied more money than he should have done with four fifteens, and also with less grudge of his commons, for to this charge paid none but men of good substance, where at every fifteenth are charged poor people which make more grudging for the paying of sixpence, than at this time many did for the paying of six nobles.

The chronicler also exaggerated the people's loving demeanour, for resistance to benevolences was widespread, if unorganized. In 1483, and later, the Exchequer was still prosecuting men for non-payment of that of 1475 and, although in 1495 parliament passed an act to enforce payment of the benevolence of 1491, Sir John Heron's notebook reveals that as late as 1505 contributions were still unpaid in 'every shire in England'.

V

Continuous progress has never been a conspicuous factor in English history, particularly the history of government finance. The later middle ages saw a marked break in development, so much so that the years 1461 to 1509 formed a period of remarkable unity in the financial history of the English monarchy — the period of a whole experiment in miniature, a system which Edward IV developed and brought to maturity, which Henry VII continued and refined and, in the opinion of many of his subjects, exploited to the point of gross abuse.

By the mid-fifteenth century the English acting through parliament (paradoxically enough earlier called into being at least partially for their exploitation) had resolutely denied their kings any significant calls upon their property. The vital condition of this restriction lay in the country's geographical position. As John of Gaunt, Shakespeare's 'time-honoured Lancaster' proclaimed, it lay secure in the protection of the sea, serving 'as a moat defensive to a house, against the envy of less happy lands'. The English were not only secure, they had become thoroughly insular. Fourteenth-century enthusiasm for war against France quickly declined into indifference, if not downright hostility, early in the fifteenth century. In spite of the existence of a small war party whose vociferous propaganda has misled generations of chauvinistic historians, by the 1420s the English upper classes in the Lancastrian parliaments had made it amply clear that they would not support expensive, foreign military ventures potentially profitable only to the royal dynasty, a small minority of the greater and lesser nobility, the few thousand men-at-arms who took part in them and merchants who profited from war contracts.

After the Norman and Gascon debacles of 1450 and 1453, the monarchy therefore, in effect, abandoned its continental ambitions. Royal fears rather than dynastic ambitions spurred even Edward IV's notorious campaign of 1475 and, if this experience served to prove anything at all, the squalid course of its financial preparations showed that not even a propaganda campaign with a marked emphasis upon the needs of defence would deter the king's subjects from blatant chicanery and evasion when it came to paying the taxes which their own representatives had voted in parliament. Henry VII was even less successful in wringing war taxation from a reluctant people and, although the fluctuations of continental politics obliged him, from time to time, to take a small force abroad to save himself from the consequences of a dangerous diplomatic isolation, the fiscal exigencies of such comparatively minor military activity produced domestic tensions dangerous to a king but insecurely seated upon his throne. Taxation for aggressive warfare by this time the English would not tolerate and appeals for taxation for defence they found almost totally unconvincing.

Therefore, one of the king's two major functions — defence — had become a comparatively minor preoccupation at least in his subjects' minds, if not in his own. By 1404 the Commons were convinced, by 1450 they were adamant, that his own resources, if carefully guarded, were adequate for his other main task — the preservation of internal order and the maintenance of a reasonable degree of justice — a contention which Edward IV tacitly admitted in a speech to the Commons in 1467.

With such a case and such strong feeling against them, neither Edward IV nor Henry VII was sufficiently secure or commanded sufficient support to risk the the political resentment which an aggressive forward policy in taxation would have brought upon them. What success could be achieved on these lines is shown by the record of the Catholic monarchs, Ferdinand and Isabella, in Spain, who between 1474 and 1504, are said, by means of more efficient administration at a time of growing national wealth, mainly that of Castile, to have forced up the yield of taxation from less than 900,000 to 26,000,000 *réales*. Even allowing for the fact that England was smaller and poorer, Henry VII's income of £113,000 a year was meagre indeed compared with the £800,000 which the king of France commanded and the £1,100,000 which the Emperor enjoyed by the 1520s. He was most definitely not among the financial giants of the European monarchs.

Freed from the millstone of foreign war, by developing the crown lands, and possibly by a more effective exploitation of the customs system, the monarchy freed itself from its mid-fifteenth century poverty. Beginning his reign deep in debt Edward IV was the first English king since Henry II to die solvent — even to leave a 'treasure' — albeit a sum of unknown extent for it quickly disappeared in the troubles which followed his death. And that with an income from taxation amounting to only half that which Henry IV and Henry V had enjoyed!

Henry VII is generally supposed to have done even better, to have left an enormous hoard to his son. In the later part of his reign natives and foreigners universally supposed Henry to be rich. In 1497 the Milanese ambassador wrote home that his fortune amounted to 'six millions of gold' and the duke of Saxony heard that Henry was 'the richest lord that is now known in the world'. Such rumours were probably given the widest currency when Henry VIII revived them a generation later in a vicious slander — an accusation (in 1529) against the fallen Cardinal Wolsey that he had squandered a mighty treasure which the king had inherited from his father. Cold, prosaic fact is far less interesting. Possibly Henry VII left a hoard of jewels and plate worth about £300,000, but certainly not much more than £10,000 in hard cash. All in all, no more than about three years' income.

Moreover, although the Commons had forced the king to 'live of his own', the situation was by no means as clear cut as this terse expression on the surface implies, for 'his own' was mutable and was by no means completely his own. Changing patterns of trade, the still comparatively low levels of efficiency and honesty, the greed of subjects to share the royal possessions, severely limited the possibilities of exploitation and therefore of revenue.

The growth of the domestic cloth industry at the expense of exports in raw wool with, by comparison, a minute export tax, had reduced the customs revenues to about four sevenths of their fourteenth-century peak. Customs valuations remained far below the commercial value of the merchandise concerned and, in spite of incessant efforts for stricter supervision, merchants and officials at all levels continued to evade and to cheat. Some of the local officials were decidedly shady by any standards and even the most trusted supervisors at the centre feathered their own nests without a qualm.

So the monarchy was forced back upon the revenues from feudal rights and crown lands. In spite of bitter complaints about the exploitation of feudal tenures, escheats and incidents, they were not at this time bringing in a large income. Henry VII's vindictive, sporadic exploitation of his rights as and when he could in a sea of evasion was no substitute for a general firm application of the law, which apparently prevailed only after the compromise of 1540.

The problem of the crown lands was not peculiar to England, though it probably existed in a more acute form here than elsewhere. In spite of the establishment of more lucrative systems of taxation abroad, by the end of the fifteenth century demands were being loudly made all over Europe that kings should live of their own and subjects were clamouring for acts of resumption in Scotland, France, the Netherlands and Spain. In Sweden an act of resumption was passed as late as 1680.

Even here, however, the crown lands had to be used for contradictory purposes — to provide, as the Commons themselves insisted, a maximum cash income and, through patronage, to pay for the loyalty of the king's supporters, a function which absorbed no inconsiderable part of their potential yield. It was never an easy matter to strike a nice balance between their financial and their political functions. In spite of their demands that the king should 'live of his own', the propertied

classes were almost as selfish about yielding him his own just dues as
they were in paying taxes. Loyalty to the king and the common good,
though theoretically debated in high-sounding tones, in practice, as
often as not, had to be bought — bought with the grant of estates,
pensions and lucrative offices which tended to the king's impoverish-
ment. On the one hand too great an emphasis on revenue and undue
meanness towards local *potentiores* undermined the position of the
dynasty; on the other a lavish generosity aroused the resentment of
wider circles of people asked to make up royal deficits by way of
taxation.

Edward IV and Henry VII took little from their subjects in the way
of direct taxation. Those same subjects widely evaded their feudal
obligations. Except for wool, the trading community paid derisively
low customs duties upon their merchandise. Office holders absorbed
at the very least one fifth of the revenues of the crown lands. In spite of
all this, both kings passed from this life with an evil reputation for
avarice, partly because, faced with such adamantine passive resistance, they (and especially Henry) had pressed demands for money in
harsh, arbitrary ways as and when they could, breaking the spirit
though not the letter of justice. A near contemporary poem, *The
Lament for the Soul of Edward IV*, made the king mourn:

I stored hucches, cofers and chyst
With tresore takyng off
My commyalte
Ffore there tresore that I toke
There prayers I myst.

After Henry VII's death, Lord Mountjoy wrote to Erasmus that the
whole land rejoiced for avarice had been banished, Sir Thomas More
welcomed the advent of a new age free from extortion, delivered from
'the sly, grasping hands of many thieves', and Edmund Dudley, in the
Tower of London under threat of execution for his part in the late
king's manipulation of 'exquisite means', wrote down for the sake of
his soul (and Henry's) a long list of what he condemned as unjust
extortions, with pungent comments that make it crystal clear that the
king had continually and relentlessly overstepped even Dudley's idea
of the threshhold of decency. And Dudley's own conscience was, to
say the least, by no means particularly squeamish.

While Henry was still alive Dudley had managed to smother his
qualms in the collection of a considerable fortune. He had entered the
royal service thirteen years before a comparatively poor man. He died
with a hoard of £5,000 in cash and estates in thirteen counties — all
gained from the pickings of office, and, if some contemporary
comments can be believed, by methods far from fastidious.

The wheel had come full circle, from bitterness against royal extravagance in 1450 to bitterness against royal 'avarice' in 1509. Given the dualistic, contradictory attitudes of the propertied classes towards the royal finances, the golden mean could hardly coexist with solvency. The Yorkist and early Tudor monarchy was thus entangled in a spider's web of financial restriction. The fly was not devoured but it could hardly move with comfort!

4 Religious Life

I

The Christian life has taken many forms—the revolutionary enthusiasm stained with the unedifying revolutionary bickering of the Acts
of the Apostles, the arrogance of a Constantine, the humility of a
St Francis or the ferocious bigotry of a Cardinal Carrafa—and
succeeding generations have often viewed with profound distaste and
a distressing lack of Christian charity the spirituality and the rituals of
their immediate forbears. Such revulsion had become unusually
strong and articulate in the generations of the late fifteenth and the
early sixteenth centuries. Many high-minded clerics then outspokenly
condemned various aspects of the church they both loved and
chastened and the Protestant reformers of the following decades
developed their condemnations often with an almost licentious fero-
city. More than three centuries of acrimonious polemics prolonged
the debate, Protestants refusing to concede the possibility of virtue to
any aspect of the church from which they had seceded, Catholics—all
too often in a blind, sentimental defensive reaction—refusing to
admit even its blatant shortcomings. Recent studies, in a calmer
atmosphere, freed from such ancient passions, have put an end to
such vicious polarization of opinion, providing detailed reconstructions of institutions, of the lives of lay and clerical groups, against
which to test the interested, emotional observations of reformers and
propagandists. Upon such reassessments this chapter is largely based.

II

The church was not, as popular opinion all too often assumes, a
monolithic authoritarian institution, in a uniform condition all over
Europe, dominated by an omnipotent papacy imposing its supreme

105

will through a rigid hierarchy of bishops and ecclesiastical courts, the obedience of which it completely commanded. True, in one sense the church was an all-embracing institution, its membership compulsory, 'the congregation of the faithful in the unity of the sacraments', as Conrad of Gelnhausen had written earlier in the fifteenth century. Within this unity the pope possessed an *ordo pastoralis*, the power to define doctrine and exercise the cure of souls, and an *ordo jurisdictionis*, an authority to govern those temporal institutions through which the church expressed its divine mission. Only the *ordo pastoralis* remained intact, even though, as always, imperfect in its expression, for over a long period the hostility of secular authorities had notably eroded the *ordo jurisdictionis*.

The *ordo pastoralis* remained unimpaired, for unity of faith was essential both for the assurance of personal salvation in the life to come and for prosperity in this terrestrial sphere. Heresy was a monstrous, unnatural, unspeakable thing, a pollution of mankind which would bring the divine retribution of physical disasters upon the deviant community as well as eternal damnation upon the deviant soul. At the same time, whatever its subtle theologians defined, the church being an all-embracing institution could never impose any uniformity of belief and practice upon a human 'congregation' comprehending everyone from the highly intelligent and the highly educated to the illiterate peasant and labourer. Circumstances forced it, however reluctantly, to tolerate many different levels of religious experience, from the highly abstract metaphysical-cum-theological speculations of the theologians to the gross superstitions of a population steeped in the remnants of semi-pagan practices.

Belief among educated clerics had become less superstitious, more rational than in earlier centuries. Although unimpeachably orthodox, the views of several of the fathers of the Council of Constance (1414 – 18) came very close to some of the condemned opinions of John Wyclif. The fathers had cautiously, unobtrusively, developed attitudes which the sixteenth-century Protestant reformers would ultimately carry to extremes. Jean Gerson, Pierre d'Ailly and Nicholas of Clémanges were all extremely sceptical about 'modern miracles', deprecated an excessive emphasis upon good works and, in particular, upon the efficacy of pilgrimages. D'Ailly denounced the proliferation of images and pictures in churches, demanded a prohibition upon the creation of new shrines and a reduction in the number of canonizations on the ground that it was 'vain to preach to the outer man if Christ does not resound within him.' Rome, to some extent, shared their desire to restrain the vagaries of popular piety. The English, in particular, burned with a desire for miracles at the tombs of their unsuccessful politicians but, to their eternal credit, a long line of Popes adamantly refused to canonize such dubious political figures as Edward II, Thomas of Lancaster and Henry VI.

The higher ranks of fifteenth-century clerics had abandoned the grosser beliefs of even their educated predecessors. They would have been horrified by the grossly superstitious bad manners of the Blessed St Hugh of Lincoln (1135? – 1200) when a guest of the monks of Fécamp. His hosts, as an unusual favour, permitted their distinguished visitor to see their most venerated relic, the arm of St Mary Magdalen. His piety having swamped any sense of decency, St Hugh took his knife, cut the bandages in which the arm was wrapped and tried to break a piece off. Finding it too hard he attacked the relic with his teeth, 'first with his incisors, then with his molars', and thus detached two precious fragments.

The attitudes of the *avant-garde* theologians had only the slightest effects, if any at all, upon the outlook of the multitude, who would still have sympathized with St Hugh's pious robbery. Unrecognized miracles, those unrecognized and refused authentication by authority, were probably more numerous than ever before. In 1513 John of Trittenheim wrote, with a good deal of exaggeration, that only the simple and the poor, who believed in miracles, still practised the traditional religion of the church. He castigated advanced theologians for creating an undesirable gulf between educated clerks and most ordinary Christians. Against such a background one can justifiably see the Reformation, when it came, as the revolt of an already long-developed reaction of professional theologians and some of the more highly educated of the laity against the excesses, possibly even the growing excesses, of popular piety.

The English were completely steeped in this universal popular attitude. Moreover, the minds of the erudite as well as those of the ignorant had from the earliest times infused the Christian story with their own contemporary mores — a habit of mind which, remaining as strong as ever in the late fifteenth century, threw a bizarre chivalric garniture over the characters of the Gospel story. The author of the *Boke of St Albans* (attributed to a Mistress Juliana Berners and printed at St Albans in 1486) snobbishly described Christ and the Apostles as gentlemen of coat armour. Even a moderate Erasmian like John Fisher, bishop of Rochester (1504 – 35) was convinced that Martha was a noblewoman who possessed the castle of Bethany by inheritance. Numerous poets and playwrights depicted the Saviour as a triumphant knight. In the Townley cycle of plays the Harrowing of Hell became a tournament in which Christ jousted with Satan for possession of man's soul:

Therefore till Hell now will I go,
To challenge that is mine.

In the alliterative poem *Death and Life* (*c*. 1450) Life descended from heaven to fight a brazen, personified Death. Death claimed to triumph on Calvary, but Life countered:

> Of one point let us prove or we part in sunder
> How did thou joust at Jerusalem with Jesu my Lord?

Life contended that once the spear had pierced Christ's side his Godhead shone forth, Death fled to his hell hole to hide from the wounded knight, only for the wounded paladin to pursue and defeat him utterly.

Late-medieval religion, as Martin Luther found to his almost unbearable cost, laid a heavy load psychologically (and it may be said financially) upon the devout. The sword of God's wrath, the prospects of Purgatory and Hell, always vivid in the mind, were to be bought off with righteous conduct and good works. Puritanism, in the sense of abstinence from joy, was certainly not a Protestant invention. Many theologians had expressed extremely forthright opinions on the very small numbers of mankind who would ever attain the bliss of Heaven. Even St Thomas Aquinas, moderate as he was in so many things, contrasted the very few saved with the legions of the damned. *Jacob's Well*, a fifteenth-century collection of sermons, relates the story of a king who never laughed: set about with perils in a body of rotten bones, above him the sword of the wrath of God waiting to smite him and the pit of Hell waiting to burn him for ever more, in the horrific contemplation of man's general doom, how could he laugh?

Fortunately some authorities took a less gloomy view. The immensely popular tract, *Dives and Pauper*, debated the subject. The rich man, citing a batch of authorities including St Augustine, condemned the wickedness of miracle plays and dancing on Sundays. Pauper, with unusual historical sense, contended that St Augustine, while condemning lascivious, pagan dances and plays in which some Christians had mistakenly taken part, had supported 'honest dances and plays done in due time and good manner', that God had ordained 'rest, mirth, ease and welfare' on holidays as a token of the 'endless rest, joy and mirth and welfare in heaven's bliss that we hope to have without end', and humanely and sensibly added that the faithful needed such foretaste of their heavenly joys, for hope and expectation too long deferred inflict immense physical and spiritual harm. The weekly sabbath should, therefore, be man's regular foretaste of the joys that will never end: 'We honour it and God, and we do ourselves good, by celebrating it with mirth, such as miracle plays and dancing.'

A long tradition, however, convinced most confessors and their penitents that it was not enough to placate God's wrath by austerities.

They must purchase his mercy by good works, often expensive good works. Charities, votive lights, intercessory prayers and, above all, masses, all possessed a market value to be assigned to particular purposes, the expedition of plans in this world as well as the more speedy relief of the soul from purgatorial fires. This attitude had received a most blatant formulation in 1348 in Edward III's foundation charter for St George's Chapel, Windsor, in which the king openly proclaimed his foundation a bargain with God, 'a good way of merchandise whereby with a happy bartering transitory things are given up in exchange for things eternal'[1] — the lavish endowment of a collegiate church in return for heavenly blessings upon his worldly enterprises.

The vast majority of people probably still looked upon 'merchandising with God' as essential, particularly to ensure the progress of the soul from purgatory — an attitude strongly revealed in the foundation, varying with social status and riches, of colleges and chantries, in less expensive endowments for masses and votive lights, and in the theology of the morality and the mystery plays with their overwhelming emphasis on good works. The foundation of collegiate churches and chantries never ceased and by 1529 there were at least 2,374 cantarists singing their masses in perpetual foundations, not to mention an unknown number in establishments of a less permanent character which have left little or no trace of their existence. At the time of the dissolution of the monasteries under Henry VIII, even more with the destruction of the chantries under Edward VI, the cessation of prayers for the dead profoundly disturbed a great many people. The foundation of a chantry was not cheap. It cost at least £200 to meet the original expenses and provide a sufficient endowment to support a single priest; but it cost far less than the small proprietary monastery or monastic cell that had been the almost indispensable sign of religious respectability for a well-to-do landowner three centuries or so earlier. The new movement brought into being a wider class of founders, so much so that the fifteenth century has been called one of the great ages of religious benefaction. And if founders were always primarily concerned with their souls, their endowments produced, even though in a haphazard and completely unplanned fashion, useful social results — from a lavish royal foundation like Eton College, begun by Henry VI and ultimately, though somewhat reluctantly, allowed to continue by Edward IV, to Archbishop Rotherham's chantry and school in Rotheram town. In the towns numerous gilds provided similar, and in some ways, even wider services. At Stratford-upon-Avon the gild of the Holy Cross was so

---

[1] 'Et quia bona est negociacio per quam transitoria declinantur et aeterna felici commercio subrogantur.'

rich and powerful that it more or less took over the town government. Even small parishes had their religious gilds. A little town like Bodmin in Cornwall possessed as many as forty and by the time of the Reformation there were at least one hundred and sixty in London alone.

At the same time the great ecclesiastical reform programme of the thirteenth century, directed by papal decrees and strongly influenced by Franciscan gentleness and contemplation, had gradually modified the predominently liturgical ethos of earlier times to develop, in the long term, a type of piety more humane, more contemplative, often tinged with mysticism, with an increased emphasis upon the redemptive passion of Christ rather than upon the earlier, harsher contemplation of God the judge.

Amongst the literate and even, to some extent, the non-literate laity, piety was more informed than it had earlier been — informed by the production of religious tracts and sermons. The printing presses of the 1470s and the following decades found a whole corpus of manuscript devotional literature waiting for wider dissemination. Manuals of piety and devotion were extremely prominent in the output of the earliest English printers.

The pre-Reformation church has generally been accused of failure to provide adequate instruction through sermons. This sweeping condemnation is certainly unjust. The fourteenth century had been almost as great an age of sermons as the seventeenth was to be — an age during which the friars in particular had developed most effective techniques of popular exposition, providing instruction in matters of faith and excoriating, in the frankest language, the shortcomings and the vices of every social class. Though far less is known of the fifteenth century, decline seems improbable. For the first time, it became customary to preach within the parish churches. Until then, except in friary churches, preachers had generally delivered their exhortations out of doors, often from the steps of the churchyard cross. Many churches, like Wainfleet St Mary in the Lindsey March, were remodelled during this period to allow ample space in a great nave and aisles for a preacher and his congregation. John Stowe, the Elizabethan antiquary, claimed that in 1450 William Lichfield, the rector of All Hallows the Great, London, left 3,083 manuscript sermons at his death, and Lichfield was only one of a group of like-minded Cambridge graduates, all incumbents of city livings in the 1440s. Bishop Pecock (died 1457), first aroused the anger of the righteous by ostentatiously and provocatively proclaiming that bishops had better things to do than to preach. There was certainly no dearth of sermons in the greater towns. Even there, however, and even more in the rural areas, sermons were not the weekly events

which they became in more modern times. They were often associated
with the greater festivals like the Rogation Day processions and like
some of the performances of religious plays with fund-raising efforts
for the church — or what nowadays might be called charity sermons.
Most of the preachers came from outside the parish, monks or friars
from houses a few miles away. The capacity to preach was not widespread among the run-of-the-mill parish clergy. But, after all, we
should remember that both the Protestant churches and the reformed
Catholic church in the sixteenth century found it a matter of great
and prolonged difficulty to provide an educated, preaching clergy in
the rural areas. As late as 1583 only one sixth of the English clergy
were licensed to preach.

III

The quintessence of piety, the rare, almost indefinable quality of
religious experience, reflects always the complete human spirit, the
inter-penetration of the tenets of faith, social conditions, education,
temperament and deep, even bizarre, psychological cravings. In the
last resort we can never analyse the yearnings of the soul with mathematical precision. The piety of divers men is still best realized in all
the crudity or all the subtlety of their own thoughts and practices.

King Henry VII, though deeply pious, was hardly surrounded by
an aura of any delicate spirituality. Appropriately enough for a
monarch notorious in his passion for financial accounts, 'merchandising' religion was marked indeed in his relations with the deity,
showing devotional avarice at its most pronounced. During his
lifetime, demanding the prayers of the clergy in all the monastic,
collegiate and cathedral churches of England, he made sure of the
resources of these 'milites Christi', as Henry V had been in the habit of
calling them, by enforcing them under legal indentures in exactly the
same way that he provided for the recruitment of troops. In his will he
left funds for the foundation of hospitals, for the celebration of ten
thousand masses within three months of his death, at sixpence a mass,
twice the usual rate, and he combined good works with propaganda
for his dynasty by giving to every parish and friary church equipped
only with a wooden pyx, a pyx of silver gilt emblazoned with the royal
arms.

The attitudes of his mother, Lady Margaret Beaufort (a more
complex character than the standard accounts of her life indicate),
well repay description. Four times married, the first time at the age of

seven or eight, a mother at thirteen, taking vows of chastity before her fourth husband's death, for years she followed an austere, even strenuous, regime of piety in an ambience of the utmost splendour and the most impressive business efficiency.

During one period of five or six weeks her household expenses amounted to the enormous figure of £551 14*s*. 2*d*. — a rate, if it were typical, reaching nearly 40 per cent of the cost of the royal household itself under the economical Edward IV. Lady Margaret had carpeted her rooms, hung them with fine tapestries (one of Nebucanezer, another of Paris and Helen). The draperies of her bed hung in folds of splendid white damask. Her plate and jewels were copious and magnificent, her dresses sumptuous though somewhat sober.

Surrounded by this aristocratic opulence, in her later years she adopted a religious round that would have taxed the energies of a nun cloistered in one of the more austere orders. As her confessor, Bishop John Fisher, described it, rising somewhat after five, after hearing the Mattins of Our Lady and the Mattins of the Day, she 'heard four or five masses upon her knees, so continuing in her prayers and devotions until the hour of dinner, which of the eating day was ten of the clock and upon the fasting day eleven. After dinner truly she would go to her stations to three Altars daily; her dirges and commendations she would say and her evensongs before supper.' When her rheumatism permitted it she would end the day[2] with 'a large quarter of an hour' upon her knees in her chapel. She rigidly kept the feasts of the church and ate only one meal a day during Lent.

Tears, one of the most respectable contemporary marks of piety, Lady Margaret produced in copious measure — 'mervayllous wepyng' at her confessions and her communions. By carrying over this lachrymose habit to more secular occasions, she may, indeed, have been more than a bit of a bore to the worldly. All her pious religious exercises never saved her from a constant tendency to anxiety. If she was not fretting over current troubles she was generally prognosticating those to come and she could hardly enjoy a great occasion without wallowing in a gloomy dejection. She cried at her son's coronation and at his wedding and added general prophecies of doom to her tears at her grandson's coronation.

Her benefactions, as one would expect, were munificent. Her main expenditure was originally intended, in a somewhat old-fashioned way, for the monks of Westminster Abbey but Fisher instead persuaded her to direct it to the scholars of Cambridge. In 1505 she refounded God's House as Christ's College and was interested enough to keep rooms there for herself and Fisher and to

---

[2] One wonders how acutely she suffered from her rheumatism during the morning!

occupy them from time to time. About a year before her death (29 June 1509) she began, with the bishop of Ely, to plan the transformation of the ancient, but badly administered, Hospital of St John the Evangelist, into St John's College. Both her colleges, together with Queen's, were to become centres of the new humanistic piety associated with the small group of English pre-Reformation Catholic reformers. However, at the time of her death, she had failed to make provision in her written testament for St John's. Her executors first ran into trouble with her grandson, Henry VIII, but Fisher's determination ensured that her plans went on. The buildings alone cost £5,000 before they were completed in 1516 and Lady Margaret's money, together with gifts from the king and Fisher secured an endowment of £537. To the same end as her colleges — godly life — she endowed her readerships in divinity at both Oxford and Cambridge and her preachership at the latter university.

At the same time she joined her piety to sound business instincts. Although once in a moment of quixotic and unrealistic exaltation she offered to become a washerwoman in a crusader camp if the kings of Europe sank their differences and organized an expedition to the Near East, her estates were well run. She became more or less the expert on protocol and etiquette at her son's very formal court — in spite of his careful attitude towards money it was one of the most splendid in Europe — took a normal, contemporary interest in patronage for her friends and dependants, adamantly prosecuted in the parliament of Paris a family ransom case of more than fifty years' duration and was held in considerable respect and demand as an arbitrator. To get her own way with her last husband, the earl of Derby, she was not above secretly asking the king, her son, to issue her own wishes to him in the guise of a royal command.

Like her son 'more studious than learned', she lamented her inadequate command of Latin (she knew just enough to understand the liturgy and the rubric), but translated books of piety from the French in which she was fluent. Fisher wrote for her the long, devotional treatise 'Concerning the Seven Penitential Psalms,' printed by Wynkyn de Worde in 1509; the treatise was, in fact, a rewriting of sermons which he had already preached before her. For her day, indeed, she read widely, did not consider herself above the occasional romance and had a decided inclination for 'skipping' passages that bored her.

She was an utterly conventional, humanly good woman, remarkable only in the extremities of her piety and the intensities of her feelings, with eyes austerely fixed upon the prospect of celestial bliss, living in terrestrial mansions of the greatest splendour, never realizing for one moment that the wealth which surrounded her might conflict

with the Gospel Story. We may yet endorse the verdict of the Blessed
John Fisher, in a memorial oration (like contemporary plays and
sermons, replete with confidence in the pre-Reformation spirit of the
combination of good works and divine grace):

> Who may not now take evident likelihood and conjecture upon this that the soul of
> this noble woman which so studiously in her life was occupied in good works and
> with a fast faith of Christ and the Sacraments of his Church was defended in that
> hour of departing out from the body and was borne up into the country above with
> the blessed angels deputed and ordained to that holy mystery. For if the hearty
> prayers of many persons, if her own continual prayer in her life time, if the sacra-
> ments of the church, if indulgences and pardon granted by divers popes, if true
> repentance and tears, if faith and devotion in Christ Jesus, if charity to her neigh-
> bours, if pity upon the poor, if forgiveness of injuries, or if good works be avail-
> able, as doubtless they be, great likelihood and almost certain coniecture we may
> take by them, and all these that so it is in deed.[3]

The Lady Margaret was by no means alone in her style of life. That of
her near-contemporary, Cecily, duchess of York, was remarkably
similar. Cecily based her daily round upon an equally firm concentration on the religious life and it was only a little less austere than that of
Lady Margaret. We know much more in detail about the Duchess
Cecily's reading than that of Lady Margaret. While it included the
familiar *Golden Legend* of Jacob of Voragine (*c.* 1275), that traditional compilation of saints' lives, it centred round devotion to the
Holy Name of Jesus (an especially English cult) and upon mystical
writers, particularly Roger Hilton and the pseudo-Bonaventure,
freely translated as *The Mirrour of the Blessed Lyf of Jesu Christ*, by
Nicholas Love, the Carthusian prior of Mount Grace—a book
probably more popular than any other in the fifteenth century.

Hilton's work, *On Contemplative and Active Life*, was the perfect
manual of instruction for this type of existence for the author had
originally addressed it to a magnate to show how a great man could
lead a life continually directed to prayer and meditation amidst all
the duties of a secular existence. These mystical writers, indeed,
conveyed distinctly monastic ideals to the faithful laity, producing
that distinctive religious aura of the later middle ages, the *devotio
moderna*—austere, compassionate, contemplative, pietistic—a
trend very strong indeed in English religious life from the late fourteenth century onwards, though it never developed the more
organized form of religious communities like the famous group at
Deventer in the Netherlands.

In the Lady Margaret and the Duchess Cecily the religious instinct
was too strong to have developed entirely from reaction to secular

[3] 'Morning Remembrance Had of the Month Mind of the Noble Princess Margaret Countess
of Richmond and Derby', in *The English Works of John Fisher*, Early English Text Society
XXVII (1876), p. 309.

misfortunes, but one may be permitted to wonder if there was not something in the existence of these rich, well-educated, aristocratic women, their lives battered by the insecure, political adventures of their families, that reinforced their attraction to so austere and disciplined a piety?

Lower down the social scale, among the modestly prosperous, reactions were cruder. The story of the pilgrim related in *Davies'* *Chronicle* demonstrates a powerful emphasis upon good works without a trace of the pious contemplation of the *devotio moderna*. The attraction of pilgrimages was very much on the wane among the upper classes by this time. Only the numerous shrines of the Virgin still retained their former popularity, for the English had always been peculiarly devoted to Mariolatry. Our Lady of Walsingham was probably the only major pilgrimage centre in England where the takings remained high. They still ran at an average of £260 a year on the eve of the Reformation[4] when St Thomas of Canterbury was taking in as little as £36. People of modest means, however, still felt a strong urge to pilgrimage and for those who could not afford the expensive trip to Jerusalem, even on the famous Venetian 'package tour', Rome and St James of Compostella remained extremely popular.

Davies' story once again shows the values of the market place at their crudest. About Michelmas 1456 a shipman arrived at Weymouth from St James of Compostella and lodged with a brewer, a 'Dutchman' (that is German) who had been with him on the pilgrimage. As he lay awake in the night he saw a wraith all clothed in white sitting on a bench near his bed. The shipman was too terrified to speak and the wraith vanished, but came again a second night, after which second vision the shipman told the Dutchman who advised him to go to confession. At confession, the priest counselled him, if clear in conscience, to be of good heart and should the wraith appear again, to demand what he was in the name of the Father, the Son and the Holy Ghost.

The third night the spirit appeared again in a great light and the shipman duly asked the question:

The spirit answered and said, 'I am thine eme, thy father's brother.' The pilgrim said, 'How long is it ago since thou died?' The spirit said, 'Nine year'. 'Where is my father?' 'At home in his own house,' said the spirit, 'and hath another wife.' 'And where is my mother?' 'In heaven', said the spirit. Then said the spirit to the pilgrim, 'Thou hast been at St James: trowest thou that thou hast well done thy pilgrimage.' 'So I hope,' said the pilgrim. Then said the spirit, 'Thou hast do to be

---

[4] Edward IV had been assiduous in his visits there but he may have been unusual in such devotions.

said there three masses, one for thy father, another for thy mother and the third for thyself: and *yet thou haddest let say a mass for me. I had to be delivered of the pain that I suffer* [my emphasis]. But thou must go again to St James, and do say a mass for me, and give three pence to three poor men.' 'Oh', said the pilgrim, 'how should I go again to St James? I have no money for mine expenses, for I was robbed in the ship of five nobles.' 'I know well this,' said the spirit, 'for thou shalt find thy purse hanging at the end of the ship and a stone therein: but thou must go again to St James and beg, and live of alms.' And when the spirit had thus said, the pilgrim saw a devil draw the same spirit by the sleeve, for to have him thence. Then said the spirit to the pilgrim, 'I have followed this nine year, and might never speak with thee unto now; but blessed be the house where a spirit may speak and farewell, for I may no longer abide with thee and therefore I am sorry.' The pilgrim went into Portugal and so forth to St James as the spirit had him commanded; wherefore I counsel every man to worship St James.

With such an emphasis upon ritual and works, people felt the deepest anxiety about the number of services and their proper conduct. In the late thirteenth century Archbishop Peckham had insisted upon mass in parish churches once a week but, by this time, two centuries later, what had formerly satisfied an exceptionally conscientious reforming prelate no longer satisfied many laymen. Parishioners were demanding daily masses and attending Mattins and Vespers as well. In 1472 those of Hustwaite in north Yorkshire complained that because the chaplain serving the cure there celebrated mass three days a week, Monday, Wednesday and Friday, in a chapel at Carleton, on those days no mass was celebrated in the parish church 'to the great peril of the parishioners there'. At Louth about 1500 there appear to have been Mattins and Evensong and 'Our Lady Mass' every day and on Tuesdays and Thursdays mass was sung 'in high choir with plainsong'.

Altars, masses and, consequently, clergy had proliferated enormously in the greater, and even in some of the lesser, churches. By the Dissolution there were more than twenty altars in Durham Cathedral, mostly sited in the transepts and in the Chapel of the Nine Altars. York Minster boasted a grand total of fifty-six perpetual chantries and there were as many as eighty others in the city's forty-one parish churches. At Lincoln between the three Morrow Masses at 5 a.m. and High Mass at 10 or 11 the cathedral staff celebrated no fewer than thirty-seven masses every day. Even a single, fairly small, parish like Great Hale might have as many as four chantries, all with their daily masses. Obviously the expectations and the demands of the pious layman had reached no mean proportions.

IV

Ideals and practice can, of course, be very different things. Only an analysis of the ecclesiastical hierarchy at all levels can reveal the extent to which the church met, or failed to meet, the expectations of the various sections of its flock.

The chain of command in the church was extremely defective. The late-medieval papacy was limited on all sides in the powers which it could exercise either for good or evil over the local churches, and nowhere were its powers more restricted than in the remnants of its jurisdiction over the *ecclesia anglicana*. Administratively the popes had never effectively controlled the church at the local level. Individual churches from small chapels to great cathedrals had originated and developed as legally and financially independent corporations, with their own endowments under their own control. They were in many cases subject to the rights of lay patrons, the descendants of their founders who were all too prone to abuse their rights of appointment to the advantage of their families and friends under the convenient and almost unquestioned assumption that the descendants of those who endowed a church were entitled to benefit from the investment for ever more.

Moreover, the church had steadily lost ground before the secular state. During the thirteenth century, influenced by the rediscovered political works of Aristotle and the revived study of Roman law, the secular state had greatly expanded its pretentions to independent judgment and authority against the church and, from a practical point of view both church and state had immensely expanded their administrative capacities and financial resources. As compared with earlier stages of development, in the later middle ages two much more formidable administrative machines jealously competed with each other for power and jurisdiction. In this prolonged rivalry the state inexorably gained the upper hand. No one, except heretics, denied the pope's *ordo pastoralis*, but almost everywhere, to a greater or lesser degree, the state encroached more and more upon his already incomplete command of the *ordo jurisdictionis*, and nowhere perhaps was this *ordo jurisdictionis* more drastically reduced than in fifteenth-century England. There, the monarchy almost completely triumphed.

Pope Martin V (1417 – 31) remarked: 'It is not the pope but the king of England who governs the church in his dominions.' His successor, Eugenius IV (1431 – 47) bitterly added that in his day there was only one Englishman 'like the phoenix' at the papal court and he quite correctly claimed that hard-headed Englishmen no longer went to Rome because there was nothing to be gained from going there. Contacts between England and Rome had been reduced to a minimum. There were rarely more than five or six Englishmen in Rome at a time, because papal patronage in England had disappeared almost to vanishing point. Successive popes now obediently followed the wishes of the king in making and translating bishops. Although popes technically 'provided' every English bishop to his see, they never disputed the king's own nomination. The papacy was equally powerless in the matter of lesser benefices. The late fourteenth-century Statutes of Provisors effectively blocked any exercise of papal patronage in the *ecclesia anglicana*. The popes could no longer support part of the curial bureaucracy on English benefices. They could not even appoint Englishmen themselves. When Pope Sixtus IV (1471 – 84) wished to reward John Doget, the archbishop of Canterbury's nephew and Edward IV's own ambassador to the Curia, recognizing his inability to intrude Doget into an English benefice, he provided him to canonries at Cambrai, St Omer and Antwerp with the reservation of a prebend in each. In England the pope's authority had been reduced to that of a mere ordinary for granting dispensations — granting permission to regulars to hold secular benefices, to abbots and priors to hold churches *in commendam*, dispensations to hold two or more incompatible benefices simultaneously, to resign or exchange benefices, for appropriations, for the foundation of colleges, allowing the possession of personal altars or for altars to be placed otherwise than towards the east — all minor matters that any well-run 'licensing authority' could have dealt with competently enough.

In the preamble to his famous Act in Conditional Restraint of Annates in 1532 Henry VIII announced his gracious determination to release the English church from 'the intolerable and importable yoke' of papal fiscalism. This mendacious propaganda libelled a papal yoke that had been light indeed. Between 1450 and 1530 the popes demanded a subsidy from the English clergy on twelve occasions. Only twice did they respond. A generous estimate of the sums flowing from England to Rome in the half century before the Reformation amounts to no more than £4,816 a year, mostly for fees, common services and annates[5] paid on the acquisition of benefices worth more than twenty-four florins — less than 40 per cent of the money the king himself was taking from the clergy in fines for the restitution of episcopal and monastic temporalities and the proceeds of clerical

---

[5] The first fruits or one year's revenue paid to the pope by bishops and certain other classes of benefice holders on their appointment to a see or a benefice. For exact definitions of these dues, see J.J. Scarisbrick, 'Clerical Taxation in England, 1485 – 1547', *JEH* XI (1960), pp. 43 – 4.

taxation. Even this figure excludes unknown profits like the payment of benevolences and 'amicable grants' to the king and under Henry VII, in spite of his immense piety, the definitely simoniacal sale of benefices. It also fails to take into account that the monarchy drastically exploited the church by paying its councillors and servants by means of appointments to bishoprics, deaneries, prebends and valuable rectories in which they were obliged to neglect their clerical duties in order to fulfil their secular obligations to the king.

Rome was, thus, a faint distant court, a negligible factor, for either good or evil, for either decadence or reform, in the life of the *ecclesia anglicana* — and consequently traces of any anti-papal feeling were negligible. Strong resentment does not arise between bodies having very little contact with each other.

Lay opinions about the papacy varied from contempt for petty restrictions to an almost superstitious dread of its command of supernatural powers. In 1468 – 9 one section of the London cordwainers obtained a papal bull forbidding Sunday work in the craft and prohibiting the making of shoes with 'pykys' (that is pointed toes) more than two inches long 'upon pain of cursing'; and 'some men said that they would wear long pykys whether the pope will or nill, for they said that the pope's curse would not kill a fly.' On the other hand, at least one Italian observer thought papal support a great asset to Henry VII politically. In September 1497 Raimondo De'Raimondi de Soncino, the Milanese ambassador in England, wrote home to Ludovico Maria Storza:

> The pope is entitled to much praise, for he loves the king cordially, and strengthens his power by ecclesiastical censures, so that at all times rebels are excommunicated. The efficacy of these censures is now felt by the Cornishmen, who are in this trouble that all who eat grain garnered since the rebellion, or drink beer brewed with this year's crops, die as if they had taken poison, and hence it is publically reported that the king is under the direct protection of Almighty God.

The Supreme Pontiff, the Vicar of Christ, had descended into a bizarre mixture of a minor licensing authority, a convenient rubber-stamp for major royal appointments, an object of derision for those determined, come what may, that they would be fashionable and a convenient miracle-worker against provincial rebels. No one yet, except Lollards, thought it worthwhile to launch a direct attack upon this remote relic of a once venerable authority.

V

So the king of England, having excluded the pope from any major exercise of patronage, controlled the bishops and, controlled very much in his own interests, one of the wealthiest sections of the entire European church. Though endowments varied widely from as much as £3,580 a year at Winchester to a miserable £131 at Bangor, the most wretched of the universally poor Welsh sees, the English bishoprics were exceptionally affluent before the Reformation. Of the forty richest sees in the whole of Christendom twelve were said to have been in England—an amazing number considering the small size of the country—and eleven of these were worth over £1,000 a year[6] at a time when Sir John Fortescue wrote that £5 clear was a good income for a yeoman, and men with less than £20 a year felt entitled to claim the status of 'gentleman'. The state, in comparison with the higher ranks of the church, was unduly poor. After the vast, but abortive, disendowment schemes proposed by the Lollards between 1396 and 1414, no one before Thomas Cromwell in the 1530s had the courage to take away from the plenty[7] of the one to supplement the penury of the other, so it was by no means entirely unfair, following a tradition accepted for centuries to exploit the endowments of the church indirectly by making bishops serve the state.

The Yorkist kings appointed nineteen bishops.[8] Only four came from noble families. One of these, Lionel Wydeville, was the king's stepson. The other three came from families of only minor aristocratic importance. Nine came from gentry families, one from merchant stock and five were of unidentified or minor origins. Three were monks. All were university educated, twelve at Oxford, five at Cambridge and two abroad, one of whom also studied at Cambridge. Nine held degrees in law, seven in theology, one in both law and theology. Only one held no degree higher than Master of Arts.

---

[6] The figures of bishops' incomes are taken from the *Valor Ecclesiasticus* of 1535 and therefore may not be completely accurate for the period before 1509. The order, however, tallies reasonably well with a list, of *c.* 1460, of assessments for papal *servitia*. These latter are reduced to round figures and probably blur the precise difference in the value of the sees. It therefore seems preferable to use the 1535 figures, keeping in mind the possibility of fluctuations in the intervening years. See *English Historical Documents* IV 1327 – 1485, ed. A.R. Myers (1969), p. 725.

[7] In the 1530s Bishop Tunstall of Durham, with an income of £2,821 a year, claimed that he could live comfortably and carry out his duties on half the amount—and that in an epoch of rising prices.

[8] I have excluded from this study bishops appointed before 1461 and their later translations.

At present we know far less about the social origins and early lives of most of the thirty-three men Henry VII appointed to the bench. Aristocrats he notably avoided, appointing only one, his stepbrother, James Stanley, the sixth son of Thomas, earl of Derby, by his first wife, Eleanor Neville, the sister of Warwick the kingmaker, to the rich diocese of Ely in 1500. Five others came from gentry families, three from merchant stock and three were Italians.[9] One was a native of Normandy. The remaining twenty came from minor or so far unidentified families.[10] A great increase in the number of the religious is particularly notable. Henry VII appointed ten as against only three during the Yorkist period. Fifteen of these men went to Oxford, five to Cambridge. Five studied at foreign universities, including one who also went to Oxford and one to Cambridge. Two others also held degrees but their provenance is unknown, and for another four no information is so far available. Fifteen held degrees in law, eight in theology and one in medicine — as notable an increase in the proportion of lawyers as in the proportion of the religious.

Difficult though it is to generalize about so diverse a group of men, some fairly broad remarks may be safely ventured. Appointments once again came firmly under the king's control, withdrawn from the aristocratic spoils system which had prevailed for a time under Henry VI in the disturbed days of the 1440s and the 1450s. Henry VI, who was well aware of the abominable defects of the system of appointments, in spite of his piety had done nothing whatever to remedy them. Although after 1461 the majority of appointments were still made basically for secular purposes, there was only a single hint (and only a hint) of simony[11] and even Lionel Wydeville, Edward IV's stepson, unlike some of Henry VI's aristocratic appointments, was not preferred below the canonical age.

As far as academic qualifications went, they were a well-educated group of men, though their learning was less that of a high 'liberal' culture than a practical training enabling them to function successfully in the highly competitive world of ecclesiastical and royal administration. Degrees in law certainly predominated yet, though the appointment of theologians decreased as time went on, law was by

---

[9] All three were the king's choice not the pope's. They received their appointments for services rendered or to be rendered at the Papal Curia. As Richard Pace wrote to Wolsey in 1514, it was necessary for the king to have one or two prominent men resident at the court of Rome.

[10] The figure is therefore, perhaps, somewhat misleading.

[11] John Kingscote, a somewhat obscure cleric (although a friend of the famous Thomas Chaundler (1419 – 90), the warden of New College, Oxford) appointed to Carlisle in August 1462, and consecrated in October, was granted the temporalities of the diocese *sede vacante* from May of the same year to repay a debt of £600 due to him from the king and the king's father.

no means so completely predominant as historians have so often claimed.

However, the lawyers triumphed financially, for they attained the greatest worldly success. Their preferment generally relegated the monks and friars to the poorer sees, particularly to the undesired, undesirable, barbarous Welsh sees with their wretched hundred or so pounds a year, and to the better, yet still comparatively poor dioceses of Carlisle and Hereford, though this was not invariable. The most prominent exception was Henry Deane, the Austin prior of Llanthony, an ecclesiastic highly praised by the saintly John Fisher. Deane rose from the economic misery of the diocese of Bangor, with £131 16s. 3½d. a year, through Salisbury, to the splendid £3,233 18s. 2d. which Canterbury[12] provided, the first monk to have become archbishop since the appointment of Simon Langham in 1336. Deane, however, for a monk had quite an exceptional career as a royal administrator, being first chancellor, then deputy-governor and judiciary of Ireland, then chancellor of England, besides being employed on diplomatic missions.

The plum bishoprics indeed fell into the laps of the lawyers and civil servants. During the whole period twenty-nine bishops served the king before they obtained the coveted mitre. Nineteen were lawyers, only eight theologians. One was a doctor of medicine, one a master of arts. Sixteen lawyers as against only four theologians entered sees worth more than £1,000 a year. Three lawyers and four theologians had to content themselves with less than a thousand. The master of arts was lucky with over £1,000, the doctor of medicine unfortunate with less.

Far from unlearned, three of the bishops were authors and at least nineteen were known as patrons of education and donors of books to libraries. With some exceptions their style and interests remained conventional, with only a minority, generally among those appointed after 1490, interested in the New Learning. John Alcock,[13] Henry VII's chancellor and the founder of Jesus College, Cambridge, the only lawyer who was at all scholarly, wrote at least two devotional works and numerous sermons. Even the ferociously Protestant ex-friar John Bale, to borrow the words of the seventeenth-century Thomas Fuller, 'though generally bitter drops nothing but honey on his memory, commending him for a most mortified man, given to learning and piety from his childhood, growing from grace to grace, so that in his age none in England was higher for holiness.'

William Nix[14] was a scholar of a sound traditional type. Bishop

---

[12] Bangor 1494, Salisbury 1500, Canterbury 1501 – 3.
[13] Rochester, 1472, Worcester, 1476, Ely, 1486 – 1500.
[14] Norwich, 1501 – 6.

FitzJames,[15] a considerable preacher of sermons before royalty, was most unsympathetic to the New Learning and very much disposed to make trouble for his dean, John Colet, who was. Another deep conservative, William Smith,[16] in addition to benefactions to Oriel College and Lincoln College, Oxford, joined with Sir Richard Sutton in the conversion of Brasenose Hall and adjacent halls into Brasenose College to propagate traditional studies in scholastic philosophy and theology.

The *avant-garde* minority proved equally active. Archbishop Neville of York, one of the pioneers of the revival of Greek in England, encouraged the studies of John Shirwode.[17] Shirwode, unusual in his wider contacts, spent nine years at the Roman Curia. He acquired a knowledge of Greek and wrote elegant letters in the new humanistic Latin. One modern scholar, Count Roberto Weiss, has described his library as the most interesting in fifteenth-century England.

Richard Fox[18] was more torn between two worlds though ultimately borne upon the same fresh wind. Having originally planned a college at Oxford for students from St Swithin's Priory, Winchester, his friend Bishop Oldham[19] (another lawyer like Fox himself) dissuaded him from spending his money upon 'a company of bussing monks'. Instead, in 1516, he splendidly endowed Corpus Christi for a president, twenty fellows, two chaplains and two clerks 'to provide for the increase of learning and for such as who by their learning shall do good in the church and commonwealth'—a statement very much in the modern, Erasmian spirit of Christian humanism. To this end also he established public lectureships in Latin, Hebrew and Greek—the first official recognition of the Greek language in either university—and ordered the college to give special prominence to the study of the humanities. Even so, although it is less often remembered, he did not completely turn his back on monasticism for he was a benefactor of both Glastonbury Abbey and Netbury Abbey.

In the end these bishops may well have left their most distinctive mark as builders. At least twenty-five out of fifty-four of them spent money in this way—and some of them spent colossal sums. Archbishop Warham[20] wrote in his will that it would be no more than just to free his executors from any charges for dilapidations as, over the years of his episcopate, he had spent £30,000 in repairs and in building new houses in his diocese. The octogenarian, Robert

---

[15] London, 1501 – 28.
[16] Coventry and Lichfield, 1493, Lincoln, 1495 – 1514.
[17] Durham, 1483 – 94.
[18] Exeter, 1487, Bath and Wells, 1492, Durham, 1494, Winchester, 1501 – 28.
[19] Exeter, 1504 – 19.
[20] London, 1501, Canterbury, 1503 – 32.

Sherborne,[21] who held the bishopric of Chichester (with a modest income of just over £600) was the most passionate builder of them all. He was expert enough as an architect to supervise the erection of fortifications for the king, and although he spent very little time in the seventeen or more benefices which he held during the course of his life, most of them owed him something in the way of new buildings or improvements to old ones. It was even said that when in Rome on a prolonged diplomatic mission his mania still pursued him and that, even there, he built a chapel. Ecclesiastics, especially, seem to have favoured the new fashion for domestic buildings in brick. In about 1470 Bishop Waynflete[22] erected a brick tower at Farnham Castle. About 1495 Morton[23] built the gate-house of Lambeth Palace and the western range of the Old Bishop's Palace at Croydon and somewhat later Alcock built Jesus College, Cambridge, in the same materials.

Appointed as they were, involved as they were with royal administration, prelates could hardly avoid political entanglement, and their records were far from courageous or high-minded. James Goldwell[24] and Robert Stillington[25] were ambitiously squalid political intriguers. Goldwell, while Edward IV's envoy at the papal court, working completely against the king's policy, secretly obtained a dispensation for the duke of Clarence's marriage to Warwick's daughter, Isabella Neville, and Stillington disclosed (or possibly invented) the story of Edward's pre-contract of marriage to Lady Eleanor Butler which enabled Richard III to invalidate his nephew's claim to the throne. Stillington's pupil John Alcock, without whose knowledge (according to the Croyland Continuator) Stillington did nothing, had been principal tutor to the prince of Wales at Ludlow, and lived on to be tutor to Henry VII's son, must have known of the plot, but made no recorded protest. John Shirwode knew the physician, John Argentine, who gave such a foreboding report of the fate of the Princes in the Tower to Dominic Mancini. After all this Stillington and Shirwode officiated at Henry's VII's coronation. Richard in the parliament of 1484 deprived three bishops (John Morton of Ely, Peter Courtenay of Exeter and Lionel Wydeville of Salisbury) of their lands on suspicion of treason. All the rest, however, seem to have accepted his activities without protest.

Did these rich, successful, highly-placed ecclesiastics ever agonize over their pusillanimous conduct in the long watches of the night? Did conscience ever murder sleep? The historian longs to know, but never

[21] St David's, 1505, Chichester, 1508 – 36.
[22] Winchester, 1447 – 86.
[23] Ely, 1479, Canterbury, 1500 – 1503.
[24] Norwich, 1472 – 9.
[25] Bath and Wells, 1465 – 91.

can know, if episcopal estates were more potent than the perfumes of Arabia in washing away the guilt from, at least, collusive hands. Outwardly these successful, career ecclesiastics sported minds that could accommodate to circumstances like a well-fitting glove. Like the contemporary nobility to whose ranks they had risen, like *nouveaux-riches* acquiring the vices rather than the virtues of their models, they were rarely, if ever, prepared to sacrifice their affluence to principle. Prepared like kings themselves to recognize the judgment of God in political change, they would certainly have agreed with the imaginary speech which Sir Thomas More put in the mouth of John Morton talking to the duke of Buckingham in 1483:

> Surely my lord [the bishop said] folly were it for me to lie, for if I would swear the contrary, your lordship would not I ween believe, but that if the world would have gone as I would have wished, King Henry's son had had the crown and not King Edward. But after that God had ordered him to lose it and King Edward to reign I was never so mad that I would with a dead man strive against the quick. So was I to King Edward faithful chaplain and glad would have been if his child had succeeded him. How be it if the secret judgement of God have otherwise provided: I purpose not to spurn against a prick, nor labour to set up that God pulleth down.

By the standards of the day Morton's attitude was respectable enough!

In less dangerous circumstances, in the performance of their ecclesiastical duties their attitudes shaded into infinite variations. Richard Bell[26] ranked as one of the most outstanding abbots and prelates of the northern province. Archbishop Warham had an extremely high reputation for piety, charity, and the patronage of scholars. On the other hand John Shirwode,[27] the humanist bibliophile, theologian bishop of Durham, was easily bored by routine. Having, as he said, 'a quick and rather hasty tongue', he vowed, under a penalty of resigning his benefices and becoming a Carthusian monk, to say all the services with as little speed as possible, weakened and, in desperation, obtained a papal mandate for the commutation of his vow into less disastrous, but still financially expensive, works of piety.

The bishops as a whole have, perhaps, been unduly castigated for absenteeism, but it is impossible to say what proportion of them were persistent absentees. Some of them, even if they acquiesced in the disreputable political conduct of the powerful, were troubled in conscience by their enforced neglect of their dioceses. William Smith of Lincoln, who was by no means a complete absentee (he visited the see as often as he could), once wrote to Sir Reynold Bray lamenting his neglect during his ten year stint as president of the Council in the Marches of Wales. Richard Fox, one of the most notorious absentees, set a scandalous example of neglect. He held in succession the

---

[26] Carlisle, 1478 – 96.
[27] Durham, 1484 – 93.

bishoprics of Exeter, Bath and Wells, Durham and Winchester, all rich and each of them richer than the last. At the end of his career, after three decades as a royal councillor and secretary, at the ripe age of seventy-four, in April 1522 he wrote to Cardinal Wolsey a conscience-stricken lament about his neglect of his ecclesiastical duties. He had never even set foot in the dioceses of Exeter and Bath and Wells, and for the last ten years of his life he was totally blind — after years as an absentee bishop, for years an incubus upon the see of Winchester.

Scandalous though this may be to modern minds, we must not exaggerate. Administratively, absenteeism was not the disaster which it might appear at first sight. The diocesan courts and bureaucracies were highly developed and sophisticated, run by deputies and officials, men of similar stamp to the bishops. They hoped to profit, through promotion, in the same way in the same world. All of them, the bishops themselves, their deputies and their official staffs, performed their duties effectively enough by the standards of the day and they did so at least without the intolerable fanaticism which so often forms a less acceptable face to enthusiastic piety. Yet, all allowances made, the effects of the system on clergy and laity alike were spiritually deadening. The bishops themselves had no contact with parish life. With no practical experience of the immediate problems of their clergy and being so often absent, they could give no living present example of the Christian life.

Subordinate bureaucrats are all too often prone to play safe by taking the line of least resistance and legally trained bureaucrats were especially prone to do so in an extremely litigious age. They neither could, nor probably were they very much inclined, to stand up to the injustices of the great or their dubious use of patronage, as a resident, magnate bishop might well have done. There is, however, another side to the picture. After the Reformation complaints were heard that some theologian bishops with no legal training were decidedly incompetent in running the business affairs of their sees.

VI

Ecclesiastical officials exercised their rods upon the faithful through a complicated network of courts — the audience court, the consistory, the archdeacon's court and the court of the bishop's commissary within the archdeaconry, the jurisdiction of these last two often overlapping in the most confusing way. It is hard to grasp the ubiquity of these courts today in a permissive age in which most churches have declined into mere voluntary societies exercising only such restraints as opinion in their congregations feels inclined to concede, with the ultimate sanction of complete freedom to depart from an anti-pathetic organization. The minutely severe moral supervision of the Christian populace, far from being the invention of sixteenth-century Puritan reformers, was as old as the Acts of the Apostles. In the fifteenth and early sixteenth centuries men and women were only marginally less acquainted, if at all, with the ecclesiastical courts than they were with the manorial courts. The ecclesiastical courts dealt with matrimonial and testamentary affairs, with the non-payment of tithes and mortuaries, moral offences and the breaking of fasts and feasts — a combination of instance and official cases. Churchwardens were obliged, at least in theory, to see that no fair, market, dancing or drinking took place in the churchyard (which was consecrated ground), to see that there were no absentees from church in the ale-house during divine service, to report to the archdeacon on his visitation all brawlers, drunkards, breakers of the peace and adulterers. People found working on the Lord's Day could be fined and beaten. Durham records reveal that in 1451, two women, Isabella Hunter and Katherine Pykeryng, found guilty of washing clothes on the festival of St Mary Magdalen, received two fustigations 'cum manipulo lini'.

The widespread activities of these church courts and their officials could be extremely costly for suitors and delinquents who, often and correctly, claimed that their procedures were both vexatious and expensive. Officials, especially in the archdeacons' courts, were undoubtedly guilty of marginal, or worse, false, citations for the sake of corrupt financial gain. The excessive zeal and corruption of petty officials brought disrepute and hatred upon the church courts, so that many people lost sight of the church's pastoral vision in resentment against its discipline.

VII

Traditional, conventional ideals of life for the parish clergy among whom these people lived in the closest contact were exceedingly high. As set out in John Myrc's standard treatise, *Instructions for Parish Priests*, the existence of the clergy who lived up to its exacting standards would have exhausted both the physical and spiritual strength of the most vigorous. Their labours would vastly have exceeded those of the Psalmist who enjoined praise of God seven times each day. Besides the mass so jealously demanded by their parishioners, all the clergy of the parish, including those who served the chantries, were supposed to gather together each day in the chancel to recite at intervals the seven canonical hours, beginning with Mattins at daybreak, followed by Prime, Tierce, Sext, None, Vespers and Compline, to say or sing the Antiphons of the Virgin and take part in processions. In addition they were supposed to give communion to their parishioners once a year, confess them three times, to preach four times in the year,[28] perform baptisms, burial services and memorial masses, not to mention special celebrations on at least thirty-seven major feasts throughout the year, the five days after Christmas, four at Easter, three at Pentecost and the feast of the dedication of the church.

Economic necessity burdened even more heavily such already strenuous days. In a poor agrarian economy the incumbent had to collect his tithes and, if a rector, farm his glebe. Though forbidden to farm anything other than the glebe, vicars (who generally were not entitled to glebe lands) and lesser secular clergy often had no option but to follow worldly occupations in order to survive, taking leases of rectorial tithes, renting farms, becoming merchants in a small way. The incumbent of Surfleet in Lincolnshire traded in hemp, corn and cattle, and most probably as a result of these commercial activities said his offices at irregular times. The curate of Barton-on-Humber was 'a common fisherman in the Humber, in English wading' and no doubt the tides left his hours even more unreliable.

Heavy parochial duties, the need to farm, numerous masses in the special foundations of colleges and chantries demanded a large number of clergy. By this time quite small parishes had a surprising number of chantries. In any church a priest and his parish clerk were the essential minimum staff, but most had an incumbent (resident or otherwise), a parochial chaplain who was a priest and sometimes a deacon or sub-deacon. Many had far more. A number of prosperous villages in the deanery of Holland in Lincolnshire had between eight and thirteen resident clerks—the incumbent, and parochial and chantry chaplains. The number of fifteenth-century choir stalls in large urban churches, like St Botolph's, Boston, shows the large number of clergy and clerks in minor orders who had to be seated for the services. At the end of the century the Gild of St Mary at Boston supported ten chaplains, a choir and a junior supporting staff and the Corpus Christi Gild another nine chaplains.

In the whole of England and Wales there were about 8,600 parishes, of which a little over 3,300 were vicarages. There were, in addition, over 260 colleges of secular canons, including 20 cathedrals,

[28] But see above, pp. 110–11.

and an unknown, though very considerable number of perpetual chantries, plus a figure, again unknown, for chantry foundations of a temporary kind, of which few traces have survived. Altogether there may have been as many as 30,000 or more secular priests in England and Wales. Considering the number diverted to administrative and secular employment with the bishops, the king and, to a lesser extent, the nobility and the greater gentry, and in view of the enormous proliferation of services, their numbers were probably not excessive. In some dioceses, indeed, especially in the southeast, there may have been a shortage of clergy.

Most of the clergy were very much local men. Nobles appointed their sons to rich parochial benefices for the sake of the income and never intended that they should reside. They were, however, such a tiny minority that noble influence upon the parishes was negligible. The knightly and gentry classes provided far more and these classes also provided many of the non-residents. There was also a very small number of manumitted villeins. The majority of the clergy most probably came from middling stock, but any convincing statistical analysis is so far impossible.

The pre-Reformation clergy endure an unenviable reputation — the result of outspoken contemporary criticism of their inadequacies and a long tradition of Renaissance and Protestant scorn. Simon Fish, in his notorious propagandist tract, *Supplication for the Beggars*, collected venomous gossip and may therefore be written off as a witness to the general condition of the parishes. Far more serious, clerics and laymen of impeccable orthodoxy launched vigorous attacks in the hope of improving standards. William Melton, a Cambridge don before he became chancellor of York Minster, wrote a treatise for ordinands in 1494, and about 1510 deplored the ignorant hordes who, he thought, shamed the church by their inadequate learning and their lack of discipline. A little later, John Colet, the humanist dean of St Paul's, complained that ordination examinations merely tested technical competence and completely neglected considerations of devotion and godliness — an opinion endorsed by Sir Thomas More in his controversy with Tyndale. More saw little hope of higher standards as long as there were so many priests: in Utopia the priests were excellent because they were so few — an almost hopeless argument for, without cutting down the number of services which both popular, and some forms of educated, piety demanded, it would have been next door to impossible to reduce the number of priests. More, Melton and Colet saw the uneducated priest as an active menace to true piety. A priest who never read could have little reflective insight to offer his people. Steeped only in rigid dogma, he could compel only the observance of dogma — a priest who, in the language of the humanists, proclaimed the 'law' rather than inspired faith, a type of piety which both Catholic humanists and, later, Lutherans, deplored and attacked.

Catholic reforming criticism of ordination examinations was largely true. It resulted, to a great extent, from the limitations which the current system of patronage imposed upon the freedom of the bishops. In some dioceses the bishop may have been the greatest individual patron, but he rarely, if ever, controlled more than a proportion of the benefices. In some dioceses the monasteries were collectively the greatest patrons. Neither bishops nor monks, however, were entirely free agents. Nobles and gentry also controlled advowsons and they and the king, the greatest patron of all, brought pressure to bear upon the ecclesiastics to promote their own nominees.

In the eyes of many families the priesthood was a career rather than a vocation. Parents chose it for their sons, often at an early age, just as they pushed daughters into nunneries to avoid dowries, and many patrons regarded benefices as existing for their own advantage rather than the good of the church. The bishops were powerless to deny installation of the nominees of patrons entrenched behind indefeasible legal rights, if those nominees possessed the bare canonical requirements. The influence of the laity was sufficiently strong in parochial appointments for us to blame them in great measure for the deficiencies which prevailed. A single family could develop a complete stranglehold upon a benefice. Between 1445 and 1552 all the known rectors of Prestwich in Lancashire were members of the patronal family, the Longleys. Critics of the church could be distinctly two-faced in this matter. The 'sublime and literate persons', to use a contemporary phrase, who were so scornful of the attainments of the run-of-the-mill clergy, were well enough aware on which side their own bread was buttered to refrain from attacking the basis of the system. Colet in his famous Convocation sermon of 1512 attacked churchmen for running 'almost out of breath from one benefice to another', asking 'what other things seek we nowadays in the church than fat benefices and high promotions?' A cynical observer could truthfully have replied that the dean of London might well have begun by casting the beam out of his own eye. In 1485 his cousin, Sir William Knyvet, had presented him to the Suffolk rectory of Dennington, five years later his father, Sir Henry Colet, gave him the rectory of Thurning in Northamptonshire and until 1505 he had held the living of Stephney, near his father's house and most probably in his father's gift. John Colet, unlike less delicately minded folk, was never undignified enough to be out of breath running after fat benefices. His family connections saw to it that he just sedately walked into them.

Again, the level of education varied in different dioceses. By this time, graduates no longer seem, as earlier in the century, to have found it difficult to persuade patrons to confer benefices upon them; to that extent laymen had responded to the more enlightened views of the hierarchy. In the enormous diocese of Lincoln, stretching from the Humber to the Thames, the proportion of known graduate clergy in the parishes, educated men fit to debate the theories of the schools, rose from about 14 per cent at the beginning of the fifteenth century to over 30 per cent in 1500. In the diocese of Canterbury in Archbishop Bourchier's time (1450 – 83) they numbered about one fifth, in Tunstall's London (1522 – 30) about one third, in Norwich between 1503 and 1528 only one sixth. On the other hand, in the northern archdeaconry of Richmond (always a clerical black spot), as late as 1525 – 6 there were none at all.

These figures are minima and, as they stand, they are misleading owing to problems of identification. They include only Masters of Arts. Ecclesiastical records reserved the designation *magister* for those who had obtained this second degree. All others were lumped together as *domini*. Therefore, among the other incumbents there must have been both BAs and a number of others who went up to the university for a year or two without taking a degree, for Hastings Rashdall estimated that only one third of those who matriculated ever took the BA degree and only one sixth went on to the MA.

Even so, the utility of a full university education at the parish level may be considered dubious. Late-medieval university courses were long, expensive and, at the higher levels, extremely technical. A graduate who had endured the eighteen years necessary to complete the full sequence of courses in arts and theology may have been successful enough in city rectories preaching to sophisticated urban audiences, but this type of erudition must have been largely wasted on peasants and yokels. This was not a problem peculiar to the later middle ages. After all, modern intellectuals may admire the baroque eloquence of John Donne's sermons but one may wonder what they meant to the farmers and labourers of his then rural church on Paddington Green. The work of the country parson demanded training of a much more practical type — the practical, vocational training provided for the first time in the Catholic world by the Council of Trent when it ordered the establishment of a seminary in every diocese, a sensible provision completely unknown in the English church until the foundation of two small theological colleges at Chichester and Wells in 1839 and 1840.

Those who could not afford a university education, or even a limited period at a university without proceeding to a degree (it cost at least 50s. a year to live in Oxford or Cambridge), benefited, like the laity, from the unparalleled expansion of grammar school education in the late fifteenth and the early sixteenth centuries. It is therefore difficult to agree with a hoary, somewhat naive, tradition that at this time their educational standards were falling below those of their parishioners. Both, after all, enjoyed the same educational opportunities, either equally extensive or equally restricted, according to schools existing in the districts in which they lived. The educational standards of individual clerics were as diverse as those of individual laymen and it is after all by no means unknown even today for some parishioners to be better educated than their parson — a situation not always producing an anti-clerical derision. The root of the evil was lack of vocational training. There was no concerted plan or blueprint for training the parish clergy. The graduate clergy at the outset of their careers were as ill-prepared, possibly even less well-prepared, for their specialized task as the non-graduates, who had probably served some kind of informal apprenticeship as an altar boy or acolyte in the parish, acquiring their Latin at the grammar school or from the priest or chaplain.

Like the demands of their parishioners, their standards had certainly risen over those of previous centuries. At least in the diocese of Lincoln the clergy could now celebrate the holy offices without egregious error. Devotional works could be had for as little as a penny and editions of saints' lives and the articles of faith at a price within the reach of most priests. The new printed books, however, lacked bindings, were easily destroyed and as often as not were never mentioned in wills — and wills, unfortunately, form our principal source of evidence. Taking this limitation into account, their evidence is quite impressive as to numbers but somewhat depressing as to content. Of the clerical wills proved in the consistory court of Norwich between 1500 and 1550 (admittedly the evidence is somewhat late), one in five mentioned books. Most were those of non-graduates and almost half those of unbeneficed clergy. By far the most common were books of sermons, of a deeply conservative, old-fashioned kind, showing no signs of the great advances in biblical scholarship characteristic of Erasmian humanism or even of the proto-humanism of fifteenth-century England. Books of the pre-1500 era must have been even more conservative — an impression confirmed by the output of the English printing presses. Two fifths of the works which Caxton printed between 1474 and 1490 were long-established traditional works of devotion. Those of his successor, Wynkyn de Worde, contained an even higher proportion of works of the same kind. The Bible, in whole or in part, was noticeably absent. In its terrified reaction from Lollardy the English hierarchy had discouraged translations. In Germany twenty complete translations and numerous incomplete editions were printed between 1466 and 1522. In the same period England saw not one. Even so, by this time it was more probably traditional attitudes and expense rather than the difficulties of Latin (though admittedly the Latin of the Vulgate is not easy) which caused continuing ignorance of the sacred text. The Bible was, after all, an enormous and expensive book compared with the small devotional works which both the clergy and the laity were buying in fair numbers. Melton and Colet, fully aware of the position, lamented the use to which the printing presses could have been put and, most emphatically, were not. Yet Melton and Colet and their like were only one wing of reforming opinion. Even Sir Thomas More favoured restricting Bible-reading to the upper classes. As we have seen from the divergent intellectual and religious tendencies of the bishops, as expressed in their libraries and in their educational endowments, this was an age of uncertainty, intellectual change and divided opinions, in which some well-enough educated men clung to traditional standards as vehemently as others rejected them. The small English intellectual *avant-garde*, mainly clerical, remained very much a minority. The more conservative majority of educated clerics and laymen seem to have been well enough content with 'the good old standards'.

The better training and deployment of a high-grade clergy was a matter of centuries. Beginning in the later thirteenth century, it came to fruition in both Protestant and Catholic lands only several generations after the advent of the Reformation, and the adequate staffing of rural areas proved to be particularly intractable and prolonged. John Calvin, even in the tiny territory of Geneva, with all the violent enthusiasm of early Calvinism and a vast influx of learned refugees to draw upon, found it difficult to persuade educated clerics to reside in the state's mere fourteen rural parishes. They always wanted to commute from the city itself. In England as late as 1551, Bishop Hooper's visitation of his diocese of Gloucester revealed (among other deficiencies) that out of 311 clergy, 106 could not recite the Ten Commandments accurately, 10 could not even repeat the Lord's Prayer and 34 were ignorant of its authorship; they showed a deplorable lack of familiarity with the Scriptures and that complete absence of the habits of reading and study which Melton and Colet had so ardently advocated forty years earlier. They were still without a basic, not to say critical, grasp of the tenets of faith. The immediate effects of the Reformation, with successive purges of the more ardent clergy and the complete absence of any reform in the church's administrative system, particularly in the matter of patronage, may indeed have led to a short-term deterioration.

Economically, the different levels of the parish clergy fared very differently and benefices themselves varied tremendously in value. The first step in the humble parson's career was a parochial chaplaincy—an unavoidable stage except for the graduates and the well connected who were often preferred to benefices before ordination. A chaplaincy could last for some years, sometimes for many years, occasionally for the exceptionally unfortunate, even for life. At Riston, in Yorkshire in 1494 the chaplain, Robert Wod, was described as 'senex et valetudinarius'. Under Henry V a statutory maximum of 8 marks a year had been laid down for their pay. A very low estimate for their annual needs would be about £4 8s. 4d. and at the end of the fifteenth century, when their numbers appear to have been somewhat declining, the average pay was under £5. Parochial chaplains were, therefore, necessarily possessed by a burning desire to obtain a benefice.

Dr Peter Heath has estimated that a rector or a vicar could reasonably have supported himself and his household, paid a chaplain and an occasional pension to a former incumbent, could have met the liturgical expenses (the cost of bread, wine, oil, chrism, candles and incense) and paid for the frequent repairs which poorly constructed medieval buildings needed, with £15 a year. Unfortunately only a small minority attained even these modest stipends. Probably three quarters of all the parishes in England were worth less than £15, half were not worth £10 and many produced less than seven. Many of the beneficed clergy must have lived under considerable financial strain, quite unable to fulfil the ecclesiastical obligation of setting aside one third of their incomes for alms and hospitality. Moreover, clerical taxation grew heavier from about 1460 and heavier yet again from the mid-1490s. The phrase 'Poor as a parson's page' had long since achieved the status of a proverb.

Housing was generally reasonably good in spite of immense variations. The usual type of parsonage consisted of two floors, with a hall and four or five other rooms, and differed only slightly from those first systematically described in the glebe terriers of Elizabethan and Jacobean days. Owing to the needs of the glebe and the incumbent's farming activities, such dwellings were more working farmhouses than the modest country houses or villas of the eighteenth and nineteenth centuries.

Judged by later standards, clerical observances and behaviour were by no means unduly low. Historians have, for example, expressed themselves over-severely upon the problem of absenteeism. The predominent cause was office-holding, though a certain amount also derived from old age and ill-health and from licences issued to clerics by the bishops to improve their standards by study at the universities. No precise measurement for the whole country is possible. In

Canterbury in 1511 somewhat less than 14 per cent were absentees, though in 1518 there was a much higher proportion of one quarter in the diocese of Lincoln. It seems reasonable to regard this as a maximum figure. Later in the 1530s and the 1540s the number of dispensations for non-residence became greater than ever before. In the supposedly 'reformed' church deterioration grew worse and worse until by 1827 less than half of its 10,000 incumbents resided in the parishes. In this matter pious Anglicans had little reason to sneer, though sneer they did, at the record of their Catholic predecessors. After all, in the early nineteenth century there was far less excuse for absenteeism than in the late fifteenth and the early sixteenth centuries when the administrative needs of both church and state drew away the clergy from their parishes. Nor, probably, did absenteeism make much difference to parochial standards. It is true that there were some scandalous cases, but in the Norwich visitation of 1499 in only two out of forty-eight parishes was the fact of absenteeism combined with accusations of neglect. Deputies and chaplains were obviously performing the duties reasonably well.

In these circumstances, considering the arduous liturgical duties of the parson, his involvement in agriculture, so similar to that of his parishioners, and the close, almost stifling contacts of small communities, surely the assiduous conduct of the services, a high standard of morality and a decent degree of sociability were more important in a village or a little town than the higher standards of education and study the reformers were demanding.

Complaints were usually hurled at the clergy under the headings of negligence, incontinence and violence. Negligence certainly existed, though it is impossible to say how widespread it was. Incontinence may well have been a serious problem, though, again, evidence for its extent is unreliable. 'Priests' whore' was a common term of abuse, but the English hierarchy never condoned the existence of concubines and nothing in any English see even remotely approached the scandalous situation in Constance in the early sixteenth century. There it was alleged that the clergy of the diocese begat 1,500 children a year, for each of which the bishop exacted a cradle fee of four gulders—a yearly take of 6,000. As one outraged pamphleteer, Sebastian Meyer, wrote: 'There are hardly two pimps in the whole bishopric who take in so much!' Many of the English clergy were certainly violent. They shared with the rest of society one of the most deplorable characteristics of the age, for, by modern European standards, all social groups, from the aristocrat to the labourer, were appallingly unrestrained in their day-to-day behaviour. The clergy who staffed the rural parishes shared to the full the lives, the habits and the temptations of those among whom they worked, but by the standards of their own day they were neither abnormally deficient in self-control nor in discipline imposed from above. Even complaints about parochial chaplains are far from numerous and their parishioners did not widely condemn them.

Evidence from the ecclesiastical courts becomes extremely valuable at this point — the evidence of cases involving benefit of clergy and purgation. By the fifteenth century the trial and conviction of criminous clerks took place in the Court of King's Bench. The question of benefit of clergy was raised only after conviction and clerical status then had to be proved in the same court. Status proved, the court handed over the convicted clerk to the bishop. In 1462, Edward IV's charter of liberties reversed this, conceding what the church had been trying to claim since the twelfth century, allowing the accused cleric to prove his clergy before indictment and, if successful, to be tried in the church courts only; but in fact the charter seems to have been completely ignored in practice.

The next step, purgation, formed a species of second, rather archaic form of trial in an ecclesiastical court. It was not merely a clerical anachronism: similar procedures were still available in the secular Court of the Upper Exchequer. The process obliged the accused person to produce a number of people of good standing prepared to affirm upon oath belief in his innocence. In theory it required at least six clerical compurgators for fornication and twelve for adultery. In practice, defendants often got away with the support of no more than six or eight made up partly of clergy and partly of laymen of superior status. The procedure was by no means the formality it is so often alleged to have been. Contemporaries took it very seriously. Then, if purgation failed, punishment could be severe — often a long term of imprisonment, usually shackled and always on an austerely meagre diet. In the diocese of York four to eight years was the average term of imprisonment for a criminous clerk who failed the test of purgation.

Between 1452 and 1530 the surviving registers of the archbishops of York, which cover forty-nine years, record sixty-two purgations, less than two a year for the entire diocese. Only six of these were those of professed clergy. Of the remaining fifty-two, twenty-eight were those of gentlemen, yeomen, husbandmen and labourers. Five came from the textile trades and there were a butcher, a chapman, a goldsmith and a wire-drawer. These 'criminous clerks', pleading benefit of clergy, were, although in minor orders, really criminal laymen, battening upon and exploiting the privileges of the church. It was probably they rather than the clergy as such who aroused the reforming indignation of the House of Commons. The scandal lay not in the priesthood itself: it lay in the crowded, shady fringes of the sub-clerical world. Even so, contemporaries exaggerated both the extent of the scandal and its threat to the social order. Although the scale of the problem was small, too small to matter where the genuine clergy were concerned, the church defended the privilege with an obstinacy as blind as it was foolish, perhaps fearing that to give way here might provoke wider attacks upon clerical privilege.

For those in major orders, the real priests, one last timidity vitiated the practice of a reasonably strict discipline—the reluctance of the bishops, except in cases of flagrant non-residence, to exact the final penalty of deprivation—an understandable reluctance in view of the fact that the parson's benefice was his freehold and patrons were morbidly jealous of any interference with their rights. Even so, the hierarchy showed the same lenity towards the unbeneficed. They may, in the end, have been too afraid of damaging clerical prestige in general by bringing such public shame upon offenders. Short of these extremes, however, the church was reasonably diligent in its discipline.

Any final judgement must, obviously, be to some extent impressionistic and subjective, but in all humanity a historian should firmly rule out the scurrilously vicious hostile gossip and sneers of Simon Fish and his like a generation later. 'Maria Monk' type of literature can no more be accepted as evidence than 'what the girl said' in cases of rape. Clerical disorders on a significant scale certainly existed, yet, at the same time, the lay world, knowing nothing better, tolerated, with some protest, even worse disorders in its own ranks—disorders which would be quite unendurable today. Irresponsible though it may be not to judge at all, it is surely even more irresponsible (and unhistorical) to demand later, more refined, standards from societies in earlier stages of development. A ferocious anti-clericalism had risen to vicious peaks in certain parts of the country in the 1420s and again in the 1450s. In the 1450s a group of Kentishmen had howled for castration for incontinent clerics. Later, tensions undeniably existed in many parishes. When have they not? But general resentment seems to have died down. From the 1460s anti-clericalism appears to have been dormant in most parts of the country, perhaps to revive again in the two decades after 1510 when the clergy more vigorously pressed their financial demands upon the laity to protect their own economic standards in a period of rapidly rising prices.

Given the general conditions of the times, the only immediate scope for improvement lay in the abolition of the minor orders, the adoption of clerical marriage—both matters outside a unilateral English decision—and in the uprooting of the deleterious system of lay patronage—a nettle which neither Catholic nor Protestant reformers, in spite of their awareness of its evils, ever had the moral courage to uproot and throw upon the flames. The early sixteenth-century reformers who loudly attacked their fellow clerics for running after benefices generally maintained a remarkable silence about the lay property rights which made the clerical rat-race possible. Like Fabrice del Dongo in the *Chartreuse de Parme*, they shuddered at the thought of simony but avidly took what they thought to be their due reward as relations and clients of the powerful.

VIII

The religious have also, like the parish clergy, suffered condemnation by somewhat unrealistic standards. Historians, perhaps, have accepted too readily contemporary criticism by humanists and by nineteenth-century historians nostalgic for the earlier middle ages. The piety and the religious tone of the educated upper classes had, as we have seen, developed from the liturgical and contemplative practices of monasticism and some, particularly women, whose circumstances allowed it, imitated a monastic regime in their house-holds; but very few of their males at this time, in England, entered monasteries, though the nunneries continued to attract aristocratic women.

Monastic life had taken a milder tone from that of earlier ages and, faced with this mutation, modern judgements have been contra-dictory and confused. Ecclesiastical historians, reared in the somewhat artificial religious heroism inculcated in many seminaries, have found the milder cloister life of the later middle ages lacking in genuine spirituality as compared with the austere period of the twelfth century when in Cluniac houses, in their prime, the liturgical day was so crowded that there was little time for either contemplation or study. All too often, in discussion, the distasteful aspects of this earlier monasticism tend to be overlooked — its inhuman corollary, the conscription of oblates and the arrogant near-conviction in some quarters that only the religious could attain salvation.

Some contemporaries held similar views and, at the other end of the spectrum some *avant-garde* bishops held the conservative intel-lectual atmosphere of the monasteries in some derision. It may indeed seem unduly sentimental to defend a form of the Christian life which many distinguished Catholics in the early sixteenth century them-selves regarded with distaste — a distaste profound enough for Cardinal Pole and his reforming friends in Rome in 1536 to recommend in the *Consilium de emendanda ecclesiae* the abolition of the majority of the orders, a reduction in the numbers of the rest and their concentration in fewer houses.

Dom David Knowles, the most learned and judicious ecclesiastical historian of the last generation, himself a Benedictine monk, sorrowfully and magisterially condemned an era of monasticism 'sitting upon its lees', in 'an atmosphere of indefinable spiritual rusticity', where the numbers of the lukewarm surpassed the numbers of the fervent, a generation living in somewhat disreputable ease in the last days before the swelling of Jordan, the last days in the vineyard before the pressing of the grapes of wrath.

A large volume of contemporary opinion and evidence could easily be cited to uphold the attacks of sixteenth-century reformers and the strictures of modern critics. By this time English monasticism had developed upon a quiet calm middle road, very different from the wide extremes of the European orders. English conventual life never sank to the appalling levels of degradation of the Spanish Franciscans. When Cardinal Ximenes (1436 – 1517) began to reform the order, four hundred Andalusian friars fled to North Africa and converted to Islam rather than give up the embraces of their concubines. Nor, on the other hand, except to a very small degree, did English religious houses ever experience the revival of monastic life taking place in various parts of Europe. Nothing in England could compare with the reforms of Johan Busch and the Congregation of Windesheim. Henry V's attempted reform of the Benedictine order had ended in nothing and of the more austere 'modern' orders there were only Henry's Brigittine foundation at Sheen, seven Carthusian houses with their proud boast, 'nunquam reformata quia nunquam deformata', and six houses of Friars Observant encouraged by Henry VII.

Black spots there certainly were, like the abbey of Dorchester-on-Thames which had passed through generations of financial scandals and loose living. In Bishop Oliver King's opinion the monks of Bath Abbey maintained so excessive a standard of living that he had no compunction in ordering them to cut their expenses by half to help meet the cost of rebuilding their ruinous church. Guilt-ridden monks themselves bore witness to their own maladjustment, like the bored inmate of Christchurch, Canterbury, who wrote, echoing the words of the poet Hockleve 'Excess at board hath laid his knife with me' — and had done so for two full decades; the Croyland Chronicler in the late 1460s was not ashamed to note (as perhaps a really strict monk ought to have been) that Brother Lawrence Chateres had left £40 to refresh the brethren with milk of almonds on fish days and he gave considerable space in the chronicle to describing the way in which the almonds were to be provided.

Indeed, the richer houses were among the pioneers of comfort, as earlier they had been of good sanitation. Abbots built pleasant lodgings for themselves. In the richer monasteries senior monks lived in suites of rooms, attended by their own servants like Oxford and Cambridge dons in more opulent days. They went on holidays, drew wages and accumulated nice little personal libraries. Only a proportion, probably a small proportion, of convents could afford such standards. Yet after all a certain dignified ease hardly constitutes depravity, nor does it necessarily lead to 'spiritual rusticity'. Erasmus, a professed monk after all, developed his intellectual distinction in at least equal comfort elsewhere, and then denounced monasticism partly because he had a profound distaste for communal life of any kind, whether in the cloister, an Oxford college, or the house of the printer, Aldus, in Venice. Against Simon Fish's attacks upon 'abbey lubbers' and 'sturdy, idle, holy, thieves' (in which latter category he generously included the entire clergy and all their connections, rich or poor), one should remember that many founders had intended their monks to enjoy a high standard of living and had endowed their abbeys at an appropriately affluent level. Standards change with the generations and in an age of rising upper-class comfort it is hardly likely that all laymen thought it proper for monks to endure the more primitive standards of earlier times. To admire such attitudes is to be somewhat unrealistic. One can after all look back with some amusement to the days less than fifty years ago, when elderly Cambridge dons saw no need to disfigure ancient fabrics with bathrooms for either themselves or undergraduates, and nuns in charge of Tuscan boarding-schools strengthened the same line of thought with the argument that true spiritual purity itself disposed of the possibility of unpleasant corporal odours.

We may also perhaps speak from numbers, from the unexpected, and too often ignored, testimony of Henry VIII himself and from an examination of particular houses. The religious orders maintained a powerful attraction for most classes except the nobility. By the early fourteenth century the population of monks, friars and nuns had reached about 17,500—a maximum almost exactly coinciding in time with the maximum growth of English population. At the same time the figure for the monks themselves had fallen during the previous century because many recruits to the religious life had then preferred to enter the new orders of friars, with their more exciting missionary vocation, as compared with the enclosed, liturgical and contemplative life of the monastery: a new generation found the *vita evangelica* more stimulating than the traditional *vita angelica*. By 1370 the Black Death and subsequent outbreaks of bubonic and other 'plagues' had reduced these numbers to almost half. From then onwards, however, the religious population so increased again that by the early 1420s they had climbed a quarter to one third above this earlier nadir. Although from that point the rise continued more slowly, by the end of Henry VII's reign there were more monks, nuns and friars in the kingdom than at any time since the great mortality of 1349 — probably over 12,000 — an increase far greater in proportion than the increase in the population of the country as a whole.

If the experience of Durham Priory, the greatest of the northern houses, is not untypical (and episcopal records of ordinations in other houses suggest that it is not), recruitment policy, so far from relying upon desperate efforts to keep up the establishment, became deliberately restrictive. True, the social base had changed. Here, as elsewhere, monks from aristocratic families had become as rare as water in a desert. The Durham brethren mostly came from the *valecti*, the sons of the middling rural income group. Between 1400 and 1529 numbers at Durham remained remarkably stable, at a figure between 66 and 70 — about 40 in residence at the mother house, the rest in the cells. The prior and chapter seem to have evolved a very sensible policy of admitting no more and no fewer novices than the resources of the community could decently sustain — 'a thoroughly conservative admissions policy which aimed at replacing one dead colleague by a new one.'

In 1536 Henry VIII and his advisers, thinking at first in terms remarkably similar to those of the exactly contemporary *Consilium de emendanda ecclesiae*, planned a sensible moderate reform by cutting out undoubtedly superfluous religious establishments and concentrating the religious population in a smaller number of houses. While condemning the lax standards of the smaller houses, the preamble to the dissolution act of 1536 went out of its way to lavish praise upon the 'divers great and solemn monasteries of this realm wherein (thanks be to God) religion is right well kept and observed'. The criterion for abolition — an annual income of less than £200 — though chosen for administrative convenience, was not entirely irrational. Individual monasteries were isolated institutions and, in spite of bishops' visitations and the periodic general chapters of the particular orders, they never achieved anything approaching a common standard of life, observance or culture. Conditions differed immensely from convent to convent. A small, poor community of a dozen monks or less, desperately struggling to make ends meet in a dilapidated house, often deserved the charge — and worse — of 'indefinable spiritual rusticity' and their guilt was far from being a recent development. To do the inmates justice, locally recruited as they were, completely ignorant of a wider world or any higher standards, they were totally unaware of their own comparative degradation. It is quite possible, even probable, that the original, humane reforming plan of 1536, by transferring the inmates of such establishments to greater and more reputable houses, would have eradicated the worst deficiences and demonstrated to the ignorant and to the innocent a higher level of the religious life than they had ever known. But all came to an end when the original plan degenerated into a squalid financial scramble which led to total dissolution.

In some of the greater houses monkish learning was not to be despised.[29] English monasteries in the fifteenth century for the first time erected separate buildings to serve as libraries and some of them housed from 900 to about 2,100 volumes — figures which should be multiplied four or five fold for most volumes contained from two to as many as ten items, which in a modern library would be bound in separate covers. Such libraries greatly surpassed those of the Oxford and Cambridge of the day. Prior Sellyng of Canterbury (1472 – 94), influenced by Archbishop Neville of York, was one of the first men to reintroduce Greek studies into England. Sellyng, however, was exceptional and humanists in general castigated the religious for the conservative nature of their scholarship. It was a castigation echoed generation after generation by classical scholars, often the more pedantic and least generally cultivated of their kind, who have judged the condition of fifteenth-century English intellectual life solely on its backwardness in classical studies, when even in contemporary Italy such studies were still those of an *avant-garde* minority. Other, if more conservative, interests are surely worthy of some esteem.

Abbot Kidderminster of Winchcombe (1488 – 1527) organized a course of study for his community of twenty-eight monks, with three of the brethren, including the abbot himself, lecturing several times a week on the Old and New Testaments and on the Sentences. Later, Kidderminster, with some pardonable exaggeration, wrote that his abbey 'had all the appearance of a young university, though on a minute scale', and his monks enjoyed a high reputation at Oxford.

Nor was the intellectual level of the monks of Durham to be condemned. Although comparable figures are lacking for the second half of the fifteenth century, between 1383 and 1441 at least 51 (and probably a good many more) out of 132 of them spent some time at Durham College in Oxford, their own special, well-endowed foundation, studying mainly philosophy and theology. Many of these monk-students stayed there only a year or two and, like many lay students at the time, did not proceed to degrees. At Durham itself they possessed

[29] For the following examples see D. Knowles, *The Religious Orders in England* ii (1955), pp. 331 – 53; iii (1959), pp. 87 – 90, 91 – 5; R.B. Dobson, *Durham Priory, 1400 – 1450* (1973), chapters 2, 4 – 6, 10; E. Searle, *Lordship and Community: Battle Abbey and its Banlieu, 1066 – 1538* (1974), pp. 418 – 37.

a library of almost six hundred volumes. In the later part of the fifteenth century it was kept up to date (if again in a thoroughly traditional way) with new, and better, printed editions of the good old standard texts—Origen, Jerome, Ambrose, Augustine and Aquinas. And if at Durham, as elsewhere, most of the new additions were bequests made by individual monks rather than purchases from the common chest, we might, after all, remember that until very recent days of abnormal university affluence many a small college library depended upon the gifts and legacies of its alumni.

In Oxford the significance of the monks may well have been seriously underestimated. Hastings Rashdall's prejudiced anti-clerical opinion that monastic colleges at Oxford and elsewhere 'possessed little or no importance in the history of learning or education' has at last been challenged. Among other things, the monks at Oxford appear to have become numerically more significant as the number of monastic colleges increased, simultaneously with a probable decline in the university population. Their importance in the study of theology is unquestioned. About two thirds of the doctorates in that subject went to monks and friars.

The religious were deeply involved, both economically and socially, in the fabric of local life. In some areas they aroused the same resentment as other landlords and many parishioners detested their activities as impropriators, putting vicars and curates into valuable rectories on low stipends and neglecting chancels—a sore point with villagers proud of their churches. On the other hand the spokesmen of the Pilgrimage of Grace protested that local people would be deprived of both jobs and charity if monastic estates passed into the hands of absentee, lay landlords. At Battle the abbey was vital to the local economy. The monks made valuable investments, among other things in a tannery. They were far and away the biggest customers in the town and its surrounding liberty, spending £600 to £650 a year between a large number of tradesmen. The abbey recruited its officers as well as the brethren mostly from a local oligarchy of burgess families. Other burgesses held lucrative sinecures as well as the working posts, and some fifteen or twenty had the right to dine in the monastic hall as esquires or valets of the house. Others fed in the kitchen, infirmary or guest house. Their liveries were sufficient to clothe entire families and they were generally educated in the abbey school. The craftsman, the tradesmen, the more educated burgesses, even rudimentary local 'bankers', were in an intricate, involved manner both the servants and the parasites of the monastic establishment. The Dissolution, in putting an end to the abbey, also profoundly changed the local economy and the local social fabric, depriving Battle of its role as a centre of education, of loans, of quality and luxury craftsmanship. Like Croyland, in similar circumstances, Battle, deprived of its abbey, swiftly declined into a mere sleepy, little market town.

Durham had an equally intimate relationship with local society. On a larger scale than Battle, the town was less a centre of commerce than a centre of ecclesiastical administration and consumption, benefiting from the presence of the bishop's administration as well as the abbey. At Durham even wider ranges of local society battened upon the brethren. Here the local gentry, often supported by their magnate patrons, in season and out of season demanded lay offices and ecclesiastical benefices in the abbey's patronage, to such an extent that Prior Bell wrote in March 1476:

> I and my brothers are so oft times called upon in such things by divers lords of right high estate that we may not have our liberty to dispose such small benefices as are in our gift to our friends, like as our will and intent were for to do, as God Knoweth and me repenteth.

The monks of so great an establishment needed a large staff to defend their interests: officials to supervise their estates, ecclesiastical lawyers trained in canon and civil law to frustrate episcopal and other ecclesiastical encroachments, gentry (*generosi*) learned in the common law to conduct the extensive litigation inevitable to large-scale property-owning at this period. At a lower level, mothers, fathers and sisters of the monks obtained places in the monastic almshouses and small gifts of money in charity from the obedientiaries.

From one point of view the monks, like the king and nobility, were the victims of an insidious spoils system. From another such a legal and social network was essential for both their protection and their popularity. Society worked upon the bland assumption that the well placed had the right to benefit from their connections to the greatest possible extent. It would have been folly to resist the deeply ingrained, unquestioned conventions of a society based time-out-mind upon a reciprocating network of kinship, lordship and friendship — friendship not in its exclusive modern meaning of emotional affinity but of a group combined for its mutual benefit.

There is, after all, some evidence to be set against the distaste of progressive humanist Catholics and the diatribes of early Prostestant opponents of monasticism, and vehement revolutionary minorities always make more noise and more impression than their numbers warrant. One need not always admire the intolerance of a bigoted *avant-garde*. One might, after all, recall the opinion of Martin Luther who, in spite of his personal disapproval, saw no objection to monasticism for those who felt the call to such a way of life. In England, it is true, less than twenty religious houses (both of monks and friars) were founded in the century before the Dissolution. After all there was no need of them for, with the decline in population, there were many empty cells in the greater houses. The number of postulants suggests that to the middling ranks of society the monastic vocation still held forth a strong appeal. Although many laymen, even those holding lucrative monastic offices, cast covetous eyes upon monastic estates, we have no means of knowing whether *active* disapproval of the religious life was at all widespread, or even the extent of lay indifference to it. It is necessary to be cautious about the extent to which contemporary writers expressed more than mere sectional opinion. In spite of competition from parish churches, collegiate churches and chantries, the flow of legacies and bequests never dried up. Bishop Fox may have been one of the new humanists, but it was touch and go whether he founded an Oxford college for monks or a college to propagate the New Learning. It was the same with Lady Margaret Beaufort. Although his friend Erasmus disapproved of monasticism, Sir Thomas More, at an early stage in his career, seriously considered life in a Carthusian cloister and in his *Utopia* drew considerable inspiration from the ideals of monasticism. Such people were less vehement opponents of the old ways than people severely torn by divergent tendencies in a changing world.

At the grass roots the monasteries of Lancashire, though some of their inmates were loose in morals and lax in observance, had lost neither the respect nor the affection of local people. The citizens of Durham and Battle, profiting as they did, were well enough satisfied with the monasteries in their midst and at the Dissolution the burgesses of Tavistock must have viewed with some dismay the closure of the monastic school in which most of them had been educated. Many local commissions reported much more favourably than Cromwell's agents upon the houses which they inspected. At Northampton they extolled St James' Abbey, explaining that its alms relieved 'three or four score folks of the town and country adjoining daily .... There are many poor in Northampton and they are greatly relieved by the house.' The cessation of prayers for the dead seriously disturbed the minds of many people and some in the later sixteenth century, disappointed by some of the results of the Reformation, looked back with a heartfelt nostalgia to the monastic foundations.

IX

The same verdict of modest satisfaction, varying in different areas from enthusiasm to acute discontent, may well be true of the church as a whole. Though contemporaries may not have been aware of it, standards had improved. Non-residence and pluralism, prominent though they were, had diminished from the excesses of the thirteenth century and were considerably below the appalling levels of later days. The qualifications of the majority of the resident clergy at least met the requirements of canon law, many of them much more than that. Instruction through sermons had become far more frequent than is generally acknowledged and well adapted to the needs of the congregations. A number of new liturgical feasts, like the Transfiguration, the Visitation, the Name of Jesus, the Crown of Thorns and the Compassion of the Virgin, became widespread and popular during this period.

More remunerative, if not more arduous, roles certainly syphoned off the ablest clergy from the parishes to cathedrals, courts and palaces, where they imbued diocesan administration with a disciplinary, legalistic atmosphere rather than a pastoral vision. In the courts people certainly resented their expensive, and sometimes corrupt, activities, though accusations of undue delay in procedure seem to have been exaggerated. Anti-clerical feeling was certainly present, though it had diminished from the vicious levels of the 1420s and the 1450s.

There may have been something of a revival of Lollardy towards the end of the century. After the death of the great heresiarch, John Wyclif, distinct groups of Lollards existed; among them were a number of educated Oxford clerics like Nicholas Hereford and Philip Repingdon and a group of well placed laymen including several household knights of the young Richard II, but generally the movement appealed to the poorer, underprivileged members of society. Most of the clerical group, who were prominent and obvious targets, soon recanted under persecution. Episcopal persecution against the Lollards in the countryside, however, varied from diocese to diocese and in some it does not seem to have been particularly vigorous. Until the later fourteenth century England had always been singularly free of heresy. There was no tradition of repression, so much so that the habit and its techniques were remarkably underdeveloped as compared with those of some continental countries. Moreover some laymen seemed to have had strong sympathies for Lollards and were inclined to protect them, thus limiting the activities of the bishops.

Attitudes changed, however, when in 1414 Sir John Oldcastle's rebellion linked heresy with sedition. This was a supreme disaster for the Lollard movement for in place of the hitherto sporadic persecution by the bishops a vigorously directed government campaign of repression smashed what unity and elementary central organization the movement had, up to that time, possessed. From this time onwards, it lost any powerful lay backing that had once sustained it and became largely an underground movement. Though there was a belated political Lollard plot as late as 1431, it was easily suppressed.

The loss of any powerful lay sympathy deprived Lollardy of political influence and the even earlier loss of its learned adherents deprived it of any real intellectual or doctrinal coherence; consequently popular Lollard attitudes tended to become ever cruder. The movement came to consist of scattered communities mainly of tradesmen — weavers, wheelwrights, smiths, carpenters, tailors and other craftsmen, with a sprinkling of priests, merchants and professional men; it seems hardly to have touched the peasantry. Although various groups, particularly in the Chiltern area of Buckinghamshire, in Kent round Tenterden, Cranbrook and Benenden, in London and Essex, Berkshire and the west Midlands, were able to keep up some communication with each other, it proved impossible to maintain any consistent body of doctrine. Lollardy became an underground, pertinacious rather than an heroic faith, surviving in the traditions of particular families or groups of families. As Dr J. A. F. Thomson has remarked, later Lollardy became 'a series of attitudes from which beliefs evolved rather than ... a set of doctrines'.[30]

Like most biblical fundamentalist movements, it developed a highly eccentric fringe. In general, however, its tendencies combined scriptural fundamentalism with a kind of crude commonsense rationalism, condemning transubstantiation, the cult of the saints, the doctrine of purgatory and indulgences.

Recorded persecutions were very few in the middle years of the fifteenth century. Then from about 1486 prosecutions once again increased. In 1494 evidence of Lollard opinions at Oxford seriously disturbed Bishop Alcock. In 1511 – 12 there were seventy-four abjurations in the diocese of Coventry and Lichfield, ninety-six in Salisbury between 1491 and 1521 and three hundred in Lincoln between 1511 and 1521. Lack of vigorous ecclesiastical counteraction in mid-century may have allowed Lollardy to revive again but it is impossible to guess to what extent the increasing number of prosecutions was due to greater vigilance and severity on the part of the bishops or to a genuine resurgence of heresy.

Lollardy had its effect, though only a limited effect, upon the development of the Reformation. The acute anxiety which it bred in the hierarchy made them over-wary of even limited, orthodox reform and so piled up resentment. On the other hand Lollards were too low in society's ranks to have brought about any reformation by themselves and they were too early to have exploited the printing presses

[30] J.A.F. Thomson, *The Later Lollards, 1414 – 1500* (1965), p. 244.

which were so vital to the spread of Prostestantism. Later in the
sixteenth century John Bale and the great martyrologist John Foxe
admired the Lollards because they wanted to establish a convincing
ancestry for their own Protestantism and even claimed the Wars of
the Roses as God's punishment upon England for rejecting Wyclif's
teaching. However, earlier reformers like Friar Barnes had been
somewhat contemptuous of the Lollard versions of the Scriptures and
other Lollard writings. On the eve of the Reformation, although
there may have been many sympathizers, convinced heretics still
formed only a small proportion of the population even in London.
Lollardy provided a background for Lutheranism and to some extent
merged into it, but it was too weak in itself to supply anything more
than fertile soil.

   People do not spend vast sums of money upon institutions of which
they profoundly disapprove. The amount of money lavished on
building demonstrates a pride and enthusiasm far beyond the limits
of a mere approbation. Roughly speaking the twelfth century saw the
great age of monastic building, the thirteenth and early fourteenth
centuries that of the cathedrals. In the later middle ages parochial
churches and parochial chapels came into their own. In the late
fifteenth century, continuing to 1529, parishioners all over the country remodelled or completely rebuilt their churches on the most
lavishly magnificent scale—churches as far apart as St Mary
Redcliffe, Bristol, St Wedreda, March (with its splendid angel roof),
St Lawrence, Ludlow, St Mary's, Bury St Edmund's, St Mary's,
Saffron Walden. Norwich, with its multitude of possibly fifty-six
churches—two hundred people were enough to form a congregation—rebuilt, in whole or in part, at least nine of them between
1460 and 1529. One might almost call the decades before the
Reformation the period of 'the great rebuilding' of parish churches.

   Nor was building confined to splendid urban churches. The
villages of Somerset are especially notable for fine churches of this
period and in Devon and Cornwall nearly every parish church was
rebuilt or refurnished at this time. In these latter counties, too, and in
Lancashire, scores of little private oratories and chapels were erected,
attached to remote, lonely houses or built at crossroads to serve
districts far distant from parish churches. Numerous parishes in
Cheshire remodelled the interiors of their churches, added aisles,
towers and much new heraldic glass. From about 1450 many church
houses were erected—buildings for the communal purposes of the
parish or district. Once again they are mainly found in the southwest
(there are sixty-four in Devonshire alone), erected because in a
countryside of scattered farms and hamlets it was desirable to have
some specialized building for communal activities.

Parishes raised building funds in various ways. They enthusiastically organized church ales, often in friendly cooperation with neighbouring parishes. Parish gilds staged profitable plays. Between 1425 and 1475 in various villages in the Midlands half the fines levied in the manorial courts went to fabric funds. The rich, even merchants so often supposed to have been anti-clerical, made lavish contributions. At Lavenham in Suffolk the lower levels of the church tower were begun between 1486 and 1495, its super storeys completed between 1520 and 1525. The wealthy clothier, Thomas Spring III (died 1523), left £200 for its completion and for building a chapel to house a monument for himself and his wife. Thomas Spring II had earlier given a vestry, the earl of Oxford gave money and in 1504 another clothier John Rusby left a legacy of £200.

The account book for the rebuilding of Bodmin Church in Cornwall between 1469 and 1471 — and that, be it noted, during one of the peak periods of the Wars of the Roses — demonstrates the extent of fervent local enthusiasm. It was an expensive business. Nineteen masons were on the site during the three years the work lasted, though not all of them were employed simultaneously or regularly. The new church cost £268 17s. 9½d. — an enormous sum of money at a time when a two-storey stone house, eighteen feet high, with walls three feet thick on the ground floor and two feet six inches on the second storey, containing a hall, a parlour and rooms above and four fireplaces, cost less than £30 to erect.

There may have been a papal indulgence at Bodmin though there is no record of it, and the parish obviously levied a compulsory rate, for the accounts contain a list of defaulters and some were even distrained. Nevertheless, popular enthusiasm is obvious enough, possibly whipped up by the town's forty religious gilds. People freely contributed according to their means, giving their labour and materials as well as cash. The vicar contributed his year's stipend. Others gave windows, timber, lambs, a cow and even a goose. One old woman, on top of her subscription, sold her 'crockke' (brass cauldron) and another old woman managed to rake 3½d. together. The maidens in Fore Street and Bore Street gave subscriptions over and above those collected from the gilds of the virgins in the same streets. The accounts end with a list of 460 individual contributors — surely nearly all the adults in the small town of Bodmin. A parish dissatisfied and disapproving of the general condition of the church would hardly have done so much.

An equal enthusiasm appeared on the other side of the country at Louth in Lincolnshire. There, when the marvellous three-hundred-foot spire, begun in 1501, was completed in 1515 at a cost of £305 with the placing of the weathercock on the eve of Holy Rood Day,

Will Aylby, parish priest, with many of his brother-priests there present, hallowing the said weathercock and the stone that it stands upon, and so conveyed upon the said broach: and then the said priests singing *Te Deum Laudamus* with organs: and then the kirkwardens garte [made] ring all the bells, and caused all the people there being to have bread and ale, and all to the loving of God, Our Lady and All Saints.[31]

Sources are meagre, contemporary opinions few. Arguments from silence are proverbially deceptive, but such contemporary criticisms as survive from late fifteenth-century England are moderate in tone, in no way resembling the vehement anti-clericalism, the violent anti-papalism or the wild, fantastic millenarian dreams of late fifteenth-century German prophetic literature. Dare we draw the conclusion that criticism of abuses was less violent because the *ecclesia anglicana* was less corrupt than the German church; that anti-papalism was rare because the papacy was deprived of any real influence for good or evil; that criticism and resentment went little further at the grass-roots level than the usual burden of complaint and bickering always found among some of the members of any long-established institution; that such grumblers did not necessarily share the more advanced views of the Colets, the Meltons and the Mores, demanding advances upon those not inconsiderable improvements which had already taken place?

The shrewd Venetian ambassador, writing in 1497, described the piety, the religious practices and, somewhat enigmatically, the doubts of the English:

They all attend Mass every day, and say many Paternosters in public (the women carrying long rosaries in their hands, and any who can read taking the office of Our Lady with them, and with some companion reciting it in the church, verse by verse, in a low voice, after the manner of churchmen), they always hear Mass on Sunday in their parish church, and give liberal alms, because they may not offer less than a piece of money, of which fourteen are equivalent to a gold ducat; nor do they omit any form incumbent upon good Christians; there are, however, many who have various opinions concerning religion.

It is a picture of a society punctilious, even ardent, in its religious devotions, in the reading of pious, but unintellectual works of edification, reproduced for wider audiences by the presses of William Caxton and Wynkyn de Worde. What the 'various opinions' concerning religion were—heresy, possibly the survival of Lollardy, or anti-clericalism or both—we may never know. Superior people may find such a spiritual ambience dull and uninspiring. It was certainly not the heroic piety of the dark ages. Nor did it pour upon the world the idealism of the High Gregorian movement, bravely struggling to establish reforming ideals amid seas of corruption. Sixteenth-century

[31] Quoted from A.G. Dickens *The English Reformation* (1964), p. 10.

reformers despised its cloistered monks. Even the evangelical activities of the Franciscans and the Dominicans fell short of the energies and activities of the new Theatines, Barnabites and Jesuits. St Carlo Borromeo, as well as Calvin, would have frowned upon the deficiencies of its secular clergy. Both Catholic and Protestant reformers strove to inculcate higher, more rigid standards, firmer definitions of doctrine, to repress mere external observance in favour of a more thoughtful, interior spiritually, to impose more puritan standards of social conduct upon both clergy and laity. Though propagandists, particularly ecclesiastical propagandists, may favour the notion, revolutions, both religious and secular, do not rise like phoenixes from the cold ashes of decadence. That reformers could aspire to higher standards (far in advance both in spirituality and practice of those of the twelfth and thirteenth centuries) and that they succeeded to some extent, after heroic evangelical endeavours, was surely, in part, the result of the already rising standards and growing aspirations of the pre-Reformation decades. The Reformation was hardly a sudden revolution, a triumphant leap of religious athleticism from a deepening abyss of corruption. It was far more, both in its Catholic and Protestant forms, the bloom of the rising clerical standards and lay expectations of its preceding generations.

5 Education and
the Arts

I

In 1407 William Thorpe claimed that in any group of twenty pilgrims less than three could repeat one of the commandments, the Pater Noster, the Ave Maria or the creeds. Surely anyone who could read could have passed so elementary a test.

During the following century both contemporary statements and circumstantial evidence point to a much wider extension of literacy. In 1497 the Venetian envoy stated that ladies took Books of Hours to church to read during the mass. Pews with book rests appeared for the first time in English churches and the fashion for wider windows and immense clerestories, glazed with paler glass than ever before, may well have developed in part to allow more light for reading. Unless the ability to read had become fairly widespread, the practice, quite common during the Wars of the Roses, of posting up propaganda bills and distributing them by hand would have been pointless.

In 1485 when Henry VII obtained a dispensation for his marriage to Elizabeth of York from the papal legate, James, bishop of Imola, confirmed by Pope Innocent VIII in a bull of 27 March 1486, he immediately prepared an English version of the letter for general circulation. It was printed the same year by William Maclinia and further editions were issued in 1494, 1495 and 1497. This English translation of the problems of the succession and disorder which had long beset England, formulating the theory of peace to come as a result of the union of the houses of Lancaster and York—a theme which was to be repeated in similar terms for more than a century—was one of the earliest examples in England of the use of the printing press for propaganda purposes.

By 1458 foreign merchants were already established as wholesalers of books in England and by the 1470s the reading public was sufficiently large to absorb from the new printing presses more numerous copies of the well-established, traditional works already popularized by the scriveners. In 1487 the London goldsmiths decided to accept as apprentices only boys who could already read English. In 1488 – 9 Caxton thought it worthwhile to rent a shop at Westminster for a week during the parliamentary session. Three years later a certain Hugh Parsons of St Bride's parish, Fleet Street, prosecuted Elizabeth Johnson for having stolen from his house sixty copies of a book called *De Novis Tenuris* and sixty more of another called *Le Fox* besides two bales of paper. Progress over the century had indeed been so great that Sir Thomas More claimed that more than half the people in the country could read. However his guess should not be taken too seriously as he could not possibly have known. It may be that his figures applied only to London for there may have been, as in every aspect of life during this period, considerable regional variations. Literacy may have been less the further the distance from the capital. As late as 1560 as many as 92 out of the leading 146 gentry of Northumberland could not sign their own names, nor could one of the MPs for Berwick. In any case knowledge spread further than literacy for, by the time of the Reformation, literate villagers read aloud to the illiterate. Both were capable of theological argument and both went to the stake for it.[1]

II

The widening educational opportunities which provided this spreading literacy increased in the most haphazard and localized manner. Men who had made fortunes elsewhere, mindful of their own earlier difficulties, often endowed schools in the places of their birth. As Archbishop Rotherham, looking back to his boyhood, wrote in the statutes (1483) of the school which he founded at Rotherham:

> We stood in that time without letters. We should have stood there illiterate and rough for many years had not it been that, by God's grace, a man learned in grammar arrived, from whom, as from a primal font, we were by God's will instructed and under God's leadership came to the state in which we now are, and others arrived at greater positions.

So the archbishop, mindful of his own earlier good fortune, gave his endowment to provide permanent opportunities for future generations.

Archbishop Rotherham's foundation was unusual for an endowed school in that it provided primary education and a kind of business curriculum as well as the more formal Latin studies necessary for

---

[1] I owe this point to Professor A.G. Dickens.

entrance to the universities. Generally, however, little is known about primary schools, then called reading or song schools; in the Tudor period, when local clergy often taught in them, they came to be known as petty schools. Such establishments formed a more or less despised sector of the educational system, a sector which attracted few endowments or benefactions. What little we know, however, shows that song schools took in children between the ages of about seven and ten and, in addition to the 'song' essential for religious purposes, first taught them the alphabet from a 'primer' — a religious miscellany a few pages long, containing, besides the alphabet, the basic prayers, the elements of the faith and the simpler liturgical devotions for laymen such as the Hours of the Virgin Mary. Owing to the lack of any specialized textbooks or readers for these elementary pupils they developed their reading from service books. Thus the Latin service books prepared a child for entry to the more advanced studies of the grammar school. Even for the child whose ambition rose no further than the reading of English, such acquaintance with Latin service books would be useful aid to devotion in later life.

Children may have learned writing in some of these schools, possibly more often at a later stage. However, as the 1518 statutes of St Paul's School, London, demanded the ability to write as well as to read from prospective entrants, this suggests that the song schools were expected to teach writing. A few of these primary schools also taught grammar while alternatively some of the grammar schools dealt with the more elementary stages.

Unfortunately, we have no idea of the number of these primary schools. Nine of the secular cathedrals[2] supported them. There were certainly song schools in many cities and towns. Others were attached to monasteries and collegiate churches and an increasing number of chantry priests taught other boys as well as their choristers. Parish chaplains, parish clerks and men in minor orders also provided a good deal of instruction privately and informally. In 1489 a gentleman at Ticehurst in Sussex left a house to the church for the use of any priest who would undertake to teach and in 1529 the convocation of Canterbury recommended the parish clergy to teach in their spare time.

Far more information exists about the country's grammar schools but still too little to see the system in anything like completeness. The earliest grammar schools may have originated in the cathedrals, for their own clerical purposes but admitting other pupils too. Somewhat later they developed in the county towns, major ports and some of the larger centres of commerce. By the thirteenth century they were

[2] Cathedrals the chapters of which were composed of secular clergy as distinct from those composed of monks.

spreading to some of the smaller towns. Most of them seem to have charged fees for teaching. Because of the small number and the very uneven distribution of these schools many boys had to seek their education away from home and, at this stage, benefactors preferred to grant endowments to provide poor boys with food and lodging which, with bed and board at 8*d.* a week, was a far more serious financial burden than the generally modest teaching fees of 4*d.* to 8*d.* a quarter. Such relief for poor scholars became a recognized form of social piety and a means of salvation. Piers Plowman thought of it as one of the charities which drove hovering devils from deathbeds and secured for the soul a rapid passage to the bliss of Paradise.

The endowment of schools to provide free teaching began in the fourteenth century, to become a popular form of charity in the fifteenth. Between 1450 and 1509 benefactors founded and endowed at least fifty-three schools or endowed older foundations.[3] They provided annual funds ranging from £10 to £35 19*s.* 11*d.*,[4] with masters' salaries ranging from £4 6*s.* to £12 6*s.* Such pay, though far from affluence, compares very well with the stipends of the parish clergy.[5] References exist to at least eighty-five schools (not all of them endowed) between 1450 and 1499 and to one hundred and twenty-four during the following three decades. For over five centuries bene-factors provided endowments for hundreds of schools all over England and this flood of educational endowment began its first strong flow in the fifteenth century not, as generally supposed, in the age of the Reformation.

Even so, our knowledge of the network of grammar schools is woefully incomplete. Property-holding and regulation both leave records. Before the Reformation neither church nor state concerned themselves with the control of education or the licensing of school-masters. Therefore we have little or no information about the numerous unendowed schools which must have existed and the number of private schoolmasters teaching for fees may well have exceeded the number of those teaching in the endowed foundations.

To sum up, after 1406 when a statute declared the freedom of every man regardless of social status to educate his children, thus freeing the progeny of villeins from seigneurial restrictions, education was in theory available to all and as the fifteenth century wore on free instruction became available over wider and wider areas. In practice, however, access to education was much more limited, much more a matter of chance. The children of the well-to-do could acquire a

---

[3] A few also included provision for elementary education.

[4] Jesus College, Rotheram, had the enormous endowment of £102 p.a. but this also had to provide for a community of priests as well as the school.

[5] See above, pp. 133 – 4.

grammar school education at the will of their parents; generally the sons of the poor could do so only if an endowed school or a private schoolmaster existed within daily walking distance of their homes.

III

Though its use was declining in governmental administration and in private business, Latin still remained the essential language of diplomacy and of all intellectual intercourse at the highest level just as English or French are the *linguae francae* of developing countries today. As William Wykeham in 1382 in the foundation charter of Winchester College had stated:

> Experience plainly teaches that grammar is the foundation, gate and source of all the other liberals arts, without which such arts cannot be known nor can anyone arrive at practising them. Moreover, by the knowledge of letters justice is cultivated and the prosperity of the human condition is increased.

During the last quarter of the fifteenth century methods of tuition began to change in the direction of the humanism which achieved its semi-triumph later in the sixteenth century. At first the old standard grammars remained in use, the fourth century *Donatus* for elementary instruction, for more advanced work the *Doctrinale* (*c.* 1200) of Alexander de Villa Dei. The *Donatus* and the *Doctrinale* were entirely in Latin. John Cornwall's grammar of 1346 had been the first to include some exposition in English. By the 1430s treatises with their explanatory matter entirely in English had appeared. At about the same time the first Latin-English dictionaries came on the market and in 1440 a certain Geoffrey, a Dominican recluse of Lynn, had completed the first English-to-Latin word list.

By the 1470s the practices of Renaissance Italy at last began to influence English teaching methods. Lorenzo Valla's (1405 – 57) *Elegantiae Linguae Latinae* had reached Oxford by 1474 and an English edition of Niccolo Perotto's (1429 – 80) work was published at Louvain in 1486. At the grammar school level John Ankwykyll was more responsible than any other man for propagating the new Italian curriculum. Appointed headmaster of the new grammar school attached to Magdalen College, Oxford, in 1481, two years later he published an entirely new grammar, the *Compendium Totius Grammaticae*, drawing upon the works of the up-to-date Italian grammarians and containing extracts from Cicero, Horace, Quintilian and other classical authors. After his death in 1488 the *Compendium* and other works of his were published both at Deventer

and Cologne, though we know nothing of the extent of their circulation. Ankwykyll may well have been the founding father of a group of
grammarians centred on Magdalen College School in the years
around 1500, men who became a dominant, if not the dominant,
influence in English education for the next thirty years. John
Stanbridge, Ankwykyll's successor at Magdalen, though once again
his influence remains obscure, continued his work with some success,
producing six fairly elementary grammatical works. They are the first
known to have achieved a really wide circulation through the printing
press. All the major schools, Eton, St Paul's, Magdalen and Winchester, and some of the new foundations prescribed them. In some
schools they remained in use as late as the seventeenth century. The
mere availability of such cheaper printed textbooks, enabling most
pupils to possess copies of their own, must have made the most
tremendous difference to the methods and to the ease of teaching.

By 1500 methods and curriculum were in a state of flux. Although
in remoter places the old medieval curriculum did not expire until the
second decade of the sixteenth century or even later, the classical
revival had spread to at least the more prominent of the English
schools. By the 1520s the old medieval grammars ceased to be printed
and William Lily, who had studied in Italy, swept the board with his
new grammar. In 1540 the government forbade the use of all others
and Lily's grammar proved so useful and enduring that its last edition
was published as late as 1858.

At first some of the reformers themselves were reluctant to adopt
the full Italian programme. About 1508 when Dean Colet began to
plan for his new school at St Paul's, he desired an entirely new up-to-
date grammar but rejected the Italian preference for pagan, classical
authors. He preferred his scholars to read fourth- and fifth-century
Christian Latin poets. His semi-conservative ideas did not, however,
meet the general approval and the great classical authors, Cicero,
Ovid, Horace and Vergil and modern Latin works like Mantuan's
Eclogues and the *Colloquies* of Erasmus were soon dominant in other
schools.

The teaching of English was no more than a by-product of the
teaching of Latin. A *Vulgaria*,[6] based on Terence, published by Rood
and Hunt at Oxford in 1483, claimed that it would teach boys correct
and useful expressions in both languages. After all, translation was an
essential part of teaching, so that a schoolmaster, if he were so
inclined, could insist upon good style in both Latin and English. Even
so, the general level of written English remained low and clumsy
among the semi-educated gentry and merchant classes. William

[6] A book of phrases for translation.

Worchester (1415-85?) chose to write his famous *Itineraries* in Latin and, although his Latin was far from classical, he obviously thought and expressed himself more succinctly in Latin than in English. As the influence of humanism increased, if we can judge from the more prominent authors, English writing improved. As Professor D. Hay has remarked, Sir Thomas More and those of his contemporaries who developed an English style capable of a wide range of accurate and dignified expression were to a man highly trained in the new Latin humanism, though More himself also owed a great deal to the strong, unbroken tradition of devotional writing which had earlier developed a greater range and sophistication than any other form of English expression.

IV

At the highest level, at the universities, there had been considerable expansion. Between 1400 and 1460 six new colleges had been founded at Oxford, four at Cambridge. At Oxford new foundations then ceased until after 1509. Cambridge was more fortunate, seeing King's, the re-foundation of Queen's and Christ's, the foundation of St Catherine's and Jesus and the planning of St John's between 1441 and 1505. By 1500 each university had ten colleges, though most of the undergraduates still resided in the privately run halls or private lodgings, which did not finally disappear until the reign of Queen Elizabeth I. In Oxford there were about seventy halls housing perhaps 1,200 to 1,300 students as against perhaps 200 in the secular colleges plus about 250 friars and an unknown number of the religious in the monastic colleges. The student population of Cambridge was still much smaller than that of Oxford though its numbers and reputation were growing by the end of the fifteenth century.

Nearly all the new colleges stressed graduate instruction in theology and law. The work of fifteenth-century English academics has never been adequately investigated. The Carmelite, Thomas Netter (died 1430), had been the last English schoolman to achieve an international reputation. After his death we are more or less ignorant of developments until the appearance of the humanists, Grocyn (1466? – 1519), Linacre (1460? – 1524) and Dean Colet (1467? – 1519), aided by the visits of Erasmus to Oxford (1499) and Cambridge (1511 – 14). Even their achievement should not be exaggerated. By the standards of continental humanism it was distinctly limited. Advanced though Colet's interpretation of the Scriptures may have been, Erasmus almost apologize for his Latin style and Sir Thomas More's own acquaintance with classical authors is much less impressive than his profound knowledge of the Christian Fathers.

Other developments, though hardly typical of current conditions, trailed the path of future developments. William Waynflete, in the foundation of Magdalen College, Oxford in 1448, had provided three lectureships in theology, moral philosophy and natural philosophy, thus making his college largely self-contained for teaching purposes. He also, following a much earlier precedent at King's Hall, Cambridge, made provision for the admission of twenty undergraduates, the sons of noble and worthy men, as fee-paying commoners (*commensales*) sharing in the common life of the college. By this practice and by opening the Magdalen lectures (as Lady Margaret Beaufort did at Christ's College, Cambridge) to all members of the university, he pointed the way to the late sixteenth-century triumph of the colleges with their system of the internal teaching of undergraduates which, combined with endowed university professorships, replaced the system of regent masters.[7]

At Cambridge in 1424 the University Library possessed 122 volumes.[8] By 1470 the 'Common Library' was completed and between 1470 and 1500 Archbishop Rotheram built and endowed the 'Little Library' or rare book room. By 1530 they together housed between five and six hundred volumes. At Oxford the year 1488 saw the completion of the great library over the Divinity Schools to house the bequests of Humphrey, duke of Gloucester and John Tiptoft, earl of Worcester. Even so, progress should not be exaggerated. Both these university libraries were still inferior to the collections of some of the greater monasteries.[9]

V

So during the fifteenth century educational opportunities greatly widened. More and more of the gentry were sending their sons on from private tutors and the growing number of grammar schools to the universities and to the Inns of Court for higher education. Earlier

---

[7] MAs of not more than five years' standard who had carried out most of the undergraduate teaching.

[8] Volumes at this time often contained several disparate works which today would be individually bound.

[9] See above, pp. 142 – 3.

in the century three out of four of Judge William Paston's (1378 – 1444) sons went to Cambridge. The heir, John, spent periods both at Trinity Hall, Cambridge, and at the Inner Temple and his father sent the youngest son, Edmund, to Clifford's Inn. About 1500 George Vernon and his brother from Derbyshire were both at Magdalen College, Oxford.

Higher education, however, did not mean what it would mean today. Many of these sons of the gentry spent only a year or two at the university and then left without taking a degree. Moreover, university standards were lower than in modern times. Young men in their earlier years at Oxford and Cambridge would have received the level of instruction more normal in the upper forms of today's high schools. The colleges did not cease teaching grammar until 1570. At Oxford and Cambridge boys may have received some form of business instruction outside the formal curriculum.[10] Many attending the Inns of Court never qualified as lawyers. They acquired gentlemanly accomplishments, history, scripture, music, even dancing, and the smattering of law essential for running their own lands or for obtaining lucrative jobs as officials upon the estates of the landed magnates.

William Worcester, although he himself was one of these 'gentlemen bureaucrats' employed by a great landowner, deplored their very existence as a symptom of the decadence of the times or, being in the service of the veteran Sir John Fastolf (died 1459), he professed to do so when writing propaganda on behalf of a thinning and thoroughly *passé* generation of warmongers and ex-war profiteers pressing for the renewal of the Hundred Years War. In *The Boke of Noblesse*, the best known pamphlet representing the views of this group of people, he claimed:

> Now of late days, the greater pity is, many one that be descended of noble blood and born to arms, as knights' sons, esquires, and of other gentle blood, set themselves to singular practik, strange faculties from that fet, as to learn the practique of law or custom of land, or of civil matter, and so wasten greatly their time in such needless business, as to occupy court's holding, to keep and bear out a proud countenance at sessions and shires' holding .... Who can be a ruler and put himself forth in such matters, he is, as the world goeth now, among all estates more set of than he that hath dispended thirty or forty years of days in great jeopardies in your antecessours' conquests and wars.

By this time such a Jeremiad was little more than an out-of-date conservative attack upon an increasingly lettered, civilian society, probably the most civilian society in the Europe of its day. Worcester's

---

[10] There is considerable evidence of an alternative 'business curriculum' at Oxford in the late fourteenth and early fifteenth centuries, but unfortunately we cannot write with the same confidence of the later fifteenth century.

own employer in his later years became the patron of a quite distinct, if minor, literacy circle in East Anglia.

At the higher levels, after the death of that notable early patron, Humphrey, duke of Gloucester, in 1447, the development of humanism in England was slow and erratic. From about 1440 the English court recognized the importance of a good classical style in diplomatic correspondence. Humanist interests developed in a few monasteries,[11] more so indeed, in spite of their alleged conservatism, than in some of the colleges in the universities. Although Professor A.R. Myers has dated the development of humanism in the universities to Thomas Chaundler's wardenship of New College, Oxford (1450 – 78), it was not until 1484 that Serbopoulous of Constantinople went to Oxford to translate Greek texts into Latin and in 1473 the University Library Catalogue in Cambridge listed only one humanist work, Petrarch's *De Remediis*. A few scholars like William Gray, bishop of Ely (died 1478), John Free (died 1465) and John Tiptoft, earl of Worcester (1427 – 1470), had studied in Padua. One of Tiptoft's Latin orations is said to have been so powerful that it brought tears to the eyes of that enthusiastic classicist Pope Pius II.

The latest trends penetrated the Yorkist court. Dominic Mancini wrote that Edward V gave 'many proofs of his liberal education, of polite, nay scholarly attainments far beyond his years', emphasizing the thirteen-year old boy's knowledge of literature which 'enabled him to discourse elegantly, to understand fully, and to declaim most excellently from any work whether in verse or prose that came into his hands, unless it were from among the more abstruse authors'. Henry VII's court in no way lagged behind. From 1505 the king employed Polydore Vergil of Urbino to justify his dynasty in the fashionable prose of the Italian humanists. According to the blind poet, Bernard André, Henry VII's eldest son, Prince Arthur, was immersed in a thoroughly classical curriculum. The future Henry VIII was educated in the same way. The legend that he was well lettered only because his father had originally intended him for the church appeared for the first time only in the works of Lord Herbert of Cherbury in the early seventeenth century and is quite false. The education of both boys was that of the *avant-garde* laity of the times. The contemporary poets John Skelton (1460? – 1529) and Stephen Hawes (1474 – 1521) — and Skelton was one of Henry VIII's tutors — strongly claimed that virtue and a sense of public responsibility were best achieved through the study of classical antiquity and more especially through poetry and rhetoric. Such developments, however, were still exceptional until the second decade of the

[11] See above, p. 142.

sixteenth century and a lay intelligentsia is scarcely observable until
about the third decade.

Private collections of books were growing larger. Although a few
contained a fair number of classical texts, a more conservative taste
dominated the majority. The Lancastrian royal family had been
highly educated and great book collectors. Edward IV began the
royal library which became one of the sights to be shown to foreign
visitors under Henry VII. By 1480 the Pastons possessed some forty or
more books, the results of three generations of collecting. Some men
were such eager readers that they carried books with them when they
were travelling. John Tiptoft, earl of Worcester, took some of his
books with him when, as deputy, he went on a military expedition to
Ireland in 1467, and Oxford once hailed him as the successor of Duke
Humphrey. Again in 1481, an entry in the *Howard Household Books*
lists thirteen of Lord Howard's books (all with French titles). The list
may be a rough catalogue of his entire library but, judging from its
place in the notebooks it is more likely to have been a list of the
volumes which he took with him on a naval expedition along the east
coast of Scotland. This is by no means improbable for his personal
preparations for the expedition were made on the most lavish scale.
At Christmas 1484, the notorious William Catesby, the speaker of
Richard III's parliament, brought to London four religious books,
eight books of law, a book of chronicles and a Pliny.

John Shirley (died 1456) a scrivener and a bookseller, had also run
the first English lending library in London. In 1492 Geoffrey Downes,
a fellow of Queen's College, Cambridge, when founding a chantry at
Potts Shrigley in Cheshire attached a library to it. The collection
consisted mostly of religious books; some were printed, some were
available for borrowing. They could be taken out on loan for thirteen
weeks against 'a sufficient pledge to keep them safe'. Parish libraries
also existed. William Gefferey, who died in 1503, bequeathed to the
'store' of St Mary's Church, Swansea, a copy of Higden's *Poly-
chronicon* in English, an English translation of Boccaccio called *The
Fall of Princes*, the very popular religious dialogue *Dives et Pauper*
and a Latin work, *Liber Sancte Terre*, probably a history of the
Crusades. He directed them to be chained in some suitable place in
the church for the benefit of literate parishioners. It would be rash to
conclude from so little evidence that there were minature chantry and
parish libraries all over the place, but there is equally no reason to
suppose that these tiny collections were isolated, atypical examples.

VI

The titles of Lord Howard's books—histories and French romances —like *La belle d.s. marcy* and *La Recuel des histories troianes*, give a clue to the taste of a predominantly conservative reading public—a taste very shrewdly exploited by that hard-headed businessman, William Caxton. Chauvinistic historians have greatly exaggerated Caxton's pioneering efforts. After all he did not invent printing, and even in England he was the first printer on the scene only by a mere two years. He exploited a well-established market for courtly literature and romances, a market which he understood very well for he had already been supplying it with manuscripts. He issued over thirty editions of romances, poems and histories in seventeen years and kept his press going by supporting the large demand for religious books when his aristocratic sponsors, particularly the Wydeville family, were under political clouds. Between these two types of work he ran a highly successful publishing house.

At the same time he occupied a somewhat fleeting position in the development of English culture. He shared to the full the intense craving for didacticism common to conservatives and humanists alike—that relish for the obvious that makes so many of their books so tedious and boring to modern readers. Exploiting traditional taste, Caxton began to print works from his stock of manuscripts, histories and chronicles in English, poems in the post-Chaucerian tradition and translations of French histories and romances which he judged would appeal to English tastes.

His translations form the highest proportion of his printed works. The taste and style of the luxurious ducal court of Burgundy had the strongest appeal to Englishmen. Caxton, while governor of the Merchant Adventurers in the Netherlands, had established close relations with Edward IV's sister, the Duchess Margaret, in the course of which he apparently became well acquainted with the literature in vogue among the Burgundian nobility—a knowledge which he turned to good use. While less aggressive businessmen imported Burgundian manuscripts, it was Caxton's peculiar *forte* to provide cheaper, printed translations of that particular species of literature and thus to reap the profits of a greatly extended market.

His translations exude a distinctly individual, even eccentric, flavour. Like many semi-educated men, and like many of his own generation, he adored grandiloquence, egregiously judging Chaucer to be 'the first founder embellisher of *ornate* eloquence in our English' (my emphasis). Being first and foremost a man of business with an eye on making money, he became a fast translator, intent upon speedy production. His English remained excessively close to the French constructions of his originals, introducing unusual French words and expressions, many of which, unlike Chaucer's borrowings, never found favour and remain unique to Caxton's own works. He generally needed some existing work as a basis for his writing, for without a model, his constructions became extremely clumsy — a defect which is very marked indeed in his original Prologues and Epilogues, so often composed of borrowed, ornate phrases, which he had no hesitation about repeating in different works. He never wasted what he thought was a good turn of phrase.

As an editor he was slapdash even by the standards of the late fifteenth century. He printed any manuscript that came to hand, apparently never comprehending that some were better than others. He never attempted, as even some of the scriveners had done, to standardize his orthography, so that one of the first results of the printing press in England was to encourage diversity rather than standardization of the language.

Caxton's vogue quickly vanished. Within thirty years of his death the fashion for the courtly literature of Burgundy had vanished and a new generation despised his translations. Humanism developed rapidly and with it humanist contempt for chivalric literature. Even the neo-chivalric revival of the Elizabethan era never revived his popularity. A more sophisticated age scorned his translation of Vergil's *Aeneid*. Knowing little Latin, he had translated it from an existing French translation. Even that he had treated in the most cavalier manner, adding boring passages not to be found in the original and cutting out others which presumably he disliked himself. His habit of enriching English by borrowing from French was soon transformed into a fashion for borrowing from Latin. As Dr N.F. Blake has remarked: 'Caxton was essentially a businessman all his life, and he possessed all the virtues and limitations of that class. As for his impact on English literature it would be fairest to conclude that his individual contribution to English letters is not so important as the evidence he gives of the taste and culture of the fifteenth century.'

VII

Perhaps the most popular art form of all was the art of the theatre. Few people until recently have realized the wide diffusion and the sophistication of the late-medieval English theatre, widely diffused over the countryside not merely in the greater towns. In 1511 twenty-seven villages round Bassingbourne near Cambridge combined to finance and produce a play about St George. Other East Anglian examples of the same kind of cooperative effort exist. Villages often staged such plays to raise funds for the parish and the church. In about 1490 at Bishop's Stortford, a church ale added to a collection taken at a play performed earlier in the day. On the other hand, funds could be allocated to cover the cost of producing a play. About 1450 Ipswich raised 40s. a year from grazing rights on the common marsh and the portman's meadows towards the cost of the town perfor-mances. Many noblemen and towns supported groups of players and minstrels. The *Howard Household Books* contain numerous ref-erences to the visits of such troupes and to the quite generous rewards given to them. Some of these noble companies made very extensive tours. In 1478 and 1480 the duke of Gloucester's players have been traced in places as far apart as Canterbury and New Romney in Kent and Selby Abbey in Yorkshire. Sir John Conyers's troupe also visited the abbey giving short morality plays and, when the players of the town of Beverley went there, they may have presented a section of their *Paternoster Play of the Seven Deadly Sins*.

State occasions were great excuses for 'disguisings'. In 1501 those staged for Catherine of Aragon's entry into London were stupen-dously lavish, using the most spectacular lighting. One of the devices used was a gigantic lantern which was

> cast out with many proper and goodly windows fenestered [that is paned], wherein were more than an hundred great lights: in the which lantern were xii goodly ladies disguised .... This lantern was made of so fine stuff and so many lights in it that these ladies might perfectly appear and be known through the said lantern.[12]

The most famous vernacular dramas were the mystery plays associated in many towns, especially in the north of England, with the Feast of Corpus Christi—plays which resulted from a combination of ecclesiastical and civic efforts. The scripts were the work of highly educated clerics deeply learned in doctrine, capable of writing numerous episodes for dramatic cycles of epic proportions in verse that often rose well above the merely pedestrian level, capable of moving the hearts and the emotions of large audiences. Performed in villages as well as in towns, the annual presentation became the special responsibility of the gilds. Therefore the town productions had early surpassed those of the more sparsely populated rural areas. In Lincoln production was the responsibility of a special gild of St

---

[12] College of Arms MS. 1st M. 13 f. 55, quoted from G. Wickham, *The Medieval Theatre* (1974), pp. 165–6.

Anne, the patron saint of the cathedral. More usually it rested with the craft gilds as at York, Wakefield and Coventry. The place of presentation varied. At Shrewsbury it was an amphitheatre formed from an old quarry and bounded by the River Severn. The York crafts performed the various scenes on pageants (that is waggons) which went from station to station through the main streets of the city.

Organization was complicated. Preparations and rehearsals by a whole host of people (the casts could include as many as a hundred actors and more) must have begun months ahead of time. The cycle of plays lasted for three days in Chester and a week in London. By this time, as in the political disguisings, presentation had become extremely sophisticated, with scenic marvels like rods which sprouted flowers and fruit. Horrible devils carried the traitor, Judas, up into the air. Stage properties and costumes could be spectacular, elaborate in their construction and often colossally expensive in the fabrics used.

The popular messages of the Franciscan and Dominican preachers were transformed into drama in the saint's plays and moralities like *Everyman* and the still popular *Castle of Perseverance* (c. 1450 – 25) and plays devoted to the Eucharist like the *Croxton Play of the Sacrament* of 1461. These, too, could be as elaborately and expensively staged as the mysteries.

Finally, although very little is known about them, and they survive only in extremely corrupt eighteenth-century texts, there were the plays and mummings of the folk festivals, plays deriving from very ancient fertility rites and plays of St George or plays of Robin Hood.

The late-medieval theatre did not come to an end because of any lack of popularity. Nor, contrary to long received opinion, were the first stages of its decline due to vigorous ecclesiastical repression. It is true that at home and abroad some moralists, both Catholic and Protestant, in the stricter atmosphere of the mid-sixteenth century with its growing sense of order and morality, strongly objected to the indecorous nature of many episodes. In 1548 an edict of the parliament of Paris banned all religious plays in the capital and provincial cities followed the Parisian example over the next fifteen years. However, some at least of the earlier Protestant reformers did not disapprove of the theatre as such. They even wrote plays propagating their own Protestant point of view, but their efforts in that direction were distinctly dull. Sporadic persecution certainly existed and at times actors were fined and imprisoned for heresy. Yet it was only after 1570 that church and state in England finally agreed upon total repression. It was not until 1579 that Archbishop Sandys and Dean Hutton finally put down the York plays on religious grounds.

The late-medieval religious theatre in England died a long and lingering death. The plays were viable as long as there was a genuine religious consensus. They were part of the popular religion of the later middle ages, exuding the contemporary emphasis upon good works, that emphasis which the reformers found so completely repellent. Their continuation demanded both a consensus of faith and willingness to raise money for production. Although the simpler village plays could, and often did, produce profits for parish funds, long before the Reformation the great urban productions had become as expensive as they were spectacular. Their increasing elaboration and cost led to resistence among some of the groups of people who by this time were compelled by local custom to produce them. To quote once more the evidence from Coventry, in 1531 the candlemakers' and saddlers' gilds appealed to the mayor and the leet to release them from their obligation to take part in the Corpus Christi pageants on the ground of the ruinous cost to their companies. The plays did not die out through any loss of religious faith as such. They declined because they had become so ruinously expensive that only considerable municipal and gild effort backed by ecclesiastical approval could any longer finance them. What had begun as popular productions had become a great municipal financial burden. They could continue only as long as all parties thought that they were worth while.

VIII

Gothic architecture achieved a climax of splendour and sophistication in the half century before the break with Rome. As noted elsewhere, the period was a great age of church building. Yet, at the same time, the taste of the age is difficult to visualize, even for some people to appreciate. Modern admiration for the greater medieval churches has generally taken a form which the people of the time would have regarded with incredulous derision. Their interiors long ago lost the brilliant decoration which their patrons and builders achieved at no inconsiderable cost and so intensely admired — the crimson, gold, blue and silver vaulting, the spangelled ceilings, mural paintings, the jewelled shrines, the gem-glittering reliquaries. People with so strong a sense of colour, whose more travelled members admired the high polychrome finish of Burgundian sculpture, would hardly appreciate modern enthusiasm for the scraped walls of their monuments. Even such partially restored buildings as the choir of Westminster Abbey give only an inadequate idea of their once gorgeous appearance. We can now fully recapture their luxuriant, vivid tones only from the minatures of illuminated books and these, for the general public, are the least known and most neglected heritage of western European art. Owing to their form, they can never be shown as fully as larger pictures painted on wood or canvas and even the best of reproductions rarely do them justice.

The fifteenth century in northern Europe was an age which exulted in ostentatious splendour, both ecclesiastical and secular. It was part of the era of the pageant chivalry taste, the last age of extreme Gothic splendour which, beginning in the fourteenth century, reached its fantastic climax in Henry VII's new palace at Richmond, in the ephemeral pavilions of the Field of Cloth of Gold, in the decoration of Henry VIII's Nonesuch Palace and continued well into the days of Elizabeth I. Although becoming apparent in education, the classical taste of the Italian Renaissance had not yet affected English building. In the late fifteenth century Norman architects applied superficial classical decorative motifs to numerous Gothic churches rebuilt after the devastations of the Hundred Years War. There is no trace even of this superficial classicism in English building and the tombs which Torrigiano cast in bronze for Henry VII (1512 – 18) and possibly for Lady Margaret Beaufort found no immediate imitators.

The architects of Yorkist and early Tudor England instead reached new heights of inventiveness within the Gothic idiom. The usual term 'Perpendicular' is a somewhat misleading description of the fashionable style of ecclesiastical architecture. It is true that builders now rejected the flowing curves of the Decorated Style, but it might be better, as Mr A. Clifton-Taylor has suggested, to call the latest period of Gothic 'Rectlinear';[13] for, although the use of tremendously high verticals was prominent enough, a new employment of horizontals was equally conspicuous. Horizontals appeared in transoms which arose from the need to strengthen windows growing ever wider with the use of flatter four-centred arches. Architects applied the same features to produce panelling on blank wall surfaces, especially between nave arcades and clerestories where earlier architects would have designed an arched triforium.

Perpendicular is often, and rightly, condemned for lack of imagination in its prominent window design and in its sculpture, but (influenced also by the demands of the friars for vast preaching halls) it produced superb results in its wide and lofty spatial effects, in its vaulting and in its towers. Both wood-carving and stone-vaulting now reached a peak of perfection. Wood-carving proliferated in the stalls of cathedral choirs, in the pews of parish churches, in the roofs, rood lofts, screens and pulpits of the many enlarged or refurbished

---

[13] A. Clifton-Taylor, *The Cathedrals of England* (1967), p. 198.

churches of the period, in the beautiful angel roofs of East Anglia, the rood lofts of the north and the elaborate screens of the southwest. The technical accomplishment and visual effects were often magnificent, as in the angel roof of March in Cambridgeshire (*c*. 1500) where the beams end in the gayest of angels. The effect is that of a *repoussoir*, a trick of stage scenery, in which the whole of the upper space of the nave seems to be filled with spreading angelic wings.

A group of accomplished architects, some of the most adventurous which the English architectural profession has ever produced, carried wall construction and stone-vaulting to a pitch of the most daring perfection, especially in the three finest of all late Rectlinear churches, all of them royal foundations—King's College Chapel Cambridge, St George's Chapel, Windsor, and Henry VII's Chapel in Westminster Abbey.

The first really big fan fault was constructed in the 1440s over the presbytery of Sherborne Abbey in Dorset, the most famous example at King's College by John Wastell between 1500 and 1508. Wastell was also responsible for the loveliest of all small fan vaults, that beneath Bell Harry in the crossing at Canterbury.

The most revolutionary and daring development of all was the pendant vault. Earlier experiments in wood which have now disappeared may have preceded the earliest example in stone, that of William Orchard in the Divinity School at Oxford built between 1479 and 1483. Orchard's vaulting is far too accomplished to have been built without predecessors of some kind. The most elaborate was that designed between 1503 and 1512 by William Vertue for Henry VII's chapel. Vertue's whole design was for a girderless age an astonishing feat of engineering which no late European Gothic elsewhere ever paralleled. Seen from within, buttresses blend with concave windows forming a continuous undulating wall, disguising the solidity of the buttresses to such an extent that the walls seem almost too frail to support the vault. The vault itself incorporated a series of pendants resembling stone lanterns, daringly suspended for several feet from the roof. Again at Windsor in the nave (1503) and in the choir (1506 – 11) Vertue's lierne vaults (among the most elaborate and successful ever constructed) rise from elegant shafts without capitals and achieve a most extraordinary flat pitch.

The architecture of these greater churches is an architecture of the most assured accomplishment, so much so that at times it seems almost facile. Yet pressed to the limits of structural possibility it seems an achievement of *raffiné*, almost over-ripe, taste. It was, however, the apparent facility of genius.

The domestic architecture of the upper classes showed rising standards of amenity and comfort. They had been rising for more than a century. The nobility and the greater ecclesiastics set the pace. The splendid private apartments of the nobility were already withdrawn from the noisy public halls of their vast households. Even a modest country house like Stonor in Oxfordshire had, among other rooms, a somewhat gloomy hall hung with black say, three chambers hung with red and green and a separate 'study'. By this time building was no longer dominated, or even much influenced, by the needs of defence. After the end of Richard II's reign the science of military architecture was almost unknown in England until Henry VIII, between 1538 and 1540, built between the Thames and Portsmouth a chain of coastal artillery forts in a somewhat eccentric variation of a revolutionary foreign style. The private castles built during the fifteenth century lacked the slightest military significance. Tattershall, Hurstmonceaux and Caister, all three built of brick during the reign of Henry VI, and Lord Hastings's two Leicestershire castles, Ashby-de-la-Zouche and Kirby Muxloe (another brick building), in spite of their delusive martial appearance had no military significance whatsoever. Their walls and their moats could at most have served as a protection against local riots. Some of them drew their architectural inspiration from the great houses of France and the Rhineland where such miniature palaces were the height of fashion. They were no more fortresses than the sham castles built by the rich during the height of the Victorian Gothic revival.

The owners of lesser houses abandoned even this fashionable martial pretence. When John Norreys built Ockwells during one of the most acute phases of the Wars of the Roses (it was not quite finished when he died in 1465), the design of the house, notable for its many windows, was based upon simple but harmonious mathematical ratios quite unrelated to any thoughts of defence. The main facade of the Prior's Lodging at Much Wenlock, built during the fourth quarter of the century in the Marches of Wales, one of the most disorderly areas in the entire country, is more glass than wall. When Thomas Tropenall built Great Chalfield in Wiltshire some time after 1467, it was an airy, spacious house constructed mostly of stone, though with some half-timbering. The moat on the north side was sufficiently utilitarian to drive a mill. To the south there were only stretches of water designed to make a set formal scheme of fishponds. Neville Holt on the borders of Leicestershire and Rutland and Gainsborough Old Hall in Lincolnshire are completely open, defenceless houses. That Sir Thomas Burgh chose to design Gainsborough Old Hall in this way seems to be particularly telling because his earlier house on the same site had been destroyed in a riot in 1470. In spite of that, Sir Thomas obviously did not think the addition of defences was worth the extra cost.

Merchants, if and when they could, aped the nobility in then
increasingly high standards of spaciousness and comfort. Crosby
Hall, built in the late 1460s by a very rich grocer, is a splendid
memorial of the state which a commercial magnate could afford. But
there were very few, even in London, who could afford to live on the
aristocratic scale and, faced with the problem of contracted and
expensive urban building sites, most well-to-do citizens were forced to
be content with lower standards. In the reign of Edward IV a quite
prosperous London mercer, his wife and their seven children had only
one chamber which could be used solely as a bedroom. But, then
privacy in the sense of exclusive occupation is a very recent desire. In
vast and noisy households when smaller groups withdrew from larger
groups they did not withdraw to solitude. Complete privacy in the
sense of a room of one's own was unknown, except perhaps in
monastic cells, and seems hardly to have been desired. For several
centuries to come in Italian palazzi and in great London houses, the
owners did not consider themselves hardly used in putting up with
very narrow personal accommodation for the sake of splendid public
apartments.

The councillors of monarchs were expected to sleep in their
bedchambers as Commynes did in those of Charles the Bold and
Louis XI. It was a mark of honour to invite a distinguished guest or
the leader of an embassy to share the bed of a prominent courtier.
When Louis de Gruthuyse, whose magnificent palace in Bruges had
housed Edward IV in his brief exile of 1470 to 1471, came on an
ambassy to Westminster in 1473, the royal chamberlain, Lord Hastings, took charge of him. When the time came to retire for the night,
they took a bath together followed by a collation of 'green ginger,
divers sirups, comfits and hippocras' before going to sleep.

If it is hard to imagine the splendour of the times, it is even more
difficult to see the villages as they were. If the remains of the greater
houses are few, the remains of those of the people are rare indeed.
Some of the poorest people lived in round mud huts. Indeed during
most of the middle ages the houses of the people were flimsy, imper-
manent structures, lasting for no more than one or two generations.
More permanent vernacular building seems to have begun during the
fifteenth century particularly in the southeast and perhaps in Devon.
The 'great rebuilding' of Elizabethan and early Stuart days changed
the appearance of English villages and small towns almost beyond
recognition. In the late sixteenth and the early seventeenth centuries
prosperous farmers replaced, altered and enlarged the more durable
of the late-medieval houses. Rare examples of cruck houses have
survived the 'great rebuilding' and later neglect and destruction.
Popular opinion assumes that these were the dwellings of the poor.

On the contrary they were occupied by prosperous peasant farmers, freeholders and copyholders. The one- or two-room dwelling, separated only by a thin wall from the cattle shelters, was no doubt typical. These hovels were sparsely furnished and utterly comfortless, with a chest, a table, a few stools, with bags of flock or straw for mattresses and, for the very poor and for servants, logs of wood taking the place of pillows. It was not until the later sixteenth century that any notable diffusion of greater comfort occurred. Kitchen utensils were sufficiently costly and cherished to be mentioned in wills. Smoke from a central hearth curled up to rafters hung with domestic and farm equipment. For the aristocracy and the gentry, in spite of habits and standards alien to our own, the fifteenth century can be described as the first great age of English domestic architecture. For the mass of the people there was little improvement: low, age-old standards still prevailed.

II Politics

6 Richard of York

I

The English crown was an office, the kingdom the greatest of all family inheritances. Therein lay an appallingly recalcitrant political problem. The fifteenth century knew no definite law governing the descent of the crown and most contemporary writers, their thoughts instinctively dominated by practices of landed inheritance, took mental refuge in deducing the descent of the crown by analogy with the law of real property. By the later middle ages the sanctity of the inheritance, of the 'lifelode' had become almost a religious dogma among English landed families. As the great thirteenth-century jurist Bracton had written, 'Only God can make an heir.' Unfortunately God had failed to inspire the common law with absolute precision as to the person of the heir. Not a few aristocratic families found themselves at loggerheads in deciding between the claims of an heir male (one claiming through the male line) and an heir general (one claiming through a female). Some adopted the solution, not entirely without subsequent disputes, of creating entails which allotted the title and some portion of the land to the heir male and the bulk of the property to the heir general. Such a compromise was obviously inappropriate to the crown and kingdom. They could not be thus divided.

The revolution of 1399 left a dispute of this kind inherent in English politics throughout the following century. Henry IV, duke of Lancaster, who then drove Richard II from his throne, was the son of John of Gaunt, fourth son of Edward III, and heir male of the royal line. Recognizing the ambiguity of his position, however, he declared his title in clouded phrases vague enough to avoid the major legal issue — the fact that he chose to ignore the claims of an heir general, Edmund Mortimer, earl of March, the grandson of Philippa, daughter of the great Edward's third son, Lionel of Clarence. In 1399 the earl of March was a child, unable to vindicate his neglected claim in arms or by any other means, but for a decade and a half various malcontents

175

were prepared to use his name as a cover for their own ambitions in revolts against the Lancastrian monarchs.

After the discovery of the Southampton plot on the very eve of Henry V's departure for France in 1415, aristocratic conspiracies against the Lancastrians came to an end. The most conspicuous of the plotters of 1415 had been Richard, earl of Cambridge, the second son of Edmund of Langley, Edward III's fifth son, and the widower of Edmund Mortimer's sister Anne. Richard's loyal elder brother, Edward, duke of York, perished a few month's later at the battle of Agincourt. Earl Richard's son, also Richard, therefore inherited both the earldom of Cambridge and the duchy of York.[1] Anne Mortimer had predeceased her husband and her only sister, the countess of Devonshire, died without children in 1418. Therefore when her brother, the dynastically ignored Edmund, died in 1425, the younger Richard, always known as duke of York, inherited both the dormant claim to the throne of the heirs general and the vast estates of the house of Mortimer, one of the greatest 'livelodes' of medieval England, and richer by far than the combined estates of Cambridge and York.

In spite of his descent and his father's treason, there was nothing in Richard of York's early career to suggest that he might one day revolt against Henry VI to claim his ignored royal inheritance. After 1415, for as long as Lancastrian government continued strong and successful, the later conflict between the two branches of the royal family, known since the early nineteenth century as the Wars of the Roses, was by no means inevitable and, when it came, the early stages of the conflict developed less from dynastic rivalry than from Henry VI's inability to control the disputes of his magnates. Only three years old when his father died, Richard of York was brought up in circles bound by the closest ties of self-interest to the reigning line. Treating him like any other child of the landowning classes, that is as a financial and political asset, in 1423 the royal council sold his wardship and marriage to Ralph Neville, earl of Westmorland, for 3,000 marks and in 1429 the earl's widow married the seventeen-year-old ward to her daughter Cecily, then aged nine.

Earl Ralph I of Westmorland (died 1425) had flourished exceedingly, first in the service of Richard II who had raised him to comital rank. Then deserting Richard at the critical moment in 1399, he tied his fortunes to the risen Lancastrian star. Married *en secondes noces* to Joan Beaufort, Henry IV's illegitimate half-sister, he and his wife exploited their royal connection to provide for their

---

[1] Thus, if the Lancastrian line should fail, the house of York would also be the heirs male of Edward III. They never, however, used this claim, preferring to rely upon their descent as heirs general.

numerous family (they were blest with a full quiver of sixteen children) upon the most enviable scale. Between 1412 and 1436, in the most scandalous series of child marriages in English history, their children and grandchildren entered into eleven alliances involving (on both sides) thirteen children under sixteen years old, a young man at the most seventeen, two girls of eighteen or less and two men between the mature years of twenty and twenty-three. Their names read like a galaxy of the English peerage—York, Northumberland, Despenser, Buckingham, Abergavenny, Arundel, Warwick.

Richard of York, slightly under age, gained control of his inheritance in 1432, potentially the richest subject in England with estates in three strategically vital areas, Ireland, the Marches of Wales and East Anglia. His wealth, his lands, his royal blood and his connection with the vast proliferating Neville clan and their allied families gave him an immense influence for good or evil in English political life—an influence quite impossible to ignore—and if a claim transmitted through females was valid he possessed a better hereditary title to rule England than his sovereign and cousin-german, Henry VI. Had the entire Neville connection supported him *en masse*, his power in the land would have been overwhelming. In fact they never did so. They were divided among themselves and individual members of the group were more concerned with their own landed and political interests than any dynastic dreams which Richard in later years came to cherish.

Inheritance, jointure and other settlement disputes provided a fertile source of prolonged, embittered quarrels among the Nevilles. A rancorous grudge divided Earl Ralph II from the children of his grandfather's[2] second marriage. For Joan Beaufort had obtained from her husband an excessively large jointure and settlements which handed over the greater part of the family property to her eldest son, Richard, in right of his wife, the heiress of the Montecute earls of Salisbury. These settlements left Ralph II, the heir at law, poorer in land as an earl than his grandfather had been early in life as a simple baron. By the late 1430s this embittered family quarrel passed from the limits of words to private warfare so serious that the harassed royal council found it necessary to intervene. After negotiations lasting for several years Richard of Salisbury retained most of the property, not apparently without some ill-feeling on the part of his resentful younger brothers and sisters, as well as the natural fury of the deprived earl of Westmorland.

In 1436, when he was only twenty-four, the royal council appointed Richard of York king's lieutenant in France on the death of John, duke of Bedford. For six years, since the appearance of Joan of Arc,

[2] Ralph I's eldest son died before he did and Ralph II inherited directly from his grandfather.

the tides of war had been running strongly against the English while a section of the court aristocracy and the military settlers in Normandy, who by this time alone had a strong interest in the war, tried to preserve the impossible inheritance of Henry V. Only a week before Bedford's death, English statesmen, at the Conference of Arras in 1435, rejected with insensate folly peace terms which could have left them the whole of Normandy at the price of renouncing Henry VI's pretended title to the crown of France. Burgundy, without whose support the future struggle would be almost hopeless, then deserted the English alliance. In spite of public indifference there was, so far, no large body of opinion strongly against the war. Certain politicians, in particular the earl of Suffolk, on this question more far-sighted than most, now favoured peace. It may be that the great duke of Bedford himself—and no one could assess the realities of the French war better than he—had veered round to this point of view before his death. At the same time the king's powerful uncle, Humphrey, duke of Gloucester, brash, opinionated and demagogic, refused to admit the weakness of the English in France. His blind obstinacy expressed itself in an unintelligent and vicious denigration of those who later sought to bring the war to an end through negotiations for peace—Suffolk and the Beaufort family, with whom, over many years, he had fought out a bitter personal quarrel for power at home. Richard of York, therefore, as an untried young man with no military experience took over a command which, in far more favourable circumstances, had defeated and broken the duke of Bedford, the most talented and experienced soldier-statesman of his day.

Although the aristocratic council of Henry VI's minority had ruled the country more successfully and more unselfishly than might have been expected, political and personal tension was already growing stronger when the king's tutelage came to an end in 1436. In an age when government was a cooperative enterprise between the monarch and the propertied classes, only a king of sound political judgment, seen to hold a fair balance between the conflicting interests of rival magnates, could hope to control the great and, through the great, the country. Henry VI, an intelligent, precocious child, with a somewhat premature interest in politics, in some peculiar way now hidden from sight, developed or degenerated into a man who could hardly have been worse equipped to meet the unceasing stresses of such a task. He may (though we can say no more than may) have inherited the unhealthy, neurotic strains of both his Lancastrian and his Valois forbears. A long-dominant tradition which, however, post-dates his own lifetime, depicts him imbued with all the Christian virtues which inspire the enthusiasm of the hagiographer—piety, charity, meekness, chastity and simplicity. Based in some degree on miracle-working at his tomb, the tradition in fact mainly owes its form to the pen of a hagiographer, Henry's own confessor, the Carthusian monk, John Blacman, who wrote the king's 'life' most probably in the days of Henry VII to support that king's unsuccessful petitions to three successive popes for his predecessor's canonization.

The comments of some of Henry VI's more outspoken subjects hardly support this pious alabaster memorial. The chronicler, John Hardyng, roundly stated that the king could hardly distinguish right from wrong and others took an even less benign view of his simplicity. By the early 1440s some of his subjects, from yeoman to gentleman, were getting themselves into serious trouble by calling him simple-minded and a childlike fool. As early as 1432 the ease with which any of his entourage could influence him had seriously disturbed his tutor, the earl of Warwick. When he reached manhood, before his short lapse into insanity, often his weak disposition left him malleable as wax in the hands of any man who talked to him. On the other hand, as it so often happens with fundamentally weak men, Henry from time to time plunged into fits of obstinate wilfulness acutely embarrassing to the ministers traditionally supposed to have dominated him completely — fits of self-will disadvantageous, if not at times disastrous, to the conduct both of foreign policy and domestic affairs.

York's first, brief command in France was a fortunate period for the English, though the main credit for their *revanche* at this time must undoubtedly go to his veteran subordinate, John, Lord Talbot. In 1437 York, possibly for financial reasons, resigned his commission, but after the failure (mainly due to the intransigence of the duke of Gloucester) of another peace conference in 1439, he again accepted command in Normandy for a period of five years. Judging from his actions he approached his second term of office with neither enthusiasm nor vigour. He demanded, in advance, exoneration for any failure in his new command and, for some reason or other unknown, he remained in England for a whole year after his appointment in spite of desperate clamours for his presence from the council in Normandy — clamours accompanied by predictions of dire disaster if his arrival were long delayed. Meanwhile, a combination of land forces under Talbot and a naval expedition commanded by John Beaufort, earl of Somerset, recaptured Harfleur from the French and in 1441 York and Talbot broke up the French siege of Pontoise. These successes were no more than a flash in the pan. Pontoise left their men exhausted, compelling them to fall back on Rouen, and the French soon returned and captured the town. Apart from the capture of Conches, Pontoise was the last real success. By October 1442 it was obvious that English possessions in Calais, Normandy and Guienne were all seriously threatened. The royal council faced the problem of how to deploy men and money unfortunately too scarce to cover all the danger points. They eventually decided to send an expedition to Guienne under Beaufort's command, but the final arrangements were not made until April 1443. This adverse decision in itself was exasperating to York. What followed was even worse. The council gave Somerset supreme command not only in Gascony but in the whole of France, thus placing him above York. Somerset received what men and money were available while York was starved of both. Somerset, in spite of his recent success at Harfleur, was a disastrous choice. Nearly eighteen years of demoralizing captivity as a prisoner of war in France seem to have left him, if not mentally unbalanced, at least quite unfit for an independent command. Rather than heading for the supposedly endangered southwest, with the agreement of the council he landed at Cherbourg, ostensibly to operate upon York's western flank in Maine and thus entice the French away from endangered Normandy. Instead he made off on a useless raid into Brittany (then, in fact, at peace with England), and afterwards wandered about in Maine quite aimlessly for four months, refusing to reveal his plans to anyone. He returned home to die the following year, some said of chagrin at the disgrace of failure, though one rumour claimed he was gored to death by a bull.

In spite of York's far from vigorous conduct at the beginning of his own period of office, he regarded Somerset's appointment as a disgraceful affront to his own position as king's lieutenant in Normandy. His rage was so deep and so widely known that, looking back upon these events, Abbot Whethampstede of St Albans marked the incident as the beginning of the Wars of the Roses, but his interpretation is too much a part of a highly stylized, self-conscious effort at literary drama to carry much weight. The incident may well, however, have formed the beginning of York's long and bitter alienation from the government, planting in his mind a justified sense of grievance which, nourished by later slights, grew at last into violence and treason.

Even so, it is mistaken to see, at this early date, two irreconcilable factions fighting to control the king. In spite of differences of opinion between York and the Beaufort family, the notable bitterness with which an older generation had quarrelled was so far absent. Cardinal Beaufort and the duke of Gloucester, the acrimonious enemies of twenty years' standing, fell into the background from about 1441. By the autumn of 1443 more people were prepared for peace and the council discussed plans for achieving it by means of a dynastic marriage. After the failure of negotiations for an Armagnac marriage, Suffolk, early in 1444, led an embassy to France to treat for peace, or failing that a truce, and for a marriage between Henry VI and Margaret, the daughter of René of Anjou, titular king of Jerusalem and Sicily and brother-in-law of Charles VII of France. Negotiations took place with the consent of all groups in England. Gloucester had been present at a council meeting where Suffolk, in order to cover himself from blame in the event of failure, had protested his reluctance to lead the embassy. Suffolk and York were obviously on good terms for Suffolk undertook, while in France, to forward a project for marriage between York's son Edward, then only two years old, and a princess of the house of Valois. Suffolk, at Tours, obtained the king's formal betrothal and a truce, but a truce for the short space of two years only. Though far from being a diplomatic triumph, the news was well received in both Rouen and London.

Yet, after the king's marriage, relations between York, Suffolk and Suffolk's principal supporter, Edmund Beaufort, marquess of Dorset,[3] rapidly deteriorated. Unfortunately the jejune chronicles of this period, mostly the thinnest of thin annals, tell us little or nothing of the thoughts and motives of the protagonists. The workings of their minds are impenetrable, forcing us back upon the fallible expedient of deducing motives from events.

On the wider canvas we can, however, discern the dangerous interplay of malign developments. Financial and administrative corruption provoked fierce discontent among the Commons. Henry progressively failed to control disputes among the nobility — a failure which drove them to arms to settle their personal quarrels, dragging into their affrays their local gentry affinities and thus destroying the peace and order of wide areas of the countryside. The final loss of Normandy coming as the climax to such growing discontent was a traumatic shock which provided a convincing pretext for a determined attack upon the government.

II

Towards the end of Henry VI's minority the royal demesne, one of the chief sources of the royal income, had been exceptionally large in extent and the legitimate charges upon it relatively small as the king had few adult members of his family to provide for. From 1437 onwards the dissipation of these resources became a matter of notorious scandal. Too fecklessly generous ever to refuse an eager

[3] The younger brother of John Beaufort, he was created marquess in 1443, at the time when John had been promoted to the rank of duke, and in 1445 was still further promoted to duke of Somerset.

request, Henry, inveigled by grasping courtiers and officials, alienated his estates in the most reckless way, and most of the income which the remnant produced passed into the outstretched hands of members of the royal household. At the same time the household was notorious for conspicuous waste while angry creditors clamoured unsatisfied for the settlement of their accounts. The royal debts, especially those of the household, became one of the burning political grievances of the day. Naturally, and rightly, people blamed those in power about the court for Henry's chronic insolvency. Working upon the feelings of an incapable king they had wantonly pursued their own profit with no regard for the public weal. As a contemporary squib. bitterly expressed it:

> Ye have made the Kyng so poore
> That now he beggeth fro dore to dore.

The first rumblings of the storm broke against this background of widespread discontent at financial corruption. Margaret of Anjou was probably the unwitting instrument of the tragedies which followed, though she was guiltless of the sinister designs for which later propagandists attacked her. In 1450 the Commons accused Suffolk of surrendering the province of Maine to the French as the price of her marriage. Suffolk's enemies may have believed this at the time, but in fact the accusation was false. From 1444 Henry himself was apparently obsessed with the idea of peace and from then onwards his own personal whims dictated the conduct of foreign negotiations, and, in all probability, they were conducted without the knowledge of his council.

The promise to surrender Maine came later and the French sank to somewhat underhand methods to gain it. In October 1446 a French embassy which came to England brought a letter from Charles VII to the sixteen-year-old queen expressing his strong desire for the delivery of Maine. On 22 December Henry wrote *secretly and personally* to Charles promising the surrender of the province.

Under such unscrupulous pressure from her uncle (and also from her father), working upon a husband probably already inclined to concessions which his principal ministers thought unwise, Margaret was innocently launched upon a political course which brought upon her, first the dislike, and later the hatred of many Englishmen. Precocious she may have been, though there is no evidence in trustworthy sources to indicate it. Early indoctrinated to an extreme dynastic view of politics she certainly was and, from the example of those ferociously strong personalities, her grandmother, Yolande of Aragon, and her mother, Isabella of Lorraine, she was accustomed to the idea of dominant and vigorous women taking over parts in political life which their husbands were too weak to play. Yet in this particular incident she could have been nothing more than an unsuspecting go-between. Her active and conscious role in politics began only in the next decade.

Since 1441 when his wife had been condemned for conspiring the king's death by witchcraft, Humphrey of Gloucester's political influence had been negligible. In spite of Henry's own erratic conduct of foreign policy, to outside observers the duke of Suffolk appeared to wield such overwhelming power that the Burgundian chronicler, Chastellain, compared him to a second king holding both the English and French in leash. Though hardly true of the French, Suffolk may well have been almost supreme in domestic affairs. Unfortunately for the duke, who had to bear public stigma for his master's personal actions, the promise to surrender Maine cut the ground from under Suffolk's feet and gave Gloucester the opportunity for a political *revanche* — a *revanche* as inconvenient to Henry with his politic intentions as it was to Suffolk. To forestall such a danger Suffolk determined to attack first. To accuse and condemn Gloucester, to bring about his final political ruin, the court summoned a parliament to meet at Bury St Edmunds, one of the main centres of Suffolk's influence. When Gloucester arrived at Bury on 18 February 1447, he was at once arrested and five days later he died. It is most likely that he died from natural causes, possibly a heart attack brought on by the shock of his sudden arrest, but appearances were all against his opponents. They had forbidden his own servants to go near him and he died surrounded by his enemies at the very moment when they were plotting his ruin. Foreign chroniclers proclaimed with one voice that the Suffolk clique had procured his murder. In England rumours of foul play began to circulate almost at once. Whatever the truth may be, within a decade the theory of murder became a convenient article of Yorkist propaganda.

After Gloucester's death the duke of York remained the most dangerous potential opponent of the Suffolk-Beaufort clique. So far York's rancour lay only against the Beauforts. Neither now nor later (according to surviving sources) did he ever direct against Suffolk[4] any of the deep hatred which he felt for Edmund Beaufort. As he had never opposed the court on any major question, the most that his opponents could do was to deprive him of influential positions. This Suffolk, most probably egged on by Beaufort, proceeded to do, moving hesitantly at first as if uncertain of his own intentions, trying at the same time to soften the blow. Even so, in a society where the unity of the nobility round the throne was almost a *sine qua non* of

[4] Later, in 1460, he married his daughter, Elizabeth, to Suffolk's heir, though this may have been to gain control of the Suffolk resources during a critical time.

decent political life, it was an index of the king's unwisdom that he allowed such a development.

York's five-year commission as lieutenant in Normandy expired in September 1445. He expected it to be renewed, but for two years the government procrastinated, then finally appointed Edmund Beaufort in his place. Though at the time he resented his dismissal as a deep affront, in the end it proved a blessing in disguise for the sake of his future reputation. Even in 1440 he had apparently feared the prospect of failure in France. In the following years he had only just managed to maintain the *status quo*, though admittedly this was not entirely his own fault. Fortunately for him his enemies excluded him from Normandy in time to avoid the inevitable disasters which lay ahead. No commander's name could survive the loss of Normandy. Somerset's intrigues, therefore, unwittingly served to ruin his own reputation and to preserve that of his rival.

More immediately, however, like many others who served the Lancastrians at this time, York had his financial grievances. The government had fallen badly in arrears on its commitments for his work in Normandy. In 1446 he accepted (or was forced to accept) a composition under which he received about seven tenths of the money still owing to him and remitted the rest. Although it is generally claimed the Henry VI's ministers treated York most unscrupulously in forcing such arrangements upon him, compositions of this kind were by no means exceptional. The government treated other, and some much poorer, men in the same way and one well-informed contemporary writer, William Worcester, states that such arrangements were common practice. York had to delay paying some of his followers which, of course, made him unpopular. On the other hand in 1446 and 1447 he obtained four valuable grants from the crown and certain longstanding claims at the Exchequer about his claims to land were settled in his favour. The grants were almost certainly an indirect compensation for the part of the debt which he had remitted. The Suffolk clique were giving with one hand and taking away with the other.

At this point, however, they failed to leave well alone. Rumours spread (probably deliberately inspired — not a difficult matter for accusations of corruption went with medieval financial methods almost as naturally as champagne goes with modern weddings) that York had embezzled funds in Normandy and had deliberately cheated his soldiers of their pay. These rumours York indignantly denied, claiming that his accounts had already been audited without question. Then in September 1447, seven months after the Bury St Edmunds parliament, the court sent him into a species of honourable banishment by appointing him lieutenant of Ireland for ten years — Ireland the great slum of the fifteenth-century political system.

If Suffolk and Somerset can be said to have triumphed, their time for exultation was short. Although Gloucester was dead and York out of the way, the year 1449 saw the beginning of tragedy and disaster. Long-frustrated recalcitrance at home found its opportunity for expression in disaster abroad. Suffolk's 'insaciable covetise', his notorious dissipation of the royal resources and his intolerable oppressions of weaker men in the area of his power in East Anglia, even more than the blame which public opinion allotted to him for the king's policy towards France, produced a political deadlock which, at a crucial moment, destroyed all hope of effective action in Normandy. When parliament met in February 1449 the Commons were in a belligerent mood. In spite of a special appeal for money for the war which the abbot of Gloucester made to both Houses, some of the Lords considered that any attempt to raise troops would dangerously increase disturbances at home and advised the government to deal first with problems of public order. The Commons would grant little in the way of direct taxation. At the same time they took an obstinate stand on financial matters, which hit directly and hit hard at the corrupt interests of the court group and of the household officers. The Commons bitterly resented the idea that the war should be carried on at their expense while financial scandals flourished unchecked in high places and ministers and courtiers grew fat upon their plunder of the royal estates. They insisted upon a full-scale resumption of all royal grants of land and offices as the condition of further direct taxation, and before this persistent agitation for resumption the king and his advisers, in July, dissolved parliament.

The previous March, François de Surienne, a renowned Aragonese mercenary in English pay, and a knight of the Garter, suddenly attacked and captured the Breton town of Fougères. He did so with the full encouragement of those in power in England, as part of a misguided attempt to force a change of policy upon the duke of Brittany, to coerce him to take sides openly with England against France. Had this policy succeeded it would have, in part at least, retrieved Suffolk's reputation. Its failure gave the pretext for an attack which led to his swift and terrible ruin. Charles VII of France came to Brittany's rescue by counter-attacking in Normandy. At the end of October the fall of Rouen rang the death-knell of English rule and in less than sixteen months Charles VII's armies swept the bewildered and disunited English completely out of the province.

At home a new parliament met in November. Infuriated by the government's refusal to put its house in order and by the news of the disasters coming in from abroad, the Commons were even more determined and aggressive than their predecessors had been earlier in the year. Over the Christmas recess Suffolk became seriously disturbed by the imputations circulating everywhere against him. A mob of unpaid sailors lynched Adam Moleyns, the bishop of Chichester and keeper of the privy seal, at Portsmouth on 9 January 1450 and rumour had it that the bishop, *in articulo mortis*, made a most incriminating last confession, highly damaging to Suffolk. It was too dangerous to allow such tales to spread unchecked. Losing no time, the very day that parliament reassembled, he tried to quell the murmurs swelling against him in a long speech, rhetorically and emotionally dwelling upon the loyal service which, over a generation and more, his family had given to all the Lancastrian kings, and formally demanded that this vindication of his actions be placed on record on the parliament roll.

He had wildly misjudged his ability to sway the Commons. So far from applauding this *apologia pro vita sua*, four days later they demanded his imprisonment. Shortly afterwards they delivered a bill of eight articles to the Lords accusing him of treason and, when action against him seemed to be hanging fire, reinforced it a month later with another eighteen accusations covering the widest range of corrupt and violent practices. By this time the peers were deeply divided in their attitude towards the government. Suffolk, therefore, could not rely upon their protection. To save him from a worse fate, the king used his prerogative and exiled him. A small fleet, commanded by men unknown, captured the duke's ship on its way to Calais. They gave him twenty-four hours in which to shrive himself and prepare for death, then beheaded him over one of the ships' boats and cast ashore his naked body on Dover sands.

In the fifteenth century the king had the absolute right to choose his own ministers. Nothing short of treason charges could rid the country of a minister if the king obstinately chose to support him. For this reason, in their first indictment the Commons alleged quite implausible treasons. Some of the more fantastic charges which they laid against their intended victim—that, in effect, his earlier duplicity, his later negligence and worse had been responsible for the loss of Maine and Normandy, that he had planned, with the aid of a French invasion, to depose the king—were brazen, scurrilous perversions of the truth. Wiser than many of his critics, Suffolk had insisted on the need to maintain a strong military establishment in Normandy even in periods of truce, so as to negotiate with the French from a position of strength. Parliament itself had originally applauded the capture of Fougères and it had refused the money necessary to reinforce the Norman garrisons. The loss of Normandy cannot, in the long term, fairly be blamed upon Suffolk. While not brilliant he was not incompetent. For twenty years the majority of the politically significant classes in the country had been too indifferent to the realities of the war to give the government adequate support in waging it and the revival of the French monarchy made inevitable the end of the English occupation. But now, outraged by the appallingly unexpected speed of the French advance, the Commons looked for a scapegoat on which to vent their wrath.

And yet, even if Suffolk were not guilty of treason or even of negligence in Norman affairs, his approval of de Suriennes's raid on Fougères had certainly precipitated the Norman disasters, and the Commons accusations of domestic corruption were amply justified. Besides profiting enormously, excessively, from royal grants, if even a tithe of the accusations levied against him were true, in every other way he had abused his position to bully, cheat and extort — bilking the customs on a large scale in trading ventures, perverting the course of justice, appointing sheriffs in return for bribes, terrorizing the countryside in East Anglia, attempting to rob lesser men of their estates by pretended titles and perjured juries and supporting members of his affinity in similar crimes. Much of this was notorious and, in article after article, the Commons relentlessly pressed home their charges of financial and administrative corruption. It was this aspect of Suffolk's rule which aroused such passionate resentment.

III

The final loss of Normandy in April, which people somewhat unfairly laid at his door, gave the occasion for more attacks upon the government.

There were riots in London and Kent, probably elsewhere from the beginning of the year. Suffolk was murdered on 2 May. Cade's rebellion broke out during the last week of the month. Cade was an Irishman who, claiming to be a cousin of the duke of York, assumed the name of Mortimer. A man of considerable abilities, he gave firm organization to long-seething resentment in Kent where, since the late 1430s, groups of the discontented had staged a series of riotous outbreaks which the government, at least, regarded as treasonable; and, in Kent, Lord Saye and Sele, one of the Suffolk group, and Saye and Sele's son-in-law, the sheriff, William Crowemer, seem to have conducted themselves little less oppressively than Suffolk and his affinity in East Anglia. No mere rabble led this revolt. It was not a rising of peasants who felt themselves bitterly oppressed economically like those of 1381. At least one knight, eighteen esquires and seventy-four gentlemen (or, seventy-four people who called themselves gentlemen) formed part of the well-organized and well-disciplined rebel host. The insurgents issued a skilfully drafted manifesto which clearly set out their complaints, in part economic, but in the main political. Overwhelmingly concerned with misgovernment and corruption at home, only one clause out of fifteen attacked the loss of Normandy. The rebel solution was to demand that recognized ideal of late-medieval politics — government by a broadly based group of peers, including this time the dukes of York, Exeter, Buckingham and Norfolk.

At this point, for the first time, York became the dominant figure in English politics, though we can only guess at his motives. For the next two years it becomes next to impossible to descry the fugitive fact in fogs of political scandal. The wildest rumours flew round London, heightened by political poems and broadsheets from both sides. So vicious and confused had rumours become that Yorkist sympathizers, conveniently ignoring the political affiliations of the past few years, even accused Suffolk of procuring the deaths of John Beaufort, Cardinal Beaufort and the duke of Exeter. Five years of procrastination and slights, mingled with feeble attempts at conciliation, had imposed heavy strains on York's loyalty. Now he had worse than political snubs to bear in deep suspicions of sinister schemes for cheating him of his very rights. It seemed unlikely that the king's marriage would ever produce an heir. Since Gloucester's death in 1447 York had been heir to the throne, now both the heir male and the heir general of Edward III. In their first bill against Suffolk the Commons alleged that in June 1447 he had plotted with the French ambassadors then in London to marry his son John to Lady Margaret Beaufort (later the mother of Henry VII — she transmitted to him whatever distant claim he had to the crown) and with the help of a French army to put these children on the throne.

Though the Commons may have dated Suffolk's plan too early and the deposition accusation is inherently improbable, they may possibly have been correct in claiming that Suffolk intended to divert the succession to Margaret Beaufort and his son, thus cheating York of his deeply cherished expectations. The Commons rounded off their accusations with the statement that since Suffolk's arrest the two children had been united in marriage. Melodramatic as it sounds the accusation was most likely true. The papal registers contain a licence dated 18 August 1450 permitting Margaret Beaufort and John de la Pole to *remain* in marriage. They must have been hastily and secretly married not so long before. By now York had ample cause for bitterness.

At the same time, if we can believe somewhat partisan and prejudiced accusations made about three years later, during York's absence in Ireland some of his friends, led by his chamberlain, Sir William Oldhall, went far beyond legitimate means to protect his interests, inciting Jack Cade, trying to stir up rebellion in East Anglia, Kent and Sussex, raising troops to attack the government and even counselling York to depose Henry. There were even hints that some of them were implicated in Suffolk's murder.

When, in 1459, the court drew up a comprehensive indictment of York's past offences, they accused him of complicity in Cade's rebellion. Whether that accusation was a fabrication or not, the revolt may partly explain his return from Ireland at the end of August or the beginning of September. It may be that he came hoping to assert his authority in a time of general confusion, or he may have thought Oldhall's activities too dangerous to leave uncontrolled. In any case he welcomed any excuse to escape from Ireland where his government had come dangerously near to collapse, and he feared that failure there (he said so himself) would destroy his reputation as failure in Normandy had ruined the reputation of Somerset. In the event he did not arrive until several weeks after the royal forces had crushed Cade's rebellion. His appearance touched off yet another crisis which may have been partly due to lack of communication and excessive suspicions on both sides. Protected, however, by his wife's nephew, the duke of Norfolk, and a large band of armed men, he reached Westminster in safety. There, according to accusations later made against him in 1459, in a wild fit of passion he beat down 'the speres[5] and walls of the king's chamber'. Whether this story of outrageous violence is true or not, within a week York had seized power, and his chamberlain, Oldhall, for a time, became one of the most powerful and courted men in the kingdom.

A new parliament had assembled early in November 1450. The Commons were well disposed to York for, over a week before the duke arrived at Westminster, they chose Oldhall as their speaker, although it was the first time that this war veteran, who had spent most of his life out of England, had ever been elected to parliament. As the courtiers and household officials had notoriously conspired together to evade the previous act of resumption, the Commons insisted upon a new and more rigid act. The dissipation of the royal lands which had taken place on such an extensive scale between 1437 and 1449 was now reversed.

The key to the events of the next few years lies in the mutual suspicions of York and Somerset. With Suffolk out of the way and the royal circle, though much against its will, forced into the first stages of

[5] A 'spere' was a temporary wall or partition.

financial reform, York and his friends could no longer claim that the choice between the rivals was a choice between good and bad government. The gordian knot was tied in the personal rivalries, suspicions and fears of the two dukes and it may be doubted whether in 1451 there was much to choose between them as statesmen and administrators. York was now extremely suspicious about his rights as heir to the throne. He was in debt and, as time went on, his political activities added to his debts. In addition to the money which the crown owed him, he was entitled to hereditary annuities valued at £1,000 from the Exchequer — no inconsiderable proportion of his cash income compared with that which he received from his apparently badly supervised estates, and the income from his Welsh lands may, at this time, have been seriously declining. Somerset was even more anxious about money. His main endowment as a peer consisted of royal annuities. Owing to this and an earlier settlement under which the bulk of the family estates had passed to his niece, Margaret Beaufort, Somerset enjoyed only a meagre £300 a year from land or slightly more, as against nearly £2,000 from crown annuities, pensions and offices. There was never enough ready cash at the Exchequer to meet all its creditors. Royal favour determined the order in which they were paid and each of the rivals dreaded that the other's predominance at court would cut off vital supplies.

Neither commanded the support of any large section of the nobility. As a class their fellow peers were not particularly interested in their quarrels. The aristocracy was divided, as always, by personal and local disputes. Such conflicts, among others, between the earl of Wiltshire and Lord Bonvile on the one side and the earl of Devon on the other in the southwest, the Percies and Lord Cromwell against the Nevilles in the north of England, between Lord Cromwell, Lord Grey of Ruthyn and the duke of Exeter at Ampthill, preceded the outbreak of the Wars of the Roses. The extraordinary number of peers imprisoned for violent conduct at this time is another serious pointer in the same direction. Between 1450 and 1455, the dukes of Exeter and Norfolk, the earls of Devon and Wiltshire, Lords Bonvile, Cobbam, Cromwell, Egremont, Grey, Moleyns and Say — a sixth of the peerage or so — all found themselves at some time behind bars for disreputable and violent conduct.

This increasing violence, this escalation of private feuds, deleterious as they were for the good order of the kingdom, did not themselves provoke the Wars of the Roses. Without the drive of York's political ambitions, provincial disorder might well have dragged on for years. Although the nobility knew Henry to be both wilful and incompetent he was, after all, their anointed king, and although they frequently took to arms to settle their personal quarrels, their violence did not easily rise into treason against the monarch himself. Yet the private feuds (or some of them) made possible York's later attempts to force himself into power. The younger branch of the Neville family, entirely to support their own very different ambitions, provided until 1460 a great part of the armed support which made possible his success against the king. But the peerage as a whole was far from sympathetic to the outlook of the Nevilles. York always found the greater part of the nobility uneasy and reluctant towards the measures which he adopted to press his claims, and it was the greater nobility with whom the decisions of the future would, in the last resort, lie.

Violence in London and Westminster accompanied the parliamentary sessions, but the king, recovering his nerve, refused to consent to a demand by Thomas Yonge, one of the burgesses for Bristol, that York be formally recognized as heir to the throne.

IV

After this parliamentary fiasco York, as far from power as ever, retired to his estates in the Marches of Wales. Now, he and his followers began making extensive plans for an armed rebellion, to be supported by riots and demonstrations in numerous towns in the Marches, in the southwest and in East Anglia. Oldhall and Sir Edmund Mulsho (another of the duke's council) were drumming up support in Lincolnshire, Hertfordshire, Cambridgeshire and Northamptonshire, until in November, realizing that the government was growing intensely suspicious, Oldhall fled to sanctuary in St Martin-le-Grand. York himself was sending letters to various towns — to Canterbury, Colchester, Oxford and King's Lynn — denouncing the government and hoping to whip up the sympathy of the common people. After issuing a final manifesto at Shrewbury early in February 1452, he marched south. This first attempt at rebellion badly misfired. He had misjudged his appeal for popular support and, in March, he surrendered to the king at Dartford in Kent — surrendering upon a promise that Somerset would be imprisoned and compelled to answer charges that he was responsible for the loss of Normandy and Guienne. The promise was quickly broken. York had gone much too far and now, more or less isolated among his peers, he was obliged to to swear, in St Paul's Cathedral, a solemn oath of loyalty to the king, an oath so formulated that it would have spelt ruin in case of future misconduct (if the king had the strength to enforce it) for, in effect, it imposed a suspended sentence of attainder upon him — that legal death for himself and his family which was the most solemn penalty known to the common law.

Opinion was now turning in favour of the court. Its will seemed to be reviving. The French were distinctly apprehensive of a new assault on Normandy in the second half of 1452. The government made every effort to recover Gascony and succeeded in doing so, though it failed to hold the recovered province for long. The success of the latest resumption act and public knowledge that reform of the king's hereditary revenues had begun had left the Commons more favourably disposed to the government than they had been for many years past. Goodwill towards the court was the note of the parliament which met at Reading in March 1453. The Commons made the king a life grant of the subsidy on wool, tonnage and poundage and the tax on aliens — an act of generosity for which there were only two precedents in English history — besides a grant of one and one half fifteenths and tenths and a force of 13,000 archers for defence purposes, their cost to be borne by the districts in which they were raised.[6] Those who controlled the agenda showed a marked hostility to York and his supporters. They attainted Sir Willian Oldhall, and passed an act of resumption against those who had taken the field at Dartford. Having shown his willingness to accept financial reform and having taken vigorous action in Gascony, Henry VI was rising in prestige and York was losing ground.

The events of the second half of the year shattered the prospects of this modest revival. By early August at the latest the king was insane. In October French forces finally drove the English out of Guienne. On 12 December the queen gave birth to a son, Prince Edward, who was later, as the political conflict grew more tense and embittered, stigmatized by Yorkist propaganda as the child of adultery. Prince Edward's birth made York more jealous of his rights than ever. He probably hoped even now to preserve his inheritance to the crown. After all, with child mortality at its fifteenth-century level, the birth of one son by no means made his deprivation certain. More menacing for the present was the fact that the king's madness left power completely in the hands of his opponents and he may have feared that they would seize the occasion to inflict upon him that retribution which he had so far escaped. In October Somerset tried, and failed, to exclude him from a great council, thus exacerbating his already strong fears. Pro-Yorkist sources allege that some of his tenants, councillors and friends were being subjected to severe persecution at this time. Moreover, if his own statements can be believed he was feeling the pressure of debt and, at the very least, he may have feared that his

---

[6] This force of archers was, in fact, never raised.

enemies would deny him his vital access to the Exchequer. Whatever emotions drove York on — fear or ambition or both — the events of the next few years were again to show how little support he could command.

For seven months the court refused to admit that the king was sick. Somerset and the queen (who was now taking an active part in politics for the first time) avoided any discussion of the king's conditon in parliament, but by mid-February 1454 they could evade the issue no longer. York's claims of blood could not be ignored and he wrung from the council a limited commission authorizing him to recall parliament and conduct it in the king's name — the same parliament which had earlier shown itself so favourable to the court.

Six weeks after the session opened, the Lords, unable any longer to avoid a decision, appointed the duke protector and defender of the realm. The lords were always wary of giving excessive power to any one of their number. During Henry's minority they had steadfastly refused to give either Bedford or Gloucester the powers of a regent. They were equally adamant now. They hedged in York's authority with drastic restrictions. They firmly refused him the titles of 'Tutor', 'Lieutenant', 'Governor', 'Regent' or any other name that 'should emporte auctorite of governaunce of the land'. They revived the title of protector and defender which implied a *personal* duty for the defence of the land — no more. And they firmly stated that his authority should in no way prejudice Prince Edward's rights. The appointment was to continue only until the prince came of age.

The whole atmosphere was reluctant and uneasy. No one wished to accept the final responsibility for this unwelcome decision. York, ruthlessly as he had enforced his claims, wished it put on record that he had been freely appointed by the Lords who, in turn, insisted that for their 'discharge' the Commons must concur. During Henry VI's minority when the king for other reasons had been incapable of government, the Lords had claimed that the residual authority in the state lay with them. They had now lost their former confidence. Now, in even more difficult and dangerous circumstances, when faced with the choice of supporting or rejecting a fellow magnate who had so recently come near to treason, they shuffled away.

Attendance in the Lords was normally thin during the later middle ages, though the peers generally turned up in greater force than usual during a major political crisis. This occasion formed a notable exception. An abnormally large number were, it seems, so averse to committing themselves to one side or the other at this major crisis that they stayed away from parliament altogether. They abdicated their responsibilities. As the king's nearest relation, York's claim to authority could not be denied, but the peers were unwilling to endorse it. And York wanted more than the mere acquiescence of a group. He determined to force some expression of approval for his authority from the greatest number of people who were potentially powerful in the country's affairs. Towards the end of February 1454 it was decided, for the first time in English history, to fine peers for non-attendance. Although these fines were stiff, they produced only the slightest effect. At the end of the session there were still far more peers absent than present.

Even those more courageous lords who did appear seem to have been loth to support York's pretentions but were too bewildered, or perhaps too timid, to find any other solution. It may well be that at this time, rather than in the later crisis of 1460, the Lords sold the pass to York. By abdicating their responsibilities now, in ignoring the queen's claim to the regency, they may well have given the duke the impression that, though he might fail to obtain wide approval for his actions he could, by sheer persistence, impose his will upon a reluctant, leaderless group of men.

V

York's first protectorate lasted only ten months during which, to his credit, he made genuine attempts to restore public order. Peace did not endure for long. By the end of 1454 Henry VI had recovered his sanity and by early February 1455 Somerset who, as he himself admitted, had been imprisoned in the Tower of London for his own protection, either escaped with the connivance of the duke of Buckingham, the earl of Wiltshire and Lord Roos, or the king ordered his release.

It was a personal feud which gave York the possibility of making yet another bid for power. The Percy family and the junior branch of the Nevilles (represented by the earls of Salisbury and Warwick) had become bitter competitors for power in Yorkshire and the Scottish Marches. Younger members of both families carried the feud to levels of violence probably undesired by their elders—levels of violence which led to two armed skirmishes between 1453 and 1456, besides subjecting whole stretches of the countryside to violence and terrorization. Both the Percies and the Nevilles had greatly profited from the house of Lancaster, both, therefore, might have been expected to be loyal. The junior Nevilles, however, were newcomers competing for power in an established Percy sphere of influence. In the absence of strong control by the king, the north was too small to hold them both, and their local conflict for power disturbed national politics in the most decisive way for the next few years. Moreover, the Neville earl of Warwick was quarrelling with Somerset over the division of Isabella Despenser's inheritance in south Wales. These bitter feuds drove Salisbury and Warwick (York's brother-in-law and nephew) into an alliance with the duke probably as early as April 1454 — an alliance owing less to sympathy with York's ambitions than to the wish to enlist his active support against their Percy rivals in the north and against Somerset in Wales.

After the king dismissed York from the protectorship in February 1455, he and the Nevilles left the court and they may have begun to recruit forces immediately. The king and Somerset countered these moves (the danger of which they badly underestimated) by peaceable means, by an appeal to the nobility — an appeal, however, to say the least, almost provocatively unskilful in its methods. Somerset convoked a great council to meet at Westminster in April, a meeting to which York and his friends, most unwisely, were not invited. This assembly summoned another great council to meet in May at Leicester with the declared intention of providing for the king's safety. A number of prominent knights were also summoned to this council, thus making it a wider assembly of notables. York's exclusion from the April council gave him the excuse (it may even have been a genuine fear) that the Leicester assembly was to be the occasion of his ruin. The king and Somerset, however, certainly hoped for a peaceful solution. The use of armed force was certainly no part of their original plans for Somerset was taken completely by surprise when he heard that York was marching south at the head of an armed force.

On 20 May from Royston, on the Great North Road, York and his friends sent their own proposals for a settlement to the chancellor. The following day, from Ware, they sent a letter to the king, together with a copy of this manifesto. In a very dubiously slanted 'apology', which they published in parliament a few weeks later, they claimed that Somerset, Thomas Thorpe and William Joseph intercepted these vital documents so that Henry himself never saw them. The court had already set out for Leicester and on 22 May the two parties met at St Albans, York having advanced from Ware. There was no immediate clash of arms. In both England and France a tradition prevailed that even when political action was based on armed force, mediation was desirable before fighting — a tradition not broken until 1461. At least three attempts at negotiation followed, guided on the royalist side by the duke of Buckingham, a senior statesman, who now and later, did everything he could to keep the peace. These negotiations finally broke down upon Henry's adamant refusal to surrender Somerset to his opponents. Pacific as he was, in the end he chose to fight rather than submit to dictation. Tempers rose in the Yorkist ranks as discussions spun out over several hours, and even as the last messenger was returning to the king's camp their troops advanced towards the town.

The numbers clashing in battle were small. York, at the most, led three thousand men and apart from Salisbury and Warwick the only peer known to have fought with him was Lord Clinton. The king's force was vaguely estimated at about two thousand, but it contained eleven peers, three of whom were related by blood and marriage to the insurgents. Even so, it is highly probable that this royal 'army', owing to Somerset's original misjudgment of York's intentions, was made up of little more than the peers then at court and the household retinues which normally attended them. The 'battle' lasted for only three hours. No more than 120 men, possibly as few as 60, perished on the field, but 23 of them were lords, knights, esquires and members of the royal household, including Somerset himself, the earl of Northumberland and Lord Clifford.

Though insignificant from a military point of view, the political consequences of the first battle of St Albans were disastrous. Before 1455 the king, in spite of his personal defects, had always been treated, except perhaps in York's fits of temper, with the greatest deference — the almost exaggerated deference of the most formal court in Europe. Now men had shed blood in his very presence. Restraint and a most valuable sanction had disappeared from public life.

More immediately, the battle solved nothing. The Yorkists could do no other than protest their loyalty to Henry. When parliament met on 19 July, the political problem seemed to be no nearer solution. Although the prospect of renewed fines for non-attendance brought more ecclesiastical lords to the upper House than had been the case of recent years, attendance among the lay baronage was exceedingly thin. Only 17 out of 36 peers below the rank of viscount had put in an appearance by the end of the first session, and those who did attend were as quietly disapproving towards York as they had been in the previous session. Nor were the Commons totally amenable. Although the Yorkists brought to bear all the influence they could in the course of the elections, and in one county at least their activity went beyond the bounds which local opinion considered to be decent, their success was limited and some members were distinctly uneasy at finding themselves in such an assembly.

Somerset may have been much disliked, especially in London, but there is no sign that York was widely popular. No one wished to accept responsibility for, or even to appear to condone, what was, after all, the treasonable action of rearing war against the king. As Henry Windsor very truly wrote: 'The king our sovereign lord and all his true lords stand in hele [health] of their bodies but not all in heart's ease as we are.'

York and his friends were neither numerous nor strong enough to impose their will, still less to carry revenge any further: even the heir of the slain Percy earl of Northumberland was indispensable to defend the north from the Scots. They dreaded the outbreak of wide-spread quarrels for they themselves might suffer too much in any general outbreak of recriminations. There was every likelihood of such an outbreak. Many were openly hostile. As the author of a very anti-Yorkist pamphlet, the *Somnium Vigilantis*, wrote a few years later: 'They made an end of many better knights than they were at that execrable journey of St Albans'; and Warwick and Lord Cromwell had hurled abuse at each other in the king's very presence. It was essential to promote at least the appearance of unity. There-fore, to provide for their own safety and to extinguish the fears of their opponents, the Yorkists passed through parliament a pardon for all except Somerset, Thomas Thorpe and William Joseph. By appor-tioning all tha blame on the dead Somerset and two comparatively lowly associates, those who, they claimed, had prevented Henry from giving them a fair hearing before St Albans, this act of oblivion for the time patched over the weakness of the Yorkist faction and protected all those who had taken part at St Albans against any legal conse-quences in the future. To complete the pacification, all the lords swore a new oath of fidelity to the king. On 31 July the session came to an end.

The way matters had gone could hardly have satisfied York. His success, so far, had been entirely negative. Some of his own friends were uneasy. They may have felt themselves still in danger and the attitude of the Lords was, at best, coldly disapproving. Real power they had still to gain, and to gain it, during the autumn York plotted a peaceful *coup d'état*. He determined to become protector again. Possibly making skilful use of a temporary indisposition in the king, he organized a pressure group in the Commons to force his plans upon Henry and the Lords. When parliament reassembled on 12 November, attendance in the Lords was still poor. The following day William Burley, one of the members for Shropshire, led a deputation from the Commons to the Upper House. William Burley was no political innocent. He was one of the most experienced shire knights in this assembly. He was also one of the duke of York's own council. The deputation asked for the appointment of a protector in case the king at some time ('hereafter' the parliament roll says) became incapable of transacting business and because vigorous action was needed to suppress certain riots and bloody outrages in the southwest, particularly in Devon involving the earl of Devon, Sir Phillip

Courtenay and Lord Bonvile. The deputation pressed the Lords for a decision three times in five days, on the third occasion making use of the wildest rumours which had just come in from the southwest. The Lords in fact had agreed among themselves to make York protector before the deputation's third visit and were discussing the terms of his appointment. Nevertheless there had certainly been a well-organized plot. Burley's deputation had their plans cut and dried the day after parliament assembled. Such swift action would have been impossible without consultation beforehand. Moreover, on the fourth day of the session, although he made a formal declaration of his unfitness for the post of protector, York had ready for discussion a number of articles defining the conditions under which he was prepared to exercise it. At the same time he succeeded only after a good deal of argument and on the same restricted conditions as before. Once again the Lords insisted upon safeguarding the rights of the prince of Wales.

During the next three weeks the new Protector made very full preparations to go to the southwest and to deal with the disorders there. Despite these preparations he never set foot in Devon. Without his intervention Lord Bonvile fled to the king, the earl of Devon surrendered and was imprisoned in the Tower of London. The swift collapse of the disturbances in Devonshire, which York's supporters had made so much of in forcing his claims upon the Lords, may well have been fatal to the duke's position. Many men, never well disposed to these claims in the first place, may now have felt even more strongly than before that he had unscrupulously forced the issue. The attendance of the Lords at the new session of parliament which began in mid-January was again poor. York and Warwick, according to one report, came to parliament at the head of three hundred armed men 'and no lord else' — a statement which, even if very much exaggerated, indicates that the Yorkists felt their position to be weak and they misjudged matters to the extent of making it even weaker by a tactless demonstration of armed force. There was no recorded opposition when on 25 February (1456) the king came to parliament and deprived York of his office.

Polydore Vergil and several Tudor chroniclers who followed him were convinced that York's second protectorate was 'a device politically invented' as they called it, to turn Henry into a *roi fainéant* and to leave York and the two Nevilles to run the country between them. The plot crashed on the passive resistance of the nobility and York was worse off than ever. He now faced an implacable foe in the queen herself. Since she arrived in England ten years before, a seasick bewildered bride of sixteen, she had, so far as we know, taken little part in the great political disputes, though it is possible that she may have used her influence (like every other highly placed man or woman) to obtain offices and financial benefits for her servants and dependants. After Somerset's death, her fierce maternal instincts aroused, she took the lead in opposing York to protect the inheritance of her newly born son. About this time John Bocking, in a letter to Sir John Fastolf, described her now formidable qualities: 'a great and strong laboured woman, for she spareth no pain to sue her things to an intent and conclusion to her power'. With such a woman and York now face to face, political passions, after a short interval, grew even more inflamed.

Though deprived of office, the Yorkists were in no way vindictively treated. For seven months a deceptive political calm prevailed, until the king summoned a great council to Coventry for 7 October—the first of a succession of great councils, all of them poorly attended, which were to meet in the late 1450s. Parliament was not to be summoned again until 1459. There Henry deprived the chancellor and treasurer, Archbishop Bourchier and Henry, Viscount Bourchier, of their offices, replacing them by William Waynflete, bishop of Winchester, and John Talbot, earl of Shrewsbury, two men who always remained unimpeachably loyal to the Lancastrians. Peace was preserved with difficulty but, in the end, York and Warwick again swore allegiance to Henry and all the lords present swore not to use force to settle their own quarrels. At the same time York received a stern warning not to expect a pardon if he again disturbed the peace in future.

VI

York and Salisbury soon retired to their estates, York to Wigmore, Salisbury to Middleham. Warwick crossed the Channel to Calais. Although York's two protectorates had left him politically weak, they had gained him two very important advantages—a footing in Calais and the adherence, somewhat unwilling it is true, of the Merchants of the Staple, the richest financial group in the country. Calais was an asset of the first order. The fortress could easily be held against the crown. It provided a jumping off ground for an invasion of England and its captain controlled the biggest professional military force in the government's pay.

Since 1454 York and Somerset had struggled for control of the town. Warwick had been appointed to command it early in the second protectorate. As the Merchants of the Staple were compelled by law to sell their wool there, they had the strongest interest in the security and good government of the port. To ensure its safety they made York first a short term, and then a long term, loan to pay the wages of the garrison. The second protectorate had lasted just long enough to give York control of Calais and to entangle the Merchants of the Staple almost irrevocably in his affairs. During the next three years matters drifted from bad to worse, neither side emerging with much credit. Warwick refused to give up his command and, in a desperate effort to raise money and victuals, supported the garrison by outrageous piracy, exploiting his control of the straits of Dover to attack both a Spanish trading fleet and the Hanseactic salt fleet. Meanwhile York himself continued to stir up trouble in an unsuccesful attempt to gain control of West Wales.

At the end of August 1457, the queen's reputation took a severe blow. Pierre de Brezé, the grand seneschal of Normandy, who had been prominent in the negotiations for her marriage, and who was already notorious for a raid on the Yorkshire coast in 1451, sailed into Sandwich Haven with a fleet of about sixty ships and spent the whole of a long summer day looting and pillaging the town. On its way home a Breton contingent from his fleet plundered Fowey. These outrages caused such fearful panic that the south and east coasts lived in mortal terror of more attacks. There is nothing to show that Margaret of Anjou had in any way been concerned with planning the raid or had even known of it, but her continued friendship for de Brezé left her guilty by association.

In January 1458 there came a last attempt at reconciliation, in another great council held at Westminster. Once again many of the lesser lords stayed away. Personal feuds and ambitions for power cut across each other in an atmosphere pullulating with suspicions and resentment. After several tedious weeks of negotiation the antagonists patched up their differences and symbolized their agreement in a great formal procession in St Paul's Cathedral. Henry went robed and crowned, Salisbury walked side by side with Somerset, the son of the duke killed at St Albans, Warwick with his bitter rival, the duke of Exeter, and York himself 'led the queen with great familiarity in all men's sight'.

For the next few months the course of events is impenetrably obscure. York intrigued with foreign powers, first with France, later with Burgundy. Under cover of negotiations about breaches of the truce between England and Burgundy, he reached, during the summer of 1458, some kind of vague, clandestine agreement with Duke Philip the Good. This understanding led in the autumn to secret proposals for triple marriages, involving on the English side the prince of Wales, York's son, Edward, and the duke of Somerset. If the younger Somerset really gave his approval to these plans, the episode shows how very fluid politics in England still remained even at this late date.

But not for long. By the winter and spring of 1459, a new vicious note, unknown before, ran through the murmurings against the court. The evil reputation which the royal household had suffered a decade earlier still left it a plausible target for the embittered scandal the Yorkists now spread against their opponents. The queen and her affinity were alleged to be gathering in riches innumerable. She had taken as her paramour the earl of Wiltshire, the handsomest man in England, too vain of his beauty ever to risk losing it in battle. She had appointed him treasurer and he was using his new position to enrich himself by evil and corrupt practices. The prince of Wales had been begotten in adultery and to make certain of his succession Margaret even planned her husband's abdication, but found no support for her schemes among the lords whom she consulted. So the venomous tales ran.

Margaret and York were both intriguing with the king of Scotland for help with their English schemes. Later on Yorkist politicians and writers found it very convenient to forget that it was not only Margaret of Anjou who sought foreign help at this time. By the end of April Margaret had moved to the Midlands and she had begun to recruit troops. York was in the Marches, Salisbury at Middleham, Warwick still at Calais. Possibly alarmed by the news of Margaret's recruiting, they determined to act in good time. Even so they were not swift enough to gain the advantage of surprise. Margaret seems to have got wind of their plans and set off with the prince of Wales to continue recruiting troops in the county palatine of Chester, Henry following them from Kenilworth.

News arrived that Salisbury was marching south. It seemed, at all costs, imperative to intercept him before he could join forces with York at Ludlow. Salisbury evaded the royal forces at Eccleshall, but then judged it imprudent to go on with a superior royal force harrassing his rear. He disposed his troops for battle on a slope near Blore Heath, where Henry had now caught up with the queen. The battle is said to have lasted four hours. In spite of inferior numbers Salisbury won the day and marched on to Ludlow where a number of York's friends had assembled. Fortunately for the Lancastrians, however, they could rely on reinforcements to follow them to Ludlow.

Warwick was known to be on his way with part of the Calais garrison. Commanding the Channel, he could, had he so chosen, have gone to Wales by sea. Instead he chose to land in Kent and march across England. That he was able to do so unmolested shows (as later events were to prove time after time) that given the advantage of surprise very small military forces could accomplish a great deal.

Both sides, all through the Wars of the Roses, found defence much more difficult to organize than attack.

Both sides still wished to avoid the odium of responsibility for bloodshed. As in 1455 the Yorkists tried to negotiate but failed. After their failure, they sent Henry a final letter protesting once more that they were under arms only to defend themselves against their enemies: they would fight only if compelled to do so. This last minute restraint owed less to scruples of conscience than to their knowledge that their case was desperate. Only two other peers had come forward to support York: Lord Clinton who had previously fought with him at St Albans and Lord Grey of Powys, an impoverished young man of about twenty-two. They already knew that they could not rely upon their only experienced troops. Warwick had taken a desperate gamble in bringing over to England part of the Calais garrison under the command of two famous veterans of the French wars, James Blount and Andrew Trollope. Trollope, the master porter of Calais, enjoyed an immense reputation as a warrior and his presence might well have been decisive. At the critical time the throw failed. Warwick had never managed to pay the garrison's wages. They felt little personal loyalty to the earl, not even the easy tolerance due to a prompt paymaster, and he had never been able to eliminate Somerset's followers in the garrison. The men Warwick brought to England had never expected to fight against the king. They may even have made it a condition of leaving Calais that they should not be led against him. The Yorkists, well aware of the danger, attempted deception, bringing into their camp men who swore that the king was dead. To make the story more plausible, their priests even sang a mass for his soul. Their discreditable subterfuge was a miserable failure. After dark on the night of 12 October, Trollope and many of his men went over to the king's camp. The Yorkists had lost the best-trained sector of their army, its only professional corps. Like most of the men who fought in the Wars of the Roses the remainder of their hastily collected levies were certainly ill-trained and poor fighting material. Realizing that they were now hopelessly outclassed, before dawn the Yorkist leaders fled.

On 20 November the Parliament of Devils met at Coventry. After three weeks' discussion it passed an act of attainder condemning the rebels—an act drafted with an eye to propaganda setting out a detailed schedule of York's offences since 1450. Even allowing that the triumphant loyalists put the most unfavourable interpretation they could upon every incident, the indictment was unanswerable.

York, his two eldest sons—Edward, the future Edward IV, and Edmund, earl of Rutland—the earl and countess of Salisbury, Warwick, two of his younger brothers and sixteen other people were attainted. They were to suffer the most solemn penalty known to the common law. Treason was the most heinous of all offences. Its penalties ruined the traitor's descendants as well as the traitor himself. The offender was held worthy of death 'inflicted with the last extremity of bodily pain' — disembowelling on the scaffold while still alive; his children, their blood corrupted, regarded as unfit to cumber the earth, could succeed to neither the paternal nor the maternal inheritance. The traitor died in the flesh, his children before the law.

In spite of the savagery of the legal penalties, unavoidable after condemnation, Henry was far from vindictive. After all the provocation he had suffered, he consented to act against the major offenders only on condition that he was left free to exercise his prerogative of mercy and pardon. The young Lord Grey of Powys was spared his life though his lands were forfeited under the act of attainder and the king himself refused to allow the attainder of Lord Stanley who had begun a notable career of political fence-sitting by refusing to bring his troops to Blore Heath although he had been only a few miles away at the time. The troops which York and the Nevilles had abandoned when they fled from Ludford had surrendered. A few, condemned as ringleaders, were hanged. The rest were pardoned and fined on giving surety for good behaviour. In many cases they were heavily fined — a policy which both Edward IV and Henry VII later followed in the aftermath of rebellion.

The assembly which agreed to these proscriptions was neither hand-picked nor apparently intimidated. Parliament had been hastily summoned and because of this there had been some technical irregularities in the election procedures. The stock accusation that the House of Commons was packed is dubious for it derives from a tainted source, part of Yorkist strategy in 1460 to undo the work of the Parliament of Devils. As for the House of Lords, there was no question of the king and his advisers trying to exclude opponents. There were in any case very few pronounced opponents to exclude. It is impossible, even at this late date,. to think in terms of a peerage divided into two hostile camps, Lancaster and York. Like York himself in 1454 and 1455, the royal advisers probably wished for the approval of the largest and most influential body of peers it was possible to bring together. Their success in this endeavour was in striking contrast to York's earlier failures. At least 67, out of 97 lay and spiritual peers summoned, attended. Even Warwick's brother, George Neville, received a kindly welcome from the king. The Parliament of Devils was, in fact (on the evidence so far available), the best attended parliament ever summoned by any of the three Lancastrian kings. The large numbers of lords were in glaring contrast with those of the thinly attended assemblies, both parliaments and great councils, of the previous few years. With York out of the way, the lords were prepared to demonstrate, if not some feeling of confidence in the monarchy (that surely was impossible after the political disasters of the last two decades), at least a continuing respect for the Lancastrian dynasty and its prescriptive right to the throne—feeble or wilful though its actual representative was! At the end of the parliament 34 spiritual and 32 temporal peers signed and sealed an oath pledging their allegiance to Henry and accepting Prince Edward and his issue as 'natural born' heirs to the crown—an indication perhaps that Yorkist smears about his parentage could no longer be ignored.

When the Yorkist lords stole away under cover of darkness from their camp at Ludford, York, Edmund of Rutland and Lord Clinton fled into Wales, breaking down the bridges behind them to hamper pursuit, and thence to Ireland. Edward, earl of March, Salisbury, Warwick, Sir John Wenlock and a few others made for Calais. Guided across the West Country by a Devonshire gentlemen, Sir John Dynham, they reached his mother's house at Nutwell where they remained in hiding for at least a week before Dynham managed to buy, for £73, a small ship in which they could hasten on to Calais. They put out from Exmouth so badly crewed that Warwick himself, it was said, had to steer the boat. Although Warwick had left his uncle, Lord Fauconberg, in command at Calais, the desertion of Andrew Trollope's men at Ludford must have made them fearful of their reception in the town. They arrived in time to forestall Somerset whose fleet had been wind-bound in Sandwich Haven during these critical days. Even so, the garrison of Guisnes, one of Calais' two subsidiary fortresses, admitted Somerset and remained loyal to the government until after Edward IV's accession.

Meanwhile York, in Ireland at the parliament of Drogheda, for the sake of his own immediate advantage made concessions which still further weakened the already feeble English control over the country and made the future of English government there more precarious than ever. The next Yorkist move was to destroy the Lancastrian naval defences. Sailing from Calais with a few vessels, John Dynham between four and five in the morning of 10 January 1460 surprised the whole of a recently assembled Lancastrian fleet in Sandwich Haven and bore it back across the Channel. Another hastily assembled fleet under the duke of Exeter, its sailors unpaid and unfed, failed to prevent Warwick sailing to Ireland in March for discussions with York and again failed to intercept him on his return to Calais in May.

From their bastions at Calais and in Ireland, the small group of York's active supporters, with the courage of desperate men, had won command of the sea. At home the government tried to round up and imprison Yorkist supporters in the southern and southeastern counties and, according to the very pro-Yorkist *Davies' Chronicle*, the commissioners for Berkshire carried out their work with zealous brutality at York's own town of Newbury. They executed some of his friends and plundered the other inhabitants. Such judicial terrorism was nothing abnormal by recent standards, but it made useful propaganda when appealing for support. The Yorkists were quick to play upon the drift of opinion and never ceased from making skilful appeals, blackening their opponents. For some time they had been sending letters into various parts of England, justifying their conduct and promising reforms. Now, judging the time ripe, on 20 or 21 June they sent an advance fleet to capture Sandwich. Their surprise attack was completely successful and Lord Fauconberg remained in the town preparing for the arrival of the main invasion force.

March and Warwick now issued another manifesto from Calais, an *omnium gatherum* kind of document very much on the lines of earlier Yorkist propaganda, denouncing obvious administrative corruption. Many of these charges were true enough and most of them were plausible. Over and above these accusations about domestic affairs, the manifesto vehemently stressed the loss of Normandy and Guienne — an appeal for the support of those still angry and resentful at the loss of their foreign estates. They mendaciously attacked the court's efforts to recruit troops for defence as an attempt to conscript men for a royal guard after the French fashion and accused the court of inviting the wild Irish to invade the country — both statements full of sinister implications after recent stories of Lancastrian brutality.

The last part of the manifesto was superbly skilful for it appealed with dark hints of foul play to one of the most deeply rooted emotions of the age — the near-absolute sanctity of the inheritance. In the minds of the landed classes, if not in law, the livelode, or landed inheritance was a family trust — an emotion to which York himself was very soon to appeal in making his claim to the throne. Men felt with passionate intensity that not even treason should extinguish the rights of an heir. For the first time the earls openly stated what hitherto had been only whispered, and what even propagandist chroniclers refrained from explicitly stating, that Humphrey of Gloucester had been murdered in cold blood, and that since Gloucester's death his enemies had continually, but unavailingly, tried to murder York himself. The insurgents now accused self-seeking lords about the king, in particular the earls of Wiltshire and Shrewsbury and Viscount Beaumont, of deliberately plotting the attainders of the Parliament of Devils in order to enrich themselves: no longer content with plundering the king of his lands and goods they had turned their covetous eyes upon other men's inheritances. Finally the earls once more vehemently protested their loyalty to the king himself.

This skilfully slanted appeal may have been effective for, at last, a significant part of the nobility began to come over to York's side. In the fifteen months after the flight from Ludford, fourteen peers swung over to fight for the Yorkists. Why so many turned their coats at this time is inexplicable. Some may have done so for personal reasons. On the other hand, constant dripping may have worn away the political stone. For a whole decade York had shown that he was not prepared to give anybody else the chance to govern. By 1460 some may at last have felt that, indiscreet and violent as his conduct had been, the results of admitting him to power might at least be an improvement upon the growing disorders and political chaos resulting from his exclusion. Again, the opinions of people lower in the social scale, from yeoman to gentlemen, may have begun to influence them. For many years past in some parts of the country, men had been openly contemptuous of the king's abilities. It may be that the threat to property inherent in the attainders of the Parliament of Devils aroused deep-seated fears. Yet whatever conjecture we adopt, the fact remains that the so-called 'Yorkist party' hardly existed before 1460.

VII

From this time onwards, for more than three decades, events in Europe profoundly influenced English domestic affairs. The Wars of the Roses were far from being a mere insular matter. In 1460 two questions of outstanding significance agitated the courts of Europe: preparations for a crusade and the claims of Margaret of Anjou's family to the kingdom of Naples. Both questions came to disturb English politics through the intrigues of Franceso Coppini, bishop of Terni and papal legate, who was dealing with both schemes and quite shamelessly using both to further his own obsessive ambition for the red hat of a cardinal.

Though we know that the vision of a crusade was a mirage in the fifteenth century, it was not so to many people alive at the time. The effect of the crusading dream in international politics should certainly not be underestimated. It was an important and disturbing fact. The vision of the crusade had for long haunted the chivalric imagination of Duke Philip the Good of Burgundy and the duke's pious dreams fell in with the determined policy of the pope. Although we know that Pius II (1458 – 64) was living on the eve of one of the most brilliant periods of Italian life, he was deeply pessimistic about the future of Europe, obsessed by haunting terrors that a combination of internal decadence and the onslaught of overwhelming Turkish forces upon Christendom would end in universal catastrophe.

As part of wider efforts to organize an expedition to the Near East, Pius had charged Coppini with the task of persuading the English government to send a contingent to his forces. While he was in England for this purpose, Coppini maintained a regular corres- pondence with Francesco Sforza, the duke of Milan, one of the most subtle and accomplished politicians of his day. Whether or not Sforza had worked out his plans in any detail before Coppini first came to England is unknown. Sforza soon decided, however, that he needed the support of both England and Burgundy to prevent Charles VII of France from supporting John of Calabria's claim to the throne of Naples — a matter which called for adroit planning as Margaret of Anjou was John of Calabria's sister. They schemed to have Coppini made a cardinal in order to increase his prestige and authority. Coppini would then throw all his influence on the side of the Yorkists (towards whom Duke Philip was not ill-disposed). The Yorkists, elevated to power, could then be expected to show their gratitude by invading Normandy and Gascony to divert Charles VII's attention from Naples. The destiny of the house of Anjou in England was thus linked with the destiny of the house of Anjou in Naples.

The bishop of Terni was a little man who exhibited all the vanity and self-assertiveness that often go with small stature. Within limits he was able, endowed with a lively, if superficial spirit, and a bombastic grandiloquence which strongly appealed to that other conceited and execrable stylist, his acquaintance Abbot Whethamstede of St Albans. Hopelessly out of his depth among the ruthless politicians with whom his lot was now cast, he soon found himself desperately struggling against the events which he aspired to control in physical conditions appalling to his natural timidity.

Rebuffed by Henry VI and the government, after crossing the Channel Coppini found himself at Calais while the earls were preparing for their invasion of England. On their behalf he under- took to present to Henry certain Latin articles — articles not only demanding redress for their own grievances but, falling in with Sforza's Neapolitan schemes, making their own submission condi- tional upon his providing armies for the recovery of the lost French provinces. Considering the state of England this was, as the earls must have known well enough, a scheme from cloud-cuckoo land.

On 26 June, although they were still uncertain about their reception by the people of Kent, the three earls and their followers with a force of about fifteen hundred or two thousand men embarked for Sandwich. Arriving there, they rode on to Canterbury, the captains in charge of which, probably collusively, surrendered. As their forces then proceeded to London, men flocked to their banners and by the time they reached Blackheath they led a considerable army.

Their approach terrified the London authorities who had, so far, shown no inclination to favour either side in the quarrel. The common council at first agreed that everybody should support the mayor and aldermen in efforts to dissuade the Yorkists from entering the city, but as they were not prepared to fight they were forced to admit the insurgents. Once they were admitted, the city fathers were powerless against them. The most they could do was to avoid giving them active support. Even so they had no option but to furnish carts, horses and other supplies for the rebel army. But when it came to much-needed money, they were grudging in the extreme. All they would provide was a short-term loan of £1,000, and even this they would lend only upon the security of bonds from the bishops of Exeter and Ely, the duke of York and the three earls; and for a whole year the city maintained this adamantine attitude towards money.

At this point Coppini, as papal legate, could not be refused a hearing, and he abused his position in a way which the pope afterwards roundly condemned. Sponsored by the legate, the earls before the Convocation of Canterbury swore upon the sacred cross of St Thomas that they intended nothing contrary to their allegiance to Henry VI, and Coppini himself read, first in Convocation and then afterwards to the people at St Paul's Cross, a letter which he had written to the king. He had nothing new to say, merely a reiteration of the old Yorkist demand that, in order to preserve the peace, the earls should be allowed to come to the king with an armed force. Impudently he told Henry that, if he listened to the 'ministers of the devil' who surrounded him and made the deliberate and wicked choice not to cooperate, he would stand guilty in the awful day of judgment when the legate himself would demand divine retribution upon him for spilling innocent English blood.

On the very day of Coppini's speech the Yorkists rode out of London. Henry, deterred neither by reports of swollen Yorkist forces nor by the legate's inflated anathemas, moved from Coventry towards Northampton, where the two forces met. Once again, as at St Albans in 1455, and before Ludford in 1459, the Yorkists attempted to negotiate, but to most of the king's advisers all idea of parley at this stage appeared futile. Like the street fight at St Alban's five years earlier, 'battle' is probably too grand a term for the fight outside Northampton. Lasting less than an hour it was decided by treachery when

Lord Grey of Ruthyn went over from the Lancastrian to the Yorkist side, and the losses were small.

The victors received but a sullen welcome on their return to London. The most which a contemporary poet could say of their entry was:

> The people rejoiced *inwardly*
> And thanked God of his goodness.

Although the victors brought Henry as a prisoner to London, an imposing escort accompanied him and his captors maintained all the ceremonial of royalty; early in July Warwick stated publicly in London that he and his friends 'ever bore true faith and liegance to the king's person'. The events which followed give no reason to doubt their sincerity. They give every reason to question the duke of York's.

VIII

All this time York had remained in Ireland. It is strange, to say the least, that in spite of his discussions earlier in the year with Warwick at Dublin, he made no attempt to coordinate his own landing in England with that of the earls in Kent — surely the obvious proceeding in so precarious a venture. So far as we know the duke did not even begin to make his own preparations until his friends had already won the fight for him at Northampton (10 July). Only after receiving the news from Northampton did he send Lord Clinton to commandeer ships in the Severn estuary for his crossing to England and it was not until about 8 September that he landed near Chester. In spite of his opportunist concessions to the parliament of Drogheda, the Irish gave him very little support. He crossed the Irish Sea with a mere handful of men.

After he landed his progress towards London was slow. He took over a month to reach the capital. The pace of his march puzzled people at the time, and the suspicion arises that he dallied deliberately so as to avoid meeting any of his friends before confronting parliament which had been summoned for early October. Various signs along the road to London showed that, although the Nevilles had won his victory for him, York intended to use it in a manner which he knew they could not approve for it would involve them in perjury. He usurped royal authority by holding punitive judicial sessions in several towns and, when he reached Abingdon, the duke sent for trumpeters and clariners, gave them banners with the royal arms of England, ordered his sword to be borne upright before him — the style appropriate only for a king — and rode on towards the capital.

Parliament had assembled on 7 October. On the 10th York reached London. He stayed there just long enough for a formal reception by the mayor and aldermen, then at once rode on to Westminster, with five hundred armed men behind him, trumpets and clariners sounding, the sword still borne upright before him. With this show of force and majesty he came to Westminster. Passing through Westminster Hall he strode into the parliament chamber where the Lords were in session and laid his hand on the cushion of the empty throne as if to claim it as his by right. The expected acclamation never came. In a tense and angry silence, he turned and faced the hostile rows of lords. The archbishop of Canterbury, in a tactful attempt to cover up York's gross mistake, stepped forward, greeted him and asked if he wished to see the king. York aggressively replied: 'I know of no-one in the realm who would not more fitly come to me than I to him.'

Baffled and angry, impetuous in his bitter disappointment, York ignored his dismayed friends and at once went to the king's chamber where, finding the doors barred in fear against him, he battered them down and turned out Henry into the rooms generally occupied by the queen. Only one interpretation could be placed upon actions such as these, and soon there came 'a noise through the city that King Henry should be deposed and the duke of York should be king'.

Alone in Ireland, isolated from his friends, York had brooded upon his wrongs and, brooding in isolation, his thoughts had outstripped the intentions of the Nevilles who, though intransigent and in arms against Henry, had not planned the king's deposition. Although some of his humbler friends had earlier asserted York's claim to the throne and there are hints of it in 1456 in the correspondence of James III of Scotland, until his return from Ireland York himself had never *openly* proposed that Henry VI should be deprived of the crown. On balance it seems that he quite deliberately laid his plans alone, even to the extent of deciding on the day for his coronation — plans which he concealed even from his closest supporters because he knew that they were unlikely to cooperate in them.

No one knew which way to turn or what to do. The Burgundian chronicler, Waurin, related that angry words (*grosses paroles*) passed between Warwick and the duke when he heard of York's intentions and Abbot Whethamstede reluctantly admitted that all sorts and conditions of men began to murmur against York at this time. York held the initiative but every group of people to which he turned tried to shuffle out of giving that approval for his claims which he was determined to procure. On the 16 October he sent the Lords a written exposition of his descent, claiming that Henry IV and his descendants had unrighteously usurped the crown, and asked for a quick reply. The Lords were recalcitrant and their resistance is all the more remarkable for none of York's most determined opponents was present. The Lords consulted the king. He threw back the onus of his defence upon them. The peers then plucked up sufficient courage to ask the judges to find arguments *against* York's claims. The judges, taking discretion to be the better part of valour, replied that such high matters were so 'above the law and past their learning' that only the lords of the king's blood could decide upon them. The king's sergeants and the king's attorney, when asked for their opinions, gratefully followed the evasive example of the judges.

The Lords could evade responsibility no longer. Even so, discussions went on for more than a week. Sixty-one years before, Henry IV, in deliberately ambiguous language, claimed that he had taken the throne by right of inheritance. He had left the details purposely vague. As we have seen, the claim was far from definitive. Yet after six decades, men felt that the house of Lancaster had a prescriptive right to the throne—a claim based upon prolonged tenure. Prescriptive right, in the end, however, could only be justified by success. Henry had proved too weak to govern himself and York—whether his actions could be justified or not is at the moment immaterial—had made it impossible for anybody else to govern for him. York had proved himself too intransigent to be ignored. He could only be accommodated. The Lords at last reached a compromise, set out in the Act of Accord of 25 October, that Henry should retain the crown as long as he lived, then York and his heirs would succeed. Henry yielded to the inevitable, consented that parliament sanction the award and agreed to hand over to York crown estates worth 10,000 marks a year, thus nearly doubling York's income.

York had acted against the wishes of well-nigh all. His disappointment at his limited success was deep and bitter and he expressed it with a childish and vicious ostentation. He turned Henry out of Westminster Palace and sent him to the bishop of London's house. On the night of the king's removal he ostentatiously rode into the royal palace by torchlight and 'took upon him as king and said in many places that this is ours by very right'. Nor content with the substance of power, he longed for its trappings as well. An ominous clause in the Act of Accord referring to Henry's possible abdication makes it quite possible that he did not intend to wait for the king's death.

The queen, now in the north, determined to fight for her son's rights. Many northern lords had stayed away from parliament and the earl of Northumberland and Lord Clifford encouraged her. The duke of Somerset, the earl of Devon and Sir Alexander Hody and others in the southwest recruited troops and with a force of eight hundred men marched unimpeded across the country to York. There they joined forces with the duke of Exeter (York's son-in-law), Lord Latimer (the duchess's brother) now in a lucid period between fits of insanity, Lord Neville (the duchess's half-brother), the earl of Northumberland (her nephew)—family support was far from conspicuous—and Lords Roos, Clifford, Greystock and Dacre. Within a short time they had concentrated several thousand men between York and Hull. The Yorkists had no idea of the efficiency of Lancastrian recruiting for they were astounded when the news of its extent reached London.

On 9 December York and Salisbury set out for the north, Edward of March for the west, taking independent command for the first time. They were disastrously short of money. York dared not ask parliament for a grant and London would lend no more than 500 marks. 1460 had been a year of incessant rain. The harvest had not matured, meadows and pastures were flooded, bridges, mills and houses swept away by the swollen rivers. The roads across the Midland clays were heavy with mire and in some places washed away. Making about fifteen miles a day—a very creditable performance in such circumstances—York reached Sandal Castle, about two miles from Wakefield, on 21 December. Margaret lay at Pontefract, nine miles away.

York, apparently relying upon a Christmas truce, allowed his men to scatter over the neighbouring countryside in search of food. The Lancastrians, breaking faith, moved up to Sandal Castle on 30 December. The catastrophe which followed was due entirely to York's own thoughtless impetuosity. He might have defended the castle until his scattered troops were called in. Scorning prudence he led his men in a wild rush down the slope from the castle. The Lancastrians let him reach the level ground between Sandal and Wakefield, then closed in on him 'like fish in a net or deer in a buckstall'. Within a short time York lay dead on the field, his army in full flight and an infuriated mob lynched Salisbury after the battle.

The Lancastrians were soon marching south with a large army, which contemporaries estimated at the quite impossible figure of 80,000 men. More significant than its size was the fact that it contained large number of Welsh and Scots as well as Englishmen. Margaret and her supporters, even before the battle of Northampton, had attracted men to their banners by promising them the plunder of seven southern counties. Now the northern horde swept towards London sacking the countryside on a line of march several miles wide. Even the churches were ransacked. Vestments, chalices and church

ornaments of every kind were looted 'as they had bene Paynims or
Saracens and no Christian men', as the terrified prior of Croyland
wrote.[7] Approaching London, Margaret at last realized the discredit
which the rapine of her troops had brought upon her cause. She had
let loose forces which she could no longer control and many people by
this time had come to regard the Yorkist cause almost as the defence
of the south against the north. London was terrified of being sacked.

Yet hope was rising in the city. Edward of March was at Shrewsbury. He had been recruiting troops in the Marches of Wales and was
preparing to come to the defence of London. Just as he was starting
out he heard that Jasper Tudor and the earl of Wiltshire had landed
in Wales with a force of Frenchmen, Bretons and Irish, and were
recruiting for the queen. Edward at once turned back into Herefordshire. On 2 or 3 February he defeated them at Mortimer's Cross near
Wigmore, in the greatest battle so far seen in the Wars of the Roses.
The weight of numbers was on Edward's side, but his success also
appears to have been due to the promptness and vigour of this attack.

Meanwhile Warwick dealt with affairs in London — a London
whose support was still grudging in the extreme although Warwick's
spendthrift hospitality made him popular with the mob. As the
Lancastrian army from the north was approaching London, the earl,
who was completely inept as a general (he never won a battle),
brought the Yorkist cause to the brink of disaster. After marching out
of London on 12 February he waited to intercept the queen at St
Albans. He failed to keep track of her movements and, believing her
to be still about nine miles away, he began to make some slight
changes in the disposition of his troops. Everything was in confusion
when the royal army unexpectedly burst upon him and the day was
lost.

A week or more of terror followed for the city of London. Edward
was still in the west. Warwick's fate was unknown. William Worcester
thought that Margaret could easily have taken the city during this
panic-stricken week. The city authorities, who were always more
concerned with the security of property than with the dynastic issue,
determined to bargain with the Lancastrians about conditions for
their admission. They would have admitted the queen with a token
force. Only the angry reaction of the city mob prevented them from
doing so. In the end, to her credit, Queen Margaret, knowing that she
would be unable to prevent her northern troops from sacking the

---

[7] Grantham, Stamford, Peterborough, Huntingdon, Royston, Melbourne and St Albans
were sacked but the extent of the devastation has probably been exaggerated by tradition. For
example, Dr L. Tebbut, the borough librarian of Stamford, has informed me that the town
charters, allegedly destroyed in the sack of 1461, are extant and that several buildings
commonly said to have been destroyed at the same time still existed at the Reformation.

capital, withdrew and began a long march back to York. Balked of
the riches of London, the 'northern men as they went homeward, did
harms innumerable, taking men's carts, wains, horses and beasts and
robbed the people and led their pillage into the north country, so that
the men of the shires as they passed had almost no beasts left to till the
land.'

It had been touch and go for the Yorkists. Their leadership in the
capital had broken down. Throughout the prolonged crisis the city
authorities had been hesitant, timorous and unreliable. Finding it
impossible to keep the Yorkists out of the city by peaceful means, they
had reluctantly admitted them. With ill-will they had doled out
money in driblets only to protect citizen property. They would have
done the same for the Lancastrians.

Though in no immediate danger, Edward and his friends faced a
future heavy with ruin. Margaret's army, though retreating, was still
undefeated, and the king was now with her. The Yorkists could no
longer make a pretence of acting in his name. Compromise had
proved unworkable in the past. It would certainly be impossible in the
future. In desperation, possibly as a somewhat legalistic attempt to
save themselves from the penalties of treason, Warwick and a minute
group of peers did for Edward what they had consistently refused to
do for his father—they made him king.

Warwick having joined him somewhere in the Cotswolds, Edward
arrived in London on 27 February 1461. His reign officially began five
days later. His accession, in spite of the haste and confusion in which
he assumed the title, was stage-managed in all its details with the
greatest possible care.

As Edward's father had unequivocally stated in 1460, the Yorkist
claim to the throne lay in a strictly legitimist title based upon inheritance. The right of inheritance could carry the validity of a title
through a period when it had not been effectively enforced. As York
himself had declared in 1460, 'though right for a time rest and be put
to silence, yet it rotteth not nor shall not perish.' To turn such a *de
jure* title into *de facto* possession, however, required some kind of
public ceremony. During the fifteenth and early sixteenth centuries,
many landowners, particularly aristocratic landowners, declared
(one might almost say registered) their titles to particular estates in an
act of parliament. So Richard in 1460 had attempted to establish his
inheritance to the throne in that assembly. No parliament was sitting
in March 1461; nor was there time to summon one. Some other form
of public recognition had therefore to be devised.

On the afternoon of Sunday 1 March, an assembly which may well
have numbered several thousand people drawn from the London
populace and the Yorkist army, came together on St John's Fields. To
this audience, George Neville, bishop of Exeter, the chancellor,

declared King Henry's offences and set out the Yorkist claim. Following his oration the crowd acclaimed 'King Edward' and the Yorkist captains ('captain' was a word with distinctly disreputable overtones at this time) went to Baynard's Castle (the Yorkist London house) and informed him of this acclamation. On Monday a proclamation cried in London set out his claims which, on Tuesday, a 'council', again at Baynard's Castle, approved. This so-called council, according to the *Annales* formerly attributed to William Worcester, consisted of the archbishop of Canterbury, the bishops of Salisbury and Exeter, the duke of Norfolk, Warwick, Lord FitzWalter, Lord Ferrers of Chartley, Sir William Herbert, 'and many others'—three prelates, five peers and a knight, three of whom were the new king's cousins and one (Herbert) a Yorkist retainer. Moreover, the status of the two barons was dubious: neither had yet been summoned to parliament. And who were the 'many others'? The phrase was an entirely naive attempt at deception. The 'council' was nothing more than a small Yorkist clique which happened to be in London, a mere fragment of a faction.

This rump issued another proclamation the same day that all the people should assemble to meet Edward at St Paul's Cathedral the next day. On 4 March he went in procession through London and made his offering at the Cathedral. A solemn *Te Deum* was sung and George Neville preached at St Paul's Cross. In conclusion he enquired of the crowd if they would have Edward as king. The crowd then acclaimed him. Following the acclamation Edward rode back in procession to the Great Hall of Westminster Palace. Going to that part of the hall occupied by the chancery, he there before the archbishop of Canterbury, the chancellor and 'other lords', took an oath 'that he should truly and justly keep the realm and the laws thereof maintain as a true and just king'—words which, in spite of their vagueness, reproduce the substance of the coronation oath.

Then Edward, still in the chancery, put on the royal robes and the cap of estate (a symbol of majesty held at that time inferior to the crown alone). The robes and the cap of estate were, in fact, the traditional regalia of the secular enthronement which normally preceded the religious rite of coronation. He then took his seat on the marble chair in the King's Bench. This enthronement was the symbolic mark of possession of the realm, and he was again hailed and acclaimed as king. A procession to the Abbey followed upon this secular enthronement. The abbot conducted the new king to the high altar and to St Edward's shrine, at which he again made an offering, before mounting the throne specially prepared for him in the choir. In ceremonies which closely resembled the coronation procedure, he was enthroned to the strains of a *Te Deum*. Again he declared his title by descent. Those present then chanted the refrain:

Verus Vox, Rex Edwardus
Rectus Rex, Rex Edwardus
Justus, juridicus et legitimus Rex, Rex Edwardus
Cui omnes nos subjici volumus
Suaeque humillime iuguns admittere subernationis.

This rolling, threefold, liturgical salutation was no longer acclamation: acclamation had risen into veneration of the quasi-sanctified person of the ruler. It was the age-old ceremony of lauds of majesty.

These ceremonies were hastily improvised. There were, at the most, five days between the earl of March's entry into the capital and the assembly in St John's Field. Yet despite the haste and the atmosphere of crisis which shadowed these few days, someone (alas unknown) had employed considerable antiquarian and liturgical knowledge to devise a scheme which linked the house of York's legitimist claim by inheritance with the idea of popular election and combined the expression of both with extreme public formality, splendour and dignity. The most surprising feature of all these attempts to press into service every possible justification for a change of dynasty was the adoration of the *laudes regiae*. The ritual chanting of lauds of majesty had begun in the late Roman Empire. In England it had reached its climax in the thirteenth century when lauds were frequently offered to the almost excessively pious Henry III. Thereafter the practice had declined. Lauds had been offered at Edward II's coronation; they may possibly have been heard at Richard II's. Then, for nearly a century, they disappeared completely. Their revival in 1461 must have been an act of deliberately conscious antiquarianism.

It may well be that in their enthusiasm Edward's advisers passed the limits of public comprehension. Only a few learned clerics could have understood the full significance of these ceremonies. Yet the ceremonies were brilliantly staged and Edward's legitimist title was already formulated in phrases so precisely defined that it could be set out on the parliament roll later in the year with only small verbal alterations. Such was the impression made that George Neville could write to Coppini with an air of some plausibility that Edward had been 'practically by force created king by the nobles and people universally'.

The claim he knew was false and Coppini himself, who knew better, about six weeks later wrote to Francesco Sforza: 'In the end my lord of Warwick has come off best, has made a new king of the son of the duke of York.' The acclamation in St John's Fields had been so obviously prearranged that Sir John Fortescue could later insinuate that a mere rabble had made Edward king.

IX

To say the least, the future was far from bright. Neither Richard of York nor his son ever commanded overwhelming support. York had too obviously allowed concern for his personal ambitions to swamp any sense of responsibility which he may have possessed. There is no evidence to show, as some writers have claimed, that he was more capable than his rival, Somerset, of holding the English position in Normandy. He left his first period of office in Ireland possibly just in time to avoid the odium of failure and during his second visit, after the flight from Ludford, his policy was frankly short-term and opportunist. The concessions which he hoped would make him popular would only make even more difficult the future government of a difficult land, without winning for him the military support which he so badly needed in 1460. During his protectorates he had made genuine attempts to improve public order. He had rightly encouraged the Commons in their attacks upon royal waste and extravagance and in their demands for resumption, thought he may have done so less out of conviction than as a bid to secure popularity.

His motives at various times across the years we can only deduce and, of course, they may well have changed with time. From Gloucester's death in 1447, York may have felt that hostile plots imperilled his position as heir to the throne. It is conceivable that as early as 1450 he fought back by plotting to depose the king or, at least, he made little effort of prevent his more extreme friends from doing so. After Cade's rebellion it was York, so far as we know, who dealt the first blow in the duel with Somerset which was to disturb the next two years. Provocation from the ministers in power, and later from Margaret of Anjou, he certainly received and they certainly broke faith with him. Yet is also fair to say that so great was his fear and personal rancour against the elder Somerset that he never allowed him even an opportunity to show that he was capable of giving the country sound government. The clandestine, hasty marriage of Margaret Beaufort and John de la Pole justified York's alarm that the Beauforts hoped to cheat him of the succession. On the other hand evidence, rendered sufficiently plausible by York's own conduct, that the duke's friends if not the duke himself were plotting the king's deposition and death, terrified the court. Neither York nor Somerset could ever trust the other. Only a strong king, capable of imposing his own will upon those above him, could have controlled them. Without such a personality on the throne, all the tensions and jealousies inherent in a system of personal monarchy rose to an abnormal pitch where political stalemate became almost inevitable. It is more than probable that York, even after the birth of a Lancastrian heir apparent, regarded himself as a man with a mission—to safeguard what he saw as his own royal inheritance. To that everything else must give place.

At the last, it must be confessed that we can only infer York's motives. Had he always intended to be king? Or did his ambitions grow with his frustration? Was he a leader or was he led by such enigmatic characters as Sir William Oldhall? Such questions cannot be answered. It is probable that they never will be answered. Yet, leader or led, lacking as he was in political judgment and self-control, proud and hasty, rash and impetuous, there is nothing in his record to show that he was fit to be a king. He was no less unscrupulous than his last opponent, Margaret of Anjou, but he may well have been less clever.

Nor is there much evidence that he won wide approval. The political poems which used to be cited as evidence of his popularity are nowadays regarded with some suspicion as inspired propaganda. Anti-Yorkist poems, though less numerous, certainly rest under the same cloud. As we have seen, London gave the Yorkists only the most grudging self-interested support and the Merchants of the Staple were caught in a financial net from which they could not escape. In 1459 the troops of the Calais garrison went over to the king at a critical moment and in 1461 popular support in the south most probably turned to the Yorkists more out of fear of the depredations of the Lancastrian armies than out of genuine enthusiasm. Only in Kent, that turbulent county prepared to support almost any insurgent movement, was there apparently real support.

An anonymous pamphlet of about 1460, the *Somnium Vigilantis*, sometimes rather dubiously attributed to Sir John Fortescue, observed that York and his friends had been pardoned insurrection and near-insurrection time after time. They were too intransigent ever to be trusted again. Certainly, the writer admitted, the realm would suffer, deprived of the influence and services of such eminent men, but this had become the lesser of two evils. For the sake of peace they must be crushed. Like rotten members they must be cast away.

The higher ranks of society, those whose support really counted, long remained hostile. By 1459, after ten years of intrigue, violence and treason, York had conspicuously failed to rally the peerage to his side. Salisbury and Warwick apart, only four peers are known to have fought for him. As we have seen, many stayed away from the vital parliaments of 1454 – 6 to avoid approving his actions. In 1459, 32 secular peers took a new oath of allegiance to Henry VI and Prince Edward and these included York's uncle by marriage, Lord

Abergavenny, his wife's brother-in-law, the duke of Buckingham, and his nephew, the duke of Norfolk. Only between 1459 and 1461 did a significant section of the nobility at last swing over to him. By March 1461 about 20 peers had fought on the Yorkist side but, even then, this new Yorkist faction was very thin as far as the higher grades were concerned, and only a miserable rump put Edward IV on the throne.

In spite of Henry VI's feebleness and its adverse consequences for the aristocracy, the king retained the loyalty of greater numbers. Between 1455 and 1461, 37 peers (and possibly 5 more) — the heads of 32 noble families — fought for him and, in the end, only 3 of these deserted him for the Yorkist side; 15 died for him, 12 on the battle-field, and three were afterwards executed by their victorious foes.

By early 1461 the major part of the peerage — at least 49 out of about 60 families — was in arms in the political struggle. This was the high-water mark of aristocratic involvement. Later developments were to show a remarkable contrast — a distinct aloofness from the dynastic struggle, a marked reluctance in the peers to risk their fortunes and their lives for Edward IV, Richard III and Henry VII. Never again would more than two fifths of the peerage actually fight during a period of political crisis.

As to other social groups, in some districts York may have counted upon the potential support of gentry families like the Pastons in East Anglia, families prepared to take his side if, by so doing, they could push their own local interests and rivalries. Even they, however, would follow their immediate patron (in this case the duke of Norfolk) rather than York himself. Yet in spite of the Pastons' close connection with Norfolk and intermittent sympathy for York, when the crunch came in 1459 their friends thought that they could 'no less do' than send their son, John, to join the queen in response to her summons. In Kent Robert Poynings joined in Cade's rebellion and supported York more to gain an advantage in his prolonged quarrel with the countess of Northumberland over the Poynings' inheritance than from any interest in reform or in the justice of the causes which he espoused.

Most of York's adherents came from two groups of men. Firstly, a few rather elderly veterans who had made their careers, and some of them a good deal of money, in France in the palmy days of Bedford's rule and had later served under York as lieutenant — men like his notorious chamberlain, Sir William Oldhall, Sir Edmund Mulsho and Sir Henry Redford, all members of his council. Having lost their lands some of the ex-veterans thought that they were despised and neglected by the Lancastrian government in the 1450s and possibly hoped for a policy more inclined to their interests if York achieved power. Their significance in the Wars of the Roses has traditionally been exaggerated. They were not, as a class, united. If some sided with York, others certainly fought for Henry VI at the first battle of St Albans. Nor were they numerous for the French war had been very unprofitable indeed during its last quarter of a century. A military career had no longer appealed to the hard-headed younger generation and the warriors had been a thinning band.

The other group of men, varying in rank from a peer to simple squires, like a few of the war veterans constituted part of York's affinity, some linked together by family and marriage ties, and profiting from long-standing connections with his household and estate management. Of the 14 men of less than baronial rank (the figure excludes two Neville and two Bourchier younger sons) who were attainted in 1459, 7 (and possibly four more) had ties of this kind. Yet even retainers held back at critical times. Lord Grey of Wilton to whom York had granted an annuity of 20 marks did not rally to his call in 1459. Sir William Herbert of Raglan, the steward of his lordship of Usk, and one of the richest of the Marcher gentry, after assisting him in Wales in 1455 – 6, never lifted a finger to help him between 1457 and 1460, though Herbert's brother-in-law, Sir Walter Devereux, was at Ludford. In 1459 the Herefordshire knight, Sir John Barre of Rotherwas, defected to the Lancastrians, although York had granted him a life annuity in 1453. The Yorkist 'party' of the 1450s is a shallow myth created by modern historians. York's 'affinity' (to use a more accurate contemporary term) was by no means exceptionally strong, nothing like as large and influential as the enormous, and quite exceptional, Lancastrian affinity which gave Henry of Derby a sufficient power-base to usurp the throne in 1399 and to hold it through the troubles which followed.

The reputation of York's entourage hardly compensated for its weakness. If the pro-Yorkist *Davies' Chronicle* flayed the corruption of the court, the anti-Yorkist *Somnium Vigilantis* was just as emphatic about the violence, corruption and hypocrisy of York and his friends:

> They did pretend a reformation of wrongs and extortions used as they said in this royaume, and the sovereign, the most endless misrule of all the sins of the world did rest in them and their servants.

Massive evidence supports the accusations of the *Somnium*. In spite of their numerous protestations about the need for sound finances, 'sad governance', honesty and probity during the 1450s, in practice the record of York's associates was hardly better than that of the courtiers and the officials whom they attacked. In May 1448 the tenants of Canterfewy, one of the royal lordships in Wales, complained of oppressions, including robbery and murder, by some of York's officers and tenants. In 1450 the inhabitants of the Isle of Wight had petitioned parliament against the oppressions and extortions of the poverty-stricken ex-veteran, John Newport, whom York had appointed as steward of the island, and had asked for his replacement by a rich official of the royal household who would not pillage them. In the autumn of 1450 York arbitrarily imprisoned Raymond Boulers, the abbot of Gloucester, at Ludlow and again, in 1454, as the result of a private quarrel he imprisoned Speaker Thorpe despite the vehement protests of the House of Commons. In 1450 York and the duke of Norfolk, according to *The Paston Letters*, had issued considerable propaganda in favour of better government, but Norfolk himself was twice imprisoned for violent conduct and by 1452, if not before, the evil activities of his affinity were notorious. Between 1450 and 1453 York's chamberlain, Sir William Oldhall, pursued political aims by methods little short of gangsterism. The Nevilles had joined York entirely for their own purposes and in more than one quarter their reputations were distinctly unsavoury. Salisbury possessed the greater part of a family 'lifelode' (livelihood), which by the recognized standards of the day should have passed to his nephew of the half-blood, Ralph, earl of Westmorland. According to *Davies' Chronicle*, he was so unpopular that, after the battle of Wakefield, 'the common people of the country which loved him not' lynched him — a statement which may well indicate that his record in Cumberland and Yorkshire approached that of Suffolk in East Anglia. As to his son, Warwick, the executors of Ralph, Lord Cromwell, claimed that he had forced a very unfavourable exchange of lands upon them and he cheated his own cousin, George Neville, out of his due share of the entailed estates of Isabella Despenser's inheritance in Glamorgan and Morgannwy. To look forward a little, Warwick, during the 1460s, was to becomed notorious for his 'insaciable covetise'. The soiled hands of York and his friends were far removed indeed from the lily-white purity of their public protesta- tions. As with the politicians of many countries today, high moral standards were the sticks with which to beat opponents rather than measuring rods for their own personal conduct. In 1461 the reputa- tion of the Yorkist inner group, both the quick and the dead, surrounding an inexperienced king of nineteen, could have given little cause for confidence in better government.

The young king, so far, had little to recommend him but physical beauty and a certain animal magnetism. Like his cousin Warwick, Edward of March inherited the powerful physique of their grand- father, Ralph of Raby. For those days, when most were shorter than they are today, Edward was a gigantic figure — six feet three and a half inches tall. All men admitted his extraordinary physical and sexual beauty: 'Beau prince entre les beaux du monde', as the cool Philipe de Commynes for once rhapsodized. Little seems to have been known of him outside the Yorkist armies in which he had fought during the previous eighteen months. While still earl of March, he had owned a copy of the pseudo-Aristotelian *Secreta Secretorum*, a by no means profound treatise on politics. Apart from this slender and dubious clue, there is nothing to show that he received anything like the thorough education given to his contemporaries Louis XI of France and Louis' brother Charles (Charles of France was studying Roman law at the age of twelve) — the kind of intensive grounding for kingship which both Commynes and Sir John Fortescue, in their different ways, thought essential for a future ruler. True, he had won a victory at Mortimer's Cross; but what did that really mean? Was he a precociously gifted commander or did he follow the advice of some more experienced older man? Only Coppini, at this early stage, with typical bravura wrote down his opinion of Edward's character, and Coppini can hardly be taken for an impartial judge. In the legate's opinion he was 'prudent and magnanimous' and a few months later he wrote that the population of the Kentish towns adored Edward like a god.

In spite of these extravagant remarks, the future, in March 1461, seemed far from bright. The section of the peerage which, since 1459, had swung over to the duke of York had done so more for political than dynastic reasons. Many of them, like the earl of Warwick, could have had little sympathy for his claim to the crown. They and most other people could hardly have been enthusiastic at the way so few men had so hastily placed Edward IV on the throne. They had lost confidence in Henry VI, but could they possibly have felt any greater confidence in an untried young man of nineteen? Among wider, less informed groups doubts prevailed, so much so that in 1462 even a group of peasants claimed the right to depose him should his rule prove to be oppressive!

7 Edward's First Reign, 1461 – 70

I

Edward IV's contemporary, the French *memorialiste*, Philippe de Commynes, most fervently held the opinion that God actively intervened in the affairs of princes, for the ruling potentates of this earth were far too powerful to be restrained or controlled by mortal means alone. Other men, though less explicit in their views, profoundly agreed with him. Although by this time they considered the judicial duel in civil and criminal cases to be somewhat disreputable, at the higher levels of politics they still adhered to the belief that God expressed his inscrutable judgment on the fate of princes in the clash of arms upon the field of battle.

Circumstances drove Edward to face divine judgment without delay. The Lancastrian army, though withdrawing to the north, remained undefeated — not only undefeated but attracting more and more recruits. Swift success in battle was vital both to the physical safety of the new king and to bestow manifest divine approval upon his legitimist hereditary claims. After the king's installation ceremonies the Yorkist lords dispersed to their various areas of influence to raise troops and possibly money. The later part of 1460 and the early months of 1461 saw the maximum military effort of the Wars of the Roses: in various areas there were at least 28 peers under arms for the Lancastrians and 20 for the Yorkists, at least four fifths of the surviving peerage — an aristocratic involvement in the dynastic struggle never, never to be repeated in the battles of the next three decades.

Edward, the duke of Norfolk and William Neville, Lord Fauconberg, left London between 11 and 13 March, advancing deliberately, somewhat slowly, towards the north to allow time for recruits from elsewhere to join their forces. By the time he reached Pontefract on 27 or 28 March Edward commanded an exceptionally large army by the standards of the day and the Lancastrians were probably even more numerous. The battle of Towton was far and away the greatest battle of the Wars of the Roses. It was fought on Palm Sunday in bitter northern weather, and the Lancastrian archers, blinded by the snow driven by the wind against them, failed to protect their infantry from the Yorkist charges. Even so, the fighting was long and bitter and it was only after many hours that the Lancastrian line broke and they, at last, fled the field.

Edward had won a shattering victory — a victory which for the time broke the power of the great northern families, the Percies, Cliffords, Roos and Dacres who (partly, it is true, out of fear and jealousy of the upstart younger branch of the Nevilles) had been so loyal to Henry VI, and who between them could control most of England north of the River Trent. Now, at least, it became possible for the Yorkists to subjugate the northern counties and the territory towards the Scottish border. Even so the perils of rebellion menacingly threatened the future. Diehard Lancastrains, if on the run, were still at large, to prove themselves formidable opponents both at home and in exile.

II

Edward, in spite of his victory, hung in a limbo of the tensest insecurity, facing three urgently inter-related problems: the need to broaden the dangerously narrow bases of Yorkist power, to repress continuing disorder and surviving pockets of resistance, especially in the north and west (disorder and political resistance were often far from easy for the government to distinguish) and to obtain diplomatic recognition abroad in order to prevent foreign interference in domestic affairs.

When parliament met on 4 November it was essential to give the impression of firm intentions to improve the state of the realm and to avoid any measures which would alienate a political nation whose reactions to the new regime were, to say the least, distinctly mixed. Edward, therefore, in spite of his almost desperate needs, made no demands for taxation, either direct or indirect. The speaker of the Commons made part of his opening oration a passionate exposition of the legitimacy of the Yorkist succession. This part of his speech was completely government-inspired and more or less reproduced the propagandist speeches made during the king's inauguration ceremonies the previous March. As propaganda, indeed, the speech was so effective that it became the basis of the Tudor myth of the fifteenth century — the myth which, surviving until very recently, depicted the dynastic struggle as a torrent of bloodshed and slaughter, God's righteous judgment upon a wicked country for rejecting the rightful heir and permitting the heinous sin of the Lancastrian usurpation.

The speaker, Sir James Strangways, a Neville connection, went on to express the hope that Edward would rule advised by those who had risked their lives and goods to recover his ancient title. The Nevilles and their followers, all the more so as they had only with the greatest reluctance dragged themselves into the dynastic conflict, expected and demanded all the power and material rewards befitting the members of a triumphant, if barely triumphant, faction. In addition to these views on patronage Strangways offered pungent advice upon the maintenance of public order. Edward did everything he could to show his good intentions. In an act of resumption he adopted as official policy what had begun as an opposition protest in 1449. Then on 21 December, the last day of the session, after Edward had personally thanked the members for their support, the chancellor told the assembly that the king had already issued an ordinance against maintenance and the giving of liveries and, somewhat quaintly in this context, thundered against the allegedly growing vices of dice and card-playing — possibly his own exhibition of conservative prejudice as card-playing seems to have been comparatively new in England. Altogether the royal propaganda exhibited an impeccable display of legitimacy and good intentions.

Parliament passed an act of attainder against 113 people, including 14 lay peers. Though the number may, at first sight, seem large and the policy of proscription vindictive, the number of anti-Yorkist peers, and lesser men, who were not attainted is probably the more remarkable. John Talbot, earl of Shrewsbury, Lord Ryvers and his son, Lord Scales, who had all fought on the Lancastrian side at Towton were pardoned. Lord Welles was attainted during the parliament. Though legally the corruption of blood which followed such a condemnation extinguished the rights of all descendants, his son Richard sat in this and the two following parliaments in his wife's right as Lord Willoughby.

Contemporary modes of thought assisted such swift political turnabouts. As remarked earlier, victory in arms was the supreme authentication of God's will and the battlefield almost a part of the inauguration ceremonies of monarchy. As the Almighty had shown his will in the battle of Towton many men, as Dr John Morton expressed it two decades later, were not disposed 'to labour to set up what God pulleth down'. They deserted Lancaster for a Yorkist government only too anxious to receive them. Edward's policy of mercy indeed roused discontent among some of his own supporters. As early as July 1461 it was reported from East Anglia that the common people 'grudge and say how that the king receiveth such of this country ... as have been his great enemies and oppressors of the commons: and such as have assisted his highness be not rewarded: and it is to be considered or else it will hurt.'

In some cases it proved all too true that such a policy of mercy did 'hurt', though in a rather different way. While many new adherents remained consistently and truly faithful, the loyalty of others was, to say the least, flickering. Sir Ralph Percy, a younger son of the second earl of Northumberland, slain at St Albans in 1455, fought for Henry VI at Towton, but submitted by Michelmas 1461 in time to avoid attainder. Edward took the risk of giving him command of the key fortress of Dunstanburgh. By the end of October 1462 he deserted to Margaret of Anjou, then two months later turned his coat yet again and, together with the duke of Somerset, surrendered Bamburgh and Dunstanburgh on condition that Edward left him in command of both fortresses. By mid-March 1463 he had the government's confidence to such an extent that he was given authority to receive repentant rebels, but, at about the same time, he went over to the Lancastrians yet again. Killed at Hedgley Moor the following year, he was finally attainted in 1465. Edward most probably used him both in an attempt to attract the notorious loyalty of the Percy tenants and to avoid the enormous cost of maintaining large garrisons under captains from outside the region.

Henry Beaufort, duke of Somerset, became the supreme example of the turncoat. Attainted in 1461, he remained with the Lancastrians in the Northumberland strongholds which still held out against the Yorkists. After his surrender, with Sir Ralph Percy, at Bamburgh and Dunstanburgh on Christmas Eve 1462, his captors led the duke to the king at Durham. Somerset's rank, his reputation as one of the staunchest of the Lancastrians and supposedly the paramour of Margaret of Anjou, made him the most superb advertisement for the policy of reconciliation and the king left nothing undone to show other Lancastrians that they might expect the most generous treatment if only they would conform. Early in March 1463 Edward reversed the duke's attainder and restored his estates. He supplied money on a lavish scale to meet the duke's immediate needs, granted him an annuity of £200 and another of the same amount to his mother, Eleanor, the dowager duchess. In the eyes of the world the king and the duke became inseparable friends. Edward frequently shared his bed with Somerset, took the risk of going hunting with him when three out of six of their attendants were the duke's servants. He arranged a magnificent tournament at Westminster, ostensibly to give Somerset pleasure after all his recent hardships and troubles. What Edward's real feelings were we shall never know. He was more than capable of the most extreme dissimulation and the fact that he continued to keep the duke's brother, Edmund, a prisoner in the Tower of London may well indicate that he had his suspicions.

Somerset's men formed the royal bodyguard. As an outraged London chronicler wrote, 'the guard of him was as men should put a lamb amongst wolves of malicious beasts', and the men of Northampton, with bitter memories of the Lancastrian sack of the town in 1461, were ready to lynch him.

Edward realized that he had gone too far. Recognizing danger if the resentments of his supporters became too great, he sent the duke to north Wales. The king may have regarded this as a temporary rustication to endure only until passions had died down. He did nothing to deprive the duke of the grants which he had made him but, owing to the chronic shortage of cash at the Exchequer, the duke's annuity and his mother's fell into arrears and his brother, Edmund, was still a prisoner in the Tower. Whether all these things together made the duke think that in the end Yorkist resentment would frustrate the king's generosity, that he and his family stood more to gain from a Lancastrian *révanche* with a dominating position over a grateful king and (if scandal be true) an enamoured queen, or whether a genuine remorse impelled him to desert Edward, we shall never know. Whatever his now obscure motives may have been, before the end of 1463 he fled out of Wales, rode hard for Newcastle, a town garrisoned, according to Gregory's *Chronicle*, by his own men. Recognized at Durham, and all but captured in his bed, he fled the place barefoot and in his shirt to rejoin Henry VI in Scotland. Captured and executed after a skirmish at Hexham in May 1464, he was again posthumously attainted in 1465.

Parallel with his efforts to win over former Lancastrians, Edward (for indeed he had no choice in the matter) took the speaker's advice to advance those who had supported his family. Patronage was the normal cement of any government and the aftermath of any revolution demanded its use upon a lavish scale. Influenced though they naturally were by his personal affections and dislikes, Edward based his promotions upon hard political considerations, upon the need to secure future services as well as to reward past loyalties. Some modern historians have interpreted his largesse at the highest level, over the next decade, as an attempt to create a new Yorkist nobility to counterbalance the indifference of the existing peerage — an expedient for supporting the throne by no means unique to the Yorkist era.[1]

Edward created no less than seven new barons in 1461, another six by 1470. During the same period he also created a dukedom, a mar-

---

[1]See above, p. 43.

quessate and eight new earldoms. These newly created peers, together with the Nevilles (and two of them, the northern Lords Ogle and Lumley had been retainers of Salisbury) and eight or ten of the older noble families, constituted his main support among the highest ranks of society during the first decade of his reign. It is possible to discern two groups, though in some degree they overlapped – those upon whom the king relied to dominate and discipline various areas of the countryside and a group who served to a far greater extent at court and in the royal council. The recipients of these honours were generally men rich enough in their own right to sustain their new dignities. Even so, the king deliberately built up the powers of the group marked out for local services by lavish grants of royal offices and estates in their own districts. His chamberlain, Lord Hastings, the son of a loyal Yorkist retainer and created a baron in 1461, he lavishly rewarded with grants which included the forfeited Leicestershire estates of the earl of Wiltshire, Viscount Beaumont and Lord Roos – grants so enormous that they transformed Hastings from a middling landowner into a magnate capable of dominating the central Midlands. Lord Herbert (also ennobled in 1461) gained such enormous wealth and power in south Wales that one admiring Welsh poet described him as 'King Edward's master lock' in the region. Lord Stanley, ennobled by the Lancastrians as recently as 1455, and as slippery a customer devoted entirely to self-interest as ever lived, through an accumulation of offices dominated Cheshire and part of north Wales. Lord Stafford of Southwick, another new creation, endowed with a great part of the lands of the attainted Courtenay earls of Devon, helped to dominate the southwestern counties. After his death in 1469 his mantle fell upon Lord Dynham, another of the new creations of 1461. The influence of the ex-Lancastrian Lord Scales was useful in East Anglia, that of the Greys of Ruthyn and Lord Wenlock in East Anglia. The earl of Arundel was powerful in Sussex and between them Lords Audley, Dudley and Mountjoy exerted a powerful influence in Staffordshire and on the Welsh borders.

At the centre the Bourchiers (the family of the earl of Essex who between them held several peerages), Lord Howard, Lord Ferrers of Chartley, Lord Dacre of the South and Lords Ryvers, Audley, Wenlock and Mountjoy were ready with their advice in the royal council.

The Nevilles, as befitted their decisive earlier support (self-interested in origin as this had always been), Edward rewarded on a lavish scale, though at the same time wisely restraining their more extreme ambitions. Warwick's uncle, William, Lord Fauconberg, created earl of Kent in 1461, in the following year received a grant of fifty-six manors to support his new dignity—manors in the west country forfeited by the earls of Devon and Wiltshire. His brother, John, created Lord Montague in 1461, in 1464 became earl of Northumberland, sustained with most of the Percy estates in Northumberland worth over £700 a year. Another brother, George, already placed in the bishopric of Exeter at the moment of Yorkist power in 1455, obtained the archbishopric of York in 1465.

As to Warwick himself, at the beginning of the reign the credulous statements of foreigners very much exaggerated his influence over the king. Even then Edward showed himself independent enough to avoid giving way to all the earl's territorial ambitions. The newly created Lord Herbert had been a client of both Richard, duke of York, and Warwick in south Wales. In 1461, Warwick hoped, with the king's help and grants, to rise to complete dominance in that area. Instead Edward chose to pass control to Herbert. Warwick's bitter resentment at this rebuff, never forgotten and hardly assuaged over the years, should at least have been tempered by royal grants elsewhere, so numerous that they put him in a class apart from all other men. The list of offices and estates granted to the earl is so enormous that it covers almost two closely printed pages of a modern book. Some of the patents, it is true, no more than confirmed him in old offices. Others vastly increased his power and influence in the danger zone of northern England, in line with the policy of entrusting great regional powers to a close circle of loyal supporters. All mitigating causes considered, however, the fact remains that the king was exceptionally lavish and the earl inordinately avaricious. Already the king's richest subject in his own right, now the scandal of his greed became a byword at home and abroad. An indignant English chronicler wrote that 'his insatiable mind could not be content and yet before him there was none in England of half the possessions that he had.' More precisely Philippe de Commynes claimed (though his claim may have been no more than an informed guess) that his offices alone brought him an annual income of 80,000 crowns.

Although fifteenth-century governments had no alternative but to rely upon the chain of command produced by patronage and bastard feudalism to rule the country, some historians have questioned the wisdom of the particular cast which, at this time, Edward gave to the system, claiming that an excessive proportion of the rewards available for distribution went to a precariously small number of men and 'that he might have obtained better dividends from the investment of political capital if his patronage had been spread more widely and evenly'[2]—spread more evenly among the

[2]C. Ross, *Edward IV* (1974), pp. 69 – 70, 333 – 41. See also T.B. Pugh, 'The Magnates, Knights and Gentry', in *Fifteenth-Century England, 1399 – 1509: Studies in Politics and*

gentry. It is a contention which may be true though it would be exceedingly difficult to prove and which perhaps takes too little account of the emergency circumstances of the early 1460s which demanded abnormal methods of control.

III

Public order had certainly deteriorated in many parts of the country over the two previous decades, owing less to the Wars of the Roses as such than to Henry VI's failure to control the nobility in the traditional way. While compelled to rely to a very great extent upon the local powers of his supporters, Edward reinforced them by his own example and his own activities. From the very first, true to his declarations in his first parliament, he showed a firm attitude towards disorders of any kind. In July 1461 one of his own servants, John Davy, had his hand smitten off at the standard in Cheapside for striking a man in the presence of the judges in Westminster Hall. In East Anglia the situation seems to have been particularly bad at this time (though it may merely be that we know more about it than other areas). The notorious Tuddenham-Heydon gang, which had originally grown up under the protection of Henry VI's minister, the duke of Suffolk, and afterwards of another court favourite, Lord Moleyns, had been rioting unchecked. There had been no hope of redress, for Sir Thomas Tuddenham had been treasurer of Henry's household, and Thomas Daniell, another member of this affinity, who was bitterly attacked in the political squibs of the day, had been a Squire of the Body.

At first the gentry of Norfolk feared that Edward would exploit his policy of reconciliation at their expense. In early June 1461 there was great depression when rumour went round that Tuddenham and Heydon had made their peace with the king through the good offices of his sister, Elizabeth, duchess of Suffolk, and that she had even

Society, ed. S.B. Chrimes, C.D. Ross and R.A. Griffiths (1972), pp. 91 – 3. Ross points out that under the Yorkists there was nothing comparable to Henry IV's expenditure in 1400 of £24,000 on annuities to build up a wide affinity. On the other hand it should not be forgotten that Henry IV's extravagance in this matter brought upon him great unpopularity and serious difficulties with the House of Commons because of the demands for direct taxation which partly resulted from it. Yet again this may not have been entirely a matter of deliberate choice for A.L. Brown ('The Reign of Henry IV', in *Fifteenth-Century England*, pp. 1 – 20), points out 'how few there were of the higher nobility to whom Henry could turn' in the early years of his reign, and 'only a small group of barons provided active members of the Lancastrian "establishment" ' and that 'the absence of a strong Lancastrian faction among the lords helps to explain why King Henry relied so much on knights and esquires.'

invited them to appear in her retinue at the coronation.

By July, to remedy the chronic conditions of disorder, which had reached a climax in the recent months of warfare, the Norfolk gentry were thinking of an appeal to the new king—an action which they had apparently regarded as hopeless under Henry VI. Whether or not a petition from East Anglia reached Edward is unknown. It probably did, for he was very well informed of the state of affairs there and his remedy was nothing less than to appoint as sheriff one of his most trusted officers, Sir Thomas Montgomery. In December the new sheriff, accompanied by William Yelverton, one of the justices of the King's Bench, went down to the county. Yelverton, Margaret Paston wrote, said openly 'in the sessions' that they had come to 'set a rule in the country'. Yelverton added there was not a knight in the royal household the king could worse have spared from the court at that time than Montgomery. Not only had Edward sent a trusted servant whom he could ill spare but he had personally discussed their charge at length with Montgomery and Yelverton before they left.

Sin, however, was by no means confined to one side and it was not only Lancastrians who broke the peace in East Anglia. It must have been particularly distressing to the king that some of his own supporters were drawing their weapons upon each other at such a time. Sir John Howard, an extremely hot-tempered, not to say bullying, cousin and follower of the Mowbray dukes of Norfolk, now (as on several later occasions) attempted to use his position at court in a manner which those who crossed his interests had ample cause to resent and fear. At this time he apparently thought that his services to the Yorkists (he had been knighted after the battle of Towton) would be cover enough for violent conduct, or that it might pass unnoticed in the midst of the general political turmoil. Within three months of Edward's accession the duke of Norfolk (himself, as mentioned earlier, an aristocratic thug of no mean reputation) had seized Caister Castle from the Pastons and, considering Howard's extremely intimate relations with the duke at this time, it is impossible that he could have been ignorant of the affair. Howard also made a forcible entry into one of the earl of Oxford's forfeited manors, which had long been a subject of dispute between the two families and which, being in the king's hands, had recently been allocated for the support of the royal household. According to the Pastons who, in spite of their complaints, were certainly far from blameless in the matter themselves, Howard behaved in the most violent manner at the Norfolk parliamentary election. It is impossible to arrive at the truth of the matter from two contradictory *ex-parte* statements about what occurred, but in the end Edward put both John Paston and Howard in the Fleet Prison for a time. Obviously in these early days Edward, as well as taking punitive measures against those Lancastrians who still refused to desert Henry VI, was obliged to exert firm discipline over some of his own supporters who, in the euphoria of victory, were taking vindictive action against their local rivals. If it was essential to the security of his throne that his supporters should be powerful in their own districts, it was no less essential that if possible (and it was not always possible where some of the greatest men were concerned) they should be made to exercise their power with a decent restraint.

Quick results were not perhaps to be expected. In spite of Sir Thomas Montgomery's appointment, in January 1462 Margaret Paston was writing to her husband that she had never heard of so much robbery and manslaughter before, that the people were beginning to 'wax wild', that men feared a 'common rising'. Yet Edward's intense interest in public order was no mere flash in the pan. In 1463 the king personally sat for three days in the Court of King's Bench and heard the case of a distressed widow; and on 2 December a signet warrant to the chancellor, ordering the issue of a commission of oyer and terminer to the mayor of Bristol and others to investigate riots which had occurred in the city and district, bears the endorsement in Edward's own handwriting:

> Cousin if ye think ye should have a warrant this our writing that suffice unto you ye may have one made in due form. We pray you it fail not to be done.

In 1464, once again in East Anglia, Richard Calle reminded John Paston that men had been hanged at every assize held over the last five years and Gilbert Debenham (an armigerous rogue whose own affairs would have come very badly out of any investigation) furiously accused the under-sheriff of indicting a hundred men since he came into office. When the assizes began at Melford a stern letter from the king was read out to the effect that justice should be done and that all oppressors of the people should be punished.

All through his reign Edward made the most extensive use of commissions of oyer and terminer and during the first part of his reign he was extremely active in progresses throughout his realm, mainly south of the River Trent and east of the Welsh borders. Many of these progresses were personal judicial tours, upon which one or more of the justices accompanied him. These personal efforts for the maintenance of order were so striking and so extensive that Dr J.G. Bellamy has claimed that Edward deliberately and consciously revived an earlier and more primitive idea of peripatetic monarchy, in which the king saw to the good of the realm by his personal attention to justice from area to area of the kingdom.

IV

The government was often unable to distinguish between disorder and political resistance. The repression of both went hand in hand and both combined with chronic fear of collusive foreign attacks — an almost continual nightmare which endured until the middle of 1464. In the north and parts of Wales, control remained barely nominal and even in other parts of the country it was often distressingly flimsy.

Early in 1462 these terrors reached a climax in a bizarre atmosphere of panic-stricken rumour. The government suspected that Margaret of Anjou, the duke of Brittany and Louis XI had all taken some part in fostering recent disturbances. Fear of widespread sedition became so acute that on 12 February the government appointed a powerful commission of twenty-five lords and ten judges to investigate treason and trespass in no less than twenty-five counties and eight cities, and they arrested the earl of Oxford and his eldest son. The scare began with a story that a captured spy had reported plans for a three-fold invasion of the realm. The duke of Exeter and the earl of Pembroke were to land at Beaumaris in north Wales, the duke of Somerset, Sir John Hungerford and Dr John Morton in Norfolk and Suffolk at the head of 60,000 Spaniards, and Sir John Fortescue was to lead yet another army of Spaniards and Frenchmen in an attack on Sandwich. Rumours mounted, mounted, mounted, until these three armies became no more than the advance guard to prepare the way for an overwhelming attack by Queen Margaret's father and the kings of France, Denmark, Aragon and Portugal with an invading force of 250,000 men. Even the duke of Burgundy was said to be in league with them.

The whole story was, of course, fantastic nonsense, no less in the extent of the alliances reported than in the logistic impossibility of the numbers said to be gathering for invasion. Nothing came of it. Nevertheless, Oxford and his son were hastily tried and executed for treason.

In the north of England the key to events lay in the attitude of Scotland and in the ability of the Lancastrians to take and hold the key fortresses of Alnwick, Bamburgh and Dunstanburgh — castles which changed hands with confusing rapidity until 1464. In September 1461 the Nevilles took Alnwick and Dunstanburgh, but the Lancastrian, William Tailboys, managed to recapture Alnwick during the winter, only for Lord Hastings to retake it again in July 1462.

In Scotland, the regent, Mary of Gueldres, wished to make peace with Edward, but James Kennedy, the powerful bishop of St Andrews, successfully opposed her desires, cast his weight behind Margaret of Anjou and, for some time, supported her various attempts to attack the Yorkists. In October 1462 Margaret, with a mere 800 men, sailed from Boulogne for northeastern England. This miserable little expedition was all that remained of the high hopes which had raised her spirits a few months before. Earlier in the year Louis XI of France, for his own purposes, had promised considerable help for her invasion in the hope of preventing the possible conclusion of an Anglo-Aragonese alliance which might frustrate his own schemes in Spain; intriguing in the complicated politics of Aragon and Catalonia, he was trying to gain possession of Roussillion and Cerdagne and his price to Margaret had been Calais. Over a period of four months, by the time she sailed, changing circumstances had transformed Margaret from a convenient tool of French policy into a diplomatic embarrassment and she embarked upon this pitiful expedition with the minimum help that Louis, to save his own face, could decently provide for an abandoned dupe. Alnwick, Bamburgh and Dunstanburgh opened their gates to the queen, but few people in the north rallied to her banners on this occasion — neither nobility, nor gentry, nor common people. They may well have detested her association with the ancient enemies of France and Scotland. Hearing of a Yorkist advance in strength (one contemporary source states that 2 dukes, 7 earls, 31 barons and 59 knights were with the king), within less than three weeks of her entry she abandoned the fortresses[3] and on 13 November took ship for Scotland. A storm scattered her tiny fleet but she herself reached Berwick in safety.

Meanwhile Lord Herbert and Lord Ferrers were trying to bring Wales to order. Although by the middle of 1462 they were successful in routing the Lancastrians there, except for the garrison of Harlech in the north, their success was to say the least superficial, the possibilities for future rebellion remained strong and the country for long remained vulnerable to a Lancastrian seaborne invasion.

In spite of this partial success in Wales and the recapture of the northern fortresses at the end of the year, 1462 had been a year of ceaseless anxiety, which had brought with it one political crisis after another. Yet Edward could look forward to 1463 in a mood of at least cautious optimism. Philip of Burgundy had stood firm for the house of York and a naval expedition against the French coast had taught Louis XI that it might, after all, be unwise to treat England as a mere sideshow in his diplomatic schemes.

Yet unlooked-for misfortunes followed. In March 1463 the

[3]The remaining defenders surrendered on Christmas Eve and Alnwick surrendered on 5 January 1463.

unstable, treacherous Sir Ralph Percy turned his coat yet again and allowed a force of French and Scots to re-occupy Bamburgh and Dunstanburgh and in May Sir Ralph Grey also turned over Alnwick to the Lancastrians. A large-scale Scottish invasion of the north followed these untimely events and June 1463 was an exceedingly black month for the Yorkists. Inexplicably, the Scottish troops panicked and fled at the approach of Warwick and his brother, Lord Montagu, who now swept for over sixty miles into southern Scotland, burning and pillaging as they pressed along. Lack of supplies then forced them to retire into England. Edward announced his intention of again invading Scotland but nothing came of the plan. Most probably lack of money frustrated any such punitive expedition. In June Parliament had granted the king £37,000 (the first grant of direct taxation which it has so far made to him) and the Convocation of Canterbury also granted £13,000, but probably most of the money had to be used to pay existing debts, particularly the arrears of the Calais garrison, always a pressing and urgent charge upon the government's desperately inadequate funds. Nevertheless, people noted this inactivity with marked disapproval.

Things so turned out, however, that the Scots came to terms without the need for any expensive punitive expedition. By the later part of 1463 the clouds at last were breaking for the Yorkist government. Negotiations which began at St Omer in August resulted, on 8 October, in a truce between England, France and Burgundy (Brittany was also included in its terms). It is true those terms were limited and the truce was to last for only one year, but it was a breakthrough which gave Edward a breathing-space, leaving him a freer hand to deal with Scotland and, above all, it gave the so-far hostile Bishop Kennedy the necessary push to negotiate with England.

Fortunately so, for the early months of 1464 saw a last spurt of Lancastrian activity, with a rising in Wales timed to coincide with another rising in the north, and widespread disorders in other parts of the country coinciding with both. Alarming as these events may have seemed at the time, tradition has probably endowed them with an exaggerated significance for the government had suppressed the movement in Wales by early March, and in the north in April and May routed the Lancastrians at Hedgley Moor and Hexham. These encounters hardly deserve the title of battle so long bestowed upon them for Hedgley Moor was no more than a failed Lancastrian ambush for a Yorkist escort, going north to meet the Scottish ambassadors who were coming to discuss peace terms and Hexham was a miserable little skirmish where all but five hundred Lancastrians are said to have deserted because their wages were unpaid. Then, recognizing their hopeless isolation, the northern fortresses, by the end of June, surrendered for the last time.

V

By the end of June 1464 the Yorkists seemed to be for the first time on the floodtide of success. On the first of the month Edward had concluded a fifteen-year truce with Scotland. Deprived of a refuge in Scotland, it seemed unlikely that the Lancastrians would ever again be able to take the offensive. Except at Harlech, their resistance had completely collapsed. Somerset was dead, Queen Margaret had taken refuge with her father. Henry VI was a hunted fugitive, concealed no man knew where. Negotiations had begun with the Hanseatic League, Denmark, Castile, Poland and the Teutonic Order. Louis XI, although he was openly professing friendship for Philip the Good, really wished for an Anglo-French alliance against Burgundy. Both he and Philip had now become eager for an English marriage alliance — a desire which shows the degree to which Yorkist prestige had risen since 1461 when Philip, although well disposed, had not been prepared even to consider marriage negotiations with so insecure a dynasty. The English continued with the proposals which they had put forward at the first conference of St Omer. Their aim for the time was a triple alliance between England, Burgundy and France. Good relations with their two most important, and potentially aggressive, neighbours would leave them free to deal with their improved, but still difficult, domestic problems.

In the middle of the new diplomatic *détente*, and somewhat to its detriment, and in the midst of the troubles in the north, on May Morning 1464 Edward married. According to the chronicler Fabyan:

> In the most secret manner upon the first day of May King Edward spoused Elizabeth late the wife of Sir John Grey, Knight ... which spousals were solemnized early in the morning at a town named Grafton near unto Stoney Stratford. At which marriage was no persons present, but the spouse, the spousess, the duchess of Bedford, her mother, the priest, two gentlewomen, and a young man to help the priest sing.

Edward was twenty-four when he plunged into this rash, impulsive alliance, a man so handsome and vigorous that he might have been created for the pleasures of the flesh. Rumour had spread that people feared 'he was not chaste of his living' and he may (though the matter is doubtful) have already achieved the reputation for lechery which has caused some modern historians to give him such a bad press. Edward lived in an age when marriages were nicely calculated according to social rank and by these standards his marriage was so decidedly eccentric that later on her political enemies could plausibly accuse the new queen's mother of practising witchcraft to bring it about; and at the international level it threw away a tremendous diplomatic advantage.

In spite of the sneers hurled at her *petite extraction*, then and ever since, the new queen's origins were by no means as lowly as many people have claimed. Her mother, Jacquetta, duchess of Bedford, was the daughter of Pierre de Luxembourg, one of the most powerful magnates of France not of the blood royal. Nor were her father's family, the Wydevilles, exactly 'raised from the dust'. They were a respectable enough dynasty who had provided members of parliament since the middle of the fourteenth century, a decent run-of-the-mill family of gentlemen bureaucrats who had thriven by service to the great. The new queen's grandfather had been steward to the famous John, duke of Bedford, and Henry VI had created her father Lord Ryvers as early as 1449. Her brother, Anthony, married the widowed Lady Scales probably in 1461, thus becoming a baron in his wife's right. In spite of their Lancastrian background, Edward treated them generously and, unlike some others, they returned his generosity with consistent fidelity, and Lord Ryvers was already a royal councillor well over a year before his daughter became queen.

How Elizabeth and Edward first met is unknown, but having met her the king became completely infatuated, perhaps even as the result of her refusal to become his mistress. It was said somewhat later, perhaps even at the time, that Elizabeth Wydeville, thinking herself too base to be the king's wife but too good to be his harlot, was one of the few women ever to deny Edward Plantagenet her bed. As early as 1468 the Milanese courtier-poet Antonio Cornazzano was writing: 'she still refused him even when he placed a dagger at her throat'.

The story may do no more than give a melodramatic colouring to rather squalid facts — facts, typically enough for the times, concerned with a family squabble over property. The widowed Lady Grey had solicited the help of her powerful Leicestershire neighbour, Lord Hastings, the king's chamberlain, in her attempts to gain a decent jointure against the rapacity of her mother-in-law, Lady Ferrers, who had very powerful Yorkist connections indeed, and Hastings may well have brought her case to the king's attention. Typically enough for the times, Hastings also looked after his own interests at the widow's expense,[4] which may have been the origin of the acute dislike she felt for him in later years.

[4]On 13 April 1464 Elizabeth and Hastings signed an indenture providing for the marriage of her son, Thomas Grey (or in the event of his death that of his younger brother, Richard) to the eldest daughter of Lord Hastings to be born within the next five or six years, with provision for a marriage to a daughter of his brother, Ralph, or his sister, Anne, if no daughter were born to him. If any manors or possessions which had once belonged to Sir William Astley (the great-grandfather of Elizabeth's dead husband, Sir John Grey) or any of the inheritance of Lady

Edward kept his marriage secret until September, when he was forced to reveal it at a great council held at Reading, for the lords of the council then discussed a diplomatic marriage for the king. Extreme astonishment and, most probably, hostility were their immediate reactions, but the persistence of their preliminary hostility should not be exaggerated.

When the time came, in May 1465, for his wife's coronation, Edward with his usual flair for propaganda turned the situation to good account. He invited his wife's powerful uncle, Jacques de Luxembourg, with a retinue of a hundred people. The ceremonies were magnificent. Edward created fifty Knights of the Bath, more than he had dubbed at his own coronation. In spite of his father's treason in 1462 they included John de Vere, earl of Oxford, who also acted as Great Chamberlain at the coronation. Lord Grey of Ruthyn was created earl of Kent and Warwick's close associate, Walter Blount, Lord Mountjoy.[5] No one could possibly complain that her husband heaped honours upon the new queen's family alone. Edward used his wife's coronation to show even more publicly what his pardons to individuals had shown since 1461, that he wished to let old animosities expire and to welcome all who would come in to serve the new regime.

In an age when the personal relationships between the king and the greater landowners, rather than ideology, dominated politics and the royal court was so much the centre of patronage that we can regard it almost as the stock exchange of the day, marriage with a subject was bound to raise somewhat abnormal tensions. The conventions of the day expected, even demanded, that those about the court should receive due reward and the inevitable gains of the queen's family would, to an unusual degree, attract jealous and resentful comment from other groups who, equally inevitably, wanted a greater share of the available profits for themselves. The queen was cursed with a large family and during the next three years the Wydevilles and the Greys cornered the most lucrative investments of the day, the very top levels of the feudal marriage market. By the middle of 1467 they had arranged and completed a series of seven great marriages — marriages to the exalted families of Buckingham, Exeter, Norfolk, Arundel, Essex, Grey of Ruthyn and Herbert. Their success became notorious

---

Ferrers could be recovered for the two boys, the rents and profits were to be divided equally between Hastings and Lady Grey until Thomas was twelve years old or until Richard reached the same age if Thomas should die. Hastings agreed to pay 500 marks for the marriage. If Thomas and Richard died before it took place, or if there were no female issue in his own family, Hastings himself was to receive 500 marks. It was a very hard bargain!

[5]They were already closely associated and some time before 27 November 1467 Mountjoy married Warwick's aunt, Anne, dowager duchess of Buckingham.

enough for open satire. Edward's court jester, in the king's very presence, could jibe that in some counties the 'Ryvers' were so high that it was impossible to get through them.

With a remarkable diversity of views, some historians have alleged that the blindly enamoured king allowed the queen's relations unbridled licence to indulge their ambitions and their avarice in this way, others that he married them off as part of a well-considered policy of building up a new nobility as a counterpoise to the old. Neither of these speculations seems to be very plausible. As we have seen, Edward had no wish to suppress the older nobility. On the contrary he was doing everything he could to attract them to his throne and, like other kings before him, he had already elevated loyal servants to the ranks of the peerage. It is difficult to see in the Wydeville and the Grey marriages any attempt, either short or long term, to build up an entirely new royalist 'party'. At the most the king may have hoped to strengthen his ties with men already ennobled. Lord Herbert had already been created a baron in 1461 and was already one of the king's staunchest and most influential supporters. Lord Grey of Ruthyn was cousin-german to the queen's first husband and he had been created earl of Kent before his son's marriage to Joan Wydeville. The Bourchiers (the family of the earl of Essex) were already connected by marriage with both the king and the Wydevilles.

The legend of supposed widespread hostility to all these marriages derives mainly from careless interpretation of the *Annales* formerly attributed to William Worcester. Even the very pro-Neville writer of this chronicle did not, however, cover them with a universal condemnation. He singled out four marriages for special comment, three of which in some way affected Warwick's own interests or those of near relations whose support he was anxious to retain. The Mowbray dukes of Norfolk deeply resented the marriage of their sixty-seven year-old dowager, Warwick's aunt, Catherine Neville, to the queen's brother, Sir John Wydeville, then aged nineteen. For thirty years the old woman had been a family nuisance, holding in jointure an unduly large proportion of the Mowbray family estates with which she had already enriched two successive husbands. It was not always an easy matter for a family to regain possession of jointure lands and it might well prove difficult to induce Sir John Wydeville to disgorge his elderly wife's jointure estates after her death. In fact the king does seem to have given the Mowbray family some safeguards about the future of these estates. Even so, Warwick may have felt it advisable to uphold his ducal cousin's grievance in such a matter if he hoped for the future support of a powerful nobleman.

In 1466, William Herbert's son, who had married Mary Wydeville, was given the title Lord Dunster—an incident most annoying to Warwick as he had very much coveted the lordship of Dunster, as part of his plans for increasing his power in south Wales, when the king had granted it to the Herberts in 1461. This was really rubbing salt into open wounds. More directly, the marriage of the queen's eldest son, Thomas Grey, to Anne Holland, the heiress of the duchy of Exeter, was an affront, for Anne Holland was already betrothed to Warwick's nephew, George, the son of his brother, John, Lord Montagu.[6]

There is no convincing evidence that Warwick showed his resentment immediately in spite of Stubbs's disobliging comment that he was furious at being baffled 'by the arts of a woman or the infatuation of a boy'. Even the pseudo-William Worcester referred only to his 'secret displeasure', and in only one case—that of the title of Lord Dunster—did even this biased writer claim that other members of the nobility shared his resentment. The nobility in general, in fact, seem to have accepted the consequences of the king's marriage without difficulty and some saw in the Wydeville connection a useful additional link with influence in high places. The Second Anonymous Croyland Continuator, the best informed writer of the period, claimed that the royal marriage did not originally alienate Warwick, that he showed considerable favour to the queen's kindred until he found that they supported the king's own preference for a pro-Burgundian foreign policy against Warwick's equally strong determination for an alliance with France.

This may have been similarly one-sided comment for, the rest of the nobility apart, Warwick had a justifiable family grievance in the implications of the Wydeville and Grey marriages upon the matrimonial prospects of his own two daughters and co-heiresses. A great nobleman had the traditional right to expect that the king would assist his family in such matters: that was one of the aspects of 'good lordship'. Warwick was England's premier earl and his daughters were the wealthiest heiresses in the realm. Only the major English families, so it is claimed, could provide them with suitable husbands and the matrimonial triumphs of the queen's family had swept the board clear. Only the king's younger brothers remained as possible husbands and Edward firmly set his face against marriages such as these. This argument,[7] however, can be pushed too far.

---

[6]The marriage of Catherine Wydeville to the duke of Buckingham (then a child) according to the *Annales* caused Warwick 'secret displeasure'. That of Margaret Wydeville to Lord Maltravers, the eldest son of the earl of Arundel had little effect, Arundel was Warwick's brother-in-law and he does not seem to have been at all active at court.

[7]See the arguments developed by C.D. Ross, 'The Reign of Edward IV', pp. 50−51 and T.B. Pugh, 'The Magnates, Knights and Gentry', p. 88, in *Fifteenth-Century England*, ed. Chrimes, Ross and Griffiths.

Warwick may indeed have nourished a genuine grievance in all this. On the other hand, exceptionally voluble sentiments of snobbery may have been little more than a cover for his failure to dominate Edward. Most people in the late fifteenth century seem to have held no particular prejudice against marriages between noble and gentry families if the gentry families were only rich enough. If Warwick did, indeed, object on principle to such marriages to newly created peers or mere gentlemen as being disparaging for the women of the older nobility (and few of them were anyway very old), it is somewhat disconcerting to find that within eleven years two of his own sisters and one of his aunts contracted such appalling *mésalliances*.

The Grey and Wydeville marriages cost the king very little. Nor can he be accused of wasting his substance upon either his wife herself or upon her male relations. Though magnificent, the queen's coronation was economically managed. It cost a mere £900 as compared with over £5,000 lavished upon the reception of Margaret of Anjou when she arrived in England. Elizabeth's dower was modest compared with those of her predecessors and her household was always more economically run than Margaret's had ever been.

In March 1466 her father, Lord Ryvers, replaced Lord Mountjoy, who shortly afterwards married Warwick's aunt, Anne Neville, the dowager duchess of Buckingham, in the lucrative office of treasurer of England, with its annual fee of £1,330, not to mention the fees to which its holder was entitled from the public; in May Edward raised him to the rank of earl, but he never endowed him with land. Three of Ryvers's sons, including the eldest, Anthony, Lord Scales, also received comparatively little, and the fourth, Lionel, although he became archdeacon of Oxford at the age of nineteen, had to wait until he was twenty-nine before he received the bishopric of Salisbury. The Wydevilles and the Greys may have cornered the marriage market; otherwise, by contemporary standards their royal connection brought them no more than reasonable financial advantages. With the single (and only partial) exception of Lord Ryvers himself, they never enjoyed the golden shower of lands, wardships and profitable offices which, since 1461, had fallen upon the Nevilles and upon the newly ennobled like Hastings and Herbert. Others, including the Nevilles, still received more than the Wydevilles after 1464. Jealousy may have endowed them with a reputation for avarice, but Edward saw to it that they did not exercise it at his expense. With the exception of Warwick and his marital grievances, none of the nobility who served the king, whatever their origins, could realistically complain that he had starved them of his patronage for the sake of his wife's family.

VI

The years between the surrender of the Northumbrian castles in 1464 and the beginning of certain mysterious tensions in 1467 were the most uneventful which Edward had so far enjoyed. In 1465 the fugitive Henry VI was captured at last. Despite the progressive development of Warwick's personal feud with the king, in this period of comparative calm the government attempted quite significant reforms in financial and administrative matters. In 1464, with the consent of the great council, Edward ordered a debasement of the coinage, for motives partly technical, partly political. A recent stagnation in the output of coin—Edward alleged that the English mints were receiving no gold nor silver because merchants could get more for their bullion in foreign mints—had produced an inconvenient scarcity of money. Debasement was, therefore, essential for the sake of trade. On the other hand, for political reasons, he may well have wished to destroy the Lancastrian currency and by levying unusually high seignorial charges he made a most welcome windfall profit of about £15,000.

A number of other financial measures all seem to have been part of a concerted plan of reform. Edward (or his advisers) began by introducing some sense of reality into the Exchequer. In April orders were sent to the Exchequer staff to abandon their expensive time-consuming efforts to collect hopeless debts, some of them going back nearly a century, thus uselessly annoying the debtors' heirs and hindering the efficient conduct of up-to-date affairs. The ulnage duties which had been farmed since 1426 were placed under direct administration once again.[8] As we have already noted Edward, poor as he was, had not ventured to ask for a grant of direct taxation until two years after his accession. Then until the beginning of 1465 he had collected the customs duties without bringing the matter before parliament. In January 1465 he astutely raised the question to coincide with another act of resumption, and parliament granted him the customs for life instead of for a limited term of years, which had been the usual form of the grant.[9] The following year he concluded the first act of retainer with the Merchants of the Staple, under which they took over the administration of certain parts of the customs revenues and made themselves responsible for the payment of the Calais garrison.

---

[8]This attempted reform was, however, apparently unsucessful as there was a return to farming in 1478.

[9]Only twice before had they been granted for life, in 1415 and 1453.

By 1467 Edward at last began to break even financially. In June he personally told parliament:

> The cause why I have called and summoned this my present Parliament is that I purpose to live upon mine own and not to charge my subjects but in great and urgent causes, concerning the weal of themself ...

and he accompanied this statement with yet another act of resumption.

The king's speech, indeed, was like a siren song to that particular assembly for it gave expression to a policy which parliament after parliament had loudly demanded under Henry VI. It was a subject not lightly to be mentioned to a group of people always exceptionally alert when financial matters were discussed. Before he ventured to make such promises Edward must have been reasonably certain that the effects of his acts of resumption, combined with a new system of estate administration tentatively begun as early as 1462,[10] were by this time successful enough to allow him to keep his word. Circumstantial evidence points to his ability to keep his promises. The financial year Michelmas 1466 to Michelmas 1467 was the first in which the royal household had a surplus of a few hundred pounds above its expenditure, whereas previously its deficits had run into thousands.[11]

Diplomatic affairs likewise progressed. The choice lay between a Burgundian alliance and a French alliance. Commercial elements in the country were strongly divided in their opinions. Strong anti-Burgundian sentiments among some of the London artisan groups, resentful of competition from a wide range of industrial products imported from various provinces of the Netherlands, made a French alliance feasible. On the other hand the prospects of a pro-French, anti-Burgundian alliance ran counter to other, and stronger, trading interests—those of the Staplers and the Merchant Adventurers, whose export markets and whose complementary financial arrangements made friendship with Burgundy essential, though the Adventurers also wished the government to put strong pressure upon the duke of Burgundy to reduce trade restrictions which inhibited the export of English cloth.

Towards the end of 1464 Edward IV was playing a nerve-racking double game with Burgundy, France and Brittany. By mid-September, however, he had obviously made up his mind against any alliance with France. It was an alliance which Louis XI desperately wanted, for he feared an attack on Normandy by a cruising English fleet and in France itself opposition to his centralizing policies was ominously growing—an opposition which, the following year (1465),

[10]See above, chapter 3, pp. 70 ff.
[11]See above, chapter 3, p. 83.

reached its peak in the War of the Public Weal. After coming to an agreement with the rebels, however, Louis recovered his nerve, decided to take a more aggressive line and, at the end of December 1465, formally declared war upon England, though nothing came of the declaration.

Warwick, for the time, worked hand in hand with the king, in March 1466 going abroad with an embassy to meet, first, a Burgundian mission at St Omer and, afterwards, a French mission at Calais. The meeting at St Omer was the first occasion on which the earl of Warwick ever met Charles, count of Charolais, the heir of Duke Philip the Good of Burgundy. Not only were these Anglo-Burgundian discussions completely fruitless, but according to the Croyland Continuator, Warwick took a personal dislike to Charolais, a dislike so violent that it finally tipped the balance of his relationship with the king, made him the more adamantly determined upon a French alliance and finally drive him into intransigent opposition.

For the next two years, English diplomacy remained in a condition more or less of stalemate. From October 1466 until early in 1468 Edward's sister, Margaret of York, became the focus of diplomatic intrigue. Margaret was an interesting, though by no means an entirely attractive, figure. At the age of twenty-two, at the time of her marriage, her good name was already so blown upon that she had achieved the reputation of a whore. On the very eve of her marriage her husband issued a proclamation that any man who repeated the current scandalous tales about her would be tied in a sack and thrown into the River Daame. In the luxurious and cultivated court of Burgundy in which she married she became a discriminating patron of the arts and in her widowhood 'mine old lady of Burgundy' was a formidable politican, a thorn in the flesh of Louis XI and of Henry VII of England for many years.

Immediately, however, Louis was putting up a French bridegroom for Margaret of York, proposing to offer Edward a pension of 4,000 crowns a year and offering the most favourable proposals for a commercial treaty. On the other hand, Charles the Bold, who had succeeded his father in June 1467, proved himself a formidably tough negotiator, who forced Edward to submit to some distinctly unpalatable conditions as the negotiations went on.[12] Edward, always careful of influential opinion in England, particularly that of the nobility, took the precaution during these negotiations of consulting the lords in great councils. Finally on 20 November 1467 his ambassadors signed a new commercial treaty with Burgundy to last for thirty years. Then came an unexpected, most disconcerting setback. Charles the Bold agreed on a six months' truce with Louis

[12]See below, p. 246.

XI, a truce which made Edward so suspicious of Charles's good faith that he refused to ratify the commercial treaty and, instead, appointed a new embassy.

VII

Diplomatically Edward faced the New Year in 1468 in a most unenviable position. He had played a double game with a nerve which Louis XI himself might have envied. He had rightly judged that Louis XI had proposed impossibly great commercial concessions and had therefore rejected the French alliance. In view of the conflicting interests which Edward had to face at home, however, his policy and methods could be justified only by success. He had bitterly offended the interests of the London artisans by his own concessions to Burgundy without obtaining reciprocal concessions which would have satisfied the cloth exporters. Lord Wenlock and Thomas Kent who, it is true, were very much of the Warwickite interest, claimed that men in the London taverns were saying openly and angrily that the councillors who favoured the Burgundian alliance deserved to lose their heads. Edward's policy seemed shattered, and the rift between the king and Warwick had widened. Edward must have been relieved that he had shared responsibility for his Burgundian policy with the lords in the great council.

Nor was everything smooth on the domestic front. The quieter years after the end of 1464 were not entirely free of anxieties. Late in 1466 Warwick demanded the hand of the king's eldest brother, George, duke of Clarence, for his daughter, Isabella. Though Edward rejected such a close family alliance, he had no wish to break with the earl and allowed him to go on negotiating with the French, who flattered his colossal vanity by treating him with almost royal honours and lavishing the most expensive presents on him. Yet, because Warwick would tolerate nothing less than a dominating position, the rift between king and earl, the Nevilles and the Wydevilles, rapidly widened. Probably because of their family connections at the court of Burgundy, the king employed Earl Ryvers and Lord Scales in those negotiations with Charles the Bold, which outclassed Warwick's discussions with the French.

By the middle of 1467 Edward had come to the point of showing the Nevilles that, powerful as they had become, they were still subjects and must behave as such. In June while Warwick was abroad, Edward deprived George Neville of the chancellorship probably because of his obstructive attitude towards the Burgundian negotiations. Two months later he unwisely allowed himself the indulgence of vicious irony. George Neville had been intriguing to be made a cardinal but, in September when instead the pope bestowed the coveted red hat upon the archbishop of Canterbury, Edward spitefully sent the pontifical letter to the archbishop of York.

Meanwhile, disorders, obscure and otherwise, continued. By the end of 1466 the government was disturbed enough to allow the sheriffs over a wide area funds for spying. In 1467 parliament complained of the need to repress murder, riots and other notorious outrages. In the autumn Lord Herbert, while laying siege to Harlech, the last of the Lancastrian strongholds captured a messenger from Queen Margaret. The messenger, under interrogation, accused many people of treason, and even accused Warwick himself of Lancastrian sympathies. Edward had already, in August, taken the precaution of appointing Earl Ryvers constable of England, with entirely new and quite special powers which included authority to try treason cases and, after the revelations of the Lancastrian messenger, he took the precaution of organizing a bodyguard of two hundred men.

Early in 1468, as part of an attempt to patch up an agreement, Warwick consented to attend a meeting of the royal council at Coventry from which, for the sake of peace, the Wydevilles stayed away. Though Edward had refused to allow the earl's family a royal marriage, and though he naturally refused to hand over control of his foreign policy to a subject, he went to very considerable lengths to pacify Warwick. All Warwick's grants, except those which had been made for a term of years had been exempted from the resumption act of 1467. A whole series of new grants meant that he probably lost very little, for among other things Edward appointed him constable and steward of the duchy of Lancaster lordship of Kenilworth and had granted him the wardship and marriage of Francis, Lord Lovell, one of the richest minors in the realm. The Nevilles may not have been politically dominant but the king was immensely careful to give Warwick nothing to grumble about financially.

Warwick and his friends continued to attend council meetings during the year and on some matters they were by no means uninfluential, but the pro-Burgundians succeeded in foreign policy. Edward had re-opened negotiations to such good effect that he concluded a marriage treaty on 14 March 1468 and, in spite of the difficulties of raising loans to pay the first instalments of an immense dowry of 200,000 gold crowns (£44,666 13s. 4d.), Margaret of York left for Bruges on 18 July, for marriage ceremonies of such lavish splendour that one dazzled Englishmen wrote home that the like had never been seen since the days of King Arthur's court.

Meanwhile in May Edward had declared war on France, possibly more as a defensive measure against the disappointed and furious Louis XI than with any serious intentions of conquest. He made no plans comparable with his later intensive preparations of 1472 – 5 and he may well have thought principally in terms of assistance to allies, mainly Brittany and Burgundy, who would bear the brunt of war. Both very quickly defected: Brittany in September in face of a French invasion, and in October Charles the Bold in the treaty of Peronne promised not to assist the English if they invaded France and agreed to a truce. Yet in spite of these disappointments, Edward, diplomatically, ended the year in a far better position than he had begun it. He very quickly renewed close relations with Brittany and Burgundy. He was at peace with Scotland, had signed treaties with Denmark, Naples and Castile and in October, after months of negotiation, concluded a treaty of alliance with John II, king of Aragon. Although for the moment there was little possibility of aggression, the diplomatic encirclement of France was complete.

It was well for Edward that he had secured so fair a position diplomatically for at home one of the worst scares of the reign was simultaneously reaching its climax. At the end of May or the beginning of June 1468, Hugh Mille, the son of a Lancastrian knight who had been attainted in 1461, already imprisoned in the Fleet, was transferred to the Tower of London on suspicion of treason and a week after Whitsun, a certain Cornelius, a servant of the exiled Lancastrian, Sir Robert Whittingham, was captured near Queenborough in Kent. Lack of direct evidence combined with a tangle of *ex-parte* statements makes it difficult to judge whether an extensive, well-organized conspiracy menaced the king at this time or whether the government, in an atmosphere explosive with personal jealousies and personal rivalries over-reacted under the stress of long-continued rumours and determined to remove any possible leaders of a Lancastrian rebellion. In the end general uncertainty produced conditions so laden with suspicion and terror that the actions of both Edward and his opponents (especially those of his opponents) degenerated into a vindictiveness notably absent in the civil conflicts since the death of Edmund Beaufort in 1455.

Cornelius, put to torture in the Tower of London by means of hot irons applied to his feet, accused a number of people, including a sheriff and an alderman of London, and John Hawkins, a servant of Lord Wenlock. Hawkins, also tormented on the 'brake', called 'the duke of Exeter's daughter', in turn accused another London alderman Sir Thomas Cook and 'said a good many things against Lord Wenlock' ('dixitque multa contra dominum suum proprium de Wenlok').

If this had been all, the government might well have become alarmed. Worse was to come. Early in July Jasper Tudor with a tiny French force (only about fifty men) landed near Harlech intending to join forces with its Lancastrian defendants. Although he was quickly defeated and although Harlech then finally surrendered, sinister rumours continued to spread. Jasper Tudor's arrival so soon after the revelations of Cornelius must have shaken Edward's nerves very badly indeed. Even for a man of his physical strength and equable temperament the strain of the last few months must have been harrowing. By the beginning of August he was in such a state of panic at the prospect of renewed invasion that he ordered his officers to requisition every ship in every port in the realm and by October Earl Ryvers's duties as constable had become so onerous that a special clerk was appointed to assist him.

The government ordered the arrested Londoners to be put on trial as evidence of more‘ plotting came sweeping in. Letters from Margaret of Anjou were reaching the country through a London skinner, Richard Steres, a merchant with a most suspicious past. In 1460 he had been so very pro-Lancastrian that he had been accused of attempting to murder the earl of Warwick. Arrests now extended far beyond the circle of suspected London merchants. Sir Thomas Hungerford and Sir Henry Courtenay, the titular earl of Devon, were arrested in Wiltshire and imprisoned at Salisbury. Both bore grudges against the king. Hungerford had failed to recover some of his father's lands and Edward had never reversed the attainder of Courtenay's brother and had restored to him only a fraction — possibly less than a quarter — of the family estates.

The next arrest was sensational, no less a man than the earl of Oxford whose father and brother had been executed in the invasion scare of 1462. Suspicions about Oxford must have been exceptionally disturbing and his arrest particularly dramatic after Warwick's apparent reconciliation with the king for he had only recently married the earl's sister, Margaret. The plots of Hungerford, Courtenay and Exeter seem (as far as we can see) to have had no connection with the London plots earlier in the year, but the earl of Oxford's imprisonment in the Tower, where his father and his elder brother had spent their last hours only six years before, terrified him into confessing a great deal. He revealed that John Poynings and William Alford, two young men who had gone to Bruges in the retinue of the duchess of Norfolk for the Burgundian wedding, had there been in touch with Edmund Beaufort, the titular duke of Somerset.[13] By mid-November the yeomen of the crown were riding

---

[13]The younger brother and heir of Henry, duke of Somerset, executed in 1464.

into many counties to arrest more suspects. Among them, implicated by Oxford's confession, was another prominent figure, Sir Thomas Tresham. Like Hungerford and Courtenay, Tresham belonged to a group of men whom the king had treated more cautiously and less generously than people like Somerset and Sir Ralph Percy. He had been speaker in the Parliament of Devils which had attainted the Yorkists in 1459. In turn he was himself attainted in 1461. Like Hungerford and Courtenay, Tresham had been pardoned but remained impoverished. The royal pardon did not restore his forfeited estates. He had to buy them back from various grantees. To do so he had been obliged to borrow money from friends and was probably deep in debt at this time. With such men, Edward may not have taken his policy of reconciliation far enough. It seems highly probable that the hard core of Lancastrians in exile had been trading both on the discontent of some of Warwick's friends and on that of men who had some reason to feel dissatisfied with the treatment they had received compared with others who had made their peace with the Yorkists, and who may, therefore, have been prepared to take desperate chances to recover their positions.

Oxford was soon released. His new relationship with Warwick, or the way in which he had turned king's evidence, may have saved him. Tresham was kept in prison. Poynings, Alford and Steres were all executed in London on 28 November. In January 1469 Hungerford and Courtenay were tried before a commission of oyer and terminer at Salisbury and executed on a charge of conspiring to assist Margaret of Anjou to invade England.

After these terrors the first few months of 1469 were peaceful enough — a deceptive calm before the most disastrous two years of Edward's entire reign. In February the archbishop of York received a valuable grant of land and Warwick himself was regranted certain estates on more favourable terms. Later in the month Warwick, Lord Wenlock and others were commissioned to survey the boundaries of the Calais pale. If Edward had distrusted Warwick's good faith at this time, he would hardly have allowed him to go there, knowing from experience how valuable a springboard the town was for an attack on England. Peace was broken once again when, early in April, Robin of Redesdale revolted in south Yorkshire. Warwick's brother John, earl of Northumberland, suppressed the tumult, only to be faced almost immediately by another in the East Riding led by Robin of Holderness which, according to the only contemporary source mentioning it, was intended to restore Henry Percy IV, a prisoner in the Tower of London, to the earldom of Northumberland. This John Neville had also suppressed by the end of May, and had beheaded the leader, only to be faced in early June by a new, and greater, rebellion led once again by Robin of Redesdale. Though his identity is not absolutely certain, there is some reason to believe that 'Robin' was Sir John Conyers of Hornby, the husband of Warwick's cousin, Alice, the daughter of the former Neville earl of Kent. But if Warwick was involved in any way the king so far had no suspicions of it for as late as 22 May he personally included Warwick in a commission of oyer and terminer for the whole realm and another for the counties of York, Northumberland and Westmorland and the city of York.

In his relief from the most acute of his anxieties, Edward was altogether too trusting at this time. Even so, he determined to go north himself, but immediately thinking John Neville capable of carrying out any necessary police work there, went on a progress through East Anglia combined with a pilgrimage to the shrine of Our Lady of Walsingham. Shortly afterwards his brother Clarence went to Canterbury. After spending two days there he rode on to Sandwich to meet the earl of Warwick who had returned from Calais. The archbishop of York, the bishop of London and the prior of Christ Church, Canterbury all followed. There was nothing particularly suspicious in this gathering for Warwick had either rebuilt, or refitted, one of his ships, the *Trinity*, for the king's use and a ceremony was being held for blessing the ship. Some days of vacillation followed, for Warwick and Clarence rode to London, then back to Sandwich whence, on 6 July, together with the archbishop of York and probably the earl of Oxford, they sailed for Calais. On 11 July at Calais, Clarence married Isabella Neville. Warwick had been waiting only for the necessary papal dispensation which Clarence seems to have obtained by bribing James Goldwell, Edward's own agent at the Curia.

The veil of deception was torn at last, but even before this other events had stirred the king into greater activity. By the time he had reached Stamford on 5 July he realized that Robin of Redesdale's rebellion was more than a mere series of local riots. Four days afterwards, at the latest, he began to suspect that Clarence and Warwick were intriguing against him, for he wrote letters in his own hand to both of them and to the archbishop of York, asking them to come to him as soon as possible, and dispatched them by the ever trusted Sir Thomas Montgomery.

The solution was not to be so easy. The day after the Clarence-Neville marriage the plotters in Calais dispatched to England a manifesto which they claimed to be a petition delivered to them by various of the king's subjects in various parts of England. Most probably Warwick himself was its author. A letter signed by Warwick, Clarence and Archbishop Neville accompanied the manifesto.[14] The letter announced that they intended to be at Canterbury the following Sunday and asked their 'friends' to make ready to accompany them to the king with as many armed men as they could muster.

The manifesto began in an ominous comparison of Edward with England's three deposed kings, Edward II, Richard II and Henry VI — kings who had all met their fate by estranging the great lords of their blood from their secret counsel and giving their confidence to other men whose only thought was to enrich themselves; men who had so plundered the royal estates and revenues that they had left their sovereigns too impoverished to rule effectively.

This menacing overture led to a direct indictment of Edward's own record — that he had allowed the queen's family, William Herbert, Humphrey Stafford, Lord Audley, Sir John Fogge[15] and others to enrich themselves from what should have been the inviolable inheritance of the crown, that the recoinage of 1464 had been accomplished for their benefit alone, that because of the alienation of the royal demesne the people had suffered inordinate taxation, that moneys levied for a crusade had been diverted to secular purposes, that maintenance by the king's favourites was notorious, so that no man of any estate or condition against whom the favourites bore a grudge could feel safe in life or property.

These accusations were an impudent, skilful mixture of truth, half-truth and sheer prevarication, designed to appeal to widespread popular discontent. The denunciation that Edward had spent money levied for a crusade for secular purposes was absolutely correct. On the other hand, Warwick and his friends were well aware of the quite adequate economic reasons for the recoinage of 1464 for they had approved it themselves at the time. Dubious rumours circulating some years later alleged that Sir Thomas Cook's indictment for treason was at least partly due to the avaricious malice of Earl Ryvers and his wife and Sir John Fogge, but there is no evidence that other treason indictments were due to anything but genuine fear and Warwick himself had even been a judge in the first of the treason trials of 1468. Both Warwick and Clarence knew quite well that the queen and her family had not been extravagantly endowed, that Edward had provided for her relations on the feudal marriage market rather

[14]The letter and articles are printed in the notes to J. Warkworth, *A Chronicle of the First Thirteen Years of the Reign of King Edward the Fourth*, ed. J.O. Halliwell (Camden Society, 1839), pp. 46-51. C.L. Scofield, *The Life and Reign of Edward IV* (1923) I, p. 495, calls the articles 'copies of Robin of Redesdale's manifesto'. C.D. Ross, *Edward IV* (1974), p. 130, also calls them 'a copy of the rebels' petition.' There is, however, not the slightest evidence for these statements. Sir James Ramsey, *Lancaster and York* (2 vols, 1892) II, p. 337, thought that both the manifesto and the petition were 'palpably the work of one pen'. His opinion seems to me to be plausible.

[15]Treasurer of the household, 1461 – 8.

than from the royal estates, that the king, far from dissipating his patrimony in the manner of Henry VI, had, while allowing for the essential needs of patronage (exceptionally pressing after a political revolution), built up the royal estates by acts of resumption and had begun their radical reorganization, that direct taxation had been extremely light, that if the gains of any particular group had been sensationally wasteful of the royal resources they had been those of the Nevilles themselves, and that some, at least, of their gains had been markedly distasteful to contemporary sentiment. Such had been the grant of the Percy earldom of Northumberland to John Neville, for long tradition and the practice of the century held that the forfeiture of such aristocratic honours should never be perpetual. Moreoever, the manifesto omitted other very obvious targets such as Warwick's brother-in-law, Lord Hastings, who had received enormous grants of land and had been the only private person to profit, as master of the London mint, from the recoinage of 1464. The hands which attacked Edward IV for financial waste and folly in 1469 were no more lily-white than those which had attacked Henry VI a decade and more earlier, and they now had far less justification for their mendacious abuse. With superb insolence the insurgents expertly tried to outbid the king in his own policies while pretending that those policies had never existed. Ignoring the king's speech of 1467 to the Commons, the speech which convincingly claimed that for the future he intended to live of his own, they demanded that 'a sufficient livelode and posses-sions' be established to render taxation unnecessary, and that it should be made an offence for any except the king's brothers and his children to accept grants from it. Here indeed was a case of rich prostitutes ardently embracing an exaggerated virtue!

Other accusations in the manifesto were far nearer to truth—its condemnation of disorder and its accusation that maintenance by the king's supporters had been so notorious that justice could not be had against those whom they favoured. In spite of Edward IV's own immensely hard work through his numerous personal judicial tours, he was still forced, in great measure, to work through the channels of bastard feudalism. As the house of York had never managed to build up such an immense affinity among the middling landowners as the early Lancastrians had possessed, they had to leave their more powerful followers something of a free hand to pursue their own interests and to turn a blind eye to many local injustices. Such expediency undoubtedly alienated potential support. The activities of Edward's master of the horse, Sir Thomas Burgh, helped to provoke the Lincolnshire rebellion a few months later and in 1470 the Pastons turned Lancastrian because the king had failed to interfere in their struggle against the duke of Norfolk to regain possession of Caister Castle.

On such matters independent evidence supports the accusations of the manifesto. The Commons' speaker in 1467 had complained of the prevalence of disorder in various parts of the realm and the author of John Warkworth's *Chronicle* (writing some time after 1478) claimed that by 1469 people were as disillusioned with the ineffectiveness of Yorkist rule as they had been with that of the Lancastrians a decade earlier.

At the same time Warwick's own family record was hardly a guarantee of better things. For the earl high morality was a stick with which to beat opponenets rather than a guiding light for his own conduct. His sense of reality had, at last, completely failed, if indeed, in the higher reaches of politics, he had ever acquired a sense of reality strong enough to distinguish rational considerations of policy from his own dominating inclinations and ambitions. Brought up in a background of family feuds where, to say the least, rampant acquisitiveness and ambitious injustice had, with royal acquiesence, long prevailed, he had spent his earlier active years in the atmosphere of political disintegration peculiar to the 1450s (he had been twenty-two years old at the beginning of the decade), when a show of force against an inept monarch had become an almost conventional political weapon. Judging from his actions — and we have few other means of interpreting his motives — set in this abnormal background a combination of arrogance and naïveté clouded a mind which, though superficially active and vigorous, was too deeply determined upon dominance, which from time to time paralysed whatever critical faculties he may have possessed, leaving him at the mercy of resentment and impulse and all too ready, under a king of very different character from Henry VI, to revert to the crude political methods of the previous decade. Nor did adversity ever chasten his pride. A year later, in exile, he arrogantly told Margaret of Anjou — to whose misfortunes, after all, he and his family had contributed to no small extent — that he had done nothing except what 'a nobleman outraged and disperred ought to have done'.

By mid-July several armies were marching across England. Robin of Redesdale had come far south. Clarence and Warwick were hastening north to meet him. William Herbert, now earl of Pembroke, was advancing from Wales with a band of archers, and Humphrey Stafford, earl of Devon, from the southwest with men-at-arms. One of those unlucky turns of fortune which were so decisive during these years now occurred. On 25 July Herbert and Stafford apparently quarrelled over the allocation of billets for their men in Banbury and separated in bitter anger. Herbert pitched camp on Danesmoor in the parish of Edgecote and Stafford withdrew his forces some ten or twelve miles away. Robin of Redesdale had by-passed Edward who, in spite of recruiting, up to this point remained idle at Nottingham, apparently still unable to believe in the treachery of Clarence and Warwick. Early next day Robin's men unexpectedly fell upon Herbert's camp. His forces put up a stubborn resistance but the battle was decided by the arrival of an advance guard of Warwick's troops before Stafford had time to bring his men-at-arms up to the field. Herbert and his brother, Sir Richard, were captured and hurried off to Northampton, where they were executed the following day.

Before Edward heard of their defeat he had at last set out from Nottingham to join forces with Herbert and Stafford. He had reached the hamlet of Olney near Northampton when the news of the disaster at Edgecote reached him, whereupon many of his troops deserted. Archbishop Neville rode to Olney and took him prisoner. He was taken to Coventry and a few days later to Warwick Castle. Meanwhile the victors rounded up and executed his friends. Lord Scales escaped but his father and his brother, John, captured either at Chepstow or in the Forest of Dean, were executed at Gosford Green just outside Coventry. Thomas Herbert was executed at Bristol, Humphrey Stafford taken and executed 'by the common people' at Bridgewater in Somerset.

Edward had been completely outwitted. Warwick had triumphed by cunning and dissimulation, and he had celebrated his triumphs with a monstrous vindictiveness, a vindictiveness quite unparalleled even in the struggles of the 1450s. Foreign observers were saying that he now intended to declare Edward a bastard and to depose him in favour of Clarence. But Warwick soon found that to hold Edward captive was not to hold the reality of power. If Yorkist rule was discredited enough to produce rebellions in the north and wide popular and aristocratic indifference elsewhere, it did not incline men to welcome government by a factious clique of Nevilles. By the end of two months events compelled Warwick to admit defeat. His captors became so afraid of attempts to rescue the king that they moved him from Warwick to Middleham, one of their principal strongholds in the north. It says little for Warwick's alleged popularity with the London mob that they threatened to riot when they realized that the king was a prisoner. In the north Sir Humphrey Neville of Brancepeth led a rising for Margaret of Anjou and early in September Lancastrian rebels in south Wales seized the castles of Carmarthen and Cardigan.

Warwick stood impotent before this new Lancastrian peril. As long as Edward remained a prisoner no one would join in resistance to the Lancastrians. During the second week in September, therefore, Edward was allowed to travel to York and then to Pontefract Castle. After this demonstration (even if it was not entirely convincing) that the king was a free agent, recruiting became easier. By the end of the month Warwick had suppressed the Lancastrian rising and had executed Humphrey Neville and his brother.

This one success, however, failed to solve the major problem of government and at the beginning of October Warwick abandoned his hopeless enterprise of trying to rule through a captive king. According to *The Paston Letters* Edward's captors, after inducing him to give 'fair speech and promise', just let him go. Back in London, surrounded by loyal friends, he began to assert his own will. In spite of the anxiety which he must have felt about the temper of his recent captors, he spoke in a friendly way about Clarence, Warwick, Archbishop Neville and the earl of Oxford, though some members of the royal household were gossiping with considerably less restraint.

VIII

Recent events had made some reorganization essential and Edward began a redistribution of power in Wales, in the southwest and in the north. Although he first worked out these plans with the advice of a small inner group of councillors, following his customary practice in important matters of policy once again and ever hopeful, in spite of what he must, by this time, have recognized as their indifference, he tried to obtain the approval of the nobility by consulting them in a great council. The unprecedented length of its session, from early in November to 10 February 1469, shows the importance which he attached to the restoration of unity and solidarity after the recent upheavals.

The dead Williams Herbert's son was only fourteen years old. He obviously could not effectively take his father's place as 'the king's master lock' in Wales. Edward now determined to entrust his youngest brother, Richard of Gloucester, who had reached the mature age of seventeen, with great responsibilities, appointing him for life constable of England, chief justice of north Wales, chief steward and surveyor of the principality of Wales and the earldom of March; and a little later Gloucester also replaced Warwick as chief justice and chamberlain of south Wales during the minority of Herbert's son. Lord Ferrers, Sir Roger Vaughan, Sir William Stanley and John Donne supported the young duke in some of the lesser offices, in fact probably doing most of the work for him, with John Donne specially responsible for the supervision of affairs in West Wales. In the southwest Lord Dynham gradually took the place of the dead Humphrey Stafford, earl of Devon, receiving some of his lands

and offices. Others went to John Stafford, a younger son of the duke of
Buckingham killed at Northampton, who now became earl of
Wiltshire.

The most significant part of the rearrangement, however, lay in a
reduction of the northern power of the Nevilles. Since 1464, when
Edward had created John Neville earl of Northumberland, the
Nevilles had combined the honours and influence normally divided
between the younger, upstart branch of the family and the Percies.
These arrangements spelt perpetual discontent and hostility towards
the Yorkist regime among the friends and tenantry of the Percies
whose traditional loyalties were intensely strong. At the end of
October 1469 Edward released Henry Percy IV from his imprisonment in the Tower of London, having taken from him recognizances
for good behaviour. Once released from imprisonment his restoration
was only a matter of time. It came five months later in March 1470
when Edward restored his estates and made him warden of the east
March against Scotland.

At the same time Edward compensated John Neville by creating
him Marquess Montagu. In 1471, according to Warkworth, John
Neville to justify his later rebellion 'declared to the people' that
Edward, having deprived him of the earldom of Northumberland,
made him a marquess with nothing but a pye's nest 'to maintain his
estate'. Another, anti-Neville, chronicle known as *Hearne's Fragment*
claimed that the king 'loved him entirely'. If the one statement was
mendacious, the other was implausible. Edward's action could hardly
have come as a complete surprise to John Neville and, as part of the
redistribution of influence in February 1470, he granted John Neville
twelve manors in Devon and Cornwall — a grant which can hardly be
contemptuously dismissed as a mere 'pye's nest'. Moreover, in
November 1469 the king allowed him to buy a valuable wardship for
1,000 marks and on 5 January 1470 be betrothed his eldest daughter,
Elizabeth, to Neville's son George, and at the same time created the
boy duke of Bedford. At this point the king's motives are
impenetrable. Did he expect by this royal marriage to bring back
Warwick to his side or was it a counter-move against the Clarence-
Neville marriage, an attempt to drive a political wedge between the
Neville brothers? As yet Edward had no son: Clarence married to one
Neville was the heir male of the house of York, the king's daughter
married to another would be the heir general. In view of the earlier
struggles between Lancaster and York, this opened up all the possibilities of dispute and, in view of the fact that the house of York itself
claimed the throne as heirs general, Edward, failing the birth of an
heir male, obviously intended Elizabeth and George Neville rather
than Clarence and Isabella Neville to succeed him.

IX

The king was not left in peace for long. New disturbances began even before the great council ended, though at first sight they seemed to be no more than private feuds of more of less unusual violence. During the political upheavals of the previous few months several magnates had taken advantage of the opportunity to pursue their private quarrels free from restraint by king or council. Another affray of this kind exploded in Lincolnshire in the winter of 1469 – 70. Sir Thomas Burgh, a local landowner, with the king's help had considerably built up his power and influence in the shire and in so doing had roused the resentment of established county families and, in particular, the hostility of Lord Welles, whose anger also fed upon particular grudges of his own against the king himself. It was a complicated tangle of grievances of which Warwick may have been aware through family connections.

Lord Welles's father had been killed fighting on the Lancastrian side at Towton and attainted in 1461. Welles himself, though never persecuted, had been less generously treated than many other Lancastrians. He had only gradually recovered the family properties between 1465 and 1468. Moreover, his son, Sir Robert, had tried to annul certain grants which his maternal grandfather, Lord Willoughby, had made from his estate revenues — contracts which the king had compelled him to honour.

Now Lord Welles, supported by his brothers-in-law, Sir Thomas Dymmok and Sir Thomas de la Launde, attacked and destroyed Burgh's house, Gainsborough Old Hall, and drove him out of the shire. The affray, at first, seemed to have no greater political significance than other recent riots, until Edward, possibly suspecting yet more Lancastrian machinations, decided to interfere to uphold his own interests in the county. Our knowledge of what followed derives from an official account of the rising and from a 'confession' made by Lord Welles when a prisoner and under threat of death. In spite of some adverse criticism of these sources, they seem to be reasonably plausible. No evidence exists to show that Clarence and Warwick possessed any previous knowledge of the attack on Gainsborough Old Hall. Be this as it may, at the beginning of February Clarence sent his chaplain and other priest to Lord Welles and Sir Robert Welles at Hellow. The two priests asked them to gather as great a fellowship as they could but not to 'stir' until they heard that the earl of Warwick had left London. The Welles, father and son, then spread rumours about the countryside that the king intended to go there with 'great power' with his judges and 'sit and hang and draw' a great number of the commons, probably for their earlier support of Robin of Redesdale, although pardons for those offences had already been issued. In view of the extent of Edward's judicial progresses since his accession the rumour was by no means implausible.

Shortly afterwards the king summoned Lord Welles and Sir Thomas Dymmok to his presence by writs of privy seal, presumably to answer for the attack on Gainsborough Old Hall. Sir Robert Welles, ignoring the danger in which rash actions would place his father and his uncle, went with as many friends as he could muster to Lincoln to meet one of Clarence's yeomen of the Chamber. The yeoman told Sir Robert that Clarence would now go to London to avert any suspicion the king might feel and so shield Lord Welles and delay the king's departure for Lincolnshire. Clarence's yeoman then more or less took charge of the forces which the Welles family and their friends had assembled and made many stirring speeches. Meanwhile, Sir Robert Welles himself sent a messenger to Warwick who, after some rather disturbing delay, brought back news that Warwick and Clarence would raise troops and march north as quickly as they could.

Edward had planned to start for Lincolnshire on 6 March, but delayed to meet Clarence. After a friendly meeting the king left London with Lord Hastings, Henry Percy and others. The next day, at Waltham, he heard that the previous Sunday Warwick and Clarence, in the king's own name, had commanded proclamations in all the Lincolnshire churches, ordering the commons to gather together to resist the entry of the royal forces into the shire. Worse was to follow. The next day a child sent by John Morling, Lord Cromwell's steward at Tattershall, brought the shattering news that the people were rising in force in Lincolnshire, Yorkshire and other counties.

The same day a letter arrived from Clarence saying that, although in London he had told the king that he was going to the west, to be of greater service to his brother he had now decided to join the earl of Warwick immediately. The king, still entirely unsuspecting, wrote Clarence a letter of thanks with his own hand and sent the duke and earl commissions to raise troops in Worcestershire and Warwickshire.

Edward now had Welles and Dymmok brought, under guard, from London to Huntingdon for questioning. They still maintained that they, and they alone, had stirred up the revolt. By Edward's orders Welles wrote to his son that both he and Dymmok would be executed unless Sir Robert disbanded the rebel troops at once. By 11 March the king reached Fotheringhay. The Lincolnshire rebels had passed Grantham and had turned towards Leicester, the rendezvous which Clarence and Warwick had appointed. Edward reached Stamford on Monday night, where messages came from Clarence and Warwick saying they were at Coventry and marching as swiftly as they could to join him. On his way to Leicester Sir Robert Welles received his father's letter. Faced with the agonizing choice of holding to the prearranged plan, which meant certain death to his father and uncle, or surrendering, he made a desperate attempt to save them from the axe, wheeled round and dashed for Stamford, hoping to overwhelm the king by a surprise attack. He reached Erpingham about five miles from Stamford and prepared for battle. Edward, in the sight of his entire army, immediately executed Lord Welles and Dymmok. Then, falling upon Sir Robert's troops he quickly put them to flight. They cast aside their coats as they fled — whence the battle has been called Losecote Field.

During the flight the rebel forces had used the battle cry, 'A Clarence, a Warwick'. Even after this startling revelation of treachery, Edward was still prepared to believe the best he could of the duke and earl. He sent John Donne, one of the esquires of the Body, to command them to disband their troops and come to his presence only with such retinues as their rank demanded. Even more damning evidence of their treason now appeared. One of Clarence's servants had been captured in the pursuit after Losecote Field. In his 'casket' papers were found which gave definite proof of a subversive plot. Two days later the royal forces captured Sir Robert Welles and Richard Waurine, who had commanded the rebel infantry. They then confessed — or were alleged to have confessed — that they had planned to destroy the king and set Clarence on the throne.

Isolated as they now were, their latest schemes in ruins, Clarence and Warwick had no intention of submitting. Though promising to come to the king with no more than a thousand or fifteen hundred men, they immediately set off in the opposite direction towards Burton-on-Trent. Their friends and connections were far from united. Warwick's brother-in-law, Lord Scrope of Bolton, rose in Richmondshire, only to retreat without fighting after a show of force by Marquess Montagu. After more attempts to parley, the king, who by this time was in a completely uncompromising mood, at last firmly told his brother and Warwick that the time had come when they must cease acting like independent powers. He had no intention of giving them a complete pardon until they had made at least some answer to the charges levelled against them. They must be prepared like subjects to come into his presence and prove their innocence. Instead, they fled to Chesterfield, then to Manchester where, disappointed of help from Lord Stanley, they turned toward the southwest, on the run with a price on their heads. Edward, assuming that they would make for Calais where Warwick was captain, or Ireland where Clarence was lieutenant, sent orders that they were to be refused admission if they appeared before Calais and arrested if they set foot in Ireland.

By 14 April the king had pursued the rebels to Exeter. He arrived just too late. Clarence with Warwick, and their wives and a small band of men, had reached the town first, had seized a few ships in the harbour and had embarked for Calais. A disastrous reception awaited them. The king's orders had already arrived. The garrison fired on the rebel ships as they entered the harbour. Lord Wenlock, Warwick's lieutenant in the town (Warwick was its captain) and for years one of his closest friends and supporters, refused to admit him and advised him to take refuge in France. While Warwick lay in the roads before Calais, his cousin, the Bastard of Fauconberg, played the traitor, deserted the royal fleet commanded by Sir John Howard and took over to Warwick some of the ships which Edward had assigned to patrol the narrow seas. Piracy was almost Warwick's favourite sin. He had never been able to resist its thrill. Nor was he able to do so now. Before they sailed for France he and the Bastard together captured some thirty or forty Burgundian and Breton ships. Even if piracy was the only way by which they could revictual themselves, they went far beyond the point of supplying their immediate necessities, and within a short time their ill-considered action was to prove acutely embarrassing.

Reluctantly Warwick abandoned all hope of Calais and, taking some of the captured ships with him, set sail for Honfleur, arriving about 10 May, and arriving there entirely unrepentant. Thomas Basin, the vindictive and spiteful Amelgard, a man well fitted from his own treacherous career and disappointed ambitions to understand the earl's character, claimed in his rancorous memoirs that Warwick had now already decided to offer to put Henry VI on the throne again. Characteristically enough Warwick told Louis XI that gratitude for their restoration would so banish the evil memories of the past from the minds of Henry and Margaret that they would allow him to exercise all real power and thus he would be able to bring England into the struggle with Burgundy on the side of France.

X

Fantastic as a Lancastrian restoration engineered by Warwick may seem, the idea was not a new one. Rumours of such a plan had been circulating as early as May 1467 and during the second half of 1468, or at the very latest early in 1469, Sir John Fortescue, Margaret's 'chancellor' at St Migheil-sur-Bar, had written to Gaillaume Juvenel des Ursins, the chancellor of France, ingeniously proposing in the interests of peace between France and England to restore Henry VI 'sans grant armee et sans grant frais'. This economical method of restoration involved nothing less than a marriage between Margaret's son and Warwick's daughter. At the time Fortescue had asked that his proposals should be kept absolutely secret for if details of the plan leaked out it would greatly damage Margaret's reputation. There is little doubt that Fortescue put the scheme to the French court with Margaret's full knowledge, and it was not the first time that she had approved plans which she knew quite well would outrage many of her supporters. The innermost circle of Lancastrian exiles was already inured to the idea of collaboration with Warwick and, by May 1470, the earl, possibly already in touch with them through his brother-in-law, the earl of Oxford, had no alternative but to co-operate in a last desperate gamble for power.

Warwick's arrival at Honfleur suddenly brought to Louis XI an embarrassing, disconcerting moment of decision. Since 1461 he had never hesitated to stir up trouble in England if it suited his purposes. Since early in 1467 Edward IV's attitude had aroused his fears and by May 1470 he had endured twenty months of the most acute anxiety and strain—the nightmare vision of an active combination of England, Burgundy and Brittany, a combination at all costs to be destroyed if his plans for the government of France were to succeed, even, it must often have appeared, if the French state were to survive intact. All Warwick's attempts to direct English foreign policy in favour of France had failed. A change of dynasty might well seem to be the way out for Louis. And yet, he could not act with the same precipitation as a bunch of penniless, irresponsible exiles. Charles the Bold was suspicious and alert, incensed that French officials had turned a blind eye when Warwick had taken his Burgundian and Breton Prizes into Honfleur and even continued his piratical exploits from there. He sent a vehement complaint either to Louis or to the parliament of Paris and offered Lord Wenlock in Calais a pension of 1,000 crowns.

Louis doubted, hesitated, stalled, tried to avoid any irrevocable decision but in the end Warwick's persistence forced the issue. At the beginning of June the king consented to receive him, but Warwick had gained his point at the price of creating a dangerous obstacle for the immediate future. Unmollified by Louis' desperate promises of compensation for the plundered Burgundian merchants, Charles the Bold ordered his fleet to sea. Earl Ryvers joined it with the English fleet from Southampton. The combined force burned and sacked Harfleur, carried off a number of ships, and then kept up a steady blockade of the Seine mouth.

After five weeks of procrastination Louis at last met Margaret of Anjou and Warwick and, at first, interviewed them separately. Margaret immediately agreed to a thirty years' truce with France. An inexplicable delay then occurred. More than three weeks elapsed before Warwick and the earl of Oxford were brought in.[16] The idea of collaboration with Warwick could hardly have been new to Margaret as her own chancellor, most probably, had first proposed the nauseating bargain. Yet, aware that the plan might well offend potential supporters in England, she may have hesitated when it came to the point. Nor was expediency the only reason for hesitation. Too many evil memories lay between them. Warwick had once accused the queen of plotting his assassination. She had sent one of his brothers to the scaffold. Warwick had imprisoned her husband, had slandered her reputation, had proclaimed her son a bastard. Now she may have been haggling over details in her talks with Louis or, recalling the past and the tragedies which divided her from Warwick, she may have resisted any suggestion that she entrust her son to Warwick's care.

The prince of Wales and Warwick's daughter Anne were betrothed in Angers Cathedral.[17] Warwick swore a corporal oath upon a fragment of the true Cross that he would faithfully support the Lancastrian cause. Margaret merely promised that for the future she would treat the earl as her husband's true and faithful subject and that she would never reproach him for his past actions. At the same time the Lancastrians gained the point that the prince of Wales, young as he was (he was only sixteen), was to be regent and governor when he arrived in England.

The day following the betrothal at Angers, Margaret and Warwick set out for Normandy. The omens for the success of their venture were hardly encouraging. Louis was keeping far too tight a hand upon the purse strings and by the third week in August the unpaid crews of Warwick's ships, on the verge of mutiny, cast off all restraint and plundered Valognes. The Anglo-Burgundian fleet was patrolling the Channel, capturing fishing boats and burning houses all along the coast. It was only a change of weather that gave Warwick his chance to embark, under strict orders from Louis not to attack the Anglo-Burgundian fleet unless it first attacked him. Warwick was fortunate that a violent storm scattered the blockading vessels and he could at last set sail for the Devonshire coast where he landed on 13 September.

The continental writers, Chastellain and Commynes, later

---

[16]Clarence was excluded from the first meetings with the queen.

[17]They were related in the fourth degree and, therefore, could not be married without a dispensation. They were later married at Amboise, probably on 13 December.

condemned Edward as over-confident and negligent in face of these dangers. Their strictures were both ill-informed and misplaced: rather his disasters sprang from miscalculation and unlooked-for treachery. Following his usual practice when he needed special support, he once again summoned the great council of peers for a session which lasted two days. Although relying on the blockade of the Anglo-Burgundian fleet, he made extensive preparations for defending the southwest, Kent and London, dismissed Lord Wenlock and appointed Earl Ryvers lieutenant of Calais. Towards the end of July he rode north to repress a rising led by Lord Fitzhugh, the husband of Warwick's sister Alice. It may well be that Fitzhugh's actions were a feint prearranged by Warwick to draw the king from the south for, by the time Edward reached Ripon, Fitzhugh fled with suspicious rapidity over the Scottish border. By 7 September, apparently expecting Warwick to land in Kent, Edward prepared to march south himself. He had few troops of his own in the north, mainly relying on men recruited by Marquess Montagu under royal proclamation. As he set off to London with Gloucester and Lord Hastings he sent orders to Montagu to join him and sent a messenger to Charles the Bold to ask him to keep his fleet at sea and, by doing so, cut off Warwick's retreat. Disaster came as swiftly as a flash of lightning. Late at night at Doncaster, the sergeant of the king's minstrels burst into Edward's room crying that Montagu had turned against him and was only six or seven miles away. His change of sides was utterly unexpected. Edward, after all, had begun to re-endow him with estates and he could hardly have hoped that the Lancastrians would ever give him back the earldom of Northumberland. The only explanation can be that at last the ties of blood and family proved too strong. Menaced by the immediate approach of troops raised in his own name, Edward fled. For the only time in his life he panicked and panicked badly. In spite of commissions of array which had been issued for the southwest in June, resistance to Warwick in that area had been completely ineffective. Faced with the danger that his own small force would be crushed between Warwick's forces advancing from the south and Montagu's only a few miles behind him, the king fled rather than risk imprisonment or even death. Fleeing across the Wash, several of his followers being drowned in the flight, on Michelmas Day the bedraggled army of exhausted refugees arrived at Lynn. Those who could crowded onto the few available vessels in the harbour and put to sea, leaving the rest to disperse to safety as best they could.

Warwick, by this time, had at least learned the lesson that, although the first stages of a revolt could be carried through by a small body of determined men, ultimate success depended upon the support or at least the acquiesence of a wider circle of nobility and gentry. He therefore proclaimed an amnesty for all except Henry VI's most prominent enemies and those who resisted his forces. Hearing news of Edward's flight he marched to London where his presence was urgently needed. Mobs of Kentishmen had invaded the suburbs south of the river and sacked and plundered Dutch beer houses there. Yorkist partisans had dashed for refuge to the sanctuaries and so many prominent people, including the chancellor, the keeper of the privy seal and the bishop of Ely, took refuge in St Martin-le-Grand, the greatest franchise within the city, that rents rose to unprecedented heights. Safe in a sanctuary well-to-do people could sit out a crisis in comparative comfort, waiting for times to change. Elizabeth Wydeville, who took refuge in the Westminster sanctuary, certainly contrived to maintain a fairly affluent existence. Her household had a standing order with a London butcher for two sheep a week and when her confinement was known to be near at hand Henry's council sent Elizabeth, Lady Scrope, to attend her, and gave her a reward of £10 for doing so.

As the Yorkists rushed to the sanctuaries, the criminals rushed out. A Lancastrian from the Westminster sanctuary, Sir Geoffrey Gate, appointed himself Warwick's representative in London and embarrassingly joined forces with the Thames boatmen and the Kentish rabble — and this time English as well as Dutch beer houses suffered.

Once Warwick arrived he quickly persuaded, or forced, the Kentishmen to retire to their homes and restored order in the capital. Even so he faced insuperable difficulties. Henry VI was a useless cypher. Even a loyal Lancastrian like Sir John Fortescue, with bitter memories of the ineptitude and wilfulness of his earlier reign, in a written memorandum advised Warwick to allow him as little personal power as possible, particularly in financial matters. A generation of bitter rivalries had destroyed the possibility of government by a united aristocratic council of the kind which had successfully ruled during Henry VI's minority. Although Chastellain denounced Henry VI's Re-adeption as a reign of terror, nothing could be further from the truth. Circumstances dictated moderation. Although the Chancery, the Exchequer and the law courts carried on much as usual, the government was weak in the extreme because it lacked effective support. Money was desperately short. The merchant community of London would lend very little. It may well be, as Commynes claimed, that they looked to Edward's restoration as the only hope of recovering the large sums which he owed them, and that they were encouraged by their wives with whom Edward was so personally popular. From other classes the restored Lancastrian government raised only a few hundred pounds. People refused to risk their money on Henry and funds became so desperately short that Warwick was reduced to raiding the revenues of private estates.

Clarence, already slighted, was intriguing against him. The nobility were deeply divided and many were lukewarm towards either side. Henry Percy remained suspiciously aloof. Of those with Lancastrian sympathies only Jasper Tudor, the young Talbot earl of Shrewsbury and the Courtenays seem to have been both available and active. The duke of Exeter, the titular earl of Somerset and Viscount Beaumont were still abroad with Margaret of Anjou. Lord Wenlock was still in Calais. Warwick's old friends, Dynham and Mountjoy, would apparently have nothing to do with him. The commissions of the peace and the commissions of array to raise troops were based upon extremely narrow groups of peers and even some of these, like the earl of Essex and the duke of Norfolk, were bitterly quarrelling among themselves.

The deployment of extensive patronage was vital to the success of any fifteenth-century government and particularly vital to the success of a government brought in by revolution—and all too little patronage was now available. The records of the Re-adeption Parliament have disappeared (possibly destroyed by the victorious Yorkists). Most probably, however, there were no attainders except against Edward IV himself and his brother Gloucester. It is likewise unknown whether attainders against former Lancastrians were reversed. Reversal or non-reversal, either would have caused acute embarrassment. Any action to satisfy Lancastrians by restoring their estates would have infuriated the Yorkists to whom they had been granted. So there were few forfeitures or offices with which to reward or buy supporters and Warwick with typical greed and unwisdom took for himself most of the plums available.[18] Against the conventions of fifteenth-century political life this was a totally impossible situation, and it would grow worse for the arrival of Queen Margaret and Prince Edward would certainly undermine Warwick's influence and the exiles who returned with them would, equally certainly, clamour for the restoration of their estates.

In the higher realms of statesmanship where circumstances did not force Warwick into moderation (but rather the reverse), his actions were even less sensible. As through the 1460s, foreign policy remained a key problem. He had returned to England in a dilemma from which there was no escape—pledged to a war policy dictated by the king of France, an expensive policy with no money whatsoever to pay for it,

---

[18]The offices of captain of Calais, chamberlain of England, and admiral, and the wardship of part of the duke of Buckingham's lordship in south Wales which he had been forced to surrender to William Herbert in 1461.

which would add to the indifference of the nobility the hostility of a large section of the commercial classes, if taxation were imposed to meet the costs.

XI

When Edward so hastily fled from Lynn, he barely escaped capture by the Hanseatics who had sent out vessels to prey upon English shipping in the North Sea and the Channel. He reached Alkmaar, a refugee so penurious that all he could give the master of the ship which brought him to safety was a gown trimmed with marten fur. Charles the Bold would have been better pleased to hear of his death than to hear of his landing on Burgundian soil. Edward's death would have destroyed much of the Lancastrian need to rely on Louis XI and Warwick and so might have saved him from the threat of an Anglo-French invasion. He gave his brother-in-law a far from gracious reception, refused to meet him personally, allotted him a meagre pension of 500 crowns a month (far less than Margaret of Anjou was costing Louis XI), then ignored him as far as he could and did his best to maintain friendly relations with England. As Philippe de Commynes (still at this time serving the duke of Burgundy) wrote, he 'tried all the ways possible to pacify the earl of Warwick'.

Louis XI realized perhaps far more than Warwick (after all he was much less given to political self-delusion than the earl) what resistance there would be to war in England. He did everything he could to neutralize it, offering immense concessions to English merchants trading in French territories, authorizing ambassadors to discuss the divisions of the spoils of war: they were to ask Warwick for a list of the greatest and most influential men in England and to promise them grants of land in the conquered territories. Louis was playing upon English memories of the immense potential profits of foreign conquests but this time directing English attention eastwards.

By mid-January 1471 the French ambassadors were sending home enthusiastic reports about English war preparations. Warwick in his desperation must have deluded them completely. He could scarcely have hoped to continue to dominate affairs once the queen and the prince of Wales arrived home with the Lancastrian emigrés. He had to try to keep faith with Louis for his own future depended entirely upon Louis' continued support and the king of France was not the man to underwrite failures. So Warwick declared war on Burgundy though nobody but he himself could possibly have known how he was going to prosecute it. His coffers were so bare that he could pay reinforcements which he had recently sent to Calais only be seizing and selling 17,000 crowns' worth of goods which two unfortunate French merchants had hoped to put on exhibition in London. Even in the most favourable conditions, with the full co-operation of the nobility, supported by the staff-work of a well organized royal household, it always took many months for the English to recruit and equip an expeditionary force of any size. It was quite beyond the resources of a government of three months' duration, face to face with a sullen and divided nobility, an obstructive parliament and a merchant class so hostile that it refused to lend a penny—to say nothing of the need for defence at home. Warwick deceived himself, or Louis XI, with desperate, extravagant fantasies and, in so doing, unwittingly signed his own death warrant.

The duke of Burgundy, anxious to keep on good terms with England, would never have lifted a finger to help his fugitive, embarrassing brother-in-law had Warwick shown any inclination to remain neutral, which he might well have done for a time on the grounds of the insecure Lancastrian position in England. It was Warwick's declaration of war which finally tipped the scales. So Charles, although he had issued a proclamation forbidding any of his subjects to assist Edward, secretly sent him 50,000 florins (£20,000) and secretly equipped for him three or four great ships at Veere on the island of Walcheren. Edward himself appealed for aid to the duke of Brittany and, promising them great commercial privileges after his restoration, negotiated with the Hanseatic League (alienated by Warwick's piracy) for fourteen ships for his crossing to England, and cautiously stipulated that they should remain in port for fifteen days after his landing.

After being held up by contrary winds for over a week, on 11 March Edward set sail from Flushing. On the face of things, in spite of Warwick's precarious position in England, his bid to recover his kingdom seemed to be a far from hopeful enterprise. It caused no great stir in Europe. His bargain with the Hanse to leave his line of retreat open shows that he was not convinced of success and, indeed, the first reports which crossed the Channel claimed that, defeated, he had been forced to take refuge in a church, even that he was dead.

Edward faced this turning point in his life with an army of at most 2,000 men, possibly as few as 1,200, even 1,000, partly Englishmen, partly foreigners. It may, however, be mistaken to stress these small numbers unduly. Events over the last two decades had shown more than once how small was the physical force needed to overthrow an English government and Warwick's government was unusually weak. News received off Cromer indicated that a landing in East Anglia was out of the question. All Edward's known supporters there, who had escaped to the sanctuaries, had been rounded up and imprisoned, and the earl of Oxford, though at that moment away recruiting in Essex, was keeping a close watch on the area. Frustrated, Edward sailed on to Yorkshire. On the way a violent storm scattered his fleet and one of the horse transports foundered. On 14 March he reached Ravenser, where Henry Bolingbroke had landed seventy-two years earlier, with Lord Hastings and five hundred men. Gloucester and Earl Ryvers landed several miles away at different points, and the following day these feeble forces reunited, a few hundred storm-battered troops on the wind-swept peninsula of Holderness.

Even the official account of the invasion, the *Arrivall of Edward IV*, written and sent abroad for propaganda purposes within a very short time of the events which it relates, admitted that few or none of the people of the countryside rallied to the king. In fact, Polydore Vergil later claimed that they had gathered in considerable numbers to resist him. Edward, far from scrupulous (like most people with whom he had to deal), appealed to one of the strongest sentiments of the day, so often mentioned before, a sentiment prevailing with almost adamantine fervour—the sanctity of the family inheritance, the hereditary 'lifelode', that god-made right that nothing could, or should, obliterate. If Edward's claim to the crown was disputable, his right to the duchy of York was indefeasible. Therefore, like Bolingbroke, another 'poor, un-minded outlaw sneaking home', he deliberately perjured himself by giving out that he had returned only to claim his paternal inheritance, the sacred 'lifelode' which no right-minded man could think to deny him.

At this point the restored Percy earl of Northumberland made no move to assist him. He, too, like Warwick, lay between the devil and the deep blue sea. It is said that his hereditary retinue and his tenantry were too pro-Lancastrian to permit him to give Edward any active assistance and he may still have feared Neville designs for the return of his earldom to Marquess Montagu. On the other hand, Edward had almost certainly been in touch with him from overseas. All in all, immediate resistance seems to have melted away when Edward gave out that he had returned only to claim the duchy of York and produced approving letters from Henry Percy. Even so, the north was at best neutral.

The royal forces went on but Hull refused to admit the king. York admitted him only on confirmation that restoration to the duchy of York was his entire aim. Yet the city refused entry to his troops and the *soi-disant* duke, who never lacked personal courage, went through the gates with only sixteen or seventeen men. Then by plunging deeper into perjury than ever, by professing his loyalty to Henry VI and the prince of Wales and even wearing the prince's livery of the ostrich feather, he talked over the city authorities into admitting his army. From now on Edward advanced rapidly. By 20 March he reached Wakefield and moved on to Doncaster. Marquess Montagu, who had wintered with his forces at Pontefract, made no attempt to resist him. He may have been deterred by the threat of Henry Percy's troops. Inactive though they were, according to the explanation given in the official *Arrivall* (which may have been concerned to put Percy's attitude in the most favourable light), they kept Montagu neutralized. At Wakefield the tide began to turn, though recruits still came in more slowly than the king had hoped. At Nottingham Sir William Parre and Sir James Harrington arrived with 600 men and the king advanced on Newark to flush out the duke of Exeter, the earl of Oxford and Lord Bardolf who were reported to be there with 'a great fellowship'. Rather than face the king they fled under cover of night, leaving leaderless the troops which they had recruited in East Anglia and Essex. Edward pressed on to Leicester. There Sir William Stanley (the Stanleys always managed to keep a foot in both camps and take the advantageous position just in nick of time) arrived with 300 men; 3,000 more, the greatest number yet to be recruited flocked in, all of them men raised through the influence of Lord Hastings and his retainers.

Within a fortnight of his landing, in spite of his initial weakness, Edward had marched nearly two hundred miles and had arrived before Coventry, the heart of Warwick's own territory, having built up his army to at least five or six thousand men. The earl, within the town, refused a challenge to come out and fight. Edward withdrew to Warwick and at last threw off the mask of perjury and proclaimed himself king.

Warwick, in turn, now found himself betrayed. The wretched Clarence, suffering the dismay and contempt which traitors so often and so rapidly attract found himself

> in great suspicion, despite, distain and hatred, with all the lords, noblemen, and other, that were adherents and full partakers with Henry the Usurper ... He saw also that they daily laboured amongst them breaking their appointments made with him, and, of likelihood, after that, should continually more and more fervently intend, conspire and procure the distruction of him and all his blood.

Facts support the highly emotional tone of this account. Clarence, after some delay, had been reappointed lieutenant of Ireland, but he had not been appointed joint lieutenant of the realm with Warwick, and, even after Edward's landing, he had been forced under protest, on 23 March, to surrender part of his estates to Queen Margaret and Prince Edward and accept in their place far less secure fee-farm rents. Various sources claim that Edward had sent messengers to his brother while he was still in France, that his mother, his sisters, Margaret of Burgundy and the duchesses of Exeter and Suffolk, the earl of Essex, the archbishop of Canterbury, the bishop of Bath and Wells and Lord Hastings were all at some time in touch with him, trying to convince him of his folly and imploring him not to assist in compassing the utter ruin of his family.

This combination of resentment and persuasion now succeeded. Some time after 2 April the duke joined the king between Banbury and Warwick with a considerable number of troops which he had recruited around Wells. To do him justice he tried to reconcile Edward and Warwick but Warwick rejected the proffered terms.

To have laid siege to Warwick would have wasted precious time, even if Edward had been prepared to incur the odium of inflicting serious damage upon an English town. Every day counted for Marquess Montagu had got through to Coventry and the Lancastrian forces appear to have been growing. To remain in the Midlands would allow Lancastrian forces in the south time to concentrate, while the early possession of London would mean a tremendous boost to Yorkist morale and give Edward control of important resources, particularly financial resources. So after issuing a last, unaccepted challenge to the Lancastrian forces in Coventry, a council of war decided upon a dash for the capital.

Consternation reigned supreme amongst the city fathers. On 10 April in a tense and anxious meeting they found themselves obliged to discuss hortatory letters from both sides. Instructed by Edward to seize Henry VI and keep him in safe custody, by Warwick to co-operate with Archbishop Neville in holding the city until he came to their assistance, what were the wretched men to do? Effective leadership there was none. The mayor, Thomas Stockton, as early as the end of February, feeling that the situation was getting altogether too much for his shattered nerves, had retired to bed with a strategic illness. He was still in bed in early April. The city walls were in a state of utter ruin. They could not stand a seige. Edward's march on London was too rapid to allow much time for consideration. Yet Warwick's forces were still intact and on the move not far behind the Yorkist army. At any moment, Queen Margaret and the Prince of Wales were expected to land in the west.

There were no influential Lancastrians left in the city, apart from Archbishop Neville, and the archbishop attempted to stiffen the waning courage of the citizens by taking King Henry in procession through Chepe, Cornhill, Candlewick Street and Watling Street. A small company of gentlemen went before the king on foot. Lord Sudeley bore the sword of state. He was the only peer in attendance and he had one foot in the grave. Nine years before he had already been excused attendance at parliaments and councils on the score of old age and debility. Henry, dressed in an old blue velvet gown, so shabby and so often seen before that the mob mockingly asked if it was the only garment he possessed, pathetically held George Neville's hand all the way and a gentlemen on horseback rode behind waving a couple of foxes' brushes tied to the end of a pole.[19] As the London chronicler sarcastically said, it was 'more like a play than the showing of a prince to win men's hearts'. The procession could hardly have been a more complete fiasco.

The following day the magistrates and other leading citizens sent their submission to Edward at St Albans and opened the gates to the king. After seeing Henry, who pitifully assured him that he knew he would protect his life, he went to Westminster where — most important symbolically — the archbishop of Canterbury set the crown upon his head again for a few minutes, and then went to the sanctuary to see his wife and their newly born son (his first).

On the following day, Good Friday, more friends entered the city to reinforce the Yorkist array. The same day brought the news that Warwick was advancing on the capital, possibly hoping to take advantage of Edward's well-known piety by a surprise attack during the king's Easter devotions.

Warwick once again mistook his man. The following day Edward advanced to Barnet, and late as it was when he arrived, to avoid the dispersal of his men in the town, marched beyond and so was forced to make his dispositions in darkness, with the result that the opposing lines overlapped, each army's right wing extending beyond the enemy's left at right angles to the St Albans-Barnet road. Although Easter Sunday dawned thick with mist, Edward attacked at once, against much superior forces. The misalignment of the armies told immediately. The earl of Oxford's troops on the Lancastrian right outflanked the Yorkist left which broke and fled. Oxford's elated men began to plunder in the streets of Barnet but, after some time, their captains managed to regroup about nine hundred of them and marched them back to the field. By this time the Yorkist overlapping right wing pressing upon Warwick's left had caused the battle-lines to turn to lie almost parallel with the Barnet-St Albans road, so that Oxford's returning men made contact with their own troops instead of with the enemy. They wore the de Vere badge of a star with streams. The Lancastrians, mistaking this in the mist for the Yorkist rising sun (the sun with streams) and demoralized by this apparent treason, broke and fled. Montagu had already been killed. Warwick took to his horse and fled, only to be captured, slain and 'spoiled naked' by some of Edward's men.

[19]Foxes' brushes were a symbol of defiance.

Edward returned in triumph to London, riding to St Paul's with the mayor and aldermen to make his offering (the mayor had suddenly recovered from his illness). Even in the hour of victory it was essential to prevent the spread of dangerous rumours, and the methods of publicity were crude. For two days the bodies of Montagu and Warwick, naked but for loin cloths, lay exposed in coffins on the floor of the cathedral for all the world to see before being taken to Bisham Abbey on the Thames, to be buried in the now long-vanished mausoleum of the Montagu family. Even so it was not long before the age-old, common tale was told that Warwick had only withdrawn to some remote place to recover from his wounds.

Edward, so far, had been incredibly lucky, but the test of a second Lancastrian army he had yet to face. About the time he had sailed from Flushing, the French ambassadors returning from England had told Louis that Warwick was unlikely to embark against Charles the Bold until Margaret of Anjou landed in England. He brushed aside whatever reason for delay had so far prevailed and on 24 March hurried Margaret and her party on board their ships. He was already feeling dubious about the outcome of the venture and expressed his doubts in a characteristically mean and petty way. Having bought three hundred and twenty pipes of wine for Margaret and her friends, when he heard of Edward's landing in England he ordered his agents not to deliver them. Louis was not the man to throw even small sums of good money after bad and now, as in 1462, he was quite prepared to abandon the Lancastrian cause if it proved embarrassing.

The weather, formerly so disastrous for Edward when it had scattered the Anglo-Burgundian fleet patrolling the Channel, now turned in his favour at a point possibly decisive to his fortunes. Storm after storm drove the Lancastrian fleet back into port. Had the Channel been calm, the winds fair, had Margaret been able to sail while Warwick's army in the Midlands remained intact, Edward's fate might well have been defeat. The weather kept her wind-bound in port until the 13 April, the day before the battle of Barnet. Two days after her landing at Weymouth, Edmund Beaufort and John Courtenay rode into Cerne Abbey to tell her the news of that disastrous defeat. They assured her that their cause was far from lost. Indeed they were stronger because more united with the Nevilles and Clarence out of the way. Nor were they apparently alone in holding such an opinion.

The forces immediately at command were small. If Margaret had landed with a really strong force she might have marched directly upon London. As it was there were two courses open to her. She could follow the coast through Hampshire and Sussex into Kent to join forces with Warwick's sympathizers there or turn to the Lancastrians

in the west country and then join Jasper Tudor in Wales. The queen
and her advisers chose the latter course. Sir John Arundel and the
Courteneys raised 'the whole might' of Devon and Cornwall, an area
in which Edward had significantly failed to build up a strong Yorkist
territorial affinity. In the later part of April they moved from
Taunton to Wells and then on to Bath.

Edward heard of Margaret's landing on 16 April. He ordered his
troops to concentrate at Windsor and, after a few days of hasty
preparation and planning, set out for the west, calling up the levies of
the western counties and the west Midlands. Various Lancastrian
feints deceived him for some time until, on Sunday 28 April, at
Abingdon he discerned their strategy. From then onwards, never
again diverted, he doggedly and tenaciously pursued them at a pace
almost incredibly swift. The next six days consumed a frenzied race
for the Severn Valley. On Monday Edward marched his men thirty-
three miles from Abingdon to Cirencester, Margaret and the
Lancastrians desperate to cross the river which separated them from
Wales and Jasper Tudor, Edward trying to forestall their every move.

Obtaining men, money and artillery from Bristol, the Lancastrians
made Gloucester, only to find the city gates barred and transit across
the Severn completely blocked. Pressing desperately forward to the
next crossing beyond Tewkesbury, they followed the valley road
through wooded country and narrow, stony lanes. By the time they
reached Tewkesbury, they had marched the forty-four miles from
Bristol almost without a break. Their cavalry could have gone on,
though with difficulty, but it was impossible to force the exhausted
infantrymen further along the road to Wales. Edward, coming up
from Sudbury, held a parallel course throughout the day, through the
'champaign' country, along the southwestern slopes of the Cotswolds,
a less exhausting march than that of the Lancastrians along the
narrow, stony lanes of the valley. Even so it was a long, gruelling
march of thirty miles and more, without fodder or even drink for the
horses 'save in one little brook, where was full little release, it was so
sore troubled with the carriages that had passed it'. Towards evening
Edward reached Cheltenham. He allowed his men a brief rest, but
refused to allow them to remain there for the night, pushed on
another five miles towards Tewkesbury and encamped within three
miles of Margaret's forces—too close for the Lancastrians to cross the
narrow bridges over the Swillgate Brook and the River Avon without
fear of attack.

The Lancastrian army had taken up a strong position south of the
town and a little to the east, protected in front and on all sides by
lanes, deep dykes and hedges. They may in addition have hastily
thrown up some kind of earthwork. On Saturday 4 May, Edward's

troops advanced, the king himself leading the centre, Gloucester commanding the vanguard, Hastings the rear. Crossing the Swillgate Brook by the old ford below the modern Prest Bridge, the king turned south of Margaret's troops into open ground, but foreseeing a possible flank attack posted two hundred spears near some old earthworks in the Camp Ground. Gloucester began the attack with ordnance and a 'shot' of arrows. The strength of their position enabled the Lancastrians to hold off Gloucester's forces, but Somerset (either because his men could not stand the Yorkist fire or for some now obscure strategic reason) chose to attack. Leaving his position, he wheeled down from the right upon the king's flank. Edward, turning round, crossing a hedge and ditch, supported by Gloucester drove them back up the hill. At this point the two hundred spears from Camp Ground charged Somerset's left, driving him down the reverse stop towards the Swillgate. Edward pushed deeper into the Lancastrian position and the fight was soon over. Within a few minutes the scene became a desperate slaughter as the Avon and the Swillgate made rapid flight impossible.

As with several episodes in the Wars of the Roses, a fantastic outcrop of legends grew up about the battle of Tewkesbury — legends for which there is no contemporary authority whatsoever. John Beaufort, Courtenay and Wenlock fell in battle. The Tudor chronicler Edward Hall wrote that Beaufort, suspecting Wenlock of turning traitor yet again, dashed out his brains with a battle-axe. The prince of Wales was slain fleeing from the battle, calling upon his brother-in-law, Clarence, for help. There seems to be no truth in the later story that he was captured and brought before Edward who, enraged by the prince's haughty replies to his questions, struck him across the face with his mailed gauntlet and then allowed Clarence, Gloucester, Lord Hastings and Sir Thomas Grey to slay him. Hall as usual embellished the tale, with an account of how Edward, after the battle, offered a reward for the capture of the prince. Even early in this century credulous tourists were shown, on the floor of a house in Church Street, bloodstains alleged to be those of Prince Edward slain there by the Yorkists.

The king himself caused an ecclesiastical scandal by entering Tewkesbury Abbey, sword in hand, in pursuit of fugitives and his men captured others in the town itself. Thirteen or fourteen Lancastrians were tried and summarily executed in Tewkesbury market place in spite of the fact that those taken in the abbey had been promised a pardon. The executions aroused considerable ill-feeling, so much so that Edward's official propagandist felt it necessary to give a most evasive account of what happened, stressing (correctly) that to many people the king granted a free pardon, though he had no need to be lenient for the abbey had no franchise which covered sanctuary for treason. In fact, most of those executed at this time deserved little pity. They, like the Beauforts, the Courtenays and Sir Thomas Tresham, had been given every chance to co-operate and they had responded with ingratitude and deceit.

The second battle was over. The worst danger was past, but quite menacing forces were still under arms in other parts of the country. The men of Essex, Kent and Surrey, led by the Bastard of Fauconberg, were surging round London and reports came in that Lancastrian sympathizers in the north were rising in alarming numbers. Only three days after the battle of Tewkesbury the tireless Edward began to march north, but the news of that defeat, following close upon the disaster of Barnet, so disheartened the northerners that by the time he reached Coventry Edward heard that they were already laying down their arms and he therefore left the earl of Northumberland to restore order.

Urgent daily messages poured in from the defenders of London. Although the Bastard's forces included a substantial element of gentry and yeomen and three hundred men from the Calais garrison (the only trained military group in the country apart from the small royal bodyguard), he had also gathered in a bunch of desperadoes, the sweepings of the seaports, the riff-raff of various counties and a fair sprinkling of foreign ruffians and an ill-ruled mob taking the opportunity to work off their resentment against the London victuallers. *The Great Chronicle of London* scornfully relates that when the news of the rising in London reached Essex, 'ffaynt husbands' cast away their scythes, dressed themselves in their wives' smocks, cheese-cloths and old sheets, armed themselves with clubs, pitchforks and ash staves, and marched against the capital to revenge themselves for the low prices ruling in the city for their butter, cheese, eggs and pigs.

In spite of cheese-cloths, old sheets and pitchforks, the force was menacing in the extreme. The king, taking no chances, stayed in Coventry for a few days to recruit new men, sent on ahead a picked force of 1,500 to assist the council and the citizens. Part of the depressed London mob was always ready to admit insurgents in the hope of being able to plunder the rich under cover of the subsequent disturbances. The city authorities and the rich, however, already deeply committed to the Yorkist cause by recent substantial loans, refused the Bastard entry and even potential supporters turned against him when he fired his guns into the city, setting fire to houses round the bridge and around Aldgate.

The Bastard lay south of the Thames. Ruinous as the city walls were at this time, they could not be assaulted on the river front without a siege train. He therefore marched ten miles up river to Kingston, intending to cross there, march back on the north bank and attack through Westminster. Possibly put off by negotiations with the royal council in the city, but more likely scared by the prospect of the king's approach and the certain knowledge that he would be forced to risk a battle if he stayed north of the river, the Bastard then returned south to Southwark, determined, even without a siege train, to force an entry into the city, loot it before the king arrived and carry away the plunder in ships which lay a mile or two downstream. He renewed the bombardment with sufficient vigour to burn down about sixty houses on and near the bridge, but the royal forces within the city counter-attacked and routed the assailants. The Bastard himself remained for another day at St George's Fields, when finally the advance guard which the king had dispatched from Coventry arrived. The king himself was expected to follow quickly with the largest force he had commanded since his return — 30,000 men it was said to be. Fauconberg's expedition had already degenerated into no more than a quest for loot and now all hope of plunder had vanished. The insurgents, with no chance of successfully resisting the king, dispersed whence they came — the Calais garrison across the Channel, the countrymen to their homes, and the mariners and the miscellaneous riff-raff 'drew down to the sea coast with all their ships'.

Edward rode into London on 21 May as this rabble was vanishing away, knighting Mayor Stockton, now restored to perfect health, eleven aldermen and the recorder — an unprecedented creation of civic knighthoods. In the triumphal entry Margaret of Anjou was forced to sit in a chariot enduring the last bitter dregs of the public humiliation of the defeated. The following day another procession came out of the Tower, bearing her husband's corpse through the streets of London to St Paul's. In the cathedral the dead body lay upon a bier with the face uncovered, surrounded by lighted candles, though one hostile chronicler remarked that 'glaives and staves' were more in evidence than torches. It was reported that the royal corpse miraculously bled upon the pavement there in St Paul's and again at the church of the Black Friars where the final requiems were chanted before it was taken to Chertsey Abbey for burial. It was officially given out that he had died of the shock caused by the final ruin of his latest hopes[20] — an unlikely end for man of his pious resignation. There can be little doubt — and it was widely believed at the time — that Edward had decided upon his murder, and many believed that the deed was done in the presence of, if not by the hand of, the duke of Gloucester.

[20] '... he took it to so great despite, ire and indignation, that, of pure displeasure and melancholy, he died.' *Historie of the Arrivall of Edward IV etc.*, ed. J. Bruce (Camden Society, 1838) p. 38.

If the murder was not a political necessity, it was certainly politically expedient. As the Milanese ambassador in Paris wrote, Edward had chosen 'to crush the seed' and, as an anonymous English writer observed, 'no one remained in the land of the living who could now claim the throne from that family.'

XII

Edward had triumphed over the Lancastrians and the Nevilles were ruined, but it had been touch and go. The events of the last three years had shown that the Yorkists still had only a feeble hold on the country, yet by this time the Lancastrian appeal was probably no stronger. Warkworth's statement, that by 1469 Edward IV was as unpopular as Henry VI had been a decade earlier, must be taken seriously. Only in financial matters had Edward achieved a modest success. Otherwise his commercial treaty with Burgundy had offended powerful commercial interests without completely satisfying others equally powerful. In spite of the immense labour of his personal judicial tours, he had failed to reduce disorder to a level which people regarded as tolerable and having to work through the chain of command of bastard feudalism he had been forced to turn a blind eye to some of the dubious activities of his more powerful local supporters, though in all justice, it must be said that both earlier and later kings, not only in England but all over Europe, were forced to do the same. Kent, with a long tradition of turbulence and sedition, was prepared to rise against him, chronic discontent flourished in Wales and parts of the southwest and in the north, to some extent centring on loyalty to the Percies and dislike of the Nevilles. Lancastrian sentiment remained strong.

On the other hand, events had shown that the discontented were too localized to unite in a countrywide threat to the government and even local pockets of opposition were too diverse to combine for long. In 1469 Warwick and Clarence had failed, before passive resistance, to rule in the name of a captive king. Events in Lincolnshire in 1470 had shown what discontents could develop when the central government tried to interfere in local affairs and upset the established balance of the local power structure. The rebel leaders attracted the support of eleven knights and sixteen esquires. Seventeen of them were prominent enough to sit in parliament either before or after 1470. Yet their motives were decidedly mixed. Some had ties of professional self-interest with Clarence and Warwick, others cherished Lancastrian sympathies and yet others, like the Welles family themselves, combined such sympathies with private grudges and discontent.

Perhaps the most ominous of all developments, however, lay in the declining interest of the nobility. Although, as we have seen, Richard of York's assertion of his claim to the throne in 1460 had caused general consternation and dismay and although, a few months later, his son had been put on the throne by a mere handful of nobles to escape the consequence of a desperate political impasse, between 1459 and 1461 a majority of the peerage, albeit reluctantly, had taken part in the dynastic conflict — at least thirty-five noble families on the Lancastrian side and about nineteen or twenty on the Yorkist. Thereafter their involvement rapidly declined with every succeeding armed crisis. In 1469 no more than four peers supported Warwick and two of these were relations by marriage. In 1471 no more than ten are known to have fought for Henry VI and eight for Edward IV. As far as the nobility were concerned, it was becoming a plague on both dynastic houses. After 1461 they became increasingly disinclined to risk their lives and their estates for Lancaster, York, or later, Tudor. They cared more for their local influence and their local interests and preferred to remain aloof from perilous involvement in politics at the highest level.

8 Edward's Later Years, 1471 – 83

I

During Edward's reconquest of his kingdom fantastic, contradictory rumours spread abroad, for Hanseatic, Flemish and Breton ships were scouring the Channel making it difficult to get messages through from England during these momentous weeks. Bettini, the Milanese ambassador in France, was saying that hardly a bird could pass without being taken.

The duke of Burgundy ordered great festivities as soon as he heard of his brother-in-law's triumph. Well he might! His foremost adversary, Louis XI, had played high, had played high and lost. Warwick was dead. The Angevin cause in England lay in ruins, the allied Angevin cause in Naples shattered, for in December 1470 Queen Margaret's brother, John of Calabria, had died of apoplexy in Barcelona. Edward IV had found a copy of a secret agreement between Louis and the prince of Wales for the dismemberment of Burgundy in the prince's baggage after Tewkesbury and had sent it on to Charles. Charles, more infuriated than ever, in November 1471, concluded a triple alliance at St Omer with Ferdinand I of Naples and John II of Aragon whose anti-French policy was as determined as ever. Bitterly and too late, Louis XI now regarded a truce which Charles the Bold had made with him in April 1471 as a mere delaying tactic — an opinion which the Milanese ambassador had held at the time. Not only had events completely shattered Louis' carefully laid schemes for the encirclement of Burgundy but, with the tables turned, he now lay in danger of encirclement himself.

The duke of Milan advised him to contain Edward at home by formenting disturbance in England. As late as July 1471 Louis was still sending help to Jasper Tudor to carry on his struggle in Wales. At one moment it was even rumoured that Jasper would make himself king of England. Louis, however, was not in such grave danger as he feared. In spite of Charles the Bold's urgent desires, no alliance against France which relied upon English help could possibly move

279

for a long time. The realm was still disturbed and disorderly. Edward had no war chest and Philippe de Commynes was correct in his opinion that quick decisions to make war were not feasible in England. It was always necessary to go through the long process of extracting money from a reluctant parliament.

Italian diplomacy during the fifteenth century has always been notorious for its blatant cynicism. It hardly deserves to be so specially singled out for such abuse for the rulers of northern Europe were just as unscrupulous in their diplomatic intrigues as Machiavelli and his southern contemporaries. Louis XI had wantonly interfered in English politics in the 1460s to defend his own interests, supporting and abandoning the Lancastrian cause as he saw fit, not from sympathy but to meet the short-term dictates of his own manoeuvres in Europe. In the last resort the danger from Warwick had lain in his usefulness to Louis rather than in any wide support which he commanded at home. With Warwick slain in battle, with Margaret of Anjou a prisoner in the Tower of London and the Lancastrian 'seed crushed', intervention in future would not be quite so easy. Nevertheless until 1477 the mutual fears of Burgundy, England and France would still dominate the diplomacy of northwestern Europe, each, from time to time, feeling driven to interfere in the domestic affairs of its neighbours. Then, after the death of Charles the Bold in 1477, and particularly after 1483, when Valois-Hapsburg rivalry dominated the scene, the English government, hamstrung by lack of money and threatened by foreign support for pretenders to the throne, was compelled to react to the twists and turns of European politics in an entirely pragmatic way.

More immediately, Edward sent an additional fifteen hundred men to reinforce the Calais garrison and he may also have maintained a strong fleet in the Channel. Edward and Louis each seemed convinced that time was on his side. To gain time, in spite of recent events, each was prepared to make friendly gestures towards the other. Semi-secret negotiations were soon in train and by early September 1471 these had resulted in a truce to last until 1 May 1472.

The most urgent task at home was to suppress pockets of disaffection and restore order. Towards the end of August, hard-pressed by loyalist forces, Jasper Tudor and Henry of Richmond fled from Wales to Brittany. Two royal commissions went through Kent, Sussex, Essex and the Cinque ports and heavily fined those who had taken part in Fauconberg's rebellion. The fines raised £250 from Essex and over £1,700 from Kent. Elsewhere a few prominent people were fined and possibly a few bishops, for some prelates who were pardoned made 'gifts' (*dona*) to the king.

In general, however, the king adopted a policy of mercy and reconciliation for all ranks. Seeing the hopelessness of their cause, prominent exiles like Sir John Fortescue and Dr John Morton made their peace. Fortescue soon became a royal councillor though he died two years later. There was now a splendid career ahead of Morton. He was soon enjoying the king's 'secret trust and special favour'. By 1475 Louis XI recognized him as one of the most influential of the royal councillors. By 1478 he had obtained the rich bishopric of Ely and, under Henry VII, he rose to be a cardinal and archbishop of Canterbury. Even the minor gentry of Kent and the merchants of the Cinque Ports who had chosen the wrong side in 1470 – 71 were soon taking their accustomed part in local affairs. They were too useful to be permanently outlawed for one political mistake, grave though it had been.

More and more old opponents made their peace. In the sessions of 1472 to 1475 parliament reversed twenty-three of the attainders passed in the earlier period of the reign. Certainly at this time more men were pardoned than punished. This was, perhaps, no more than the conventions of the day expected and political realism demanded. Most surprising of all, there was no repetition of the enormous act of attainder of 1461. After an astonishingly long delay only thirteen people were now attainted for their rebellion during the years 1469 – 71 and at least six of the thirteen were already dead by the time the act was passed.

II

The explanation of the king's moderation seems to lie in a calculated indulgence towards his younger brothers — an indulgence which he expected them to return with loyal provincial support, part of yet another scheme for the redistribution of territorial power. This part of his wider territorial plan,[1] however, was soon bedevilled with frustration. Considering his earlier disloyalty, Clarence would have been well advised to behave for the future with a decent circumspection if not with humility. Instead, as aggressive as ever, he pushed his own territorial and financial interests with a ruthless lack of caution. Even his basic loyalty was soon in question again. Though there is no proof of sedition rumour soon came to link his name, and to link it continuously, with treasonable activities, even with the schemes of Louis XI.

[1]See below, pp. 297 ff.

Clarence had earlier received enormously generous endowments from the king. Even in 1471 when he had to disgorge part of the estates of the now restored Percy family, Edward granted him all the forfeited lands of the Courtenay earls of Devon in Devon and Cornwall. By this time, although he had lost elsewhere,[2] Clarence was one of the greatest landowners in southwestern England and Edward naturally expected him in return for his endowment to act as a stabilizing force in the area.

In spite of these benefactions and the enhancement of his power, Clarence was morbidly jealous of any favours shown to his brother Gloucester. As part of his current redistribution of power Edward planned that Gloucester should become one of the principal rulers of northern England: the successor of the dead Warwick and Montagu, the younger branch of the Neville family, and a counterpoise to the enormous hereditary influence of the Percy earls of Northumberland. To implement this scheme in June 1471 Edward granted Gloucester in tail male Warwick's lordships of Middleham and Sheriff Hutton in Yorkshire and Penrith in Northumberland.

Clarence, who was married to Warwick's elder daughter, Isabella, was determined to obtain the entire Warwick inheritance for himself. Probably already annoyed by these grants to his brother, he fell into furious anger on hearing of Gloucester's wish to marry the younger sister and co-heiress, the now widowed Anne Neville. After failing to prevent the marriage, which took place between February and March 1472, he is said to have vowed that in spite of the wedding there should be no division of the inheritance.

The king must have found this unseemly, and politically divisive, family quarrel particularly infuriating, for his indulgence towards his brothers had lost him valuable forfeitures for treason and had led him into perversions of the common law of inheritance of a kind which, as earlier mentioned, contemporary society regarded as tyrannical. The exceptionally small number of attainders at this period was certainly the result of the desire of his younger brothers for maximum security in possession of the Neville inheritance. If the Nevilles, Warwick and Montagu, had been attainted, their lands would have been forfeited to the crown and the wives of Clarence and Gloucester could have obtained them only by royal grant. In view of the Commons' liking for acts of resumption, this would have been a precarious form of tenure as compared with inheritance at common law.

Equally important for the two royal dukes the larger part of the

[2]According to B.P. Wolffe the principal cause of the Resumption Act of 1473 was to force Clarence to disgorge the considerable gains which he had made during the Readeption. Under the act Clarence had to surrender the honour of Tutbury and other lands and offices granted him from the duchy of Lancaster — which he fiercely resented and tried to impede.

Warwick inheritance belonged, in her own right, to the Countess Anne, Warwick's widow, and many of Warwick's own estates, being held in tail male, should have descended to the heir-at-law, George Neville, the son of Marquess Montagu. In the parliamentary session of 1474 an act was passed treating the countess of Warwick as if she 'were now naturally dead' and dividing her inheritance between her daughters. A second act barred the claims of any heir male of Marquess Montagu to Warwick's own lands. The wives of the royal dukes thus prematurely gained their maternal inheritance and acquired vast estates at the expense of the legitimate heir male.

The second act stated that the king had originally intended to attaint Montagu and his heirs but had refrained from doing so at the request of Clarence, Gloucester and other lords of the blood royal. To have attainted a long list of lesser people while letting major offenders go free (even though dead) would have been even more rankly unjust than the treatment of the Countess Anne and George Neville. The escape of the Nevilles thus formed an umbrella for other offenders and the king's indulgence towards his brothers' interests lost him considerable sums of money.[3]

After such extremes of favour had been shown him, at the expense of both the king's pocket and his reputation, Clarence might well have shown enough gratitude to be loyal. Not a bit! Already early in 1472 Clarence was involved in schemes with his wife's uncles, Archbishop Neville and John de Vere, earl of Oxford. No one knows why George Neville was unexpectedly arrested on 25 April and imprisoned in Calais. Warkworth's *Chronicle* claims that he had been intriguing with the exiled Oxford who was raiding on the borders of the Calais pale. No contemporary source claims that Clarence was involved in these intrigues. Suspicion, however, remains. A few months later in November, Pietro Aliprando, the somewhat rumour-mongering papal envoy, reported from Bruges (for what the statement is worth) that Edward before invading France would have to decide about the regents and lieutenants to govern, so that he would not be overthrown by his brother, the duke of Clarence. In 1473 it was widely believed that Clarence and Oxford were in touch. Now that the house of Lancaster was extinguished Clarence was the most obvious focus for plots with which rumours consistently and continuously linked his name.

Louis XI was always deep in intrigue and generally willing to harass Edward by assisting the earl of Oxford. Before the end of 1471 both Burgundy and Brittany, in an attempt to exploit Edward's very

---

[3]Even this modest act of attainder was passed only in the fifth and final session of the parliament of 1475 — a long delay which indicates that there had been considerable argument about it.

natural resentment over recent events, were trying to involve him in anti-French schemes, but Edward also had cause to remember his initially cold reception in Burgundy during his exile. Early in 1472 Duke Francis of Brittany, badly scared by French threats against his duchy, appealed to Edward for 6,000 archers. Fully aware that French control of the Breton coast would be a serious threat to English interests, Edward met the appeal in part by sending Earl Ryvers and Sir Edward Wydeville across the Channel with 1,000 archers. The prospect of a triple alliance between Brittany, England and Burgundy once more became a feasible proposition. By August 1472 Brittany had beaten off a French attack. Edward sent another 2,000 archers and equipped a fleet for service in the Channel. At the same time Charles the Bold was trying to tempt Edward into hostilities against France with the offer of the county of Eu in Normandy in return for the service of 3,000 archers against Louis XI. On 11 September 1472 Edward concluded the treaty of Châteaugiron with Brittany, providing for an English invasion of either Gascony or Normandy by 1 April 1473. A month later he summoned parliament to ask for money for war.

Louis XI and the Hansards, who for commercial reasons of their own wished to put pressure upon the Yorkist government, now began to help the earl of Oxford. On 28 May 1473 Oxford attempted a landing on the Essex coast, a county where he held considerable estates and where he hoped for local support. Driven off by the earl of Essex, Lord Dynham and Lord Duras, he supported his fleet by piracy in the Channel until, at the end of September, he seized St Michael's Mount off the coast of Cornwall. The threat from Oxford was never very great. Seduced by the king's offer of a pardon, Oxford's men soon began to desert him and in January 1474 he was forced to surrender. He had certainly, though mistakenly, hoped for support in England. Christoforo di Bollati, the Milanese ambassador in France, had written in July 1473 that Oxford, after his arrival in England, had sent Louis XI a list of twenty-four lords and knights and *one duke*[4] who had promised to support him. Only some rather obscure statements in *The Paston Letters* mention Clarence but once again many people both at home and abroad believed him to be involved both with Oxford and with Louis XI.

[4]The editor of the *Calendar of State Papers Milanese* (p. 176) suggested that the duke of Exeter was the duke concerned but Exeter was a prisoner at this time.

III

The parliament which the king had summoned to raise money for war sat through no less than five sessions between 1472 and 1475. Both the parliamentary records and other evidence reveal a distinct lack of enthusiasm for foreign war. The Croyland Chronicler wrote that, in order to popularize the war policy,

> Many speeches of remarkable eloquence were made, both of a public and private nature, especially on behalf of the duke of Burgundy. The result was that all applauded the king's intentions and bestowed the greatest praise on his plans

and readily voted large sums of money.

The Chronicler's statement about the propaganda speeches was certainly correct, but circumstantial evidence throws considerable doubt upon the veracity of his other assertions. Fortunately, a unique document, the full text of one of these speeches, was preserved at Christ Church, Canterbury — a speech most probably delivered in the first session of the parliament (6 October to 30 November 1472), possibly by the chancellor, Robert Stillington, bishop of Bath and Wells.

The speech was long and eloquent. It covers no less than eleven printed pages. Its most remarkable feature was its emphasis on the defence of the realm. The chancellor (if indeed the speech was his) gave remarkably little space to the king's claim to the French throne. He did not even mention it until the end of the fifth page and even then he rapidly disposed of it in a mere fourteen lines. The rest of the speech was a long catalogue of defensive arguments. So many were put forward, Pelion was piled upon Ossa to so great an extent, that the entire effect is somewhat unconvincing. Although the king had extirpated the worst causes of domestic dissension (so the argument runs), 'extortions, oppressions, robberies and other great mischiefs' still abounded. If rigid justice were employed to suppress such enormities, within a few years the remedy would be worse than the disease. The violent perpetrators of these enormities were necessary to the defence of the realm. In other words many of the country's thugs were essential members of its ruling class. Their aggressive instincts could be best and most effectively employed upon foreign soil. After a successful war many gentlemen, younger sons and others, could be rewarded with land, men without a livelihood could be settled in garrisons and live upon their wages — and the chancellor clinched this part of his argument by informing his audience that since the Norman Conquest internal peace had never prevailed for long, 'in any king's day but in such as have made war outwards'.

He provided secondary reasons in plenty, all negative and defensive in tone. Possession of the French coast would make the English Channel safer for English shipping and reduce the intolerable financial burden of keeping the sea. The Scots and the Danes were threatening the country and the subtle and crafty enterprises of King Louis of France for long had been and still were a constant danger in spite of Edward's efforts to reach agreement with him. Now for the first time during the king's reign the state of the country and the king's foreign alliances combined to make the riposte of war feasible. Therefore war abroad, taking the aggressive line, was the surest guarantee against invasion and was the indubitable path to internal security and prosperity.

The speech makes a startling contrast to the earlier propaganda of Henry V. Although Henry occasionally used defensive arguments he used them only in a secondary, minor way. They never formed his main theme. Edward's argument that attack was the best form of defence was predominent throughout this speech reinforced by arguments about internal pacification and by strong appeals to the greed of those who might volunteer to take part in the expedition. Two interpretations are possible: that the emphasis upon defence was quite genuine; or that Edward was concealing dynastic motives of conquest in a cloud of spurious propaganda. Unfortunately we know nothing of the confidential discussions of the king and his councillors. As so often we can only guess at their motives.

Earlier in the century the English had quickly lost interest in Henry V's dynastic ambitions after a few years experience had shown how costly their realization would be. It may well be that Edward knew that after 1430 only a small section of the court aristocracy and those who stood to lose land grants in Normandy showed any enthusiasm for the war. In 1467 – 8 Edward's motives for war and his appeals for money had certainly been defensive. It is possible, of course, that his motives in 1472 were genuinely aggressive but, on balance, it seems more probable that the emphasis in the chancellor's speech represented Edward's true thinking, that he was scared of possible French interference and therefore tried to forestall it through aggressive measures himself.[5]

The war preparations, however, never went smoothly either abroad or at home. As in 1468 the defection of Brittany began the rot. The duke of Brittany had already signed a truce with Louis XI even before Edward had ratified the treaty of Châteaugiron. So did

[5]For more detailed arguments see J.R. Lander, *Crown and Nobility, 1450 – 1509* (1976), pp. 48 – 52, 220 – 41. For arguments in favour of the alternative explanation see C. Ross, *Edward IV* (1974), chapter 9.

Burgundy under pressure from Brittany. Edward, himself, therefore, while continuing his war preparations made a truce with Louis to last until 1 April 1471. In August 1473 English and Burgundian envoys met at Bruges but got nowhere. Charles the Bold had now become more interested in expansion towards the east — part of his hopes, in alliance with the Emperor, of elevating his duchy into a kingdom. As he increasingly concentrated his troops in Alsace for war against the Swiss, by successive agreements he extended his truce with France until May 1475. Then on 25 July 1474 he suddenly signed the treaty of London agreeing to cooperate with the English in an invasion of France before 1 July 1475.

To facilitate invasion Edward in February 1474 had already signed the treaty of Utrecht with the Hansards. As it turned out some of the rather vague terms of the treaty and its execution ultimately worked to the detriment of English merchants,[6] but at least it freed England from a prolonged commercial quarrel and an expensive, if sporadic, commercial war and allowed her to convey a large army and all its equipment across the Channel.

Further valuable alliances followed. In October 1474 a marriage treaty was concluded with Scotland under which James III's son, James, just over a year old, and the Princess Cecily, now four, were betrothed. They were to be married within six months of reaching marriageable age and there was to be a truce between the two kingdoms lasting until 1519. In May 1475 Edward reaffirmed his alliance with Ferdinand and Isabella of Spain and in the same month he concluded a treaty of friendship with Denmark. Brittany suddenly, at last, came back into the fold, promising to aid Edward's attack on France with 8,000 men and in return Lord Audley and Lord Duras were to serve under the duke with 2,000 archers. By the beginning of June 1475, after so many disappointing vicissitudes, the prospect of success at last appeared to be in sight.

If events in the diplomatic sphere were progressing well the same can hardly be said of the domestic front. The course of the war preparations shows that the political nation was far from wholehearted in support of royal policy. All the speeches in parliament had alike failed to raise any conspicuous enthusiasm. As shown elsewhere in this book,[7] between 1472 and 1475, Edward raised about £116,000 (or nearly the equivalent of four fifteenths and tenths) for the war, nearly as much as Henry V had collected during a similar period. Yet he accumulated this war chest only in the face of the most humiliating suspicion and resistance — refusal to hand over the money to the king until parliament was convinced that an invasion of France was about

---

[6]See above, pp. 28 – 9.
[7]See above, pp. 97 – 8.

to begin, extreme resistance to experiments with taxation, local delays in assessment, the refusal of local collectors to deliver proceeds to the regional repositories assigned to receive them, embezzlement by collectors, robberies by local gangs. These were years of obstruction and administrative humiliation. Even at the end of it all there was insufficient money for the campaign and Edward had to tout round part of the country himself, with immense personal trouble, raising more funds by the dubious process of a benevolence. Recruitment, which began in the middle of 1474, was more successful though once again the results demonstrate a certain lack of enthusiasm for the king's policy. Edward managed to assemble the largest army which had so far left England in the fifteenth century. He himself told the Milanese ambassador that he had raised 20,000 men. Exchequer sources (which may possibly be incomplete) showed that he paid a force of at least 11,451 combatants and Commynes wrote that there was a numerous body of camp servants. In addition there were the 2,000 archers sent to Brittany and a fleet with about 3,000 men to protect the crossing to France.

As usual during the later middle ages, the king had to recruit his forces through private enterprise. Men contracted with the king under indentures to raise contingents of men-at-arms and archers, the ideal combination for effectiveness, it was generally held, being three archers to every man-at-arms. An analysis of these contingents and their leaders shows the nature of the support upon which the king could call and the popularity, or lack of popularity, of the enterprise among various social groups in the country.

Naturally peers and royal officials were conspicuous. It was part of their traditional duty to support the king in warlike enterprises. The peers who took part in the 1475 campaign can be divided into two groups: a group closely related to the king and queen or holding appointments in the royal household who, together with officials of the household and a few from other government departments who took part, may be designated as the 'court interest'; and a second group of 'country peers'. The members of the court interest between them produced about 63 per cent of the men-at-arms and 66 per cent of the archers. They were, thus, overwhelmingly important as recruiting agents for the campaign. Eleven such 'court peers' produced 516 men-at-arms and 4,080 archers between them while twelve country peers raised only 213 men-at-arms and 1,619 archers. In addition, among the court circle the household officials produced 50 contingent leaders with a total of 270 men-at-arms and 2,587 archers and nine other officers 29 and 134 respectively.

As against these impressive totals, the contribution of the rest of the country was comparatively small: a mere 108 non-noble leaders who

raised only 220 men-at-arms and 1,693 archers between them.
Among them were 5 bannerets and 13 knights. Of the remaining 90
the official records called 52 esquires and another 6 gentlemen. There
remained 32 whose status is not given and who presumably fell below
even the rank of gentlemen. Outside the court circle and the 'country
peers', only the 18 bannerets and knights and 15 others can be
described as men who were really prominent in their own local,
county communities. Of the 90 leaders below the rank of knight, 70
led only archers and 27 of them led as few as three archers or less. This
was really scraping the barrel — a wretched total for the whole country
which seems to indicate that most people were at best indifferent if
not hostile to the war policy.

Nor was the quality of the army as impressive as it might have been.
The ratio of archers to men-at-arms was very much in excess of the
desirable level. Only in two small contingents did the figure approach
the ideal standard. For the army as a whole it was over seven to one.

The government had strained every nerve to raise money. By the
standards of the day its war propaganda had been intensive. It had
managed to raise an impressively large force. Yet it does not seem to
have aroused popular enthusiasm or to have produced an army of
high quality. The army never stood the shock of battle. One cannot,
therefore, be dogmatic about its fighting qualities, but the probabi-
lities would indicate a lack of military distinction. It was over two
decades since the English had fought a campaign abroad, and the
army of 1475, like those which fought in the Wars of the Roses at
home, was hastily recruited for a particular occasion with little or
none of the professional expertise which prolonged warfare brings
with it. Some foreigners held no very high opinion of such hastily
recruited Englishmen. In their view the English who, they said,
always demanded every creature comfort even when in the field,
became excellent soldiers only after some experience, and Englishmen were still serving as mercenaries abroad. Moreover, considering
the obsolete nature of English fortifications, they were entirely
unfamiliar with one important branch of continental warfare, the
conduct of sieges. All in all foreigners considered them more or less
useless when they first crossed the seas. The army of 1475 were certainly not the type of seasoned veterans of the earlier phases of the
Hundred Years War. One may, perhaps, conclude that they were a
somewhat dubious legion to pitch against Louis XI's professional
corps. By this time the English had lost their ancient technical
superiority over the French. It was probably fortunate for the preservation of Edward IV's reputation as a general that he never, in the
end, fought against continental professionals.

In all probability Edward originally planned to invade Normandy but changed his mind owing to the disturbing behaviour of Charles the Bold. By the end of June the transport of the army to Calais had begun. It went on steadily without interruption, partly because the French, still expecting an invasion through Normandy, had concentrated their naval patrols in that area.

Edward undoubtedly regarded the full cooperation of Burgundy in the venture as essential to success, and Burgundian cooperation was not forthcoming. Pursuing his eastern ambitions Charles the Bold at the end of July 1474 had laid seige to Neuss in the Rhineland. Though small, the city was well fortified and Burgundian losses were heavy. Louis XI's activities drew into the war against the duke the Emperor Frederick III, Duke René of Lorraine and above all the Swiss who defeated a Burgundian army at Héricourt on 13 November. The seige of Neuss dragged on and, in the end, only a French invasion of Burgundian territory forced Charles to abandon it. In July he moved to France to meet Edward, but brought with him only a small personal force — little more than a personal bodyguard, instead of the considerable army which the English had hoped for.[8]

After all his propaganda, after all the money he had wrung from his reluctant subjects, Edward dared not yet abandon the campaign. It may well be, however, that even before leaving England the king and his advisers were looking for a credible way of escape. Philippe de Commynes, who had left the service of Charles the Bold in 1472 and was now one of Louis XI's most intimate councillors, wrote that just before the invasion when the English sent Garter Herald to France to present a formal defiance, Louis in a secret interview told the herald that he knew Edward was invading only under pressure from Burgundy and the English commons and that Charles the Bold's position was already too precarious for him to give much assistance. Garter, according to Commynes, replied that to save face Edward could listen to peace proposals only after he had crossed to France and he gave Louis the names of Edward's councillors most favourably disposed to peace. Commynes would hardly have invented such a story.

So things turned out. Edward's allies had completely let him down. Charles the Bold was too involved elsewhere and Francis of Brittany, in spite of the archers which Edward had sent him, showed no sign of moving. Both Louis' desires and Edward's needs now coincided. English opinion was divided. The rank and file, who had joined the army in the hope of loot and booty, apparently wanted to carry on. Some of the lords shared the opinion that the whole enterprise would be better abandoned at once. To save face, however, the English marched through Ardres and Guisnes to St Omer, then through

[8]R. Vaughan, *Charles the Bold* (1973), pp. 344–5, however, argues that this was part of a deliberate plan.

Fauconberge and St Pol to Doulens and St Quentin. On the march Charles the Bold refused them entry to any of his towns and a treacherous so-called ally, the Count of St Pol, defended St Quentin instead of handing it over to the English as he had promised. This may well have been the last straw for Edward.

By this time Louis XI had moved up to Beauvais. The English were already short of money and it looked as if they would be left to fight the French alone, and the French were numerically far superior and probably far more experienced and better trained. All considerations now pointed to the desirability of coming to terms as soon as possible, and by 18 August the English and French had made a series of agreements which came to be collectively known as the treaty of Pécquigny. The king of France agreed to pay Edward 75,000 crowns (£15,000) within fifteen days and an annual pension of 50,000 crowns (£10,000) as long as they both lived. His heir, the dauphin, was to marry Edward's first or second daughter, and Louis was to provide her with a jointure of £60,000 a year 'after the estimation of France'. The English were to leave France as soon as possible giving hostages to be released as soon as the greater part of the army had departed. Edward also obtained a secret agreement binding each king to aid the other if 'wronged or disobeyed' by his subjects and a commercial treaty to last for seven years.

For three or four days the English army got gloriously and squalidly drunk in Amiens at French expense. Three miles down the river at Pécquigny the two kings met, for security reasons upon a bridge specially built with a screen across the centre, pierced by a trellis through which conversation could be carried on. There, after exchanging the articles of the treaty, the two kings talked alone through the trellis. The English army marched back to Calais by 4 September and the voyage home began at once. Widespread rumours on the continent predicted tumult and perils when Edward arrived home in England. Charles the Bold confidently spoke of revolution when the English heard what had happened. It was even said that Edward dared not let his brothers return before him 'as he feared some disturbance, especially as the duke of Clarence on a previous occasion, aspired to make himself king'. It is extraordinary how persistent seditious rumours about Clarence had become. From England we have only the comments of the Croyland Chronicler. According to this writer Edward did indeed fear 'mischief' and acted quickly to suppress it. If he had not,

> the number of people complaining of the unfair management of the kingdom, in consequence of such quantities of treasure being abstracted from the coffers of everyone and uselessly consumed would have increased to such a degree that no one could have said whose head amongst the king's advisers was in safety.

The king, however, appears to have been in little danger. Gloucester is said to have been against the peace but the leading councillors and captains most probably approved. At least eight of them received substantial pensions from the king of France. But there was nothing particularly unusual or reprehensible about that in those days. Lord Hastings, who received 2,000 crowns a year, was already receiving one thousand from the duke of Burgundy. Some of the rank and file took service as mercenaries with the Burgundians. The principal menace seems to have come from the depredations of disbanded soldiers in Hampshire, Wiltshire and Yorkshire and, according to the Croyland writer, Edward quickly suppressed them by making a personal judicial tour in the south and sending Richard of Gloucester to do the same in the north. He also remitted that part of the war taxation, three quarters of a fifteenth and tenth, which still remained uncollected.

In fact both king and country benefited from the results, though at the same time the whole inglorious episode brought home to the king the very definite limitations upon his power. The commercial clauses of the treaty of Pécquigny allowed a considerable expansion of English trade and the French pension lessened the need for taxation. The fiasco of war taxation must have convinced the king, as later events in 1489 must equally have convinced Henry VII, that he could not afford an adventurous foreign policy. His subjects had shown him just how reluctant they were to support him with money. It was obvious that they would be even more reluctant to do so in the future, the realization of which must surely have been a major factor in his wary, cautious approach to foreign policy during his later years.

IV

As we have already seen, persistent rumours linked the name of the duke of Clarence with sedition and continental observers believed him to be a natural focus for rebellion. Nothing was ever proved against him and in the end it was an act of judicial violence, appalling even by fifteenth-century standards, which led to his destruction. The duchess of Clarence died on 22 December 1476, a few weeks after the birth of her son Richard, who also died a few weeks later. On 5 January 1477 Charles the Bold of Burgundy was killed at the battle of Nancy. His widow, Margaret of York, who seems to have had a blind affection for Clarence, immediately conceived the unrealistic plan of marrying her brother to her step-daughter, Mary of Burgundy, the richest heiress in Christendom. Mary was already affianced to the Archduke Maximilian of Hapsburg. The dowager duchess's doting scheme would have aroused the hostility both of Maximilian's father, the Emperor, Frederick III, and Louis XI of France, scared as ever that the king of England would regain a foothold on the continent. If carried through the plan would have involved Edward IV in a ruinously long and costly war for the defence of the Burgundian territories — a war which (after his humiliating experiences of the years 1472 – 5) he knew to be totally beyond his capacities. Edward, possibly in a great council on 13 February 1477, made it quite clear that he would have nothing to do with such a matrimonial and diplomatic absurdity.

Even before this rejection of the marriage proposals, Clarence had begun to avoid the court, an ominous sign of ill-will. Frustrated abroad he vented his resentment at home and his actions rose to a frenzy of indiscretion. On 12 April two of his servants leading a gang, afterwards alleged to be four score strong, went to Cayford in Somerset and there kidnapped Ankarette Twynyho, one of the duchess of Clarence's former attendants. They carried the unfortunate woman over three counties to Warwick, one of the centres of Clarence's influence. On 15 April, all within a brief three hours, she was indicted before the Warwickshire justices of the peace of poisoning her former mistress, falsely convicted by a terrorized jury and hanged. At the same time John Thuresby of Warwick, equally innocent, was hanged for the murder of Clarence's son Richard. A third victim, Roger Tocotes, who was accused of complicity in both crimes, fortunately escaped.

The accusations, those against Ankarette Twynyho in particular, were so fantastic that only a seriously disturbed mind could have produced them. Edward had already smirched his own reputation by playing fast and loose with the common law of inheritance to satisfy Clarence's greed. Yet in spite of this and although he had to turn a blind eye often enough upon oppressions committed by magnates, in a peculiar illogical way he was proud of his reputation for justice. If he allowed Clarence to commit the crime of embracery and to commit judicial murder with impunity, his reputation and that of his dynasty would be for ever blackened. Even so by the standards of the day these were hardly offences heinous enough to warrant the infliction of the death penalty upon a prince of the blood royal.

Edward may have riposted obliquely but deliberately by bringing different accusations against members of his brother's entourage, or possibly these accusations may originally have been independently planned, merely coinciding in time with the judicial murders.

About this time an Oxford astronomer, John Stacey, was accused of

practicing sorcery and, confessing to it after a very severe interrogation, implicated another Oxford clerk, Thomas Black, and a
member of Clarence's own household, Thomas Burdett of Arrowe. A
commission of oyer and terminer which investigated these accusations
found Stacey and Burdett guilty of disseminating treasonable
writings and plotting the king's death by necromancy and other
means. On 20 May, protesting their innocence to the very last, they
were hanged, drawn and quartered at Tyburn. On the same day an
order went out to the Warwickshire justices to transfer the records of
the Twynyho and Thuresby cases to Westminster.

The day after the execution, or possibly the day following,
Clarence, for the first time for a long period, entered the council
chamber at Westminster and caused Dr John Goddard to read to the
assembled councillors a declaration of innocence which Burdett and
Stacey had made at the foot of the gallows. His choice of a spokesman
was, to say the least, provocative for Goddard was the same Minorite
friar who had preached upon Henry VI's right to the throne at St
Paul's Cross on 30 September 1470.

Under this last provocation Edward's long-tried patience finally
broke. Even so he cannot be accused of acting with furious
precipitation and destroying his brother in a fit of rage. It was a full
seven months later that in mid-January 1478 the king at last exhibited
to parliament an indictment signed with his own hand and demanded
Clarence's attainder. The indictment included a long catalogue of
old offences together with accusations now thrown against him for the
first time — direct accusations that he had plotted for the throne and,
by implication, that in return for his support during Henry VI's
Readeption it had been entailed upon him failing heirs male in the
house of Lancaster.

This accusation involved a story that obviously puzzled contemporaries. It puzzled them to the point of scepticism and it has
remained mysterious ever since. The indictment which the king
signed and which is now to be found on the parliament roll states that,
apart from his more recent and notorious crimes, in 1470 and 1471
Clarence had 'laboured' to obtain the crown and that he had since
concealed an exemplification which entailed the succession upon him
in the event of failure of the Lancastrian male line. This extraordinary tale now appeared for the first time in 1478 and independent
supporting evidence for it is entirely lacking. Warkworth's *Chronicle*
tells of such an agreement made in France between Margaret of
Anjou and Clarence, but Warkworth's narrative dates from after
1478 and his story is best regarded as no more than a garbled version
of Edward's accusation against his brother. Considering the intensely
strained relations which had existed between the queen and Clarence

during those months, any such accommodation between them was highly improbable. No London writer nor foreign chronicler heard of it at the time, and that was just the sort of highly coloured story they delighted to include in their narratives. This story of the agreement in France did not appear in print until 1580 when the Elizabethan antiquary, John Stowe (who included more and more details about the Clarence affair in each of his successive works), adopted it after reading Warkworth's still unprinted manuscript. A further elaboration mentioning an *act* of parliament in 1470-71 (Edward's own accusation never mentioned an act as such) had appeared for the first time in Hall's *Chronicle* in 1548, a possible invention which went even beyond contemporary rumours. Then in 1592, Stowe, still expanding his narratives as he widened his reading, gave an account of the exemplification, an account which is a rough paraphrase of part of the king's indictment on the parliament roll of 1478.[9]

These stories, both of the parliament of 1470 to 1471 and of the exemplification, therefore derive entirely from Edward IV's loaded accusations. Apart from Warkworth who got them from somewhat confused rumours about the indictment, no contemporary or near-contemporary ever mentioned these vital details. Like Warkworth they could well have done so, but the well-informed Croyland Chronicler, Dominic Mancini, Sir Thomas More and Polydore Vergil, one and all expressed themselves bewildered as to the real reasons for the duke of Clarence's final condemnation. Their narratives are conspicuous for their evasions, even for their hints of perjury. Even the generally confident Edward Hall threw up his hands in despair, confronted by what he called 'conjectures which as often deceive the imaginations of fantastical folks'. No contemporary, or near-contemporary, writers were satisfied in their own minds as to the real reasons for Clarence's death, but they were all reluctant to accept the king's indictment at its face value.

Their scepticism was justified for the king's indictment was ambiguously drafted with superb skill, mingling notorious facts with accusations hitherto unknown and with vaguely damaging innuendo. The exemplification was one of the hitherto unknown accusations. Nobody had ever heard of it until that time. Nobody has seen it since. If it existed, most probably somebody had fabricated the document. Possibly Clarence himself had forged it and the royal officers found it among his papers when they arrested him. His entire past showed that he would stop at nothing to consummate his inordinate ambitions. Equally his brother the king had ample motives for such action and he had earlier shown himself quite capable of perjury. Neither persistent

---

[9]For a full exposition of the evidence and arguments from it see Lander, *Crown and Nobility*, pp. 242 – 66

rumours of Clarence's seditious intrigues since 1471 nor his recent outrageous behaviour were sufficient to merit the death penalty. Only treason could slay the kindred of a king and it is possible that 'evidence' for the necessary treason was deliberately fabricated.

Clarence denied all the charges. No one spoke in his defence, parliament passed the act of attainder, and the duke of Buckingham, as steward of England, pronounced the death sentence. Even then Edward seemed to hesitate and it was only after Sir William Allington, the speaker of the Commons, a few days later asked that the verdict should be carried out that Clarence was at last executed, probably as many contemporaries believed by drowning in a butt of Malmsey wine.

Clarence was a superficially intelligent character, handsome and dangerously eloquent, but fundamentally lacking any idea of loyalty, reality or even common sense. Now aged twenty-nine, since adolescence he had been a public nuisance and a danger to a dynasty only precariously established. Fratricide may be a horrible spectacle but Clarence thoroughly deserved his fate.

V

After Clarence's death Edward's last years were secure—secure enough in the opinion of some of his subjects for his firm government to degenerate into tyranny. The Croyland Chronicler (later echoed by Polydore Vergil who seems to have been acquainted with his narrative) wrote:

> After the perpetration of this deed, many persons left King Edward fully persuaded that he would be able to lord it over the whole Kingdom at his will and pleasure, all those idols being removed [to whom] the multitude, ever desirous of change, had been in the habit of turning in times past. The king ... after this period performed the duties of his office with such a high hand, that he appeared to be dreaded by all his subjects, while he himself stood in fear of no one.

The same writer also commented upon Edward's industry and his tremendous grasp of detail. He was astounded that a man given to such fits of debauchery.

> should have had a memory so retentive in all respects that the names and estates used to recur to him just as though he had been in the habit of seeing them daily of all the persons dispersed throughout the counties of his kingdom and this, even, if in the districts in which they lived they held the rank only of mere gentlemen.

It was in these later years that he gained his reputation for harshness and avarice, by applying a much stricter supervision over the distribution of local offices, there placing his own men who kept him so well informed of local actions that nobody could do anything without his knowledge, by appointing new highly powered supervisors of the customs system and by insisting upon the exaction of his feudal rights.[10]

These years saw the climax of a new assertion of power and the final working out of the territorial dispositions which had given the king so much trouble throughout his reign — a new territorial reorganization first begun in 1471, based partly upon the creation of appanages for members of the royal family and partly, as earlier, relying upon the powers of the nobility in their own districts. It evolved into a formidable if somewhat precarious assertion of control, and its methods, like those of Henry VII some years later,[11] developed aspects so unpleasant that they resulted in an acute backlash of resentment.

In Wales and the Marches the Yorkist earldom of March included twenty-three of the marcher lordships and the civil wars brought many more under Edward's control, either temporarily or permanently. Unfortunately his 'master lock' in south Wales, William Herbert,[12] first earl of Pembroke, had been killed in 1469. Herbert's son, also called William, had been only fourteen at the time, far too young to fill his formidable father's place. Edward had at first entrusted this area to Richard of Gloucester but in 1471 he had transferred Richard to northern England. Then, with Herbert still too young to take control of the area, Edward was compelled to build up an alternative system of control. This he did so successfully that to extend it further he compelled Herbert to surrender his Welsh lands to the prince of Wales and to surrender his Welsh title in return for the earldom of Huntingdon and manors in Somerset and Dorset,[13] thus bringing more Welsh lordships under direct royal control. Finally, owing to minorities, the estates of the Stafford dukes of Buckingham were in the king's hands between 1460 and 1498, except for the years 1474 – 83 when the duke was closely allied with the royal family by his marriage to Elizabeth Wydeville's sister, Catherine. Even so, Edward never trusted him and more or less excluded him from power. So the king was the greatest landowner and the greatest franchise-holder in the area and could therefore exercise immense patronage through the distribution of offices.

Meanwhile the perennial disorder of Wales and the Marches continued, resulting to a great degree, as it had for decades, from the

---

[10]See above, chapter 3.
[11]See below, pp. 353 ff.
[12]See above, p. 228.
[13]C. Ross (*Edward IV*, p. 195) claims that the second William Herbert was 'ineffective and uninterested in his duties' but I know of no evidence for this. In 1471 Edward had somewhat oddly granted the young man (at the age of sixteen) many of his father's offices in south Wales.

negligence of absentee English magnates. The solution ultimately found was a royal solution. In the winter of 1473 – 4 the infant prince of Wales and his household, headed by Anthony, Earl Ryvers, and John Alcock, bishop of Rochester, were placed permanently at Ludlow Castle. The king appointed a council to govern the household and the prince's estates. In piecemeal fashion and rather haphazardly, the king thrust more and more responsibilities upon the prince's council including the control of the lordships of the earldom of March (1477) and a general commission of oyer and terminer.

By the late 1470s the prince's council exercised complete power in the principality, in the earldom of March and in the other numerous lordships which belonged to the crown. Although it could not interfere in the day-to-day affairs of the marcher lordships which were still in private hands, it exercised a valuable supervisory authority over them and over the Marches in general. In any case, most of these remaining marcher franchises were minor and were harmless enough by this time. In addition the council's jurisdiction covered a much wider area than is generally realized. On more than one occasion it intervened in the affairs of a city as far to the east as Coventry.

The north presented considerably more intractable problems for it was a border. A border was not the neat barbed wire fence of today's well-defined frontiers but a no-man's land many miles deep, subject to devastating raids from either side and needing a permanent military establishment. This was provided by the affinities of the local great landlords, by this time financially assisted in a very big way by the king in payments to such magnates appointed as wardens of the Marches, a vicious circle by which the Exchequer reinforced the existing powers of the local aristocracy at the expense of the monarchy. Royal authority in this area was, therefore, unusually dependent upon the cooperation of the aristocrary and political peace was more important than impartial justice.

In 1471 Henry Percy had been restored to power in the Eastern March, and throughout Northumberland. Edward now placed his brother Gloucester in the room of the dead Nevilles in the Western March, in Cumberland and Westmorland. Northumberland and Gloucester shared territorial power in Yorkshire. Between 1470 and 1483 twelve men served as sheriffs in the three Ridings of Yorkshire. Six of them were Gloucester's retainers and four Northumberland's. The duke and the earl jealously competed for local influence. In June 1474 they arranged something like a compromise when Northumberland entered into indentures with Gloucester to do him loyal service saving only his duty to the king. In return the duke promised to be the earl's 'good lord' at all times. Though technically couched in terms of lordship and subordination the agreement really established a division of power, a demarcation of influence and territory especially in the East Riding, for the duke's power was dominant in the rest of the county. Between 1472 and 1478 the king granted Gloucester increasing numbers of estates and offices in Yorkshire. To a great degree he had also taken over the former Neville affinity. In 1473 – 4 twenty-two out of thirty-six of his retainers receiving fees from the lordship of Middleham had been in Warwick's service in 1464 – 5.

In the end it was war against Scotland which gave Gloucester a more complete predominance. In 1482 the king made him his lieutenant in the north. Even greater power was to come. In January 1483 the king decided to create for him a vast hereditary palatinate, including Cumberland, Westmorland and any parts of southwestern Scotland which he conquered. He was to possess more or less the same immunities as the bishop of Durham. Moreover the wardenship of the Western Marches was granted to Gloucester and his heirs in perpetuity.

Useful though it might be for Edward to have so loyal a brother in charge in the north, his policy was in the long term extremely unwise. This was the first time that one of the wardenships of the Marches had been permanently alienated from the crown. No one, not even the Nevilles, had ever enjoyed so great an accumulation of power in the northwest before and it threatened the permanent establishment of a new magnate family with quite unprecedented powers. Only Gloucester's unexpected accession to the throne reversed a situation so potentially dangerous for the future.

Allowing for such unwise extremes in so boosting Gloucester's power, there was really no alternative to relying upon magnate government in the north. Mere officials sent into the area by the central government would have been powerless before the feuds of the borderland. The only effective way of enforcing the peace, of keeping so turbulent a countryside in some condition of order, was to give official commissions to magnates who could enforce their decisions with powers of coercion derived from their local estates, retinues and feed men, from the power of private property and local aristocratic patronage. In such an area there was no feasible alternative to government through bastard feudalism.

This apparently was not the only royal appanage which Edward intended to erect in his later years. His plans to create yet another for his younger son also involved the unscrupulous manipulation of certain aristocratic inheritances for the fulfilment of the scheme. This manipulation, with others, certainly lay behind the increasing hints of tyranny which were now being levelled against him.

In March 1475 Edward settled upon his second son, Richard, duke of York, lands forfeited by the Welles and Willoughby families under the most recent act of attainder. This destroyed the families' hopes of reversal and recovery of their properties — a hope quite usual in aristocratic families in such circumstances. Then in the will which he made before leaving for the French campaign, the king provided York with Fotheringhay, Stamford, Grantham and other duchy of York lands and certain duchy of Lancaster honours in the northeastern Midlands. Possibly had the arrangements come into effect, the lands would have been run by a council like that of the prince of Wales.

The following year Edward seized the opportunity to extend York's influence to the east. In January 1476, John Mowbray, fourth duke of Norfolk, died leaving as his sole heiress a three year old daughter, Anne. Edward, in January 1478, married her to Richard of York, then aged four. Unfortunately the child bride died in November 1481. As no children had been born of the marriage, the child widower had no right to the Mowbray inheritance which should then have passed to the heirs-at-law, John, Lord Howard, and William, Lord Berkeley, the co-heirs of a great-aunt of John Mowbray. Edward had been ruthless in making these arrangements and he now advanced with even greater ruthlessness. In 1478 he had passed acts of parliament to secure the eventual return to the infant couple of the immense jointure lands of Catherine, the aged widow of the second duke, and had forced Elizabeth, the widow of the fourth duke, to surrender to them a large part of her own dower and jointure. Now he deliberately deprived Howard and Berkeley of their rights of succession to these immensely valuable estates. An act of parliament of 1483 gave the entire Mowbray inheritance to Duke Richard for life with reversion to his heirs and then if he had none to the king himself. Possibly Lord Berkeley, whatever resentment he may have felt, could allege no genuine grievance, as five years earlier he had surrendered his claims to the king and now confirmed his surrender in parliament in return for release from bonds for £37,000 which he owed to Edward and to the Talbot family and received some little consolation in promotion to the rank of viscount. On the other hand, Edward's long trusted and loyal servant, John, Lord Howard, received nothing. The king coldly and brutally deprived him of his common law rights.

Edward seized other great inheritances during these later years. In 1473, Elizabeth Howard, the dowager countess of Oxford, was forced to surrender a great part of, if not all, her property to Richard of Gloucester — another rank injustice by contemporary standards, for the wives even of traitors were entitled by law to retain their own inheritances and jointures. The vast Holland inheritance of the dukes of Exeter was also manipulated. The unreliable duke was a prisoner in Calais. Married to the king's sister, Anne, their only daughter, also

Anne, died childless by June 1474. The duchess, having been allowed to divorce her husband, married Sir Thomas St Ledger, one of the Knights of the Body. Their infant daughter, also confusingly named Anne, was then contracted in marriage to Thomas Grey, the heir of the king's stepson, the marquess of Dorset, and in 1483 (a peak year for dubious transactions) parliament declared Anne heiress to the Exeter estates. Other people got their cut out of it, however. The act of parliament passed to confirm these dispositions provided that a part of the Holland inheritance valued at 500 marks a year was set aside for the queen's second son, Richard Grey. Elizabeth Wydeville, though she did not get this provision for her son for nothing, got it at the bargain price of 5,000 marks. Once again these arrangements completely ignored the rights of the common-law heirs of the Holland family, in particular those of Ralph, Lord Neville, heir to the earl of Westmorland.[14] It is true that because the duke of Exeter was attainted, Neville had no strict right to the inheritance but, once again, these arrangements, contrary to established convention, made it certain that the attainder would not be reversed.

Lastly, Henry Stafford, duke of Buckingham, wished to recover his family's moiety of the Bohun inheritance which, long before, Henry V had seized, giving the Stafford family much poorer lands in exchange.[15] These considerations apart, although Buckingham was married to the queen's sister Catherine, Edward, for reasons now unknown, had allowed him no political influence after he attained his majority. This, too, may well have rankled.

So Edward IV alienated at least six powerful noble families by unjust, arbitrary territorial settlements which, in their eyes, counted probably as little less than confiscations. They were deeply resented at the very end of his reign at a supremely critical moment. Richard of Gloucester was able to gain support for his plans by promising redress to the victims of his brother's greed.

VI

Edward's recent scholarly biographer has argued that the foreign

---

[14]The son of the duke of Exeter's thrice married sister, Anne, countess of Douglas, by her second husband, the earl of Westmorland. Ralph Neville succeeded to the earldom of Westmorland in 1484.

[15]The earldoms of Essex, Hereford and Northampton, the inheritance of the Bohun family, had been partitioned in 1421 between Henry V and his cousin Anne, countess of Stafford (died 1438). After the death of Henry VI in 1471, Buckingham also regarded himself as the rightful heir of the Lancastrian moiety.

policy of his later years was equally dominated by financial meanness, in particular that he was anxious to marry his daughters abroad with the dual aim of gaining foreign alliances at little or no cost, so much so that he 'allowed his own avarice and Louis' [XI] diplomatic skill to render him little more than a passive spectator of developments on the continent and unable to exploit them to his own advantage.'

This harsh verdict seems distinctly unfair to Edward for it seriously underestimates his difficulties after 1477. So volatile were the diplomatic relations of the day that it was not long after the treaty of Pécquigny before England and Burgundy were on good terms again and relations with Brittany remained friendly. The whole situation suddenly changed with the death of Charles the Bold at the siege of Nancy in January 1477, leaving his daughter Mary as his heiress. Louis XI determined to exploit the crisis by the dismemberment of Burgundy once and for all. This determination dominated Anglo-French relations for the remaining years of the two kings, who died within four and a half months of each other. It presented Edward with difficult decisions. He wished to remain on good terms with Louis, to retain the French marriage alliance and his French pension. Yet on the other hand any extension of French influence along the Channel coast might be a danger to English security and it was highly desirable for the sake of English commerce, particularly the expanding English cloth trade, to remain on good terms with the major cities of the Netherlands.

Edward has been condemned for not intervening decisively to defend the interests of Mary of Burgundy, to protect her against French aggression and, by his neglect, for putting English commercial interests in jeopardy. It should not be forgotten, however, that the legal and political situation in the Netherlands was tangled in the extreme. Louis XI and his successors who did interfere had to struggle for years to try to establish control there. Any intervention would have involved England in a long and expensive war. England had no offensive or defensive alliance with Burgundy at this time, only commercial treaties. No contemporary English writer accused Edward of neglecting commercial interests and fluctuations in trade between England and the Netherlands over the next few years cannot with any certainty be attributed to the diplomatic situation. The French had more than enough opposition to face in the Netherlands without wantonly alienating powerful commercial groups by cutting off their vital commerce.

Once again, as so often with Edward IV, we can trace adverse opinion back to the jaundiced reflections of Philippe de Commynes. According to him, the king of France had remarked that the towns of Flanders and Brabant were large and strong, neither easily taken nor easily kept, and the English did not want war on account of Anglo-Burgundian trade. Yet these thoughts prevented him neither from condemning Edward IV for not going to war, nor from censuring Louis from waging war in that area. A more active diplomacy, let alone war, might well have done far more damage to English trade, as it proved under Henry VII between 1493 and 1496.

Immediately in February 1477 Edward demanded from Louis certain guarantees for the payment of his pension, further pledges for the marriage of his daughter Elizabeth with the dauphin, an assurance that Margaret of Burgundy's jointure lands would not be affected by a French invasion and that the seven year commercial treaty should be extended to endure for the lives of both kings. Louis was reassuring and sent over an embassy to discuss commercial matters.

On 18 August 1477 the Archduke Maximilian of Hapsburg married May of Burgundy at Ghent. From then onwards until the end of 1482 both Hapsburg and Valois competed, with either bribes or diplomatic pressure, for Edward's support. Louis, at times, offered both territory in the Netherlands and a century long truce as a bait or delayed payment of his pension. Maximilian offered new commercial treaties. As we have seen Edward was really powerless to assist either. Both Maximilian and Louis changed their attitudes towards him as the fortunes of their mutual struggle in the Netherlands fluctuated. In the end the prospects of the Anglo-French marriage depended upon Maximilian's success in the war.

In August 1480 Edward signed a treaty of alliance with Burgundy. It was a last diplomatic success and it turned out to be futile. Somewhat later Edward also concluded a defensive alliance with Brittany, though he stopped short of reviving the old idea of a triple alliance between England, Brittany and Burgundy. Maximilian, in fact, received little more than permission to recruit 6,000 archers in England. Edward was still anxious for his French pension and by March 1481 he was moving towards more friendly relations with Louis. The death of Mary of Burgundy after a fall from her horse on 27 March 1482 destroyed whatever was left of Maximilian's precarious position in the Netherlands. The estates of Flanders and Brabant took charge of the children of the marriage and Maximilian opened negotiations with Louis. Louis then completely repudiated the English marriage treaty and at Arras on 23 December 1482 agreed to the marriage of Margaret of Austria and the dauphin. Edward had lost the French marriage and Louis ceased to pay his pension.

In spite of Edward's anger and immediate desire for revenge, there are signs that second thoughts soon prevailed and that he wished to maintain the Anglo-French truce. A single fifteenth and tenth which parliament voted in January 1483 'for the hasty and necessary defence of the realm' (a more or less standard and completely unrevealing formula) he may at first have intended for war against France. It is more likely, however, that he wanted money for war against Scotland.

The foreign policy of Edward's later years was admittedly inglorious but too much adverse criticism, both contemporary and modern, has sprung from a complete misapprehension of his resources. Apart from the extreme fluidity of continental affairs, given the king's financial position it is difficult to see what other line he could have taken. His experiences of the years 1472 to 1475 must have burned deeply into his consciousness. They must have taught him the lesson that he could not afford an active foreign policy which might lead to continental war. He knew full well that his subjects were not prepared to pay the price. As far as foreign affairs were concerned, it is hardly too much to say that they had castrated their unfortunate government.

Like Henry VII later, Edward IV could only react to, and try to take advantage of, the aspirations of more powerful continental rulers while at the same time trying to protect his own interests in a highly volatile and conspicuously unscrupulous diplomatic atmosphere, and he was pitted against the most unscrupulous diplomatist of all, Louis XI.

England may well have appeared to foreign observers to be stronger than she was. Foreigners combined memories of the Hundred Years War with erroneous impressions of the true internal financial situation. They mistook exaggerated rumours of royal avarice and hoarded treasure for the true sinews of war and consequently misjudged the realities of power. With these impressions they were often anxious for an English alliance or at least anxious to prevent other powers from gaining one. Rather than condemning Edward's foreign policy at the time of his death as a total and disastrous failure, it is more realistic to regard it as a vicissitude in an extremely complicated, changing situation. Only two years later, in 1485, France was sufficiently alarmed at the prospect of English support for Brittany to give modest support for Henry of Richmond's invasion. Edward died on 9 April 1483 and it has been unfortunate for his reputation that he died during one of the ephemeral downswings of foreign policy.

Edward's policy towards Scotland during the same years is far less defensible. Since 1474 his daughter Cecily had been betrothed to King James of Scotland. James III was anxious to strengthen relationships but sometime during 1479 the Scots began to raid across the border. Early in 1480 Edward, threatening war unless the Scots offered reparations, demanded that Prince James be sent to England as a guarantee of his marriage to the Princess Cecily and further demanded the surrender of Berwick which Margaret of Anjou had handed over to the Scots.

The Scots, far from pacifically inclined, in the summer of 1480 burned Bamburgh, twenty miles across the English border. James III then offered peace, but Edward resolved upon war. In the late spring of 1481 a naval force under Lord Howard raided along the Firth of Forth and a force under Gloucester and Northumberland at the same time penetrated Scotland by land, both inflicting considerable damage. James III counter-attacked across the border with three raiding parties, bringing havoc to wide areas of the countryside. The English campaign had been a complete fiasco and it had cost at least £17,000.

Border raids continued throughout the winter, the destruction of crops and cattle adding to the miseries of a bad harvest and a hard winter. In 1482 the war began again, the English supporting a pretender, James III's brother Alexander, duke of Albany, who, in return for recognition as king of Scotland promised to restore Berwick and to marry the Princess Cecily if he could conveniently get rid of his French wife. Gloucester, once again in command of the land forces, perhaps as many as 20,000 men, marched into Scotland under the most favourable conditions. Part of the Scottish baronage revolted, seized James III on 22 July and hanged many of his courtiers at the bridge of Lauder. The English forces, after looting and devastating large areas of Roxburghshire and Berwickshire, by the end of the month marched victorious into Edinburgh.

Then the volatile Albany defected. The Scots asked for terms. Although they promised the Anglo-Scottish marriage, they refused to guarantee the surrender of Berwick. At this point Gloucester, most oddly, decided to leave Scotland and fell back on Berwick where he dismissed all but 1,700 men, thus throwing away all the advantages gained in the course of the year. However, Berwick Castle surrendered after a siege on 24 August. The capture of Berwick was the only gain from two expensive seasons of warfare.

The Croyland Chronicler noted Edward's anger at such an outcome and roundly condemned Gloucester's (now) inexplicable conduct:

> What he effected in this expedition, what sums of money again extorted in the name of benevolences, he uselessly squandered away, the affair in its results sufficiently proved.

The author thought that Berwick was a trifling gain after so great an effort, and that the annual cost of its maintenance and defence was far in excess of its value. Nevertheless Edward seems to have decided to continue the war, but he died before the onset of the next campaigning season.

VII

Edward was a handome man of great personal charm, full blooded lust and love of pleasure. He dressed magnificently, even setting fashions, for during the last Christmas festivities of his life he appeared before the court in clothes of an entirely new and strange cut. It was a matter of personal inclination, though he knew well enough that magnificence in a monarch was also a tremendous political asset. His appetites were so gross it was little wonder that towards the end of his life he grew rather fat, for according to Dominic Mancini: 'In food and drink he was most immoderate: it was his habit, so I have learned, to take an emetic for the delight of gorging his stomach once more.' Indeed his death at the comparatively early age of forty may well have been due to an apoplexy caused by the excesses of high living. Numerous though rumour makes his amours, especially in his earlier years, they never, apart from his rash marriage, affected his political judgement and in his later years his devotion to the winning and charitable figure of Jane Shore, so compassionately depicted by Sir Thomas More who, after all, was no advocate of unchastity, throws a gentler light upon his character.

A lover of ostentation — perhaps to express it more kindly a lover of the beautiful and the curious — he spent considerable sums of money on building, jewels, tapestries and books, though his choice of sumptuous, somewhat second-rate Flemish volumes reveals more of the taste of the tired businessman than that of the connoisseur. On one occasion he spent £20 on three lions for the royal menagerie. Unfortunately two of them died in Spain on their way to England. His court was splendid, luxurious, extremely formal, though its rigid etiquette (already traditional by the time of his accession) was intended, like his clothes, to impress his power and majesty upon his subjects. Personal taste and political expediency coincided. Judging from his instructions for its conduct and the records of its expenses, it was also economically run. If Edward loved luxury, like Queen Elizabeth I he also intended to have his money's worth.

It was a court whose pleasures and whose rather vulgar, highly coloured pageantry were more akin to those of the Burgundians than to the refinement of the Medici and the Italian Renaissance courts of the day. Some of its major figures were a curious amalgam of traditional and newer foreign tendencies. John Tiptoft, earl of Worcester, translated Cicero's *De Amicitia* as well as being president of the Court of Chivalry and the recognized authority on jousts and tournaments. Edward's brother-in-law, Anthony, Earl Ryvers, strangely mingled worldliness with melancholy and piety. He was a highly respected politician, a man who paid close attention to the administration of his estates, a patron of Caxton and his chivalrous romances and yet at the same time an admirer of the Latin classics. He was — unusual for his class in England — a devotee of pilgrimages and so renowned for his piety that after his political murder by Richard III the Carmelite friars of Doncaster treasured his hair shirt like a relic.

Even to the more discerning of his contemporaries, Edward IV was an enigmatic figure — a compound, less unusual than many people like to think, of dissipation and ability; it was this combination which so impressed his councillor, the Croyland Chronicler, who was astounded that a man given to such fits of debauchery should have had so retentive a memory for the details of politics and administration, details of remote and often petty local affairs at that. The extensive use from the very beginning of the reign of the royal sign manual and signet amply confirms the Croyland writer's testimony. These highly personal instruments were so extensively used even down to the execution of quite minor details of administration that they can be considered as two of the main vehicles of Yorkist government. In his relations with citizens he was more genial and convivial than some of his courtiers thought dignified. Affable and patient in listening to never ending requests and petitions from self-seekers about the court and elsewhere, he softened refusals (as Machiavelli would have advised) by blaming unpleasant decisions upon his advisers. He was undoubtedly opportunist and far from scrupulous. In difficult circumstances he had no hesitation about stooping to perjury if it served his turn. In that he was no better and no worse than the men with whom he had to work. Fifteenth-century Italy did not invent the so-called *realpolitik* of the Renaissance. The greater concentration of the political scene there only made it appear more prominent. Italy had nothing to teach Louis XI, Charles the Bold, Edward IV and the men who brought him to power and those who helped him to maintain it. One and all they were far from nice in their political conduct and their occasional expressions of high morality were generally sticks with which to beat opponents rather than the principles by which they lived.

From the first he was anxious to rule upon as wide a basis of power as possible, to put down disorders and to improve the state of his kingdom, though it is true that all those endeavours were to some extent linked with the suppression of sedition. His personal attention to the problem of disorder was arduous and unremitting and he was capable of stern action even against some of his friends and supporters. Yet, at the same time, like earlier and later monarchs, he was forced to rely upon the local power of magnates, upon bastard feudalism, and in the general interests of security to turn a blind eye upon many of their less just activities. It is true that in his earlier years he failed and the 1460s may have ended with his rule almost as discredited as that of Henry VI a decade earlier. Success must be measured against circumstances and the circumstances of Edward's earlier years were overwhelmingly adverse. By his father's sudden death he was prematurely forced, even by the precocious standards of the fifteenth century, into the key position in politics in conditions which would have taxed the powers and the abilities of the most mature of statesmen. With a realm in disorder, a bankrupt treasury and the north and west still in arms against him, his most prominent supporter, the earl of Warwick, was a man of overwhelming pride and avarice, and lust for popularity. At the same time Warwick's political sense was rash and defective and he had become almost accustomed to imposing his will by violent means. Disaster could have been foretold. It was not a situation to give a young man of nineteen leisure to cultivate the gentler traits of character. In these earlier years Edward's judgment was not of the soundest and his handling of Warwick was at times evasive to the point of making a bad situation worse. At the same time his attitude towards foreign policy showed him possessed of a sounder political wisdom than the emotional personal reactions which served the Kingmaker as a basis for political action.

In these years Edward's situation of fear and uncertainty might well have led him into a panic stricken vindictiveness, but his record towards ex-opponents compares very favourably with both that of Margaret of Anjou and Warwick. From the very first he placed ex-Lancastrians in positions of power and welcomed former enemies who were prepared for reconciliation.

Even historians most hostile to him have generally allowed that Edward was one of the most brilliant generals of the day. Such eulogies may, however, be wide of the mark. It is true that he never lost a battle. On the other hand he never fought a battle against a professional continental leader and even his pursuit of the Lancastrian army to Tewkesbury seems to have been more tenacious than brilliant.

After 1471 when conditions became more favourable and he had greater scope to carry out his plans, Edward's purpose hardened and he was able to execute more resolutely policies earlier conceived. In spite of his creation of royal appanages which, had they survived, would have caused trouble to future kings, he was not well served by his family. The duke of Clarence, always a nuisance, ultimately became a menace. Even Richard of Gloucester, though always loyal, was considerably less competent than a favourable northern tradition has given him credit for.[16]

Towards the end of his life the benefits of his government were recognized by its relative popularity in spite of growing resentment against his financial stringency—a hard financial policy which, together with the end of the financial drain of the Hundred Years War abroad, had at least restored the monarchy to solvency. Yet recent revelations of his cavalier treatment of the common law of inheritance to the detriment of powerful families shows a taint of avaricious injustice overcoming political wisdom—an injustice which, as we shall see, helped to create a balance of political forces disastrous to his family when sudden death removed his own controlling hand.

[16]See below, pp. 327 – 8.

9   Richard III

I

If Edward IV had lived until his heir had attained his majority, there is no doubt that the throne would have passed peacefully and securely to Edward V. With his sudden and premature death in April 1483, leaving an heir only twelve years old, the arbiter between hostile court factions was suddenly removed, leaving a struggle for power almost inevitable. The hostility of the factions had certainly disturbed Edward himself but, as Sir Thomas More remarked: 'Yet in his good health he somewhat the less regarded it, because he thought whatsoever business should fall between them, himself should always be able to rule both the parties.' Edward, on his deathbed, tried to reconcile the conflicting parties. In the intense emotional atmosphere of the moment they promised reconciliation but their mutual suspicions proved too strong for them ever to work harmoniously together.

In 1422, when Henry V died at the age of thirty-four, a united peerage had overcome the pretentions of the king's brother, Humphrey, duke of Gloucester, to a regency and, during the child's minority had ruled the country for fifteen years with considerable success through an aristocratic council.

Conditions in 1483 were essentially different. According to a recent estimate, only about one third of the peerage families had taken an active part in the politics of the central government during Edward IV's later years, though it is probably going too far to deduce from this 'an alienation between the majority of "country peers" and the "court peers" '.[1] At most we can say that some members of the peerage owing to age, lack of ability or personal disinclination were unsuited to the life of the court and that a large number, as happened later under Henry VII, preferred to remain withdrawn, exercising their local powers in the countryside where their estates and their influence lay. Events since 1461, after all, had shown beyond doubt that the

---

[1] C. Ross, *Edward IV* (1974), p. 332.

majority of the peerage were completely disinclined to risk their lives and estates in dynastic faction fights.

If a struggle were to come it would therefore erupt within the smaller politically active section of the peerage. As we have earlier seen, six powerful families bitterly resented Edward IV's unjust manipulation of great inheritances to their disadvantage. All six would, therefore, probably support anyone from whom they might expect a reversal of the actions which had so aggrieved them. All, in fact, supported Richard of Gloucester and two of them[2] were among the small group of nine peers who fought for him at Bosworth.

There were in April 1483 two hostile groups, though events were to show that one of them was by no means united. The queen's family, the Wydevilles, had the tangible advantage of controlling the young king's person, the queen's brother, Earl Ryvers, ruling the prince's household at Ludlow. Under his patent of appointment reissued on 27 February 1483 Earl Ryvers had the right to move the prince from place to place at his pleasure, guarded by an armed retinue, for all the members of the household were to be supplied with horse and harness. As recently as 8 March the king, possibly secretly, had granted Ryvers another patent authorizing him to raise troops 'if need be' in the Marches of Wales, the traditional recruiting area of the Yorkist family. Moreover, the queen's son, the marquess of Dorset, was deputy constable of the Tower of London, and as such, controlled Edward's famous treasure hoard, and her brother, Sir Edward Wydeville, commanded part of the navy. It can be plausibly argued that the grant of such extensive powers shows that Edward IV before the onset of his fatal illness was inclined to give power to the Wydevilles.

Edward's final will is unfortunately lost. Although the evidence is not absolutely conclusive, it is generally assumed that, either in the will or in codicils added to it on his deathbed, he appointed Richard, duke of Gloucester, protector. Thus, at the last moment, and in the absence of both Gloucester and Ryvers, he suddenly reversed a political decision made only a short time before, making practically certain an open struggle for control.

Just as he had put dangerous forces into the hands of the Wydevilles, Edward had given Gloucester the power to pursue such a struggle, for during the last few years he had made his brother the most powerful magnate in the realm, and had provided him with potential allies by alienating other powerful men. As the only surviving adult male of the house of York, he was the obvious candidate for the office of protector during a minority. So that, at the king's death, Richard in the north, the Wydevilles in Wales and the

[2] Norfolk, Berkeley, and Norfolk's son, Surrey.

Marches and in London, each commanded sufficient armed force to
defy the other. Edward, in his final illness, foresaw all too clearly and
all too late the consequences of his own policy of building up the
powers of two hostile groups which only he could control. However,
the appointment of Gloucester as protector meant that the Wydevilles
would have to be content with a subordinate position.

The Wydevilles, although their greed has been traditionally
exaggerated, were certainly unpopular in some quarters. One of the
key factors now lay in the long-standing hostility between them and
Edward's chamberlain, Lord Hastings. Indeed this hostility may have
originated as far back as the early years of the 1460s when, as a friend-
less Lancastrian widow, Elizabeth, Lady Grey, had found herself
forced to pay a very high price for Lord Hastings's protection.[3] In
1471 Hastings and Earl Ryvers had been in bitter competition for the
lieutenancy of Calais. Dominci Mancini, the Italian observer,
claimed that Hastings and the marquess of Dorset had both incited
informers to spread stories of disloyalty about the other. In 1477
Hastings had been imprisoned for a short time as a result of these
activities. Ryvers, on one occasion, had spread tales that Hastings
might betray Calais. As late as August 1482 a certain John Edwards
had appeared before the royal council accused of traducing Dorset,
Ryvers and Robert Radclyf and it is highly probable that Hastings
had been the promoter of a series of slanders. They must have been
extremely serious for the council to have spent its time on the affair.

The former king's council soon met at Westminster with the queen.
Individual accounts of it, though by no means contradictory, are
incomplete, and must be patched together to make what seems to be
the most plausible palimpsest of the discussions. Again, according to
Dominic Mancini, one section considered that Gloucester should
govern because Edward IV had directed this in his will, but the predominant view was that 'the govenment should be carried on by many
persons amongst whom the duke, far from being excluded, should be
accounted the chief' — a reversion, whether conscious or unconscious,
to the aristocratic decision of 1422. According to the Croyland
chronicler all the council members ardently desired that the young
Edward should succeed peacefully — phraseology which of itself indicates the fears which then prevailed. They fiercely debated the ways
and means. The 'more prudent members' argued that the king's
guardianship should be utterly forbidden to his mother's kindred.
There followed an acute altercation about the size of the prince's
escort from Ludlow to the capital for his coronation. Lord Hastings's
demand for a moderate company ultimately prevailed after he had
threatened that if a large force were allowed he would flee to Calais, in

[3] See above, pp. 237 – 8.

fear (adds the chronicler) 'lest, if the supreme power should fall into the hands of the queen's relations, they would exact a most signal vengeance for the injuries formerly inflicted upon them by that same lord'. In the end, the queen, who did her best to quiet these dissensions, agreed to an escort of no more than 2,000 men. Such discussions, even more the events which were to follow, show an atmosphere of quite extraordinary suspicion and fear—a heavily charged atmosphere which increasingly led to the swift impulsive reactions of terror.

Meanwhile, although Hastings sent messages urging Gloucester to come to London with a strong band in order to force the issue, the duke wrote soothing letters to the queen assuring her of his loyalty and at York, together with all the nobility of the region, took an oath of fidelity to the young king. It has often been alleged that Gloucester and Ryvers now more or less competed in a race to London, each being anxious to arrive first and establish his power there. This can hardly be true, at least as far as Earl Ryvers was concerned. Although the news of Edward's death reached Ludlow on 14 April the royal party did not set out for the capital until about the 24th. Ryvers evidently planned to meet Gloucester so that they could enter London with the king together and he must have arranged the journey to suit Gloucester's convenience, for Stoney Stratford, where Gloucester finally overtook the king, while on Gloucester's more or less straight course from York was about fifty miles at least out of the most direct Ludlow to London route.

When Gloucester, and later in the day the duke of Buckingham, reached Northampton on 29 April Ryvers was there to meet them, the king having already passed through to Stoney Stratford. Having spent the evening on amicable terms with Ryvers, the two dukes arrested him early the following morning. Moving on to Stoney Stratford they there told the king a fabricated story of a plot which threatened their lives and in spite of his protests and tears arrested three of his most trusted attendants, Sir Thomas Vaughan, Sir Richard Grey and Sir Richard Hawte. The whole party then returned to Northampton. The prisoners were sent to the north, Ryvers to Sheriff Hutton, Grey to Middleham and Vaughan and Hawte probably to other places. They were all beheaded at Pontefract probably on 25 June and most probably without any form of trial.[4]

The news from Northampton immediately sent the queen and her other children, the marquess of Dorset and the queen's brother,

[4] The Croyland Chronicler states that they were executed by the order of Sir Richard Ratclyf who was bringing south for Richard troops sent at his command by the city of York. John Rous, however, states that they received some form of trial under the earl of Northumberland. The former seems to be the more likely story.

Lionel, bishop of Salisbury, flying to the Westminster sanctuary, in their haste breaking down part of the sanctuary walls to take in with them as many of their possessions as possible.

On 4 May, the day originally fixed for the coronation, Richard, with the king and Buckingham, entered London. The first council which he attended confirmed Richard's title as protector, according to the Croyland writer 'with the consent and good-will of all the lords, with power to ordain and forbid in every matter like another king, and as the necessity of the case demanded'. Although the writer referred to the precedent of Humphrey of Gloucester in 1422, unless his phrasing is mere rhetoric the parallel was by no means exact, for at that time the lords had considerably restricted Humphrey's powers.

II

After the way in which Edward IV had ignored him, the duke of Buckingham now entered a period of power and glory which must have been intensely gratifying to his vanity. As early as 16 May the protector gave him power to array (that is raise) troops in Shropshire, Hereford, Somerset, Dorset and Wiltshire. On the same day a second grant made him chief justice and chamberlain in both north and south Wales and gave him complete control of all the most important Welsh castles and lordships. Yet a third patent appointed him steward of all the Welsh castles and manors of the duchy of Lancaster and the earldom of March and in July he was granted the constableships of all royal castles and the stewardships of all royal lands in Shropshire and Hereford as they fell vacant. So great a concentration of power in Wales and the West Country was unheard-of, exceeding by far even that of William Herbert, 'King Edward's master lock' in the 1460s. Buckingham, within a few days, became a powerful viceroy over a large territory.

The king's coronation was finally fixed for Sunday 22 June and meanwhile the council (a vague word for we do not know who its members were) recommended for submission to the forthcoming parliament a proposal that the protector's office and powers should be confirmed until Edward V came of age.

In spite of this a position resembling stalemate seems to have developed. Either Richard was genuinely fearful for his position or he was already planning a *coup d'état,* for on 10 June he wrote to York asking the city authorities to send him in all haste as many well-armed men as possible 'to aid and assist us against the queen, her blood adherents and her affinity who have intended and do daily intend to murder and utterly destroy us our cousin the duke of Buckingham and all the old blood royal of this realm'. Thus far Gloucester always linked Buckingham's name with his own in accusations of conspiracy against those he intended to repress.

Richard suspected that, by this time, Lord Hastings was plotting against him, possibly communicating with the Wydevilles through Edward's former mistress, Jane Shore, now mistress to Hastings himself. The knowledge that Hastings, Thomas Rotherham, the archbishop of York, and John Morton, the bishop of Ely, were frequenting each other's houses besides meeting in the council may have been the prime cause of his suspicions. If Hastings had indeed already turned against the protector the reason must have been that he suspected him of aspiring to the throne for Hastings was especially devoted and was well known to be devoted, to the children of his former friend.

On 13 June at a meeting of part of the council in the White Tower, Richard suddenly accused Hastings, Lord Stanley, Morton and Rotheram of plotting with the Wydeville interest and accused the Chamberlain of treason. A group of waiting armed men seized Hastings, and, after giving him a short time to make his confession, led him out to immediate execution. To forestall any popular commotion a herald read out an indictment of the dead man, but people observed that it was so neatly and carefully written that it must have been prepared in advance.

After Hastings's execution a deputation led by the archbishop of Canterbury persuaded the queen to allow the young duke of York to leave the sanctuary to join his brother. Possibly she may have been reassured by the death of Hastings, whom she regarded as one of her principal foes in spite of his known devotion to her children's interest. In any case the deputation made it clear to her that, if she refused the request, they would take the boy out of the sanctuary by force. The wretched woman obviously realized that she had no choice in the matter.

Possessed of the heir to the throne and his brother, Richard could reveal his intentions. He began by reviving an old story that the children were bastards. In Clarence's last years Robert Stillington, the bishop of Bath and Wells, had told the duke that before Edward IV's marriage to Elizabeth Wydeville the king had been secretly betrothed to Lady Eleanor Butler, the daughter of the earl of Shrewsbury and the widow of Sir Thomas Butler, a precontract which made his marriage invalid and his children illegitimate. The story was dubious and even had it been true it could not have affected the status of Edward V and his brother for Lady Eleanor had died in 1468 and the princes were born in 1470 and 1472 respectively. Therefore their legitimacy can hardly be contested for their parents had lived together openly accepted by the church and public opinion as man and wife.[5]

The protector chose Buckingham as his mouthpiece. London sources claim that the duke told the story to a gathering of the mayor, aldermen and citizens, Dominic Mancini that he told it to an assembly of lords who had arrived in London for the coronation. By this time Richard had contrived an overwhelming display of force against any possible resistance. The lords had arrived in London with the considerable retinues appropriate to their ranks but Gloucester, on the pretext that so great a concentration of men in the capital might lead to rioting and plundering, persuaded them to dismiss their entourages keeping only a few attendants for their personal service. The protector and Buckingham, on the other hand, 'had summoned armed men, in fearful and unheard-of numbers, from the north, Wales, and all other parts then subject to them'. They may indeed have commanded a menacing force as great as four or five thousand men. The lords were thus in no position to resist the protector's plans.

On 22 June the conspirators staged yet another scene, riding to St Paul's Cross to hear Friar Ralph Shaa, the mayor's brother, deliver a prearranged sermon. After praising Gloucester's virtues, the friar repeated the story of the pre-contract and, according to some sources, also for good measure revived an old story that Edward IV himself had been illegitimate. Shaa drawing his conclusions claimed that Richard by descent was entitled to the crown and was fitted by his character to wear it and to exercise all regal powers. Possibly other preachers also spread the tales in similar sermons.

The way being thus prepared, three days later on 25 June, before an assembly of lords and commons originally summoned as a parliament, a petition was presented begging Richard, on the grounds of Edward IV's pretended marriage, to take the crown 'according to the election of us the three estates of the land'. According to the Croyland Continuator, rumour had it that the petition originated in the north. Be that as it may the protector and his friends must certainly have composed it and a Year Book of 1488 claims that Bishop Stillington drew it up. The following day Buckingham read the petition to a large gathering at Baynard's Castle. Richard accepted it, then rode to Westminster Hall where he formally asserted his 'rights' by sitting in the royal seat in the Court of King's Bench and declared that his accession should be dated from that same day.

[5] These conditions were enough to validate a marriage before the reforms of the Council of Trent.

III

Rewards, or bribes, began to flow even before the coronation. They continued to flow until the very end of the reign. Forfeitures under the act of attainder in the parliament of January 1484 made possible some of the later grants but in the end they did not always succeed in buying loyalty. Sir Thomas More truthfully wrote: 'With large gifts he got himself unsteadfast friendship, for which he was fain to pill and spoil in other places and got himself steadfast hatred.'

On 28 June patents passed the great seal making John, Lord Howard, duke of Norfolk and earl Marshal, Viscount Berkeley earl of Nottingham and Norfolk's son, Thomas, earl of Surrey. Probably Howard received at least part of his coveted moiety of the Mowbray inheritance towards the end of July, though the Berkeleys may have had to wait for theirs until the death of the dowager duchess Elizabeth, meanwhile being compensated with a grant from the London customs.[6] Although Richard seized the Exeter lands for the crown, he granted Ralph, Lord Neville estates worth £200 a year. Quite apart from lands which went to the Howards, during his reign Richard alienated lands worth £12,000 a year against reserved rents worth only £735 15s. Among the beneficiaries were the earl of Northumberland, Thomas, Lord Stanley* and his brother, Sir William, the earl of Huntingdon, the earl of Lincoln*, Viscount Lovell, Lord Mautravers (the heir of the earl of Arundel) and Lords Cobham*, Dacre of Gillesland, Dudley*, Dynham, Fitzhugh*, Grey of Codnor*, Lysle* and Scrope of Bolton*.[7] The gains of the Howards were enormous and continuous. In addition to some part of the Mowbray inheritance the king granted Duke John the office of lord admiral, the custody and marriage of the minor, Henry, earl of Essex and as late as 28 February 1485 another thirty-five lordships and manors and the reversion of yet five more, plus a week later a money grant of £42 2s. 5d. for six and a half years. In addition to all this in August 1484 Surrey had received for as long as his father lived the

[6] The grant of titles to Howard (*Calendar of Patent Rolls, 1476-1485*, p. 358) makes no mention of estates but granted £20 p.a. from the fee farm of Ipswich. A grant of forty-eight manors and lordships on 25 July (ibid., p. 359) most probably represents the moiety of the Mowbray estates). On 20 March 1488 (*ibid.*, p. 388) William, earl of Nottingham was granted £226 13s. 4d. p.a. from the London customs 'provided that this grant be void if Elizabeth, duchess of Norfolk, pre-decease him', which looks like a temporary compensation. The subject needs further investigation.

[7] Those marked with an asterisk received their rewards for services in repressing Buckingham's rebellion. The following were northerners—Dacre of Gillesland, Fitzhugh, Grey of Codnor, Ralph, Lord Neville, Lovell. The following proved loyal to the end and fought for Richard at Bosworth—Norfolk, Surrey, Nottingham, Lovell, Scrope of Bolton.

enormous grant of £1,100 a year from the revenues of the duchy of Cornwall. This was, in fact, little less than 48 per cent of the entire net revenue of the duchy. The king was buying Howard support upon a colossally expensive, unprecedented scale. It remains mysterious why they should have obtained so very much more than any other peerage family. Considering the extensive scale of his grants, it is little wonder that Richard soon ran into grave financial difficulties.

Buckingham's case presents peculiar features. At first sight the king seems to have included him in the general quick rewards for on 13 July a sign manual granted him the long coveted moiety of the Bohun inheritance with the provision that the grant would be confirmed in a forthcoming parliament. The sign manual, generally in such cases, was an instrument for the issue of letters patent under the great seal. In this case no letters patent were ever issued. It may well be, therefore, that Richard changed his mind.[8] If he did so, perhaps thinking that recent grants of office had already made Buckingham over-powerful, he must mortally have offended the duke.

Whatever the reason may have been, Buckingham very soon regretted his recent vital support and began to plot against the king. Richard had set out on a royal progress which, by the beginning of August, had taken him as far north as York, where he was forced to repress the troops he had sent home after the coronation for they were wreaking havoc in the area. Buckingham retired to Brecon where, according to Sir Thomas More, conversations with bishop John Morton, who had been placed in his custody after his arrest at the time of Hastings's execution, further inflamed his grudges against the king. At the same time a movement was afoot in the Home Counties to rescue the young princes from the Tower, for many men feared that they would meet their deaths at the hands of their uncle. Before the end of August Richard had heard of the plots and had issued commissions of oyer and terminer to deal with offenders. He may even have encouraged rumours that the princes were already dead in order to scotch the movement.

If he did so his attempt failed and in its failure led to even more dangerous complications. It transformed an attempt to release the princes into a conspiracy to replace Richard by Henry of Richmond. According to Polydore Vergil's later account of the affair, Henry's mother, Lady Margaret Beaufort, plotted with Elizabeth Wydeville, who was still in the Westminster sanctuary, by means of an unsuspected Welsh physician called Lewis who attended both of them and thus was able to carry messages between them. They arranged that Henry should receive Wydeville support by marrying the queen's

---

[8] Or that Buckingham was waiting for the parliamentary confirmation, though this seems less likely.

eldest daughter, Elizabeth. To have fallen in with such a scheme Elizabeth Wydeville must surely have thought her sons already dead.

As always in this series of events all is dark and cloudy. We can only guess at the feelings and the motives of the protagonists. It may be that Buckingham had at first aspired to the throne himself (he was descended from Edward III) but switched his support to Henry of Richmond when he realized that he had very little hope of fulfilling his own more extreme ambitions.

By October the princes had disappeared from men's sight and the probability is that they had been murdered. Much ink has been spilt in arguing the contrary, in attempts to rehabilitate Richard's sanguinary reputation. Yet it still remains that his nephews completely disappeared and Richard never produced them to counteract and never even took the trouble to deny the rumours of their death,[9] perhaps because he had already encouraged these self-same rumours himself. Revolt broke out in October with a premature rising in Kent about ten days before action in the west and elsewhere. Lord Stanley, in spite of his wife's intrigues, remained loyal and a number of peers who later failed to rally to his cause in 1485 now took part in assisting to suppress the rebellion. The duke of Norfolk managed to get between the rebels of East Anglia and those of Surrey and Kent and they were soon put down. In the west the heaviest rains for years, afterwards known as 'the Great Water', flooded whole areas of the countryside. Humphrey Stafford had destroyed the Severn bridges so that Buckingham's men were unable to cross the swollen river; Buckingham marched as far as Weobley, one of Lord Ferrers' manors, and marched through the Forest of Dean hoping to cross the river at Gloucester to join forces with the Courtenays in the West Country.

Buckingham had the reputation of a hard and grasping man, extremely unpopular among his estate officers and tenants, especially Welshmen. Very few of his more prominent tenants and ministers took part in the rising and as soon as he had left Brecon the Vaughans of Tretower, who had a history of fifty years service to his family, attacked the castle and set fire to its contents. Moreover, the king's excessive grants of regional offices to the duke had offended many local families like the Kemys and the Herberts who greatly desired to recover the influence of which they had so recently been deprived.

---

[9] Attempts to exonerate Richard III from guilt began in the seventeenth century with Sir George Buc, continued in the eighteenth with Horace Walpole and in the late nineteenth, with Sir Clements Markham. In the present century they have been taken up more cautiously by P.M. Kendall and less cautiously by various amateur historians. Henry VII, the duke of Buckingham and John, Lord Howard have all been suggested as the villain in the piece, but on balance the attempts to exonerate Richard have tended to be emotional and unconvincing and they have not found favour with most professional historians.

Many of the duke's troops had joined him unwillingly, even possibly under duress. Now further demoralized by the appalling weather and by the lack of enthusiasm they found in the districts through which they passed, they deserted in considerable numbers. Then bishop Morton escaped, first to Ely and afterwards to Flanders. Buckingham, realizing the hopelessness of his cause, fled into hiding in the house of one of his affinity, Ralph Banaster, who betrayed him to the sheriff of Shropshire. He was immediately tried, denied an interview which he desperately sought with the king and was beheaded on 2 November.

Meanwhile Henry of Richmond had set sail from Brittany. The same storms which caused 'the Great Water' dispersed his fleet and drove most of it back upon the coast of Brittany and Normandy. With the remainder, possibly as few as one or two ships, he attempted to land at Poole, but alarmed by the troops guarding the coast, quickly withdrew. He may also have attempted a second landing at Plymouth some time later.

IV

Two contradictory traditions about Richard III have come down to posterity, a favourable tradition from the north, a hostile tradition from the south. Richard, partly as heir of the Neville interest and partly as a result of generous patronage, was popular with certain groups of northern society. On the other hand, as Mr A.J. Pollard has shown, the notorious Tudor legend of the king's villany originated to a very great extent in his treatment of the south after Buckingham's rebellion. The hostile tradition was almost entirely a southern creation.

Richard's hand fell heavily, especially upon the southern gentry. The Croyland Chronicler, who admittedly nourished the most violent anti-northern prejudices, as violent as those of Abbot Whethamstede a generation earlier, wrote of the parliament of 1484:

> Attainders were made of so many lords of high rank, besides peers and commoners, as well as three bishops, that we do not read of the like being issued by the Triumvirate even of Octavianus, Anthony and Lepidus. What immense estates and patrimonies were collected into the king's treasury in consequence of this measure. All of which he distributed amongst his northern adherents whom he planted in every spot throughout his dominions to the *disgrace and lasting sorrow of all the people of the south, who daily longed more and more for the return of their ancient rulers,* rather than the present tyranny of these people (my emphasis).

Although the tone of this wail is exaggerated, record sources demonstrate its underlying truth. After the rebellion ninety-seven people were attained and lost their lands including Henry and Jasper Tudor, Buckingham, the marquess of Dorset and Lord Saintmount, and the estates of three bishops were confiscated.[10] The countess of Richmond was not attainted though most, but not all, of her lands were transferred to her husband, Lord Stanley, who was ordered to keep her in close confinement. The majority of the condemned were southern gentry, most of them of the rank of esquires or below. Some grants from the forfeitures, of course, went to non-northerners. Magnates also profited. The king allowed the earl of Northumberland's claim to the Bryan and Bures estates which the marquess of Dorset had disputed. Lord Stanley received estates worth £700 a year for a reserved rent of only £50. Most important of all a group of some forty northerners, mainly from Yorkshire, most of them already conspicuous in Richard's services or in the affinity of the earl of Northumberland, were granted lands, offices and annuities from the forfeited estates.

This golden shower not only provided rewards, it placed trusted northerners in key positions as sheriffs, justices of the peace and custodians of castles and provided them with the necessary local territorial bases and influence to defend the disaffected southern areas from the expected Tudor invasion.

In the southeastern area (Essex, Kent, Surrey and Sussex) Richard made Sir Robert Brakenbury from Durham sheriff of Kent and constable of Tonbridge Castle and gave him lands worth about £400 a year. Sir Ralph Ashton from Yorkshire received lands in Kent worth £116 a year and became the lieutenant of the sixty-seven-year-old earl of Arundel in the key strategic posts of constable of Dover Castle and warden of the Cinque Ports. Why was Arundel's heir, Lord Mautravers overlooked? Although he received a grant in March 1484, the king obviously did not trust him.[11] Sir Robert Percy, the controller of Richard's household, who came from Scotton near Knaresborough, became sheriff of Essex and Hertfordshire. Sir Marmaduke Constable of Flamborough in Yorkshire, one of the earl of Northumberland's most trusted retainers and now a Knight of the Body, received the honour of Tonbridge and the lordships of Penshurst, Brasted, Hadlow and Yalding in Kent. All these men became justices of the peace and commissioners of array in their counties.

---

[10] John Morton of Ely, Peter Courtnenay of Exeter and Lionel Wydeville of Salisbury. Although their estates were confiscated by a separate act of parliament they were not technically attainted.

[11] This grant does not mention service against the rebels as many of the grants at this time do.

The king made his intentions crystal clear to the inhabitants of Kent in signet letter of 22 January 1484 about Sir Marmaduke Constable:

> We ... have deputed and ordained him *to make his abode among you and to have the rule within our honour and lordships aforesaid.*[12]

And the king forbade any of the inhabitants to take the livery of or to be retained by any other men.

Similar plantations of 'foreigners' can be traced in Hampshire, Berkshire, Wiltshire and in the Isle of Wight and in Cornwall, Devon, Dorset and Somerset where forfeited estates were especially plentiful. In Devon a northern peer, Lord Scrope of Bolton, received the constableships of the castles of Barnstaple and Exeter, the stewardship of the temporalities of the bishopric of Exeter and estates in Devon, Cornwall and Somerset worth just over £200 year. Another northern magnate, Ralph, Lord Neville, the heir of the earl of Westmorland, and one of those men who had been bitterly aggrieved by Edward IV's property manipulations, received the confiscated Somerset estates of Sir Giles Daubeney and the countess of Richmond, worth about £200 a year.

The extent to which the northerners could be promoted and enriched is shown by the case of Richard's confidant, Sir Richard Ratcliffe. Sir Richard's own Yorkshire estate of Sudbury-in-Gilling was but a modest patrimony. In September 1484 the king granted him lands from the estates of the earls of Devon, mostly in Devon, Dorset and Somerset, of approximately £650 a year. In one single step the king promoted him to the ranks of the greater landowners, filling the gap left in the West Country by the attainder of the earl of Devon in 1461, though Edward IV had never completely excluded his family, the Courtenays, from power in the area.

These changes were not, of course, sufficiently drastic to substitute an alien for a native ruling group in any county. For Richard could always rely upon some of the hereditary local families. The 'foreigners' were always a small minority in their allotted districts. Nevertheless, their importance was very great for Richard appointed them to key positions. They kept guard against suspected disloyalty, kept a watchful eye upon the activities of those who were accustomed to predominate upon the local scene and who considered that they had every right to do so. From early 1484 onwards the lesser, even some of the greater, gentry of the south must bitterly have resented this northern, alien intrusion and must have longed for the return of their own ancient, rightful predominance which, it was obvious, only

---

[12] Quoted from A. J. Pollard, 'The Tyranny of Richard III', *Journal of Medieval History* III (1977), my emphasis.

a change of régime could bring to pass. Richard's government had contravened one of the most deeply rooted conventions of power, that local government should be the preserve of local families. From their point of view his rule was the rule of a tyrant. When the time came, even if they did not rush to arms to support Henry of Richmond, they were unlikely ardently to defend Richard of Gloucester.

V

Early in 1484 Richard attempted, and successfully attempted, to win over Elizabeth Wydeville. On 1 March, before parliament ended, he undertook in writing, witnessed by the lords spiritual and temporal and by the mayor and aldermen of London, to guarantee her safety and that of her daughters if they came out of the sanctuary and to give her an annuity of 700 marks a year. Elizabeth accepted the offer. She probably felt that she had no alternative. Richmond's prospects of success now looked very slim indeed and she must have wondered for how long the sanctuary would be respected if she continued to resist. So she went to Richard's court, threw over her agreement with Richmond and even wrote to her son, Dorset, advising him to change sides. Dorset indeed fled, but overtaken by Henry's messengers was persuaded to return to his side.

Rumours began to spread that Queen Anne would not live long and that, after her death, Richard intended to marry his niece Elizabeth of York. The rumours reached Richmond and set him seeking for another bride. The queen died about mid-January 1485. Such was his reputation that Richard was forced to deny another horrendous story attributed to the catalogue of his crimes, the story that he had poisoned Queen Anne in order to marry Elizabeth of York. Realizing that his wife was near to death he may have contemplated an incestuous marriage with his niece, but the rumour of poison was certainly slanderous. But slander or not, the rumour was widespread, showing what many people thought about the king, and it so seriously disturbed his northern followers, devoted to the old Neville interest which his wife represented, that on 30 March, the king himself in the great hall of St John's Priory, Clarkenwall, declared before the mayor and aldermen,

in the presence of many of his lords and of much other people shewed his grief and displeasure ... and said it never came to his thought or mind to marry in such manner wise nor willing or glad of the death of his queen.

People spreading the rumour in future were to be punished. Signet letters to the authorities of Southampton, Windsor and York, and probably other cities too, ordered the repression and punishment of those who repeated slanderous rumours about the king. Surely this was a uniquely shameful spectacle for an English monarch and shows that Richard's reputation had fallen extremely low in his own lifetime. There was really not much scope for it to be posthumously blackened by Tudor propaganda.

It was essential to his safety for Richard to get Henry of Richmond out of Brittany and to prevent him from taking an alternative refuge in France; otherwise, once more, he might use the French coast for launching an invasion of England. In June 1484, while Duke Francis of Brittany was in the midst of one of his periodic fits of mental derangement, Richard came to an agreement with the duke's treasurer, Pierre Landois. In addition to a truce to last from 1 July to 24 April 1485, Richard offered the duke the yearly revenues of the earldom of Richmond (to which the duke considered he had an hereditary title) in return for Richmond's surrender or possibly that Richmond should be kept in much straiter custody.

The plan failed. Henry was warned in time by Bishop Morton from Flanders who sent a priest, Christopher Urswyk, to inform him of the plot. Henry immediately dispatched Urswyk to the court of Charles VIII of France asking for a safe-conduct for himself and his friends to enter French territory. Under pretext of consulting Duke Francis, who had now recovered and was staying in a town on the borders of Breton and French territory, Henry sent his chief supporters there, but when they were near the border they made a sudden, and successful, dash for France. Two days later Henry himself left Vannes with only five servants, outside the town he changed clothes with one of them and by a devious route galloped for the border. It is said that he reached Anjou only an hour ahead of a party which Landois sent in pursuit. Francis II had recovered sufficiently to repudiate his treasurer's policy completely. He sent for Sir Edward Wydeville and Edward Poynings and gave them enough money to take to France those of his followers Henry had been forced to leave in Brittany.

France was always, and justifiably, suspicious of Brittany. Suspicion had reached a new height since the Anglo-Breton truce concluded in June. Therefore Charles and his council welcomed Henry and in November gave him 3,000 livres tournois to gather troops. Preparation for invasion, however, occupied a considerable time. For months King Richard had to live with the threat and he had no idea where the landing place would be. He therefore stayed at Nottingham Castle, sufficiently central for meeting invasion in either the north or south, and established posses of mounted scouts posted at intervals of twenty miles along the roads for speedy information of any attempt that would be made.

His situation became more tense and alarming as the anxious months passed by. Prominent men were fleeing to France. Prosecutions for treasons rose. Sir James Blount, the lieutenant of Hammes, one of the subsidiary fortresses of Calais, fled to Henry with his prisoner, the diehard Lancastrian earl of Oxford. At the end of May Richard appointed his chamberlain, Viscount Lovell, to command a fleet based on Southampton. A prophecy had predicted that Henry would land at Milford and it was thought to refer to Milford near Christchurch. Richard, however, had not overlooked the possibility of a landing in the great natural habour of Milford Haven for, according to Polydore Vergil he established a system of signalling lamps 'on the hills adjoining'. He had also made elaborate arrangements to defend West Wales, relying on the loyalty of William Herbert, earl of Huntingdon, whom Edward IV had deprived of power in the 1470s, but whom Richard had to some extent restored by granting him many of the offices and castles which the duke of Buckingham had occupied. He also relied on the loyalty of Sir Walter Herbert and upon that of Rhys ap Thomas, the representative of a family which had been hungry for power in West Wales for at least half a century.

Henry's tiny expedition set sail from the mouth of the Seine on 1 August and landed at Mill Bay in Milford Haven on the 7th. He had with him a force of only 2,000 men of very dubious quality — possibly some three to five hundred English refugees, possibly a small number of men provided by the king of Scotland, the remainder being a miscellaneous rabble mostly recruited in Normandy. After landing he moved to Haverford West, remaining in that area for two days without opposition. He was afraid for the attitude of Walter Herbert and Rhys ap Thomas but they with Sir John Savage, a nephew of Lord Stanley's, joined him. Shrewsbury opened its gates and he moved on towards Stafford and Lichfield. Richard, on hearing the news, sent for his supporters to join him, threatening the penalty of death for any who refused, and began to march from Nottingham to Leicester. In spite of this, prominent former supporters began to desert him. Sir Walter Hungerford and Sir Thomas Bourchier, marching with Sir Robert Brackenbury from London and gaining wind that Richard suspected their loyalty, deserted a little to the north of Stoney Stratford and joined Henry somewhere between Lichfield and Tamworth. Soon after, Sir Brian Sandford and Sir Simon Digby deserted Richard and it is possible that desertions continued until the very morning of the battle. Lord Stanley, on the pretext of illness, refused to come in and only the fact that his heir, Lord Strange, was a hostage in Richard's hands prevented him from declaring openly for Henry. Henry secretly met Lord Stanley and his brother, Sir William, at Atherstone, and there probably received their promises of support.

On 22 August, just a fortnight after Henry's landing, battle was joined near the deserted village of Ambion not far from Market Bosworth. For one of the decisive events in English history the battle, like the march of only two weeks which preceded it, was a small, even a minute affair, lasting little more than two hours. If Henry had met little opposition during his march through Wales, neither had men flocked to his banners. Only another 3,000 men had been added to his original force of 2,000. The Stanleys had brought 3,000 with them but there is no knowing how many of them took part. They must have been divided between Lord Stanley and his brother, Sir William. Sir William certainly entered the battle at a critical moment but there is no certainty that Lord Stanley himself had any part in it. He may well have stood by, fearing for his son's life. Few peers supported Richmond. His uncle, Jasper Tudor, earl of Pembroke, had landed with him in Milford Haven but Jasper Tudor's movements after that are something of a mystery. He may have been at Bosworth but no contemporary or near-contemporary source mentions his presence. The only other peers on Henry's side at Bosworth were his half-uncle, John, Lord Welles and the Lancastrian earl of Oxford. If he had landed in some other part of the country, particularly the southeast, it is possible that more of the disgruntled gentry might have come to his banners but, as it was, any general rally in his favour was notably lacking and the section of the peerage which supported him was no more than a small family group.

Contemporary sources state that Richard's army was double the size of Henry's. This is certainly an exaggeration. Plausible estimates vary between as few as 7,000 and as many as 12,000 men. Of these possibly as many as 3,000 came to the field with the earl of Northumberland. At the vital moment, Northumberland stood idly by and after the battle came in to do homage to Henry VII. He undoubtedly resented Richard's predominance in the north, based on the Neville interest backed by royal authority, and hoped that Henry Tudor would give him the rule of the north. Nine other peers supported Richard — a far better showing than Henry's but still meagre enough especially considering that six[13] of the nine had benefited from Richard's lavish grants and that four of them were amongst the notorious, hated northerners.[14] Once more the cautious, withdrawn aristocracy, caring most for their safety and for their local

[13] The duke of Norfolk, his son, the earl of Surrey, the earl of Nottingham, Viscount Lovell, Lord Scrope of Bolton, Lord Dacre of Gilsland.

[14] Viscount Lovell, Lords Scrope of Bolton, Dacre of Gilsland and Greystoke.

influence, had declined to take the risk of dynastic decisions. The choice between candidates was, after all, far from inspiring. Richard of Gloucester's reputation was tarnished beyond repair. He was a usurper. Many people were convinced that he was a murderer and many, judging by the social and political standards of the day, regarded him as a tyrant. On the other hand Henry of Richmond, though free from moral stain, was nothing more than an inexperienced political adventurer, an almost pathetic rootless exile, in whom the powerful and the rich could repose little, if any, confidence. It is little wonder that men stood aside from the conflict and refused to commit themselves.

VI

Richard was killed at the early age of thirty-two. But for his usurpation historians might have found much to commend in his career. He had been conspicuously loyal to his brother, Edward IV, and correspondingly much trusted. When he was king his single parliament produced a useful, though by no means exceptional, programme of legislation. On the other hand the opinion that he had always been on the side of justice and mercy is somewhat dubious. It is true that he had favoured the release of Archbishop Neville and that he had tried to defend the rights of the countess of Warwick when she had taken refuge in the sanctuary of Beaulieu and that, as king, he granted an annuity of £100 to the wife of the imprisoned earl of Oxford. In fact the countess's annuity was no more than the renewal of a grant already made by Edward IV in 1481. Moreover in 1478, as duke of Gloucester, he had taken over the inheritance of his mother-in-law, the dowager countess of Warwick, a takeover which he forced the unfortunate lady to confirm after he became king.

His efficiency as a soldier and as an administrator has been exaggerated. In 1475 he led a large contingent to France as became his rank but, of course, had no opportunity of showing his mettle. Later in 1481 and 1482 in an independent command against Scotland, although the details are obscure, his performance seems to have been so incompetent, the gains of the expeditions so meagre when set against the cost, that it had seriously vexed Edward IV.

Northern tradition long cherished his memory; that of the south condemned him as a villain and a tyrant. As late as Wolsey's day his good government and firm administration of justice in the north were held up as an example to others. Even so, there are strong hints that less respectable factors in his exercise of lordship may account for his popularity. The revenues of the northern parts of the duchy of Lancaster beyond the River Trent fell during the period after he became their chief steward in 1471 and in 1482 the duchy council told him in a remarkably outspoken letter that through sales of timber and other things he and his deputies had brought the lordship into 'great decay'. Historians have made a great deal of his popularity in York. He had been able to secure a number of favours for the city which undoubtedly earned him the gratitude of the ruling group in the city council. Yet other groups in the city were capable of making extremely unpleasant and hostile remarks about the duke of Gloucester. It may well be that his popularity was based upon no more than an exceptionally generous, or lax, exercise of lordship which its recipients no doubt contrasted very favourably with Edward IV's growing stringency in the exercise of his rights during his later years. Such methods may have been a good recipe for regional popularity but they were perhaps not in the long run the firmest of foundations for future government. After all, during his brief reign the wide extension of such methods in lavish grants and bribery to gain supporters by the end of February 1485 had reduced him to the highly unpopular expedient of demanding a forced loan.

Richard's court, like that of his brother, was noted for its music. Both as duke of Gloucester and as king he was a great builder. His plans for religious benefactions were magnificent indeed. He founded at least eighteen colleges and chantries, all attached to existing churches; the largest (one of the largest of the later middle ages) in York Minster was to provide for no less than one hundred priests. In no case did he ever complete the endowment but then it was common enough for plans of this kind to be completed after death by a founder's executors.

Richard's piety was more than skin-deep, more than merely conventional. In May 1484, he told Nicholas von Poppelau, the Emperor Frederick III's ambassador: 'I wish that my kingdom lay upon the confines of Turkey: with my own people alone and without the help of other princes I should like to drive away not only the Turks, *but all my foes*' (my emphasis). The insecure circumstances of his entire life, crowned with thorns by a few months of an usurper's ever threatened existence, made him, and little wonder, neurotically aware of hostility.

Diverse influences tinged his religious feeling — the rather morbid piety of the late fifteenth century, like that of the tract on the Precious Blood of Christ which William Sudbury dedicated to the king, and that of John Doget, the humanist scholar, his confessor, who was familiar with Donatello's Gattemalata in Padua. Nine of Richard's books demonstrate the type of his piety. These are not grand presentation copies, but fairly simply produced volumes obviously intended for his own reading. Only his Book of Hours is in Latin which suggests that he could read Latin only liturgically. The others include a Wycliffite New Testament, parts of an Old Testament in English, and English copy of the *Vision of St Matilda* and other works of a similar nature, books deriving from the great days of English mysticism in the late fourteenth and early fifteenth centuries.

Two extreme traits dominated Richard's religion — an obsession with sexual morality and a morbid sense of persecution. Again and again he struck a shrill note of moral indignation when he accused his dead brother of bringing down the wrath of God upon the country by his dissolute living, in accusations against the marquess of Dorset and Henry Tudor and in forcing the unfortunate Jane Shore to do public penance. In a circular letter to the bishops sent out on 10 March 1484 he stated:

> Our principal intent and fervent desire is to see virtue and cleannes of living to be advanced, increased and multiplied, and vices and all other things repugnant to virtue, provoking the high indignation and fearful displeasure of God, to be repressed and annulled.

He ordered them to see that all such sinners were 'repressed and punished condignly after their demerits'.

A personal prayer written for the king, most probably after the deaths of his wife and only legitimate son, reveals an attitude of mind more than bordering upon persecution:

> And you, O Lord, who restored the race of men into concord with the Father, and who bought back with thine own precious blood that forfeited inheritance of paradise, and who made peace between men and angels, deign to establish and confirm concord between me and mine enemies, show to me and pour out on me the glory of thy grace. Deign to assuage, turn aside, extinguish and bring to nothing the hatred which they have towards me ... And just as you freed Susannah from the false accusation and testimony ... even so, Jesus Christ, son of the living God, deign to free me thy servant King Richard from all the tribulation, grief and anguish in which I am held and from all the snares of my enemies and deign to send Michael the Archangel to my aid against them. Deign, O Lord Jesus, to bring to nothing the evil designs which they make or wish to make against me.[15]

Though it is possible to write off Richard's denunciations of other people's immorality and even his circular letter to the bishops as mere propaganda, it is impossible to treat a highly personal, specially composed prayer in this way — a prayer reading like the incantation of a litany, fraught with notes of the deepest gloom, oppression and danger, in which the highly charged reference to Susannah, *de falso criminere et testimonio,* so prominently stands out. Considering the

---

[15] The Latin prayer is printed in P. Tudor-Craig, *Richard III* (National Portrait Gallery exhibition catalogue, 2nd ed, 1977), pp. 96 – 7.

accusations against him, the knowledge that he slandered his brother's memory, the probability that he impugned his mother's chastity, that he authorized judicial murder, that he was prepared to contemplate incest, that he cheated his nephews out of their inheritance if not far worse, the prayer must indicate that either Richard thought he was innocent of the charges or that towards the end of his life he had become in the highest degree schizophrenic, a criminal self-righteously invoking the protection of the Almighty.

10   Henry VII

I

Henry of Richmond gained the English throne only because a turn of French politics had permitted him to do so. Although he marched uninterrupted across the country, he had attracted very little support. His Welshness and his appeal to the Welsh have been very much exaggerated. The English nobility stood remarkably aloof from his adventure and he owed his success to one family, that of his step-father, the Stanleys. Aged twenty-eight, he had no experience of government, not even of seigneurial administration. As Dr B. P. Wolffe has remarked,[1] hindsight has led generations of historians to exaggerate his prospects of success but, as in the case of Edward IV in 1461, the accession of so untried an adventurer could have given little comfort to nervous politicians, particularly to large property-owners. Once again the whole question of stability seemed to be thrown into the melting-pot. Henry could have had as little confidence as other people in the durability of the settlement. Although we see that the conspiracies against him were nothing like as dangerous as those of the Yorkist period, they appeared dangerous enough at the time and throughout his reign Henry seems to have attracted no great love or loyalty. In 1496 a Florentine, Aldo Brandini, who had recently been in London, told Giovanni de Bebulcho, the envoy of the duke of Milan: 'The king is feared rather than loved, and this was due to his avarice. ... The king is very powerful in money, but if fortune allowed some lord of the blood royal to arise and he had to take the field he would fare badly owing to his avarice; his people would abandon him.'

He was unfortunate in the survival rate of his children. Five out of eight predeceased him. Even in 1499 when Prince Arthur was thirteen, a group of prominent men could discuss the succession without even mentioning the prince at all[2] and the atmosphere of

[1] B. P. Wolffe, 'Henry VII's Land Revenues and Chamber Finance', *EHR* lxxix (1964), p. 230.

[2] See below, p. 347 – 8.

sedition had become so infectious that a 'crazy mawmet', a mere Cambridge student, could try to raise an insurrection by claiming to be the duke of Clarence's son.

II

Very much as with Edward IV, four inter-related problems faced the king—the power base of support, public order, finance and foreign policy.

It is difficult to define the basis of support for Henry VII for we lack the detailed knowledge of his relations with the nobility that recent research has revealed for the reign of Edward IV. Divided as the peerage had been in 1461, a much greater proportion of the nobility even so had then supported Edward than now supported Henry. Henry VII, unlike Edward IV and unlike his son Henry VIII, was extremely sparing in trying to obtain support by new creations. There were only nine new creations at most during his reign and seven of these had been made by 1488. As Professor S. B. Chrimes had pointed out,[3] only three were genuine new peerages.[4] The rest were summonses to parliament of men who had some more or less distant hereditary claims, like John Radcliffe de Fitzwalter who was summoned to parliament in September 1485 in the 'right' of his mother. In any case two of these families died out before 1509. Lord Fitzwalter was attainted in 1495 and another three families vanished by 1533. Moreover Henry abandoned the practice common since the 1430s of creating new peerages in tail male by letters patent. Only one peerage, that of Giles, Lord Daubeney (1486), was created in this way. The rest, in a more old-fashioned tradition, just received personal writs of summons. Henry gave some recognition of existing hereditary claims but he kept a free hand and avoided creating new ones. He preferred to reward loyal service with the Order of the Garter, creating no fewer than thirty-seven new knights of whom more than half were men among his closest companions in government or war.

Sir Francis Bacon wrote: 'For his nobles, although they were loyal and obedient, yet did not co-operate with him, but let every man go his own way.' Although it was written more than a century later, there is no reason whatsoever to doubt the truth of Bacon's statement. As we shall see later, towards the end of his reign Henry had brought a cowed and timid peerage under a particularly brutal and terrifying

[3] S. B. Chrimes, *Henry VII (1972)*, pp. 137 ff.
[4] Lords Burgh, Cheney and Daubeney.

form of control. Yet although he reduced them to a humiliating condition of fear and terror he never, so far as we know, attempted to interfere with their local control over the countryside in general. The Chancery still placed them on the commissions of the peace, on important commissions of oyer and terminer and, when less drastic methods of arrest had been exhausted, ordered them to see to the apprehension of malefactors.

In spite of his dubious conduct at the battle of Bosworth, Henry Percy IV, earl of Northumberland, was immediately given the wardenship of the East and Middle Marches which he held until his assassination in 1489. Henry considerably reduced the peace time pay of the wardens of the Marches, but the extent to which he relied upon ·officials rather than lords in the government and defence of the north has been exaggerated. Although the Percies were in eclipse after 1489 and the king appointed Prince Arthur as warden-general, he relied upon Thomas Howard, earl of Surrey, as lieutenant of the East March,[5] which gave the Howards the idea, ultimately unsuccessful, of trying to establish themselves as a great northern family. The king also continued to rely upon the other great northern families, the Dacres, the senior branch of the Nevilles and the Cliffords.

Over the whole country it may well be, though the matter requires much further investigation, that Henry to a much wider extent than the Yorkists relied upon the greater gentry, particularly upon members of his household. The custody of most castles and fortresses, for example, were placed in the hands of household men.[6]

III

The questions of security and public order were no less urgent than they had been under Edward IV, and they were equally inter-connected. Immediately after Bosworth Henry issued a proclamation which showed the connection very clearly indeed. One would have expected a command to the disbanded troops not to pillage. In fact, the proclamation commanded the reverse: the king

> Strictly chargeth and commandeth that no manner of man rob or spoil no manner of commons coming from the field, but suffer them to pass home to their countries and dwelling places with their horses and harness. And moreover, that no manner of man take upon him to go to no gentleman's place, neither in the country, nor within cities nor boroughs, *nor pick no quarrels for old or new matters* [my emphasis]

[5] See below, pp. 354 – 6.

[6] J. D. Alsop, 'The Military Functions of Henry VII's Household', unpublished M A thesis, University of Western Ontario, (1974).

Two years later, the year 1487 seemed to show something like a peak of suspicion and fear. The parliament which met five months after the battle of Stoke produced no less than six statutes for suppressing sedition and disorder as well as attainting twenty-eight rebels who had fought in the battle. One statute made the kidnapping of well-to-do women a felony. Another complained against 'the daily increase' of murders in the land and proposed to tighten up alleged negligence in the prosecution of such crimes. A third forbade anyone to retain the king's tenants as this had led (among other things) to unlawful assemblies and to riots. Tenants who became other men's retainers were to lose their leases. The mistakenly called Star Chamber Act set up a court manned by the chancellor, treasurer and keeper of the privy seal or any two of them who, with the assistance of a bishop and a temporal lord from among the king's councillors, were to deal with maintenance, unlawful retaining by indentures, by promises, oaths or by the giving of liveries signs and tokens, embracery, the corrupt conduct of sheriffs empanelling juries, bribe taking by juries and riots. The records of only ten cases heard by this court have survived. It is, however, possible that it exercised the criminal jurisdiction formerly, and erroneously, attributed to the Council in the Star Chamber.

Finally the same parliament established another court which showed, after so brief a period upon the throne, how terrified Henry VII had become of the very centre of power, the royal household itself. The statute setting up this court stated that in the absence of actual deeds there was no remedy against 'false imaginings and confederacies' against the king, his councillors, great officers of the household or any lords. Moreover, quarrels among members of the household had become so ferocious and their malice so great that they were likely to lead to plots to kill the king himself. Therefore the steward, treasurer and controller of the household or any one of them were empowered to enquire by twelve 'sad and discreet' persons of the check roll of the household whether any person under baronial rank, sworn and named in the same roll, had taken part in 'any confederacy, compassings, conspiracies, or imaginings' to destroy or murder the king or any of the persons before named. If enquiries suggested that anyone had taken part in such conspiracies, any two of the great officers were empowered to put the suspects on trial by a jury of twelve other members of the household, and if found guilty they were to stand convicted of felony and attaint at common law.

At various times acts were passed against justices of the peace, sheriffs, corrupt jurors, corrupt officials, against perjury and riots. Although since the middle of the fourteenth century governments had piled more and more duties upon the justices of the peace and had given them wider and wider jurisdiction, from the beginning they had been sceptical about their honesty and reliability—a scepticism which had certainly not diminished with time and which still flourished in the Elizabethan and early Stuart period. Twenty-one out of a total of 192 statutes passed during Henry VII's reign dealt with the justices. An act of 1489 condemned their negligence and partiality because of which (it was alleged) the laws were not enforced. They were charged, under threat of dismissal, to execute their duties properly. In future they were also to proclaim four times a year, under a penalty of forty shillings, that anyone wronged by a particular justice might complain to another and then, if redress were not obtained, to any justice of assize, to the chancellor or the king himself. If the king found the accusation to be true, the offending justice would be dismissed and even punished.

Professor Chrimes has not only expressed doubts about the efficiency of law enforcement under Henry VII but has even questioned whether there was any strong will or determination for stricter enforcement.[7] Several statutes tightening up the law had a limited life, being made valid only until the next parliament.[8] Both Lords and Commons, although they constantly complained, as they had complained for the greater part of a century and more, about 'lack of governance', obviously had no wish to see any great extension of the government's powers.

Enforcement was really crux of the problem. Like Edward IV in his parliament, Henry VII in 1485 announced stern measures against disorder and he exacted an oath from all the Lords spiritual and temporal, members of the House of Commons and the knights and esquires of the royal household that they would neither shelter nor aid anyone 'openly cursed' of murder, felony or outlawry but would cause such people to be arrested. Nor would they retain any man contrary to law, indulge in maintenance, embracery, riots or unlawful assembly, nor obstruct the king's officers. Again in a meeting of the justices at the Blackfriars in the first year of the reign Chief Justice Huse said:

> The law will never be well executed until all the lords spiritual and temporal are of one accord, for the love and dread they have for God or for the king, or both, to execute them effectively and *when the king on his part and the lords on their part both want to do this and do it.* [my emphasis].

There are, indeed, certain pointers that the king was not as consistent as he might have been in such matters. In prison in the first year of Henry VIII's reign, Edmund Dudley wrote that one of the main

---

[7] Chrimes, *Henry VII*, chapter 8.
[8] For example, against jurors giving untrue verdicts (1495), *Statute Roll*, c. 24, against false verdicts (1503), *ibid.*, c. 3, an act for preserving the fry of fish (1488 – 9), *ibid.*, c. 21. Also, in 1488 – 9 an act against the negligence of JPs was to last for two years only, *ibid.* c. 12.

functions of the nobility was to protect the poor from injury: what a realm there would be if the king kept 'the temporal subjects in a loving dread and has not suffered them, nor the mightiest of them to oppress the poor ... nor suffer the nobles of thy realm nor any other of thy subjects [so] to run at a riot as to punish or revenge their own quarrels'. If the king himself set the nobles the right example, all might be well. But Dudley was very well aware that Henry VII never remotely approached such a high ideal. Instead another document which Dudley himself drew up at the same time reveals with dreadful clarity that, rather than dealing out impartial justice, Henry had indulged in arbitrary terrorization and financial extortion against selected victims, both high and low, who were unfortunate enough to have attracted his personal attention.

Action through the law courts, however, turns out to have been a very different matter. The famous Council in the Star Chamber mostly dealt with suits between party and party. No single case is extant in which the government there initiated a prosecution for maintenance.[9] Nor do the common law courts show any particularly vigorous activity in such matters. Neither the Court of King's Bench nor the Exchequer were very effective. In the Michaelmas term 1488 (the only term for which the records have been investigated in detail), two thirds of the cases which came before the court were civil suits. Sentences of outlawry, seldom reversed, were imposed in most cases and the court recorded few final judgments. Even in the crown pleas only about one fifth came to any final decision. After 1490 there were a mere two actions a term on retaining and most of them ended in pardon or dismissal. After 1501 there were nine such cases in the Exchequer, none of them begun by the attorney-general. Two were never resolved, the judges dismissed another two and juries acquitted in the other five. There was only one single action for maintenance and that ended in a pardon.

Later in the Tudor period the system of penal statutes[10] and common informers became notorious for injustice and corruption, with prosecutions in the exchequer and other courts which aroused increasing resentment. This can hardly have been true in Henry VII's day. Even after 1500, when there was somewhat greater activity than before, royal officials seem to have had little interest in the enforcement of any statutes other than those relating to foreign trade and the customs system. There was certainly no army of private informers crowding into the court to lay informations. Nor were the pro-

---

[9] Professor G. R. Elton however has suggested that the court may have heard more criminal cases at the king's instance than the surviving records of only 194 cases suggest.

[10] Statutes under which informers received a part of the fine and part of the value of confiscated goods in cases of successful prosecution.

secutions particularly successful. Throughout the reign a verdict of guilty was returned in just over 37 per cent of such revenue cases and in twenty-four years they brought the king only £7,965 5s 5½d in fines and forfeitures and informers £3,062 4d in moieties.[11]

Parliament, therefore, was somewhat reluctant to extend the government's powers of coercion and the legal system was scarely harsh in the enforcement of the law. The government brought in little that was new either in law or law enforcement. Except where the king personally interfered, it was hardly harsh or ruthless, neither more nor less efficient than most previous governments. As Professor W. H. Dunham remarked of Henry VII's Star Chamber: 'The most striking characteristic of the court was its moderation. It was surely the mildest-mannered tribunal that ever sentenced a criminal, considerate in its procedure, gentle in its punishments, and failing altogether to live up to the reputation of ruthlessness that the Star Chamber has enjoyed since the seventeenth century.'[12]

Moreover, like his predecessors Henry VII had to rely upon the forces of bastard feudalism to keep order in the countryside. Several statutes during his reign dealt with the subjects of retaining and maintenance, attempting to provide for the better enforcement of the existing laws on the subject, but there was no new approach until 1504. A new statute was then, in the main, a repetition of Edward IV's act of 1468. Edward's act had prohibited retaining for any except menial and estate servants, officers and men of law. It was, however, somewhat ambiguous, for another clause mentions persons retained 'for loyal service to be done'. Henry VII's statute, whether deliberately or not is uncertain, omitted this last category. Even now retaining as such was not completely prohibited, only unlawful retaining. The penalties were those of 1468, though the methods proposed for enforcement were somewhat stricter. The new act, for the first time, introduced a kind of licensing system. Under the act men could take retainers to do the king service under a 'placard' or licence signed by the king himself and sealed with either the signet or the privy seal. Once again, however, this was one of the statutes of limited duration. It was to remain valid for the king's own lifetime and no longer.[13]

There is no evidence that the act had any great effect. Some people took additional precautions in their retaining. The Percies, for

[11] Out of 1,804 prosecutions in the Exchequer for the whole reign, 1,140 were for smuggling. In 891 cases out of the total of 1,804 the informers were royal officials and 322 cases were started by the attorney-general, thus leaving only 342, 14 a year, to the initiative of private people. J. de Lloyd Guth, 'Exchequer, Penal Law Enforcement, 1485 – 1509', unpublished PhD thesis (Pittsburg, 1967). A moiety was the common informer's share of the forfeiture.

[12] C. G. Bayne and W. H. Dunham Jr, *Select Cases in the Council of Henry VII*, Selden Society LXXV (1956), p. clxxii.

[13] See also above, p. 335.

example, duplicated some of their household and estate offices to maintain the number of their retainers without breaking the law. The only known prosecution of a peer was the notorious case of George Neville, Lord Burgavenny, in 1506, whose loyalty the king may have suspected. The accusations against him, somewhat late in the day, alleged that he had been implicated in the Cornish rebellion of 1497. Enormous fines were imposed upon him.[14] Yet subsequent events ironically enough show how vital retaining was to the monarchy. In 1510 Henry VIII granted Burgavenny in reversion for life the constableship of Dover and the wardenship of the Cinque Ports and in 1512 in preparation for the war in France issued him a licence 'to retain as many men as he can get in Kent, Sussex and Surrey and elsewhere ... and he shall give them badges, tokens and liveries as he thinks convenient.'

It may well be that here, as in other matters, Henry VII chose to avoid direct confrontations in the law courts, preferring to pounce upon selected individuals in a cat-and-mouse manner. Certain entries in Edmund Dudley's notebook suggest that a few people at least compounded with the king for retaining offences. Henry certainly did not solve the problem. All the Tudors continued to issue licences for retaining well into the reign of Queen Elizabeth I though it is true that these licences came to be more and more restricted to men holding office under the crown.

IV

Various statutes show the government to have been frightened of large assemblies of people. Even hunting parties they thought could lead to sedition. In the minds of the king and his advisers, disorder and sedition were very much interrelated problems; so were security, finance and foreign policy. The plots of pretenders drove a fearful king (whether wisely or unwisely) to expensive interventions in European affairs, the financing of which produced a perilous backlash of resentment, even revolt, at home. The general trends and the details of Henry VII's finances are dealt with elsewhere so that here it will be necessary only to indicate their very intimate connection with foreign policy and security.

The first conspiracy against the king, led by Viscount Lovell and Humphrey and Thomas Stafford, the sons of Sir Humphrey Stafford of Grafton, occurred as early as Easter 1486. Lovell and the Staffords

---

[14] See below, p. 359.

burst out of the sanctuary at Colchester where they had taken refuge after the battle of Bosworth but their petty rising quickly collapsed. Lovell fled and disappeared. The Staffords were captured, Humphrey was hanged and his brother Thomas, pardoned.

A far more dangerous conspiracy arose the following year and its origin lay in Irish politics. The Yorkists had been popular in Ireland. After 1447 Richard of York, to gain support for or at least acquiescence in his own schemes, had more or less allowed free rein to the independent aspirations of the Anglo-Irish lords — a policy which Edward IV had been quite unable to reverse. Gerald FitzGerald, the eighth earl of Kildare, had become in effect king of Ireland, supported by all the other great families except the Butlers. To maintain their independent position the FitzGeralds and their allies chose to adhere to the Yorkists and to defy the new dynasty. They selected as their puppet a child about ten years old called Lambert Simnel, the son of a baker. A twenty-eight-year-old priest, Richard Simons, trained him to play the part of the earl of Warwick, the son of George, duke of Clarence. The real Warwick was, of course, a closely guarded prisoner in the Tower of London but the conspirators claimed that it was the prisoner who was the impostor.

Rumours of the plot were circulating by the end of November 1486 and they probably reached the king's ear in the New Year. In February Edward IV's nephew, John, earl of Lincoln, fled to the Netherlands where he joined Viscount Lovell, who had now reappeared, at the court of Margaret of Burgundy. Lincoln's aunt, the dowager duchess ('mine old lady of Burgundy' as the Pastons called her) was, in her widowhood, a formidable politican who, in spite of her niece Elizabeth's marriage to Henry Tudor, was always eager to ferment plots for a Yorkist restoration. On 5 May with the dowager duchess's support Lincoln and Lovell landed in Ireland supported by some 2,000 German mercenaries led by a professional soldier, Martin Schwartz. On 24 May the conspirators crowned Lambert Simnel in Dublin with a gold circlet taken from a statue of the Blessed Virgin Mary and then accompanied by a force of half-naked Irishmen landed on 4 June at Furness on the Lancashire coast where they expected the support of a local knight, Thomas Broughton. Marching south they encountered Henry and his forces at Stoke near Newark, on 16 June. Lincoln, Martin Schwartz and Thomas Geraldine, the Irish leader, were all killed. Lovell was either killed or fled and completely disappeared, this time without any future trace. Simons was imprisoned for life and Simnel contemptuously relegated to the position of a scullion in the royal kitchen, later to be promoted to king's falconer.

Although a battle for survival within two years of his accession must deeply have disturbed the king's peace of mind, the conspiracy was of small significance. The invaders attracted very little support even in those parts of Lancashire where Sir Thomas Broughton's influence was strong. It would have been impossible without the German mercenaries and the 'wild Irish' and their employment was hardly likely to encourage the English to join in. Pro-Yorkist feeling never seems to have been very strong. The nobility had given little support to dynastic conflict after the peak period of 1460 to 1461 and, in spite of the survival of a certain amount of Yorkist sentiment among officials of the former regime, it may well be doubed if there was anything like a 'Yorkist party'. Irish lords would always rise to stave off the prospects of firmer English government. 'My lords of Ireland, you will crown apes at last,' Henry once sarcastically remarked. The dowager duchess of Burgundy would support almost any anti-Tudor conspiracy and members of the de la Pole family, the descendants of Edward IV's sister, Elizabeth, were always tempted to advance claims to the throne. Even so, Irish lords and a few ambitious and disgruntled relations hardly formed a Yorkist faction. Among the nobility, though a number of men of lower rank may have been less cautious, there was now no more of a Yorkist party than there had been in the early 1450s. Apart from the de la Pole earl of Lincoln, Viscount Lovell was Lambert Simnel's only prominent adherent and, apart from the dubious case of Lord Burgavenny, Lord FitzWalter was the only peer who later supported Perkin Warbeck. Lord Audley, who joined the Cornish rebels in 1497, had no apparent Yorkist connections.

Henry VII, however, was not to know this. His early experiences had bred in him an intense wariness and caution. He was only too well aware with how little support he had gained the throne and, as Bacon claimed, how distant and aloof the nobility remained. Although he was willing to employ ex-Yorkist servants, the slightest suspicion of disloyalty was always enough to bring about their immediate downfall. As under Edward IV foreign interest made these conspiracies (on the whole rather feeble conspiracies) the more dangerous. Foreign interests were so prominent that until the last years of his reign his foreign policy was always influenced by the possible consequences of Yorkist plots or the effect of possible support for pretenders upon domestic security. In his anxiety to avoid needless risks, perhaps he sometimes became too cautious and too ready to sacrifice the country's commercial interests to bring pressure to bear upon foreign powers, particularly the rulers of the Netherlands, to surrender potentially dangerous pretenders to his throne.

Although Richard III had dropped his brother's aggressive policy towards Scotland, James III viewed the change of dynasty favourably. He may even have allowed a Scottish contingent in France to take part in Henry VII's invasion. Henry maintained agents in Scotland and in June 1486 made a three year truce with James. James himself would have preferred a more permanent settlement but dared not go further for fear of domestic opposition. Negotiations for a marriage alliance followed but in June 1488 rebels defeated James at the battle of Sauchieburn and afterwards murdered him. After this setback the best that Henry could do was to maintain subversive agents in Scotland by the distribution of pensions. Soon, however, he was able to conclude another three year truce with the government of the fifteen-year-old James IV. No more was yet possible and the truce left Anglo-Scottish relationships delicately and dangerously poised.

Meanwhile Henry had to face the problem of Brittany. The king owed his preservation from the Yorkists between 1471 and 1484 to Duke Francis II of Brittany. On the other hand he owed his success in 1485 to France. After the death of Francis II on 9 September 1488, Anne of Beaujeu, the French regent, aspired to take control of Brittany for her brother, Charles VIII. As France since 1478 had a already overrun part of the Netherlands, French expansion west-wards along the Breton coastline, giving them control of the Breton ports, would be yet another threat to English security. Whichever side Henry chose the other was bound to accuse him of ingratitude. More-over, if he declared for Brittany the French were quite likely to support another pretender as they had supported Henry in 1485.

Even so in the treaty of Redon (February 1489) Henry undertook to support Anne, the new twelve-year-old duchess, though at Breton expense. Brittany was to pay any English soldiers who were sent there. He was fortunate about six weeks later to conclude the treaty of Medina del Campo with Spain, which included an undertaking that neither side would harbour or help the other's rebels. In January 1489 Henry also met his third parliament from which, in spite of the terms of the treaty of Redon, he demanded special taxes amounting to £75,000 for the defence of Brittany. The Convocation of Canterbury also agreed to raise another £25,000. Parliament granted the tax extremely reluctantly, imposing restrictions just as humiliating as those which the parliament of 1472 – 5 had earlier imposed upon Edward IV. This time evasion was far more successful and far more extreme than it had been in the 1470s. No more than £27,000, possibly as little as £20,736, was ever collected from the lay grant. Even so, disastrous events followed from the collection of the tax. On 28 April when the earl of Northumberland attempted to explain the need for taxation to a crowd at Topcliffe in Yorkshire, the angry mob assassinated him while his own highly paid retinue stood idly by.[15]

Henry also managed to negotiate a pro-Breton coalition with the Emperor Maximilian, but on 6 December 1491 the duchess Anne married the king of France. The Breton cause was lost and French influence along the southern coast of the English Channel dangerously extended.

Henry had lost his first continental diplomatic round and English taxpayers had once again, and even more emphatically, repeated the lesson of the 1470s — that they would hardly permit their monarch an active foreign policy if he called on them to pay for it — a lesson which they were to repeat even more menacingly eight years later.

Yet in spite of the dangerous tensions which an active foreign policy produced at home, Henry was convinced that his own security was even more dangerously threatened without one. Between the devil and the deep blue sea he was forced to judge between domestic and foreign dangers. Very soon the danger once again took the form of a pretender, and, this time, a far more dangerous pretender than Lambert Simnel had ever been.

In October or November 1491 Perkin Warbeck, the son of John Osbec, the controller of Tournai, appeared in Cork masquerading as Richard, duke of York, the younger brother of Edward V, whose murder in the Tower, though generally assumed, had never been proven. For the next few years Warbeck's recognition by various foreign powers dictated Henry's foreign policy and, indirectly, produced the most dangerous revolt of the entire reign. Henry's acute anxiety about him can be shown, perhaps, by a small but significant event. The king liked to gamble though he generally staked only small sums. One day the accounts record a loss at cards of cards of £9 with the note, 'this day came Perkin Warbeck.'

Charles VIII of France was certainly implicated in the origins of the plot. Warbeck was a useful counterpoise against further English interference in Brittany. The dowager Duchess Margaret may also have been involved in the early stages. Although he never spoke English well, Warbeck had been able to accumulate a good deal of information useful for his role especially from Sir Edward Brampton, a converted Jewish Portugese merchant who had risen high in the favour of both Edward IV and Richard III. Brampton had fled to the Low Countries after Bosworth. There he had employed Warbeck, whom he took with him on a voyage from Middleburg to Lisbon in 1487.

Although the earl of Kildare was possibly implicated, the Irish gave Warbeck no very warm welcome. By 1492, despairing of much

---

[15] Northumberland was also personally unpopular. Many men in the north seem to have resented his betrayal of Richard III.

support there, he made his first overtures to James IV of Scotland. As Henry VII was again intervening in Brittany in support of the Duchess Anne, albeit with very little effect, Charles VIII invited Warbeck to France and treated him with princely honours. In October 1492 Henry invaded France and laid siege to Boulogne but, like Edward IV in 1475, swiftly turned warfare into negotiation and on 3 November concluded the treaty of Étaples. The treaty partially removed French restrictions upon English merchants. It was financially advantageous for the French agreed to pay for the cost of the war, the money which Anne of Brittany owed to Henry and the arrears of Edward IV's pension. Henry netted an immediate total of about £159,000 and both Charles and his successor, Louis XII, continued to pay the pension regularly. The treaty marked the end of one phase of Henry's foreign policy. The Breton question was finally settled. Anglo-French relationships were for the time stabilized and the idea of an Anglo-Spanish marriage alliance was first put forward. Above all the French agreed not to assist any English rebels and expelled Warbeck from the court.

Nevertheless Warbeck continued to be a dangerous menace. His earlier overtures to James IV paid dividends when he was obliged to leave France. First of all, however, he turned to the ever implacable Margaret of Burgundy who could now train him for his part by priming him with recollections of Edward IV's court and details about the Yorkist family. The Archduke Philip and his father, the Emperor Maximilian, now on bad terms with Henry VII, soon extended their protection to him, but at first put the blame on Margaret, saying that it was quite impossible for them to control her actions. Henry retaliated by forbidding trade with Flanders, banished all Flemish merchants from England and ordered the Merchant Adventurers to move the seat of their operations from Antwerp to Calais. This trade embargo continued from the summer of 1493 until February 1496 and it was not the only extended period during which Henry was prepared to sacrifice English commercial interests to his feelings for dynastic security. These drastic pressures for the time only made matters worse. In November 1493 in Vienna Maximilian recognized Warbeck as the rightful king of England and by the following summer was prepared to give him material assistance.

Henry became thoroughly scared by more plots at home, plots which involved the family of his stepfather, the Stanleys, the family which had really put him on the throne. As early as March 1493, the earl of Derby's younger brother, Sir William Stanley, had employed Sir Robert Clifford to go to the court of Margaret of Burgundy to contact Perkin Warbeck. This Clifford did in June of the same year. At some stage Sir Robert Clifford informed the king of the whole

Stanley plot, following which in February 1495 Sir William Stanley was arrested, put on trial and executed.

The entire episode has its elements of mystery. Clifford may have played a double game. He may have been in Henry's pay all along. At any rate Henry pardoned him and rewarded him with £500 for his revelations. Nor is it impossible that the Stanleys themselves were merely playing safe, trying to keep a foot in every camp, taking out a kind of insurance policy against future disaster in unpredictable times. They were quite capable of such action. Ever since their ambiguous conduct at Blore Heath in 1459 their reactions in every dynastic crisis had been shifty and uncertain.

Henry's espionage had been effective. Stanley's downfall and the arrest of other conspirators broke the plot in time. When Warbeck, with a small expedition from the Netherlands, attempted to land at Deal in Kent on 3 July he found no local support. His men were soon surrounded and captured. Abandoning them to their fate, for the second time he made for Ireland. Received by the earl of Desmond, he attacked Waterford for eleven days until it was relieved by a force under Sir Edward Poynings. Seeing no hope left in Ireland, after sending messages to James IV, he set sail for Scotland.

James had been intriguing with Margaret of Burgundy in 1489 and 1490 and in 1491 he had renewed a treaty with France undertaking to attack England if that country made war on France. Later James had swung more in Henry's favour and after the treaty of Étaples he had agreed to a truce until April 1494, later extended for a further seven years from June 1494. Henry's envoys took immense trouble and expense during these prolonged negotiations, the results of which were encouraging enough for the king in June 1495 to make proposals for a marriage treaty between his daughter, Margaret, and James.

After the complete collapse of the plot at home, Warbeck's failures in Kent and in Ireland and the feeling that the time was ripe for a firm Anglo-Scottish alliance, it was all the more galling that when the pretender landed in Scotland in November 1495 James IV acknowledged him as Richard of York and in December married him to his own kinswoman, Catherine Gordon, the sister of the earl of Huntley. Such a match could hardly have been possible unless James, for the moment at least, had believed Warbeck's claims to be genuine.

Warbeck, in Henry's eyes, continued to be a dangerous menace, though English foreign policy was also governed by other considerations. From 1496 Charles VIII of France turned his mind to dynastic ambitions and to conquests in Italy, which led to Henry's inclusion in the Holy League with the Empire, the pope, Venice and Ferdinand of Aragon against him. At this Charles once again began to intrigue, offering to buy Warbeck from James IV. The same year saw the conclusion of the important commercial treaty, the Intercurcus Magnus. Yet the support of James IV and Margaret of Burgundy for Warbeck and fears of conspiracies of unknown dimensions frustrated Henry's ambitions for a Spanish marriage treaty the first idea of which had been mooted as far back as 1489. Ferdinand of Aragon now refused to make such an alliance under the shadow of dangerous threats of this kind. Henry became so desperate that he even entertained a scheme for kidnapping Warbeck while at the same time making further overtures to James IV and putting in hand preparations to resist a possible Scottish invasion. James IV in the end decided upon an invasion, having first obtained from Warbeck a promise of payment of 50,000 marks within two years to cover the cost of the expedition and a guarantee for the return of Berwick to Scotland.

Assisted by a meagre force sent by Margaret of Burgundy, a rabble of about 1,400 men of diverse nationalities set out on 17 September 1496. The expedition proved an utter failure, raising no response whatsoever south of the border. After penetrating for about four miles and capturing a couple of watch towers the Scottish force retreated homewards.

Indirectly this Scottish invasion triggered off the most dangerous domestic crisis of the reign. Preparations to resist it had cost a great deal of money. When parliament met in January 1497 the Commons voted the king large sums to cover the cost — no less than two fifteenths and tenths, without the usual deduction of £6,000 for the exemption of impoverished and decayed places, plus the equivalent of two further fifteenths and tenths to be assessed on people with incomes of more than 20s a year from land. Reaction to this essential taxation shows how little England can be considered a united country at this time for the men of Cornwall rose in revolt rather than pay taxes (which their own representatives had voted in parliament) for the defence of the distant north. Resentment against the cost of defending the dynasty had proved to be a far greater incentive to rebellion than any shadowy pro-Yorkist sentiment.

It must have been terrifying to the government that an insurgent rabble of possibly 15,000 men under the insignificant leadership of a mere blacksmith, Michael Joseph, and a lawyer, Thomas Flamanck, and armed only with bills and bows, without cavalry or artillery, could march from Cornwall to Kent without interruption. James Touchet, Lord Audley, was the only peer to join them and he had no known Yorkist connections. Lord Daubeney quickly came down from the north and defeated the rebels at Blackheath. About a thousand were killed. the rest surrendered or fled. The episode drove Henry to renew his negotiations for a firm settlement with James IV so as to avoid the costs of any future war on the northern border. Once again events had amply proved (if Henry needed further proof by this time) that it was dangerous to levy taxes even for the defence of the realm, let alone for the pursuit of a foreign policy leading to any expensive commitments in Europe.

Fortunately James IV had also come to realize the folly of costly hostilities with England. He decided to abandon Warbeck and began negotiations which, in September 1497, resulted in a seven year truce, leading in 1499 to the first full peace treaty with Scotland since 1328. Under the terms of this treaty James was to marry Henry's daughter, Margaret, and the marriage took place in 1503.

In July James IV had got rid of the now embarrassing Warbeck by hiring a Breton vessel to take him away from Scotland. Warbeck once again landed at Cork towards the end of the month, but finding his third landing in Ireland even less welcome than his previous appearances had been, set sail with two small ships and a pinnace and a mere 120 men. He landed in Whitesand Bay near Land's End on 7 September hoping to profit from the now notorious discontent of Cornwall. Possibly from three to four thousand countrymen joined him. Exeter drove him away and Taunton refused him entry to the town. Warbeck soon fled before advancing royal forces, then surrendered and made a full confession of his entire imposture.

Henry was generous. Warbeck was treated as a member of the court.[16] Foolishly he attempted to escape, but he was recaptured at Sheen on 9 July 1498, made to repeat his confession and, having been twice put in the stocks in London, was imprisoned in the Tower. There he was in contact with Edward, earl of Warwick, the totally innocent son of the duke of Clarence, now aged twenty-three, who had been a prisoner ever since Henry's accession. What happened next is obscure and ever will be. Either charges were concocted against Warbeck or he drew Warwick into some kind of crazy plot. In either case his fate was sealed. In mid-November he was charged with attempting to escape and hanged by the end of the month. At the same time a grand jury brought in a charge of treason against Warwick—a charge which he admitted and he was shortly afterwards beheaded.

Even now, threats to the dynasty were by no means over. New menaces came from the de la Pole family. After the battle of Stoke, John, earl of Lincoln, the heir of the duke of Suffolk, had been attainted. With the death of his father the duke, sometime in 1491-2, the third son, Edmund, was treated in a distinctly peculiar way. In 1492-3 on payment of £5,000 the king allotted him certain of the

---

[16] As he was not an English subject it would have been difficult legally to have accused him of treason.

family estates as though his brother had never been attainted and reduced him in rank from duke to earl of Suffolk. This reduction in both rank and estates must grievously have rankled in his mind — a mind with a tendency to violence somewhat abnormal even by the standards of those days. For several years he remained loyal, even leading a contingent of troops against the Cornish rebels in 1497. Then in the Michelmas Term 1498 an accusation of murder was brought against him in the Court of King's Bench. Although promptly pardoned, he took furious offence and fled to Flanders. In September 1498, in Guisnes, near Calais, he was persuaded to return. Even after this he remained in favour until July or August 1501 when he and his brother, Richard, again fled, this time to the court of the Emperor Maximilian whose aid they sought in launching a new conspiracy in Earl Edmund's favour.

Sir Francis Bacon alleged that Henry VII's mind was always 'full of apprehensions and suspicions'. In his earlier years, if contemporary witnesses can be believed, he had kept his fears well under control and he had tended to be exceedingly suspicious of rumour-mongers and tale-bearers. By this time he was already in an enfeebled state of health, possibly suffering from the tuberculosis that finally killed him. From now until the end of his reign his earlier, and more generous, instincts deserted him. He became almost pathologically frightened and brutally suspicious both of his somewhat withdrawn nobility and of his higher officials.[17] Moreover, the prospects for the future of his dynasty suddenly became more precarious than for many years past. In June 1500 his third son, Edmund, had died. In April 1503 calamity struck again. His eldest son, Prince Arthur, died less than five months after his marriage to Catherine of Aragon.[18] Prince Henry, aged only ten, was now the sole survivor of three boys. Henry may well have been a delicate child and his parents anxious about his survival. According to the Spanish ambassador, after the queen's death[19] the king so greatly cherished the heir to the throne that he was brought up with extreme care in the kind of seclusion normally reserved for young girls.

The atmosphere of febrile uncertainty and intrigue in high places which fed Henry's growing fears (though it hardly justified his growing political brutality) is well illustrated about this time, if a spy's report can be believed. The spy reported that Sir Hugh Conway, the treasurer of Calais, in conversation with other officials of the Calais garrison, alleged that even before Prince Arthur's death men

[17] See below, pp. 351 ff.
[18] The marriage treaty had been signed on 1 October 1496, the marriage by proxy took place in May 1499 and the marriage on 14 November.
[19] Queen Elizabeth died 11 February 1503.

prominent about the court had been somewhat boldly and freely speculating about the prospects of the succession. In the course of the conversation at Calais Sir Hugh stated that some time earlier at the royal court various unnamed 'great personages' when discussing, in his presence, the king's feeble health, spoke of the duke of Buckingham saying that he was a noble man and would make a royal ruler. Others there were (said Conway) 'that spoke likewise of your traitor, Edmund de la Pole, but none of them ... spake of my lord prince.'[20]

If all this can be believed, at least a decade and a half of Tudor rule had produced remarkably little sense of dynastic devotion to the family of an adventurer who had gained the throne as a pawn in one of the vicissitudes of French foreign policy.

Edmund de la Pole continued to be a nuisance abroad for several years. Henry made tremendous efforts to get him out of Flanders, once more prohibiting trade with the Netherlands in order to do so — a prohibition which this time lasted for three years. It says a great deal for Henry's fears that he was prepared to inflict such potential damage on English commerce to force the surrender of a comparatively minor political embarrassment of this kind.

At last chance provided the opportunity. In 1506 when the Archduke Philip and his wife, Joanna, were sailing from Zeeland to Spain a storm forced their fleet to take refuge in Melcombe. They remained in England for three months and before they left Philip agreed (among other things) to a commercial treaty remarkably favourable to England and, with guarantees for his safety, to the surrender of Edmund de la Pole. De la Pole remained in the Tower of London until 1513 when his brother, still at large, got himself recognized for a time by Louis XII of France as King Richard IV, whereupon Henry VIII executed his prisoner.

Even after the deaths of Warbeck and Warwick and the surrender of Edmund de la Pole, Henry VII still dreaded conspiracy. *The Chronicle of Calais* records under the year 1507:

> Sir Richard Carew, knight lieutenant of the castle of Calais, brought out of England by the king's commandment, the Lord Marquess Dorset and the Lord William of Devonshire, the earl of Devonshire's son and heir, which were both of kin to the late Queen Elizabeth and her blood. They had been in the Tower of London a great season. They were kept prisoners in the castle of Calais as long as King Henry VII lived, and should have been put to death if he had lived longer. They were brought into the castle of Calais the 18 of October the 23 of Henry the seventh.

[20] The report was presented to the king by a spy called John Flamank about 1504. Printed in J. Gairdner, *Letters and Papers etc.* I, pp. 231 – 4, A. F. Pollard, *The Reign of Henry VII from Contemporary Sources* (3 vols, London, 1913 – 14) I, pp. 240 – 50. Gairdner dated the document *c.* 1503, but Pollard suggested 1504 at the earliest. The conversation between the great men at court was alleged to have taken place when the king lay sick at his manor of Wanstead. Henry bought Wanstead in 1499. See also Chrimes, *Henry VII*, p. 308, n. 1.

After the death of Prince Arthur in 1503, Ferdinand and Isabella were anxious to retain their English alliance. They first instructed their ambassador to reclaim the instalment of Catherine of Aragon's dowry which they had already paid, to demand the allocation of her English jointure and her return to Spain. At the same time they instructed the envoy to try to arrange a marriage with the young Prince Henry. Such a treaty was arranged in September. A papal dispensation was to be obtained for the marriage and it was to take place as soon as Henry was fourteen, that is in 1505.

Spain's position in the international sphere, however, very much changed with the death of Isabella of Castile on 26 November 1504. The union of Aragon and Castile had been a purely personal union and Isabella's death left the control of Castile disputed between her widower, Ferdinand, and her heiress, Joanna, and Joanna's husband, the Archduke Philip of Hapsburg. This dispute made Ferdinand a figure very much reduced in international power and influence. If his position in Castile was undermined, Aragon would sink to the status of a third class power. Henry VII now became anxious to maintain a balance between England, France, Spain and the Netherlands. The death of his queen, Elizabeth of York, in February 1503 meant that he was a widower capable of making a new diplomatic marriage himself—a situation which he began to exploit with almost feverish activity.

He considered various schemes, none of which came to anything. 1505 was a busy matrimonial year. His first scheme (1505) was to marry Ferdinand's niece, the widowed Queen Joanna of Naples, but he abandoned the plan in March 1506 when he heard that Ferdinand had made an alliance with France and had married Louis XII's niece, Germaine de Foix. Maximilian offered Henry his daughter, Margaret, the widow of Philibert II of Savoy and Louis XII proposed his niece, Margaret of Angoulême. The most serious project seems to have been the proposal for Margaret of Savoy for, bearing in mind English commercial interests and the schemes of Edmund de la Pole, Henry particularly wanted to re-establish good relations with the Emperor Maximilian and the Archduke Philip. In his last years Henry's foreign policy was becoming exceedingly expensive. He was prepared to back up his diplomacy with considerable sums of money. Between 1505 and 1509 he provided £342,000 in cash, plate or jewels for the Hapsburgs. These advances were termed 'loans' but Henry could never have hoped to get repayment from the impecunious Hapsburgs. Most modern historians have misunderstood these transactions, not realizing that the oldest meaning of the term 'loan' was that of a gift or a grant from a superior. In the royal accounts of this period the word was often used in the sense of 'imprest'.

In February 1506 in the secret treaty of Windsor, Henry finally committed himself to the Hapsburg cause against Ferdinand in Spain, recognizing Philip as king of Castile and undertaking to assist him there, in the Netherlands and in the Channel with military and naval aid if necessary. Then on 25 September the Archduke Philip died and the whole situation changed with drastic suddenness. His death opened up the possibility that Henry might marry Philip's widow, Joanna, or put through an alternative scheme, the marriage of Henry's daughter with Philip and Joanna's son, the Archduke Charles.

During these twists and turns of policy Henry appeared at his worst in his treatment of Catherine of Aragon. By June 1505, the date stipulated for her marriage to Prince Henry, the king had changed his mind and was anxiously wooing the Hapsburgs. Greatly resenting Ferdinand of Aragon's French alliance and French marriage, the king was now reluctant to allow the Spanish marriage to take place. On his father's instructions the prince made a declaration protesting against a marriage treaty which had been made while he was under age. Henry's hostility continued after the Archduke Philip's death. He stopped Catherine's allowance of £100 a month, forced her to give up her household at Durham House and to live in impoverished conditions at one or another of his royal residences. Admittedly at this time Catherine was a difficult and querulous character but there was really no excuse for this shabby treatment. His attitude only changed in 1507 when he wanted Ferdinand's agreement to the proposed marriage of his daughter, Mary, to Ferdinand's grandson, the Archduke Charles. Yet in the end it is possible that on his deathbed he repented of his behaviour and told his son to marry Catherine. That at least was Henry VIII's own explanation to Margaret of Savoy when he decided to marry soon after his accession.

In his last few months Henry remained uncommitted to any of the European powers, but they all wished to be on friendly terms with him. Their attitude may have been due in part to misjudgment. Foreign observers were impressed by an apparent, superficial strength, by the absence of garrisons and the lack of any standing military forces in England. Moreover, abroad Henry was held to be exceedingly rich. Rumours of his treasure hoard were grossly exaggerated and his 'loans' to the Hapsburgs confirmed foreign delusions about his wealth. Foreigners, in fact, were not to know how precarious the bases of his finances were. When Henry died in 1509 he had reason to be satisfied with the results of his foreign policy. Although he had twice, for long periods, sacrificed English commercial interest to dynastic fears and dynastic safety, he had finally achieved a secure international position. He no longer feared foreign military intervention in his internal affairs. He was respected, his judgement was shrewd and his diplomatic skill had become considerable. Realistically, knowing his true financial weakness, he had attempted no great schemes, no grand designs of military conquest. His policies had been essentially cautious and pragmatic, more or less a series of reactions to external pressures. As such they had been successful.

V

If Henry's reign ended upon an optimistic note in foreign policy, the same can hardly be said of domestic affairs. The last few years of his reign, like those of Edward IV, saw an intensification of most of his worst characteristics — characteristics which his subjects saw as a combination of avarice and tyranny. It may be (though this can be no more than conjecture) that badly deteriorating health intensified the suspicions and anxieties which he had been forced to endure during the whole of his reign, that the 'many years together full of broken seas, tides and tempests' which Bacon described were, in the end, altogether too much for him. Polydore Vergil remarked that his subjects showed greater inclinations to treason than ever before and that from about 1502 he 'began to treat his people with more harshness and severity than had been his custom in order (as the king himself asserted) to ensure that they remained more thoroughly and entirely in obedience to him'.

Similarly Edward Hall, writing in the 1540s, claimed that by Henry's reign many persons had become so accustomed to civil dissension that they 'could not live well in rest, and less forbear their usual custom of moving strife and daily debate'. Hall also claimed that in his last years the king 'determined to make low and abate the courage of his subjects and vassals, especially of the richer sort' by a stricter enforcement of penal statutes. He later commented that Empson and Dudley were responsible for the work and that they empanelled perjured juries for the purpose. Hall's attitude was somewhat ambiguous for in another section of his chronicle he stated that the king maintained rigid justice, imposing fines for the sake of public order and that it was only those who suffered who accused the king of basically avaricious motives.

Debate upon Henry's policies had begun thus early and it has continued ever since. Of the unpopularity of Empson and Dudley there is no doubt whatsoever and Dudley accumulated a considerable fortune for himself, part of it certainly by means of corruption and extortion. As noted elsewhere, however, Henry and his agents certainly did not work through the rigid enforcement of penal statutes in the common law courts; what little legislation there was for the better enforcement of the crown's feudal rights was timid and limited in scope, and Henry was not conspicuously more successful than Edward IV had been in his exploitation of the crown lands.

Yet in spite of this, Henry died with an atrociously unsavoury reputation for avarice, a reputation far worse than that of Edward IV. Unable, for fear of causing political resentment and unrest, to reform the antiquated system of taxation or even to impose direct taxation at all frequently, he had resorted to what Sir John Fortescue called 'exquisite means' to raise money. His subjects certainly thought that he exploited the crown lands too harshly. He sold offices extensively at prices ranging from £1,000 for the mastership of the rolls to between £80 and 20 marks for clerkships of the peace in various counties. His greed overcame his deep, if conventional, piety and drove him into the sin of simony when he demanded 1,000 marks for the deanery of York and £300 for the archdeaconry of Buckingham. Like his predecessors (and there was nothing new in this) he sold his favour in matters of justice particularly where family disputes about land and inheritances were concerned. On 7 December 1506 Lord Conyers paid him 20 marks for 'a letter of justice' to the justices of the peace in Lincolnshire. The following February the earl of Northumberland paid £100 'for the king's favour in the matter between him and Sir John Hotham and so to be dismissed out of the Sterred Chamber'. In January 1508 Lord Henry Stafford agreed to raise the enormous sum of £400 (to be paid in instalments over two years) for the king's lawful favour 'in the matter concerning Sir William Gascoigne'. In 1506 even the king's stepfather, the earl of Derby, promised him a present of land worth £50 a year if councillors appointed to settle a lawsuit between the earl and one Thomas Middleton about lands in Westmorland and Lancashire reported in his favour and there is a strong suspicion that Middleton offered a similar bribe in the same case.

Although Henry's profits from the system caused intense resentment, as Dr E. W. Ives has suggested[21] something of a jungle law prevailed in this sphere. Henry, knowing that he was widely cheated, exacted scandalously high sums from his feudal tenants whenever he saw the chance—exactions which roused the indignation of the victimized who saw many of their neighbours escaping.

During his later years Henry harassed and persecuted all sorts and conditions of people to such a degree that his activities revolted even one of his own principal agents. When Edmund Dudley was imprisoned in the Tower of London in 1509 he drew up a list of no less

[21] E. W. Ives, 'The Genesis of the Statute of Uses', *EHR* lxxxii (1967).

than eighty-four cases in which he stated that the king's purpose was 'to have many persons in his danger at his pleasure', many of whom, in Dudley's opinion, he had treated with excessive vindictive harshness, 'much sorer than the causes required'. Dudley commented that 'the abbot of Furness had a hard end for his pardon for he paid and is deemed to pay 500 marks for a little matter'; 'one Hawykyns of London, draper, upon surmise of a lewd fellow, paid 100 marks for a light matter'; Sir Nicholas Vaux and Sir Thomas Parr paid 9,000 marks upon 'a very light ground'; 'one Sims, a haberdasher without Ludgate, paid and must pay £500 for light matters only upon a surmise of a lewd quean' — so the discreditable list runs on.

Henry's 'tyranny' came out most strongly in the matter of attainders and in his treatment of the nobility, especially towards the end of his reign. Although, with reservations, he was merciful to the Yorkists who were attained in 1485 (twenty attainders out of twenty-eight had been reversed by 1495 and two more by the end of his reign), his record towards opponents compares ill with that of Edward IV. Unlike Edward, Henry VII continually resorted to attainders. Henry attainted 138 people in the course of his reign against Edward's total of 140. Each king reversed respectively 46 and 42 attainders which had passed at his own instigation. But whereas under Edward, after the mass attainders of 1461-3 only twenty-seven new names were added to the list, Henry followed each crisis of his reign with new proscriptions. Only one of his parliaments, that of 1497, was free of attainders and his last, that of 1504, saw fifty-one, the greatest number in any parliament of his reign.

Perhaps it is unfair to pass such judgement on numbers alone for Edward never had to face a major conspiracy after 1471 and the attainders which could have resulted from the crisis of 1469 − 71 were restricted for political and family reasons.[22] There were, however, other significant differences. As so frequently remarked, contemporaries felt very strongly that attainders should not be permanent. They regarded landed estates as the possession of a dynasty which should not be permanently forfeited as a result of the political miscalculations of a single member of the line. Under the conventions of the day restoration could ultimately be expected, even if long delayed.

Edward IV, so far as we can see, generally accepted these conventions. Practice changed very much for the worse under Henry VII. Petitions presented in his day show that many offenders when suing for reversal had to compound with the king beforehand and were forced to agree to only a partial restoration of their property in return for pardon — a practice which had been quite exceptional under

---

[22] See above, pp. 281 ff.

Edward IV unless the wording of the parliament roll conceals such transactions.[23]

Henry VII attainted nine noblemen in the course of his reign. He reversed five of these attainders and his son one more. Only one of these restorations, that of Walter Devereux, Lord Ferrers, reversed for his son, John, was in any way complete. The rest all showed considerable reservations.

For example, John, Lord Zouche was attainted 1485. In July 1486 Henry granted him a pardon under the great seal after he had produced sureties in 2,000 marks to be of good behaviour. The pardon was limited in scope. It obviously did not restore Zouche's property for when the attainder was reversed in the parliament of 1487, the act permitted Zouche to inherit only the lands of his grandmother, Elizabeth, the wife of Lord Scrope of Bolton. The king still withheld his paternal inheritance. This the king conceded only in another act eight years later in 1495 and conceded at a very considerable price. In November the same year Zouche sold five manors to Sir Reynold Bray for £1,000, 'since Sir Reynold helped to obtain grace for Sir John from his liege lord to repeal the attainder and recover his land'. The king had previously granted Bray these five manors from the Zouche inheritance and he now obviously obtained a secure title to them by paying Lord Zouche far less than their true market value. The act also protected the interests of Henry's chamberlain, Giles, Lord Daubeney and his heirs, in certain lands which the king had granted them. The act stated that Zouche might recover these properties if he could persuade Lord Daubeney to sell them back to him. Three other prominent royal courtiers had also profited from Lord Zouche's misfortunes. Some of his lands were still in the hands of the descendants of Sir John Savage, Sir Richard Edgecombe and Robert Willoughby in 1523. Henry, to the profit of his friends and councillors, in defiance of strongly held political and social conventions, had extorted a very high price for the reversal of Lord Zouche's attainder.

The story of the Howard family is curious indeed and, in some ways, even more revealing. John, duke of Norfolk, had died fighting for Richard III at Bosworth Field, and together with his heir, Thomas, earl of Surrey, also at Bosworth, was posthumously attainted in the parliament of 1485. At first the rumour went round that Henry intended to execute Surrey. Instead he was imprisoned in the Tower of London under a form of pardon, the limited terms of which left him completely at the king's mercy. There he remained

[23] A few of the attainted under Edward IV bought back some of their lands from royal grantees, but there are only two cases (and those quite minor) and neither concerning members of the peerage where the actual enrolled petition specifies a reservation for a particular grantee.

until January 1489, when he was released after swearing an oath of allegiance. The parliament which met the same month as his release reversed the attainder, but reversed it with wide reservations. He was restored to the dignity of earl of Surrey only. The king denied him the higher title of duke of Norfolk. Moreover, the king restored to him only the lands to which he was entitled in his wife's right and lands which he might inherit from relations other than his dead father. Oddly enough, considering the king's frequent practice of reserving grants already made from forfeited estates, Surrey also received back those of his lands which had been granted to the earl of Oxford and Lord Daubeney. Within a mere three months of his release from the Tower of London, the king sent him to the north to quell the unrest there after the assassination of the earl of Northumberland at Topcliffe. In the second session of the same parliament which met later in the year, Surrey received his reward in an extension of the terms of his reversal. He now received the hereditary lands of the Howard family except for those which the king had already granted away. These he might buy back with the king's agreement. Even this settlement meant drastic limitations for it did not include the share of the Mowbray estates which his father had received from Richard III together with the title of duke of Norfolk.

Further service followed when Surrey became lieutenant to the infant Prince Arthur in the wardenships of the eastern and middle Marches. In the spring of 1491 he put down a second rising (possibly no more than an unusually large riot) at Ackworth near Pontefract. The following year parliament passed another act in his favour. At last Surrey was permitted to inherit all his property except that, once again, grants from it which the king had already made were to remain valid, though any rents reserved to the king were in future to go to the earl. By now Surrey had recovered all the Howard family lands and such estates of the Mowbray inheritance as the king had not already granted away. The king, however, by certain legal concessions in the act made it easier for him to negotiate with the grantees to buy them back.

Henry recognized loyal service. Yet he was cautious and grudging enough in rewarding it, tantalizing Howard with the prospect of restoration stage by stage. Surrey never recovered the immense grants from the crown lands which had so greatly enriched his family under Richard III. These had been the abnormally large gifts of a usurper bribing support. Their return was hardly to be expected. Surrey ultimately got back the hereditary Howard estates and the moiety of the Mowbray lands to which he was entitled at common law, that common law inheritance which Edward IV had unwisely denied to his father, thus driving him to support Richard III. Even so Henry was not prepared to offend other supporters by revoking outright grants which he had made from Surrey's estates. Nor did Henry ever restore the title of duke of Norfolk. That only came back to Surrey following nineteen more years of service as soldier, ambassador, councillor and administrator after his defeat of the Scots at Flodden Field.

Howard's case and those of lesser men, both peers and gentry, show that Henry (as Edward IV had done only in a much smaller degree) came to operate attainders as a stern system of discipline and control, a system of probation. Under both kings men had to 'work their way back' to favour and restitution. Yet Henry was far more arbitrary than Edward in his operation of the system, imposed harsher conditions by far and was much more inclined to let his friends, courtiers and councillors profit at the expense of the unfortunate who had committed political mistakes.

In Henry's last years attainders came to be accompanied by a second, almost equally terrifying system of control — a system imposed upon much wider groups of people through bonds and recognizances. Bonds and recognizances were everywhere a common-place of fifteenth-century life. It was standard practice on many estates to demand bonds, supported by mainpernors or guarantors, as a condition of appointment for officials. The Exchequer generally demanded them from the customs staff. Similarly bonds and recogni-zances were extremely common among private people, binding them to keep the peace towards each other, guaranteeing the execution of family settlements and commercial transactions.

They had also been used to a limited extent for political and social purposes during the whole of the fifteenth century. Henry VI and his council during the period of his personal rule between 1437 and 1458 had used such methods in their attempts to quell the growing recal-citrance and violence of the nobility. Edward IV, except for routine administrative matters, employed such instruments somewhat sparingly, putting only six peers and a peeress under financial bonds of any political significance, though other bonds concerning seven noblemen dealt with legal arbitrations and the keeping of the peace and one guaranteed the sale of certain estates to the king. Considering the short period of his reign, bonds and recognizances were much more numerous under Richard III. Oddly enough in view of the political tensions of his reign, none of the seven bonds which he took from noblemen dealt directly with the problem of allegiance, although bonds for this purpose were certainly taken from commoners. All in all during the Yorkist period some twenty nobles, including one woman, the countess of Oxford, gave bonds or recogni-zances of some kind, ten for themselves and ten on behalf of other people. By 1486, therefore, the nobility were quite accustomed to such practices. They were part of the normal fabric of their lives. Looking forward, however, they would hardly have predicted the monstrous extension of the system which took place from about 1502.

Its brutal ramifications best appear through examples. In 1505 Lord Clifford gave the king a recognizance for £2,000 that he would keep the peace for himself, his servants, tenants and 'part-takers' towards Roger Tempest of Broughton, and that he would try within forty days to bring before the king and his council 'such as were present at the late pulling down of Roger's place and house at Broughton'. In 1508 Lord Willoughby de Broke gave a recognizance for 1,000 marks, the condition being payment of £2,000 within two months of warning by the king's letters missive or privy seal. Recognizances such as these were the simplest type and affected single persons only. Others, which one might call 'composite recognizances,' could involve a number of people and one man's misbehaviour or failure to carry out the conditions of the bonds could associate all sorts of people in financial peril.

Territorial rivalry and bad blood had long prevailed between the Percies and the archbishops of York. In 1504 as a result of their latest series of disputes, the earl of Northumberland and the archbishop of York each gave a bond of £2,000 to keep the peace. Two years later the earl gave a recognizance of £200 for the payment of a debt of £100 by his probable relation, William Percy, and in 1507 another of £100 as a guarantor for the safe keeping of Castle Cornet, Guernsey, by Richard Weston; in the same year he replaced the earl of Kent in giving a bond of £200 for Sir Nicholas Vaux as keeper of Guisnes.

All these examples except the one involving the archbishop of York were matters more or less, of administrative routine, but the earl was already in really deep trouble. In 1505 he was condemned to pay the enormous fine of £10,000 for 'ravishing' Elizabeth Hastings, that is, for interfering in some way with royal rights of wardship. One story has it that Northumberland abducted the girl while she was suffering from measles, whereof she died. The king suspended the fine 'during his pleasure' when the earl agreed that he and four other people would enter into a recognizance of 6,000 marks to pay 3,000 marks in annual instalments of 500 each Candlemas.

The king was still not content. In November 1507 he tightened the screws. On the tenth of the month the earl was forced to give a further recognizance of £5,000 payable at the king's pleasure, stiffened ten days later by yet another stipulating that the money should be paid the same day. Even worse, on 13 November the earl had to levy a fine to put certain of his estates into the hands of feoffees until £5,000 of his fine had been paid by half-yearly instalments of 500 marks. More-

over, payment of the remaining £5,000 was still to be at the king's
pleasure.

Again, the harshness of these methods is shown by the way in which
the king treated William Blount, Lord Mountjoy, the student and
later the patron of Erasmus and the companion of the child Prince
Henry. Apparently loyal enough, he had served in the army against
Perkin Warbeck in 1497. In May 1503 Henry appointed him keeper of
Hammes Castle, one of the subsidiary fortresses of Calais. Under his
indentures of appointment he gave a recognizance of 10,000 marks
himself and he had to find guarantors in a similar sum that he would
keep the castle safely and surely to the king's use, deliver it up when
required to do so in writing under the great seal or the privy seal,
appear personally before the king and council upon reasonable
warning under any of the king's seals and keep his allegiance. In the
end Mountjoy's guarantors put up a total of 8,180 marks. There were
no less than twenty-eight of them involved, including five other peers,
the earl of Shrewsbury, Viscount Lysle and Lords Burgavenny,
Hastings and Strange. Then Mountjoy had to produce another
recognizance for £1,000 to find substitutes in the event of death and
for allowing the castle treasurer £200 from the local revenues towards
the cost of repairs. Mountjoy did, later, find four replacements,
including the marquess of Dorset, the earl of Arundel and the earl of
Kent. Nor were these the only recognizances in which Mountjoy was
involved for there were at least another twenty-one in which he was, at
various times, concerned.

In the first decade of the sixteenth century, the list of nobles under
bonds and recognizances, either for their own good behaviour or that
of others, reads almost like a roll call of the English peerage — the
duke of Buckingham, the marquess of Dorset, the earl of Kent, the
earl of Northumberland, the earl of Shrewsbury, the earl of Arundel,
Viscount Lysle, Lord Strange, Lord Hastings to name only a few. All
in all as a result of these activities out of 62 peerage families[24] in
existence between 1485 and 1509, a total of 46 or 47 were for some
part of Henry's reign at the king's mercy. Seven were under attainder,
36 gave bonds and recognizances of whom five were also heavily fined
and three more were at some time under subpoenas which carried
heavy financial penalties. Only 16 (possibly only 15) remained free of
these financial threats.

Some historians who earlier noted a few of these bonds concluded
that Henry's motive was pure avarice. Their conclusion was most
probably erroneous. Owing to the unevenness of the financial documents which record such transactions and the cancellation of many of

[24] The parliamentary peerage was, in fact, somewhat smaller than this figure suggests as,
owing to extinctions and new creations, not all of them were members of it at the same time.

the bonds within a short time after the king's death, we shall never know how much money the king made, or intended to make, out of the system. Edmund Dudley, however, recorded that in spite of the enormous sums set down on paper Henry intended to exact no more than £2,000 from the earl of Northumberland. The earl, however, was not to know this and after the strain and humiliation of the previous four years he must have been intensely relieved, if not over-joyed, at the king's death. He could not have lost more than £1,000 by the time Henry VIII cancelled his recognizances in 1509. In the Michelmas Term 1507 the Court of King's Bench had fined George Neville, Lord Burgavenny, the grand total of £70,650 for unlawful retaining—a fine which no subject alive could possibly have paid at the time. In the end the king accepted as parcel of the debt the sum of £5,000 to be paid in instalments over ten years. By the time of Henry's death he had probably paid no more than £1,000 and Henry VIII quickly cancelled Burgavenny's bonds. His income is unknown. It may possibly have been somewhat over £1,000 a year. Whatever Burgavenney's income was, the prospect of paying over a very large proportion of it to the king for over ten years must have been shattering to contemplate.

The shadow of ruin more likely than the money involved was the king's objective. Bacon's surmise that the nobility, though not actively disloyal, continued to be wary and withdrawn throughout the reign is most likely to be correct. Polydore Vergil knew what he was talking about when he wrote that Henry about 1502 began to treat people more harshly in order to keep them in obedience to him, for his date coincides exactly with the remarkable increase in the number of bonds and recognizances from then onwards enrolled on the close rolls of the Chancery. Henry's aim seems to have been to keep his nobility (and other people[25]) in subjection through legal terrorization and the dread of financial ruin. It was little wonder that John, Lord Mountjoy, advised his son to beware of the royal service, that it was unwise 'to be great about princes for it is dangerous'.

There had always been a strong arbitrary element in English king-ship. Monarchs had always interfered with the process of justice, tinging it with favour through their own will, especially where their richer subjects were concerned. Over the centuries the royal favour or displeasure had affected the great landed fortunes and the power which they carried with them. King John had forced men to seal deeds allowing him to seize their lands at his pleasure. He, too, had imposed tremendous fines upon his tenants-in-chief and had manipulated such debts for political purposes. Edward I, by an arbitrary 'arrange-

---

[25] He also exacted recognizances from bishops and many gentry but these still need to be investigated.

ment' of escheats had on very flimsy pretexts deprived the common law heirs of great families of their inheritances to the profit of the royal house and its members. So did Edward IV, only to a lesser degree. Though the use of bonds and recognizances was well established at all levels of society during the fifteenth century, the degree to which Henry drove the system had been unprecedented since the days of King John. His combination of harsh fiscal measures through haphazard, arbitrary 'exquisite means' with his measures *in terrorem* over a great many people was producing an intense backlash of resentment by the time of his death. Edmund Dudley in his last days bore conscience-ridden witness to the king's injustices. Lord Mountjoy and Sir Thomas More, freed from fear and restraint, excoriated the system and its vile corruptions and rejoiced in its end in the prospect of new and more liberal times to come.[26] Edward IV, Richard III and Henry VII all to a greater or lesser degree came to be condemned for tyranny.

The whole system sounds revolting. Indeed, it was! But how else perhaps, other than by fear, could Edward IV and Henry VII have controlled such a mob of aloof, self-interested magnates? After all, the entire justification for the presence of the nobility lay in its potential fidelity and its governing capacity. If its loyalty were not willingly given there could be no alternative to coercion.

One may well ask why the nobility submitted to such treatment, but no contemporary expression of opinion now survives. The late K. B. MacFarlane, who once wrote that Henry VII almost 'governed by recognizance',[27] in his later years also thought that the nobility, suffering considerably from the consequences of treason and forfeiture from the late fourteenth century onwards, had grown progressively more reserved and timid in their attitudes towards the crown.

Even if this is true (and like most theoretical judgments of this period it is no more than an informed guess), one may legitimately speculate how much longer the system could have continued. The advisers of the young Henry VIII certainly took the course of immediately relaxing its tensions. They at once subjected the 'bye-courts', that is mostly the special agencies responsible for the revenues and for the collection of debts, to the Exchequer with a very considerable loss to the royal income. While mixing mercy with a fair financial and administrative caution, they equally swiftly relaxed the brutal system of recognizances. Henry VIII issued a general pardon but, for the time being, merely 'respited divers recognizances and other weighty matters' concerning fifty people including ten

[26] See above, p. 103.
[27] *English Historical Review* LXXXI (1966), pp. 153–5.

aristocrats, three of them being women. As late as 1512 Thomas
Lucas, Sir James Hobart, Henry VII's former attorney-general, and
the late king's executors were ordered to investigate debts due upon
recognizances and other instruments. Such discrimination was no
more than wise for the majority of bonds and recognizances had
always been made for purposes recognized as legal and just.

Even so, Henry VIII cancelled at least forty-five recognizances
during the first year of his reign and a further 130 over the next five
years. No less than fifty-five were explicitly stated to have been
unjustly extorted. Even if he did not abolish it completely, Henry
reduced the system *in terrorem* over peers to minute proportions.[28]
From the beginning coldly and distantly regarded, at the last Henry
VII must have passed to his tomb unregretted and unlamented by
most of the political nation. With the relaxation of financial pressure
in the administration of the crown lands and the emergence of the
peerage from the valley of the shadow of the late king's legalistic
brutality, a new reign of appeasement, possibly even of aristocratic
reaction, had begun.

[28] A few only of the recognizances *in terrorem* were allowed to stand and Henry VIII
obviously made some distinction between recognizances for good behaviour in office and those
of a more directly coercive nature, for example, Lord Mountjoy had to give new recognizances
for Hammes and for victualling Calais but other recognizances were cancelled.

11 Conclusion

By the late fifteenth century England was, by contemporary standards, a fortunate and peaceful country. Both native and foreign writers stressed the high standards of material comfort enjoyed by almost all classes — a high standard due, in the case of the majority, to the favourable balance (alas, to be only temporary) between agrarian resources and population, the result of the long-term effects of the plagues which had begun in the middle of the fourteenth century. At the same time the worst of the agrarian slump which had earlier affected many areas of the country was now over. The rent rolls of the greater landlords had begun to increase, even if so far to only a small degree, while the disastrous prices rises which so depressed the condition of the masses in Tudor times still lay in the future. From the 1470s the export trade in woollen cloth began the more or less steady expansion which was to reach boom proportions in the 1540s.

We are by this time well aware that the long tradition of atrocities committed during the Wars of the Roses originated in highly tendentious Yorkist propaganda in 1461, reinforced by the chronicle of a terrified monk of Croyland and exaggerated rumours picked up and still further inflated by foreign ambassadors in France and the Netherlands. For mid-Tudor consumption Edward Hall took over the theme in a tale of misery, murder and execrable plagues which, he claimed, was beyond the wit of man to understand or his tongue to declare. Shakespeare, to meet the dramatic needs of the stage, dropped all qualifications to produce an atmosphere of tragic horror which until very recently dominated all discussion of the subject.

Contemporary evidence gives the lie to this hoary and persistent myth. The period compares very well with ages past in England and contemporary conditions in other parts of Europe. From time to time small numbers of foreign mercenaries were brought into the country, but they were never numerous enough to become a menace to their employers or a scourge to the general population. England, unlike France and Italy, never offered even the ghost of a prospect of a long and profitable career to a military entrepreneur. There were nothing like the bands of mercenaries who, during various phases of the Hundred Years War, had terrorized whole regions of France or regular troops like those of the king of France himself who, according to the *Cahier* of the third estate of the Estates General of Tours in 1484, mercilessly fleeced and ill-treated the unfortunate peasantry in the districts where they were billeted, whom they were supposed to protect.

Nothing in fifteenth-century England could compare with the trails of devastation left by William the Conqueror on his march from Dover to Canterbury and on towards London in 1066 or with his devastations in the north in 1069 to 1070 when, according to Ordericus Vitalis, 'innumerable multitudes, particularly in the county of York' had perished through his actions by famine and the sword. The horrors of war were mild as compared with the ravages of the Scots in the north of England during the early fourteenth century or the devastations of the English over whole areas of northern France during the period of their 'scorched earth policy' after 1435 — or with the miseries they inflicted upon each other two hundred years later in the seventeenth-century civil war.

No English sources describe continuous military raids and the violent price fluctuations which they caused like those chronicled year after year for the Paris region in the *Journal of the Bourgeois of Paris* for over forty years in the first half of the fifteenth century. Nor was there anything like the 'Burgundian vintage' of 1465 during the War of the Public Weal, when in early September the Bretons and the Burgundians ravaged all the vineyards round Paris, cutting down the grapes, green as they were, for their own immediate drinking. Nothing even approached the condition of Gascony at the end of the Hundred Years War (1453), when 30 per cent of the villages in the area were ravaged or seriously damaged.

In Wales Denbigh was burned twice, once in 1460 or 1461, again in 1468. One tradition attributes rebuilding upon a new and better site to this latter catastrophe but another merely states the cause to have been greater convenience. Looting there was. It can never be absent from any war. Tradition, however, has grossly exaggerated the sack of Stamford by Margaret of Anjou's northern troops. The very indignation which these troops drew upon themselves surely indicates how unusual such atrocities were. The lack of up-to-date fortification demonstrates the peaceful condition of the English countryside. There were about one hundred or so walled towns in late medieval England. Of these, only the walls of Alnwick were completely built after 1400. Coventry was an exception which tends to prove the rule. The city authorities constructed different sections of the walls in erratic spurts between 1356 and 1534. The wonder was that they were

ever completed. Some of the smaller towns like Richmond and
Warwick lost their defences completely. In any case most English
urban fortifications had always been amateurish and ill-designed as
compared with those of the great royal, or even private, castles. A few
towns — Lynn and Canterbury among them — strengthened their
defences during the 1450s or slightly later, but such additions or
reconstructions as they made to the old-fashioned layout of their walls
and towers were too hastily carried out and too shoddy to have been at
all effective. In 1460 the defences of the landward side of
Southampton were described as 'so feeble that they may not resist
against any guns' shot and so thin that no man may well stand upon
them to make any resistance or defence'.

The obsolete, ruinous defences of London may well in part account
for the pusillanimous readiness of the city fathers to negotiate to keep
out both Lancastrians and Yorkists. In 1478 when an ambitious
mayor planned to rebuild the walls, the project petered out upon the
indifference of the citizens and their reluctance to pay for the heavy
cost of the proposed reconstruction. They correctly judged the
improbability of a long siege and that, ruinous as they were, the walls
of London were still solid enough to serve as a protection against local
disorder or the incursions of the perennially restless inhabitants of
Kent. The city fathers obviously thought the risk of assault from more
professional legions minimal as compared with the immense cost of
refortification. Even in the ports the government could encourage
maintenance and rebuilding only by making grants to the local
councils from the fee farms and the national customs. Such indifference to military architecture must have had a salutary, though now
unquantifiable, effect upon the economic life of English towns. They
escaped the serious drain upon their resources which the cost of building immense new systems of fortification imposed upon urban
communities in other parts of Europe.

The building economies of governments (royal castles were also
falling into ruin) and the negligent indifference of town authorities
were, after all, justified in their optimism for the armies of the Wars of
the Roses were as unprofessional as their numbers were limited. Far
earlier, soon after the death of Henry V, the quality of the English
forces abroad had shown a marked and progressive deterioration.
From the 1430s their numbers had been small and no convincing
evidence has yet been adduced to show that their pitiful remnant after
1453 contributed to the beginnings of the Wars of the Roses. Except
at Towton in 1461 the numbers locked in battle on English soil were
small, ranging from a few hundreds to less than 20,000 men in
individual engagements. Nor were the so-called campaigns of long
duration. According to one modern computation, the total period of

military activity between the first battle of St Albans (1455) and the battle of Stoke (1487) amounted to no more than twelve or thirteen weeks — twelve or thirteen weeks in thirty-two years. Most people seem to have gone as quietly about their own business as they could. Even in the peak period of the conflict between 1460 and 1461, although rival gangs in some parts of the country took the opportunity of paying off old scores against each other and terrorizing their more peaceful neighbours, most people probably suffered more from the dreadful weather — weeks of torrential rain and floods — than from the war. Philippe de Commynes, ill-informed though he was in detail about English affairs, for once was correct when he wrote:

> As I observed before, England enjoyed this peculiar mercy above all other kingdoms, that neither the country, nor the people nor the houses, were wasted, destroyed or demolished: but the calamities and misfortunes of the war fell only upon the soldiers, and especially on the nobility.

Even financially the people suffered less. After the peak period of Henry V's military effort, war taxation was light. The English had developed a successful resistance to anything like realistic assessment, and the government's demands could have had nothing like so depressing an effect upon the peasantry as those of Edward I, when for two decades they had endured heavy taxation and the abuses of purveyance to cover the costs of war or threatened wars in Wales, Scotland and Flanders. We hear no complaints in the fifteenth century, as we do in this earlier period, of war taxation so grinding men down into poverty that they were forced to sell their farm stock and even their seed corn to meet the king's demands.

This is not, however, the same thing as saying that England was a peaceful place in which to live. While it escaped the horrors of war prevalent elsewhere, the general levels of disorder and of violence among all social classes were, by modern standards, execrable. Sir John Fortescue (1385/95? – 1479) bragging of superior English valour, actually boasted about the English preference for burglary as against the French penchant for larceny and further boasted that more men were hanged in England in one year for robbery than were hanged in France in seven. The Venetian ambassador of 1497 thought that violent crime was exceptionally widespread in England, partly because the judicial powers of the nobility were so limited:

> There is no country in the world where there are so many thieves and robbers as in England: insomuch that few venture to go alone in the country excepting in the middle of the day, and fewer still in the towns at night, and least of all in London.

After listing various ways of evading justice, including sanctuary and benefit of clergy, he went on:

> But, notwithstanding all these evasions, people are taken up every day by dozens, like birds in a covey, and especially in London: yet for all this they never cease to rob and murder in the streets.

Despite Fortescue and the Italian envoy most English sources give a much less gloomy picture. In *The Stonor Papers* there are no hints whatsoever of any danger to travellers. There are only seven such references in *The Paston Letters*, but three of these cases belong to 1451 and 1452, two others to 1453 and 1454 and the last pair to 1461 and 1471, so all took place in times of exceptional disturbance. The Pastons as a matter of course sent valuables and money by the common carrier between Norfolk and London. Significantly there are very few references to robbery in estate accounts, for if robberies occurred bailiffs and receivers, in order to cover themselves, would surely have reported them to auditors.

The English never stopped complaining about lack of governance. At the same time they were extremely suspicious of any extension of powers which would have enabled their governments to deal more effectively with the problems of disorder. In spite of waves of complaints, we should not despise Sir Thomas More's statement that Edward IV left his realm 'in quiet and prosperous estate'. Evidence upon such a subject is always bound to be conflicting. Possibly the most we can say is that by the turn of the century the revived monarchy, now controlling the forces of bastard feudalism to a reasonable extent, had reduced the country to a state of public order which most people at the time regarded as tolerable.

Most people except the obscure, and possibly growing, congregations of Lollards and a minority of humanist reformers seem to have been fairly content with the state of the church although many resented the discipline of the ecclesiastical courts. They certainly raised large sums of money for church-building and architecture, both ecclesiastical and domestic but especially ecclesiastical, reached a phase of the most accomplished maturity. Educational facilities were expanding, the curriculum changing and broadening into the new humanism which, for the first time in England, was to produce a lay intelligentsia in the 1520s. Meanwhile both ecclesiastical and lay culture were in a state of flux, conservative tendencies only gradually giving way to new trends of thought.

Although Erasmus and later writers held somewhat more favourable views the observations of foreign writers on English manners and customs at this time were remarkably antipathetic. The English had no small opinion of themselves. According to the Venetian ambassador they were 'great lovers of themselves and of everything belonging to them: they think that there are no other men but themselves and no other world but England.' They had a profound antipathy to foreigners and thought that anybody forced to live abroad would be better dead. The ambassador (and others) tartly refused to take them at their own valuation. He added that they were given to fine clothes, polite in their language and quick at anything they put their minds to. They were devout. They had a high reputation in arms though even on campaigns they demanded every comfort and good eating. They were so fond of food that they would rather entertain a man lavishly than give him so much as a groat to help him in any distress. Their licentiousness was a byword, but either they were the most discreet lovers in the world or quite incapable of love for nobody had ever seen an Englishman in love. The women were especially violent in their passions and, although their husbands were extremely jealous, in England 'anything may be compensated in the end by the power of money.' Above all, the English were neurotically tense and suspicious in all their relationships, quite incapable of establishing sincere, enduring friendship one with another. They would never, according to the ambassador, discuss either public or private affairs together in the same trusting way as Italians were accustomed to do.

In 1473 the papal envoy, Pietro Aliprando, had remarked: 'In the morning they [the English] are as devout as angels, but after dinner they are like devils .... They do not keep faith and are evil islanders, who are born with tails ... and they are so bad they cheat all the world with their eating and drinking.'

Nicholas von Poppelgau visited England in 1484 and a few years later wrote a travel diary with comments equally unflattering to the English. They exceeded the Poles in ostentation and pilfering, the Hungarians in brutality and the Lombards in deceit. The women, though very beautiful, were astoundingly imprudent and brazen. They were rich and hospitable but their cooking was poor and English avarice made everything astonishingly dear.

An English dinner party must have been a dreadful occasion for if the cooking was poor the conversation was even worse. More than one observer noticed the extraordinary silence of the guests. Once the food was on the table they stopped talking and did nothing but eat — an unsociable habit which still prevailed as late as the Elizabethan period.

Finally, the monarchy which ruled over this (to foreign eyes) supremely unattractive race, like every other monarchy in Europe, shared its powers with the aristocracy, major and minor, peerage and gentry. In spite of the revival of royal power after 1471, in spite of the outward appearance of one of the most lavish, ostentatious and formal courts in Europe, the monarchy remained financially weak, too poor in face of its subjects' admantine resistance to taxation to renew earlier dreams of foreign conquest, too hamstrung to do anything more than react in a pragmatic, defensive manner to threats of foreign aggression and self-interested foreign support for pretenders

to the throne. Nor would subjects pay for any extension of the
monarchy's powers and services at home. In fact the majority of
people were probably incapable of thinking in such terms at all. Their
ideals demanded no more than a long continued tradition laid
down — a tradition expressed in Edmund Dudley's trite and morali-
zing pamphlet *The Tree of Commonwealth* — that if every man
conscientiously did his duty in his own divinely allotted sphere of life
all would go well in the land. Such a conception meant that the rich
should 'have the rule' and that it was their bounden duty to rule justly.
'Government was a function of property' and that, given the social
hierarchy of the day and the lack of any police force or standing army,
could only mean government through clientage, through the more or
less controlled forces of bastard feudalism, supervised by a hardworking king capable of arbitrating fairly in the disputes of the aristocracy, while at the same time capable of imposing a fair degree of
awesome discipline upon them.

Even so, the English monarch was probably less constricted than
foreign kings. In France kings had to fight civil wars with magnates
who possessed vast provincial concentrations of estates and who were
supported by strong provincial loyalties — loyalties often merging with
emotions of separatism. No English lawyers would ever have claimed
as some Norman lawyers did: 'Le duché n'est pas du royaume.' Very
few of the English nobility wanted to make war upon the king. English
magnates, unlike their French counterparts, could not afford it, for
their estates, instead of being concentrated, were widely scattered in
different parts of the country, so that civil war might only too easily
cut them off from some part of their vital revenues. Their ambition
was to share in the spoils of the royal administration or to be left undisturbed to wield their local territorial influence or both.

Only by accepting these conditions could the government carry out
its distinctly limited functions — defence and the maintenance of an
acceptable level of public order. In 1473 during disturbances in the
southwest Edward IV wrote under his signet and sign manual to John
Cheyne, the sheriff of Devon, ordering him to quell rumours that the
rebel earl of Oxford had landed, forbidding him to make any
assemblies of people or to allow any to be made and telling him for the
moment to do nothing but 'sit still and be quiet.'[1] The words might
well apply to the domestic aims of government in general. Both
Edward IV and Henry VII, surrounded as they were by insecurity and
conspiracies, anxiety and danger, and restricted by their limited
resources, must have been reasonably satisfied if they could, with the
co-operation of the nobility and the greater gentry, get the country 'to
sit still and be quiet.'

[1] Quoted from D.A.L. Morgan, 'The King's Affinity in the Polity of Yorkist England', *TRHS*,
5th series XXIII (1973), p. 17.

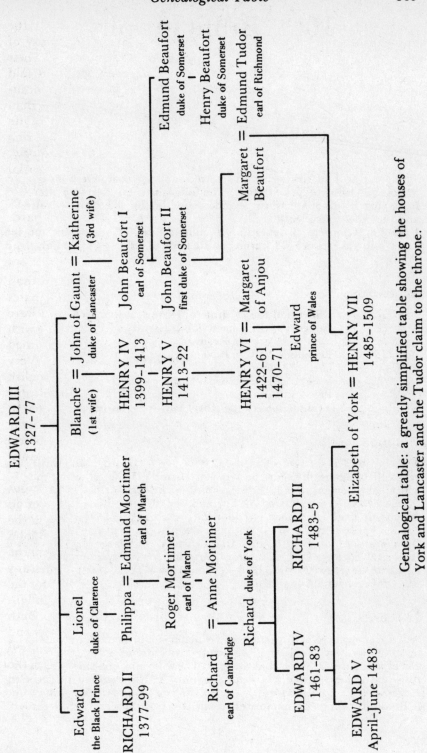

Genealogical table: a greatly simplified table showing the houses of York and Lancaster and the Tudor claim to the throne.

10.   Bibliography

The great bulk of writing on this period makes a complete bibliography impossible owing to lack of space. The following list is therefore offered as being, in the author's view, the soundest combination of both older valuable and the most recent work.

1 Guides. 2 Sources. 3 General. 4 Economic Life. 5 Government and the State. 6 Royal Finance. 7 Church and Religion. 8 Education and Culture. 9 Politics.

Abbreviations

BIHR	Bulletin of the Institute of Historical Research
BJRL	Bulletin of the John Rylands Library
EHR	English Historical Review
EcHR	Economic History Review
HJ	*Historical Journal*
JEH	Journal of Ecclesiastical History
PP	Past and Present
TRHS	Transactions of the Royal Historical Society

1   Guides

E. F. Jacob, *The Fifteenth Century, 1399 – 1485* (Oxford, 1961) contains a very full bibliography. For the reign of Henry VII the following may be consulted: Conyers Reed, *Bibliography of British History: The Tudor Period, 1485 – 1603* (Oxford, 1959) and the shorter lists in M. Levine, *Bibliographical Handbooks: Tudor England, 1485 – 1603* (Cambridge, 1968). These may be brought up to date by reference to the 'Annual Bibliographies of British and Irish History' published by the Royal Historical Society. C. L. Kingsford, *English Historical Literature in the Fifteenth Century* (Oxford, 1913, reprinted New York, 1964) is still worth study for its detailed comments.

2   Sources

Apart from printed archival material which it would be inappropriate to list in a bibliography of this kind, contemporary chronicles and collections of correspondence are somewhat meagre. The following collections of narratives and letters, however, are most useful: A. Hanham (ed.), *The Cely Letters, 1472 – 1488* (Oxford, 1976); *Oeuvres de George Chastellain*, ed. M. le Baron Kervyn de Lettenhove (Brussels, 1863 – 5), useful for Margaret of

Anjou; *Chronicle of the Rebellion in Lincolnshire, 1470*, ed. J. G. Nichols (Camden Society Miscellany 1847); *Collection of Ordinances and Regulations for the Government of the Royal Household* (London, 1790); A. R. Myers, *The Household of Edward IV* (Manchester, 1959); P. de Commynes, *Mémoires*, ed. J. Calmette and G. Durville, (3 vols, Paris, 1924 – 5), translated by S. Kinser and I. Cazeaux (South Carolina, 1969), vivid but prejudiced against Edward and unreliable in detail; *An English Chronicle of the Reigns of Richard II, Henry IV, Henry V and Henry VI*, ed. J. G. Davies (Camden Society, 1856), violently pro-Yorkist; R. Fabyan, *The New Chronicles of England and France*, ed. H. Ellis (London, 1811) and *The Great Chronicle of London*, ed. A. H. Thomas and I. D. Thornley (London, 1938); R. Flenley, *Six Town Chronicles of England* (London, 1911); Sir John Fortescue, *The Governance of England*, ed. C. Plummer (Oxford, 1885) and *De Laudibus Legum Anglie*, ed. S. B. Chrimes (Cambridge, 1942) are the best reflections of a contemporary upon politics and law; W. Worcester, *The Boke of Noblesse*, ed. J. G. Nichols (London, 1860) represents the viewpoint of the pro-French war groups; *The Travels of Leo of Rozmital*, ed. M. Letts (Hackluyt Society, 2nd series CXVIII, 1957) is interesting on conditions in England and on the Yorkist court; 'Gregory's Chronicle' in *The Historical Collections of a Citizen of London*, ed. J. Gairdner (Camden Society, 1876); E. Hall, *Chronicle* (first published 1548), ed. H. Ellis (London, 1809) contains useful information not found elsewhere but needs to be used with caution; *Hearne's Fragment*, ed. T. Hearne (Oxford, 1719), very anti-Neville; the 'First and Second Anonymous Croyland Continuators', in *Rerum Anglicarum Scriptorum Veterum* I, ed. W. Fulman (Oxford, 1684), trans. H. T. Riley, *Ingulph's Chronicle of the Abbey of Croyland* (London, 1854) — the Second anonymous Continuator, one of Edward IV's councillors, gives by far the fullest contemporary account of the Yorkist period; *Mémoires d'Olivier de la Marche*, ed. H. Beaune and J. d'Arbaumont (Paris, 1883); *Historie of the Arrivall of Edward IV in England and the Finall Recouerye of His Kingdomes from Henry VI, A.D.M.CCCC.LXXI*, ed. J. Bruce (Camden Series, 1838) is an official propaganda account; J. Molinet, *Chroniques*, ed. G. Doutrepont and O. Jodogne (3 vols, Paris, 1935 – 7); St Thomas More, *The History of King Richard III*, in *the Complete Works of St Thomas More* II, ed. R. S. Sylvester (Yale, 1963) is more careful in sifting rumour from truth than is generally admitted; C.A.J. Armstrong, *The Usurpation of Richard III* (2nd edn, Oxford, 1969) prints a most vivid account of the earlier part of Richard III's reign by a visiting Italian, Dominic Mancini; *The Paston Letters*, ed. J. Gairdner (4 vols, Edinburgh, 1910) are indispensable; only two volumes of a new three volume edition, ed. N. Davis, *Paston Letters and Papers of the Fifteenth Century* (Oxford, 1971, 1977) have so far appeared-the introduction is most valuable; see also *The Plumpton Correspondence* ed. T. Stapleton (Camden Society, 1839) and *The Stonor letters and Papers*, ed. C.L. Kingsford (2 vols, Camden Society, 1919); *Historical Poems of the XIVth and XVth Centuries*, ed. R. Hope Robbins (Columbia UP, 1959) provides useful material but the introduction is unfortunately out of date; J. Rous, *Historia Regum Anglie*, ed. T. Hearne (Oxford, 1745); *Three Fifteenth-Century Chronicles*, ed. J. Gairdner (Camden Series, 1880); J. Warkworth, *A Chronicle of the First thirteen Years of the Reign of Edward IV*, ed. J.O. Halliwell (Camden Series, 1839), somewhat confused in its chronology and pro-Neville; J. de Waurin, *Recueil Des Croniques et Anchiennes Istories de la Grant Bretaigne a Present nomme Engleterre*, ed.

W. Hardy (5 vols, Rolls Series, 1864 – 91) contains valuable information but at times is somewhat confused on details and geography; *Registrum Abbatiae Johannis Whetehamstede Abbatis Monasterii Sancti Albani*, ed. H.T. Riley (2 vols, Rolls Series, 1872 – 3) useful for events leading to the revolution of 1461; William Worcester, Annals formerly attributed to, in *Letters and Papers Illustrative of the Wars of the English in France* II, part 2 (Rolls Series, 1864) decidedly pro-Neville in tone; Polydore Vergil, *Three Books of Polydore Vergil's English History, comprising the Reigns of Henry VI, Edward IV and Richard III from an early translation*, ed. H. Ellis (Camden Series, 1844) and *The Anglica Historia of Polydore Vergil, 1485 – 1537*, ed. D. Hay (Camden Series, 1950), incorporating a valuable oral tradition; *Memorials of King Henry VII*, ed. J. Gairdner (Rolls Series, 1858) gives much original material including the *Vita* by Bernard André; see also E. Dudley *The Tree of Commonwealth*, ed. D.M. Brodie (Cambridge, 1948); *Calendar of State Papers and Manuscripts Existing in the Archives and Collections of Milan* I, ed. A. B. Hinds (London, 1912); *Chronicle of Calais in the Reigns of Henry VII and Henry VIII*, ed. J. G. Nichols (Camden Series, 1864).

3 General

A standard work covering the period up to 1485 is E. F. Jacob, *The Fifteenth Century, 1399 – 1485* (Oxford, 1961). The corresponding volume, J. D. Mackie, *The Earlier Tudors, 1485 – 1588* (Oxford, 1952) is now badly out of date in its interpretations. C. L. Kingsford, *Prejudice and Promise in Fifteenth-Century England* (Oxford, 1925, repr. London, 1962) remains useful and interesting. Short good accounts are found in A. R. Myers, *England in the Later Middle Ages* (2nd edn, London, 1963) and G. A. Holmes, *The Late Middle Ages, 1275 – 1485* (Edinburgh, 1962). Differing and contrasting analyses can be found in F.R.H. Du Boulay, *An Age of Ambition: English Society in the Late Middle Ages* (London, 1970), J.R. Lander, *Conflict and Stability in Fifteenth Century England* (3rd edn, London, 1977) and *Politics and Power in England, 1450 – 1509* (London, 1976), D.M. Loades, *Politics and the Nation, 1450-1660* (London, 1974), A.J. Slavin, *The Precarious Balance: English Government and Society, 1450 – 1646* (New York, 1973), C.L.S. Davies, *Peace, Print and Protestantism, 1450 – 1558* (London, 1976) — all give useful interpretations. A.R. Myers, *English Historical Documents* IV, 1327 – 1485 (London, 1965) and C.H. Williams, *English Historical Documents* V, 1485 – 1558 (London, 1967) are splendid collections of extracts from contemporary documents with valuable analytical introductions.

4 Economic Life

The only modern work to attempt an overall interpretation is A.R. Bridbury, *Economic Growth: England in the Later Middle Ages* (London, 1962), stressing advancing prosperity. E. Miller, 'The English Economy in the Thirteenth Century', *PP*, no. 28 (1964) has criticized it for pressing too far anachronistic conceptions of economic growth. It has also been criticized as over-optimistic. R.E. Glasscock, 'England circa 1334', and A.R.H. Baker, 'Changes in the Later Middle Ages', in *A New Historical Geography of England*, ed. H.C. Darby (Cambridge, 1973) are reliable surveys. However, a good general survey is still badly needed and things must still be pieced together from monographs and articles. M.E. Beresford and J.K. St. Joseph, *Medieval England: An Aerial Survey* (Cambridge, 1958) contains useful information, plans and photographs. W.G. Hoskins, *The Making of the English Landscape* (London, 1955) brilliantly surveys changes in the countryside. P. Laslett, *The World We Have Lost*, (2nd edn, London, 1971) deals mainly with the seventeenth century, but many of its perceptions apply equally well to the fifteenth.

The following provide a selection on particular topics and regions:

Population and prices

J.C. Russell, *British Medieval Population* (Albuquerque, 1948) is a valuable study though its statistics have been severely criticized. M.M. Postan, 'Some Evidence of Declining Population in the Later Middle Ages', *EcHR*, 2nd series II (1949 – 50); J.M.W. Bean, 'Plague, Population and Economic Decline in the Later Middle Ages', *EcHR*, 2nd series XV (1962 – 3); S.L. Thrupp, 'The Problem of Replacement Rates in Late Medieval English Population', *EcHR*, 2nd series XVIII (1965); J. Cornwall, 'English Population in the Early Sixteenth Century', *EcHR*, 2nd series XXIII (1970). J. Hatcher, *Plague, Population and the English Economy, 1348 – 1530* (Economic History Society, Studies in Economic and Social History, 1977) summarizes and criticizes most recent work on this subject. R.S. Gottfried 'Epidemic Disease in Fifteenth – Century England', *Journal of Economic History* XXVI (1976) and 'Population, Plague and the Sweating Sickness: Demographic Movements in Late Fifteenth – Century England', *Journal of British Studies* XVII (1977) provide interesting new evidence. The same author's *Epidemic Disease in Fifteenth-Century England: The Medical Response and the Demographic Consequences* (Leicester and New Brunswick, N.J., 1978) discusses population trends between 1430 and 1480 from an extensive investigation into wills, mostly East Anglian; but he admits considering the limitations of the evidence, that his conclusions cannot be regarded as definitive. Y.S. Brenner, 'The Inflation of Prices in Early Sixteenth – Century England', *EcHR*, 2nd series XIV (1961 – 2), and 'Prices and Wages in England, 1450 – 1550', *BIHR* XXXIV (1961). I. Blanchard, 'Population Change, Enclosure and the Early Tudor Economy', *EcHR*, 2nd series XXIII (1970) provides a new interpretation on the problem of enclosures. E.H. Phelps – Brown and S.V. Hopkins, 'Seven Centuries of the Prices of Consumables, Compared with Builders' Wage Rates', *Economica*, new series XXIII (1956), reprinted in *Essays in Economic History*, ed. E.M. Carus-Wilson, II (London, 1962). R.S. Schofield, 'The Geographical Distribution of Wealth in England 1334 – 1649', *EcHR*, 2nd series XVIII (1965) compares wealth at different periods on the basis of taxation returns; though his statistics are dubious his conclusions about regional changes in wealth are valid. W. G. Hoskins, 'Harvest Fluctuations and English Economic History, 1480 – 1619', *Agricultural History Review* XII (1964), reprinted in *Essays in Agrarian History*, ed. W. E. Minchinton, I (Newton Abbot, 1968), is interesting for price fluctuations and living standards. T. A. Lloyd *The Movement of Wool Prices in Medieval England*, *EcHR* Supplements, no. 6 (1973).

M. Beresford, *The Lost Villages of England* (London, 1954), now supplemented by M. Beresford and J. G. Hurst, *Deserted Medieval Villages*, part 1

(London, 1971), deal with wool production and the enclosure movement. Also P. J. Bowden, *The Wool Trade in Tudor and Stuart England* (London, 1962); J. Thirsk (ed.), *The Agrarian History of England and Wales* IV (Cambridge, 1967), though dealing with the Tudor period is useful. The companion volume for the later middle ages has yet to appear. For recent criticism of these works and new theories on the causes of enclosure see Blanchard, 'Population Change, Enclosure' Lloyd, *The Movement of Wool Prices.*

Regional Studies

The following are a selection from many valuable studies of particular estates and regions: J. M. W. Bean, *The Estates of the Percy Family, 1416 – 1537* (Oxford, 1958); F.R.H. Du Boulay, *The Lordship of Canterbury: An Essay on Medieval Society* (London, 1966); 'A Rentier Economy in the Later Middle Ages: The Archbishopric of Canterbury', *EcHR*, 2nd series XVI (1963 – 4) and 'Who were farming the English Demesnes at the End of the Middle Ages', *EcHR*, 2nd series XVII (1964 – 5); E.M. Carus-Wilson, 'Evidence of Industrial Growth on some Fifteenth-Century manors', *EcHR*, 2nd series XII (1959 – 60), reprinted in *Essays*, ed. Carus-Wilson, II; R.R. Davies and J. Beverley Smith, 'The Social Structure of Medieval Glamorgan: Bro Morgannwg and Blaenau Morgannwg', in *Glamorgan County History* III, *The Middle Ages*, ed. T.B. Pugh (Cardiff, 1971); H.P.R. Finberg, *Tavistock Abbey* (Cambridge, 1951); J. Hatcher, 'A Diversified Economy: Later Medieval Cornwall, *EcHR*, 2nd series XXII (1969) and *Rural Economy and Society in the Duchy of Cornwall, 1300 – 1506* (Cambridge, 1970); B. Harvey 'The Leasing of the Abbot of Westminster's Demesnes in the Later Middle Ages', *EcHR*, 2nd series XXII (1969); R.H. Hilton, *The Economic Development of Some Leicestershire Estates in the Fourteenth and Fifteenth Centuries* (Oxford, 1947); I.R. Jack, *The Grey of Ruthin Valor* (Sydney UP, 1965); A. Jones, 'Land and People at Leighton Buzzard in the Later Fifteenth Century', *EcHR*, 2nd series XXV (1972); A.J. Pollard, 'Estate Management in the Later Middle Ages: The Talbots and Whitchurch, 1383 – 1525', *EcHR* 2nd series XXV (1972); T.B. Pugh, *The Marcher Lordships of South Wales, 1415 – 1536* (Board of Celtic Studies, University of Wales, History and Law Series, no. 20, 1963); J.T. Rosenthal, 'Fifteenth-Century Baronial Incomes and Richard, Duke of York', *BIHR* XXXVII (1964) and 'The Estates and Finances of Richard, duke of York (1411 – 1460)', *Studies in Medieval and Renaissance History* (University of Nebraska) II (1965). For criticism of Dr Rosenthal's conclusions see C.D. Ross, 'The Estates and Finances of Richard, Duke of York', *Welsh History Review* III (1966 – 7). This review article also brings together a good deal of comparative material. R.A.L. Smith, *Canterbury Cathedral Priory* (Cambridge, 1943). C. Rawcliffe, *The Staffords, Earls of Stafford and Dukes of Buckingham, 1394 – 1521* (Cambridge, 1978) is useful for politics as well as estate administration though some of its political conclusions must be used with caution. K.B. McFarlane, *The Nobility of Later Medieval England* (Oxford, 1973), chapter 5, stresses the harsh efficiency of landlords, while C. Dyer, 'A Redistribution of Incomes in Fifteenth-Century England', *PP*, no. 39 (1968) and B.J. Harris, 'Landlords and Tenants in England in the Later Middle Ages: The Buckingham Estates', *PP*, no. 43 (1969) deal with peasant resistance to rents and seigneurial exploitation.

Trade and towns

E.M. Carus-Wilson and O. Coleman, *England's Export Trade, 1275 – 1547* (Oxford, 1963) provides an indispensable volume of statistics though the introduction wrongly discounts the effects of smuggling. The best general works are E.M. Carus-Wilson *Medieval Merchant Venturers* (London, 1954) and E. Power and M.M. Postan, *Studies in English Trade in the Fifteenth Century* (London, 1933). For the volume of trade see also P. Ramsey, 'Overseas Trade in the Reign of Henry VII: The Evidence of Customs Accounts', *EcHR*, 2nd series vi (1953 – 4). Works on shipping are limited but see D. Burwash, *English Merchant Shipping, 1460 – 1540* (Toronto, 1947); G.V. Scammell, 'English Merchant Shipping at the End of the Middle Ages: Some East Coast Evidence', *EcHR* 2nd series XIII (1961) and 'Shipowning in England, circa 1450 – 1550', *TRHS*, 5th series XII (1962).

The following are good accounts of particular branches of trade: A.R. Bridbury, *England and the Salt Trade in the Later Middle Ages* (Oxford, 1955); E.M. Carus-Wilson, 'The Effects of the Acquisition and the Loss of Gascony on English Trade', *BIHR* XXI (1947); M.K. James, *Studies in the Medieval English Wine Trade*, ed. E.M. Veale (Oxford, 1971); N.J.M. Kerling, *Commercial Relations of Holland and Zealand with England From the Late Thirteenth Century to the Close of the Middle Ages* (Leiden, 1954); M.E. Mallet, 'Anglo-Florentine Commerical Relations, 1465 – 1491', *EcHR*, 2nd series XV (1962 – 3); M. Mollat, 'Anglo-Norman Trade in the Fifteenth Century', *EcHR*, XVII (1947); E. Power, *The Wool Trade in English Medieval History* (Oxford, 1941); E.M. Veale, *The English Fur Trade in the Later Middle Ages* (Oxford, 1966).

For urban life and the varying fortunes of different towns: J. Cornwall, 'English Country Towns in the 1520s', *EcHR*, 2nd series XV (1962 – 3) R.B. Dobson, 'Urban Decline in Late Medieval England,' *TRHS*, 5th series XXVII (1977); and C. Phythian-Adams, 'Urban Decay in Late Medieval England', in *Towns in Societies: Essays in Economic History and Historical Sociology*, ed. P. Abrams and E.A. Wrigley (Cambridge, 1978) break new ground on this important topic. J.N. Bartlett, 'The Expansion and Decline of York in the Later Middle Ages'. *EcHR*, 2nd series XII (1959 – 60); A.F. Butcher 'The Origins of Romney Freemen, 1433-1523', *EcHR*, 2nd series XXVII (1974); E.M. Carus-Wilson, *The Overseas Trade of Bristol in the Later Middle Ages* (Bristol Record Society, no. 7, 1937); 'The Overseas Trade of Late Medieval Coventry', in *Economies et Sociétés au Moyen Age: Mélanges offerts à Edouard Perroy* (Publications de la Sorbonne, 1973) and *The Expansion of Exeter at the Close of the Middle Ages* (Exeter, 1963); O. Coleman, 'Trade and Prosperity in the Fifteenth Century: Some Aspects of the Trade of Southampton', *EcHR*, 2nd series XVI (1963); A.A. Ruddock, *Alien Merchants and Shipping in Southampton, 1270 – 1600* (London, 1951); M. Dormer Harris, *Life in an Old English Town: A History of Coventry* (London, 1898); C. Pythian-Adams, 'Ceremony and the Citizens: The Communal Year at Coventry 1450 – 1550', in *Crisis and Order in English Towns, 1500 – 1700*, ed. P. Clark and P. Slack (London, 1972), a fascinating, unique account of the rituals and *mentalité* of provincial urban life; W.I. Haward, 'The Trade of Boston in the Fifteenth Century', *Associated Architectural and Archeological Societies Reports and Papers* XLI, part 2 (1933); J.W.F. Hill, *Medieval Lincoln* (Cambridge, 1948); S.L. Thrupp, *The Merchant Class of Medieval London* (Chicago, 1948); V.

Parker, *The Making of King's Lynn: Secular Buildings from the Eleventh to the Seventeenth Century* (King's Lynn Archeological Survey Series I London and Chichester, 1971); C. Platt, *The English Medieval Town* (London, 1976).

A. Bossuat, 'Le rétablissement de la paix sociale sous le règne de Charles VII', *Le Moyen Age*, 4th series IX (1954) gives an analysis of the effects of the Hundred Years War in France which is most useful as a contrast with the effects of the Wars of the Roses in England.

5 Government and the State

B. Wilkinson, *Constitutional History of England in the Fifteenth Century, 1399 – 1485* (London, 1964) has translated a splendid collection of documents, but his theories have not met with general approval.

The effects of the Wars of the Roses, disorder and military fortification are dealt with in Bridbury, *Economic Growth* B. H. St. J. O'Neil, *Castles and Canon* (Oxford, 1960); W. H. Dunham Jr, *Lord Hastings' Indentured Retainers, 1461 – 1483* (Transactions of the Connecticut Academy of Arts and Sciences, XXXIX, 1955); K. B. McFarlane, 'The Wars of the Roses', *Proceedings of the British Academy* L (1965); and J. R. Lander, *The Wars of the Roses* (London, 1965) and *Conflict and Stability*.

The Role of the Nobility and Gentry

The following books and articles deal with the position of the nobility and gentry and their functions in government: K. B. McFarlane, *The Nobility of Later Medieval England* (Oxford, 1973) provides a completely new approach to the formation of the late medieval nobility and their role in government, war and politics. T. B. Pugh, 'The Magnates, Knights and Gentry', in *Fifteenth-Century England, 1399 – 1509: Studies in Politics and Society*, ed. S. B. Chrimes, C. D. Ross and R. A. Griffiths (Manchester, New York, 1972) is a splendid analysis of political influences. J. H. Hexter disposes of traditional theories on the decline of the nobility and Yorkist and Tudor reliance on the middle classes in *Reappraisals in History* (London, 1961), chapters 4 and 5. The best analyses of bastard feudalism are G. A. Holmes, *The Estates of the Higher Nobility in Fourteenth-Century England* (Cambridge, 1957), much of the text also relevant for this period, and Dunham, *Lord Hastings' Indentured Retainers*.

J. R. Lander, 'Attainder and Forfeiture, 1453 – 1509', *HJ* IV (1961) and 'Bonds, Coercion and Fear: Henry VII and the Peerage', in *Florilegium Historiale: Essays Presented to Wallace K. Ferguson*, ed. J. G. Rowe and W. H. Stockdale (Toronto, 1971), both reprinted in J. R. Lander, *Crown and Nobility, 1450 – 1509* (London, 1976), contain additional material.

J. Cornwall, 'The Early Tudor Gentry', *EcHR*, 2nd series XVII (1964 – 5) is a well-informed analysis. The following are valuable regional studies showing variations caused by the differing composition of local ruling groups: R. R. Reid, *The King's Council in the North* (London, 1921), an old but still valuable book; F. W. Brooks, *The Council of the North* (Historical Association Pamphlet, G 25, revised edn, 1966); M. E. James, *Change and Continuity in the Tudor north: The Rise of Thomas First Lord Wharton* (Borthwick Papers, no. 27, York, 1963) and *A Tudor Magnate and the Tudor State: Henry Fifth Earl of Northumberland* (Borthwick Papers, no.

30, 1966); C. F. Richmond, 'Fauconberg's Kentish Rising of May, 1470', *EHR* LXXXV (1970); R. L. Storey, 'The Wardens of the Marches of England towards Scotland, 1377 – 1489', *EHR* LXXII (1957) somewhat exaggerates the decline of magnate influence. P. Williams, *The Council in the Marches of Wales Under Elizabeth I* (Cardiff, 1958) and J. Otway-Ruthven, 'The Constitutional Position of the Great Lordship of South Wales', *TRHS*, 5th series VIII (1958) discuss Edward IV's policies in the area. The same period and later policy and conditions in this area are dealt with in T. B. Pugh, 'The Intenture for the Marches between Henry VII and Edward Stafford (1477 – 1521), Duke of Buckingham', *EHR* LXXI (1956); *The Marcher Lordships of South Wales* (Cardiff, 1963); and 'The Marcher Lordships of Glamorgan, 1317 – 1485', in *Glamorgan County History*, III; R. A. Griffiths, *The Principality of Wales in the Later Middle Ages: The Structure and Personnel of Government* I, *South Wales, 1277 – 1536* (Cardiff, 1972); R. Robinson, 'Early Tudor Policy towards Wales', Bulletin of the Board of Celtic Studies XX, XXI (1964 – 6); J. B. Smith, 'Crown and Community in the Principality of North Wales in the Reign of Henry Tudor', *Welsh History Review* III (1966 – 7); J. A. F. Thomson, 'The Courtenay Family in the Yorkist Period', *BIHR*, XLV (1972).

M. Keen, 'Brotherhood in Arms', *History* XLVII (1962) and J. Hurstfield, 'Political Corruption in Modern England', *History* LII (1967) discuss the highly personal relationships prevalent in politics and government at this time. Professor Hurstfield's article is reprinted in *Freedom and Corruption in Elizabethan Government* (London, 1973), part 3, chapter 5. W. T. MacCaffery, 'England, the Crown and the New Aristocracy', *PP*, no. 30 (1965); J. Russell Major, 'The Crown and the Aristocracy in Renaissance France', *American Historical Review* LXIX (1963 – 4); and P.S. Lewis, 'Decayed and non-Feudalism in Later Medieval France', *BIHR* XXXVII (1964) provide good material for contrast with later English and contemporary French government.

The Legal System

The following deal with law or the legal system: C. Ogilvie, *The King's Government and the Common Law* (Oxford, 1958); T. F. T. Plucknett, *Early English Legal Literature* (Cambridge, 1958); M. Blatcher, 'The Working of the Court of King's Bench in the Fifteenth Century', *BIHR* XIV (1936 – 7), (summary of an unpublished London PhD thesis); N. Pronay, 'The Chancellor, the Chancery and the Council at the End of the Fifteenth Century', in *British Government and Administration: Studies Presented to S. B. Chrimes*, ed. H. Hearder and H. R. Loyn (Cardiff, 1974); M. Hastings, *The Court of Common Pleas in Fifteenth-Century England* (Cornell, 1947); J. B. Aurutick, 'Commissions of Oyer and Terminer in Fifteenth – Century England (unpublished London M Phil thesis, 1967); B. H. Putnam, *Proceedings Before the Justices of the Peace in the Fourteenth and Fifteenth Centuries, Edward III to Richard III* (London, 1938); A. F. Pollard, 'The Growth of the Court of Requests', *EHR* LVI (1941); I. S. Leadam, *Select Cases in the Court of Requests, 1497 – 1569* (Selden Society, 1896); C. G. Bayne and W. H. Dunham Jr, *Select Cases in the Council of Henry VII* (Selden society, 1958). The introduction needs to be read with G. R. Elton's criticism in 'Henry VII's Council', in *Studies in Tudor and Stuart Politics and Government* (2 vols, Cambridge, 1974). S. E. Lehmberg. 'Star Chamber, 1485 – 1509', *Huntingdom Library Quarterly* XXIV (1960 – 1).

The following deal with the complications of the law of real property, trusts and uses: W. H. Holdsworth. *The History of English Law* IV (3rd edn, 1945); J. M. W. Bean, *The Decline of English Feudalism, 1215 – 1540* (Manchester, 1968); D. Sutherland, *The Assize of Novel Disseisin* (Oxford, 1973); K. B. McFarlane, 'The Investment of Sir John Fastolf's Profits of War', *TRHS*, 5th series VII (1957); S. E. Thorne, 'English Feudalism and Estates in Land', *Cambridge Law Journal*, (1959); J. L. Barton, 'The Medieval Use', *Law Quarterly Review* LXXXI (1965). J. G. Bellamy 'Justice Under the Yorkist Kings', *American Journal of Legal History* IX (1965) gives a very good account of Edward IV's personal efforts to improve public order. The same author's *Crime and Public Order in England in the Later Middle Ages* (London, Toronto, 1973) is the only modern book which deals comprehensively with this important topic. The following are also useful: E. W. Ives, 'Promotion in the Legal Profession of Yorkist and Early Tudor England', *Law Quarterly Review* LXXV; (1959) 'The Reputation of the Common Lawyer in English Society, 1450 – 1550', *University of Birmingham Historical Journal* LXXV (1959); and 'The Common Lawyers in Pre-Reformation England', *TRHS*, 5th series XVIII (1968).

Government Departments

On various departments, J.F. Baldwin, *The King's Council in England during the Middle Ages* (Oxford, 1913) needs complete revision of the chapters covering this period. It is corrected by J. R. Lander, 'The Yorkist Council and Administration, 1461 – 1485', *EHR* IXXIII (1958) and 'Council, Administration, and Councillors, 1461 – 1485', *BIHR* XXXII (1959), both reprinted in *Crown and Nobility*; R. Somerville, 'Henry VII's "Council Learned in the Law"', *EHR* LIV (1939); and G.R. Elton, 'Why the History of the Early Tudor Council Remains Unwritten', in Elton, *Studies* J. Otway-Ruthven, *The King's Secretary and the Signet Office in the Fifteenth Century* (Cambridge, 1939); A.R. Myers, *The Household of Edward IV* (Manchester, 1959); D.A.L. Morgan, 'The King's Affinity in Yorkist England', *TRHS*, 5th series XXIII (1973); J.C. Sainty, 'The Tenure of Office in the Exchequer', *EHR* LXXX (1965).

Parliament

J.C. Wedgwood, *History of Parliament, 1439 – 1509* (2 vols, London, 1936, 1938), contains a mass of useful information but also numerous inaccuracies. The Lords are best studied in J.E. Powell and K. Wallis, *The House of Lords in the Middle Ages* (London, 1968); J.S. Roskell, 'The Problem of the Attendance of the Lords in Medieval Parliaments', *BIHR* XXIX (1956); H. Miller, 'The Early Tudor Peerage, 1485 – 1537', *BIHR* XXIV (1951), summary of unpublished London MA thesis); W.H. Dunham Jr, *The Fane Fragment of the 1461 Lords' Journal* (London, 1935).

For the Commons see J.S. Roskell, 'The Social Composition of the Commons in a Fifteenth-Century Parliament', *BIHR*, XXIV (1951) and *The Commons in the Parliament of 1422* (Manchester, 1954). The scope of both these works is far wider than their titles indicate. A.R. Myers, 'Some Observations on the Procedure of the Commons in Dealing with Bills in the Lancastrian period', *Toronto Law Journal* III (1939). The pioneer work on borough representation was M. McKisack, *The Parliamentary Representa-*

tion of the English Boroughs During the Middle Ages (Oxford, 1932) but this now needs correction from Roskell's works. See also N. K. Houghton, 'Theory and Practice in Borough Elections to Parliament During the Later Fifteenth Century', *BIHR* XXXIX (1966). There are also good accounts of elections, patronage and influence in C. H. Williams, 'A Norfolk Parliamentary Election in the Fifteenth Century', *EHR* XL (1925); K. B. McFarlane, 'Parliament and Bastard Feudalism', *TRHS*, 4th series XXVI (1944); R. Virgoe, 'Three Sufolk Parliamentary Elections of the Mid-Fifteenth Century,' *BIHR* XXXIX (1966); Sir J. G. Edwards, 'The Huntingdonshire Parliamentary Election of 1450', in *Essays in Medieval History Presented to Bertie Wilkinson*, ed. T. A. Sandquist and M. R. Powicke (Toronto, 1969); A. Rogers, 'Parliamentary Elections in Grimsby in the Fifteenth Century', *BIHR* XLII (1969); P. Jalland, 'The Influence of the Aristocracy on Shire Elections in the North of England, 1450 – 1470', *Speculum* XLVII (1972) and 'The Revolution in Northern Borough Representation in Mid-Fifteenth-Century England', *Northern History* XI (1976). H. L. Gray, *The Influence of the Commons on Early Legislation: A Study of the Fourteenth and Fifteenth Centuries* (Harvard, 1932) is still useful in spite of somewhat exaggerated conclusions based on too narrow an interpretation of diplomatic investigations. A useful corrective is H. M. Cam, 'The Legislators of Medieval England ', *Proceedings of the British Academy* XXXI (1946), reprinted in *Lawfinders and Lawmakers* (London, 1962).

6 Royal Finance

The only full treatment, F. C. Dietz, *English Government Finance, 1485 – 1558* (Urbana, 1920) is notoriously unreliable. For acts of resumption and the crown lands the works of B. P. Wolffe are indispensable: 'Acts of Resumption in the Lancastrian Parliaments', *EHR* LXXIII (1958); 'The Management of English Royal Estates under the Yorkist Kings', *EHR* LXXI a(1956); and 'Henry VII's Land Revenues and Chamber Finance', *EHR* LXXIX (1964); *The Crown Lands 1461 – 1536* (London, 1970). *The Royal Demesne in English History: The Crown Estates in the Governance of the Realm from the Conquest to 1509* (London, 1971) revises the above-mentioned articles in the *EHR*, but at the same time the articles and book contain different information and to some extent supplement each other. See also W. C. Richardson, *Tudor Chamber Administration, 1485 – 1547* (Baton Rouge, 1952) and J. Hurstfield, 'The Revival of Feudalism in Early Tudor England', *History* XXXVII (1952). For the customs system N.S.B. Gras, *The Early English Customs System* (Harvard, 1916). H. S. B. Cobb, ' "Books of Rates" ' and the London Customs, 1507 – 1558', *The Guildhall Miscellany* IV no. 1 (1977) and E. M. Carus-Wilson, 'The Aulnage Accounts: A Criticism,' *EcHR* II (1929) deal with the inadequacies of the system of indirect taxation and probems of under – valuation De Lloyd Guth, 'Exchequer Penal Law Enforcement, 1485 – 1509' (unpublished University of Pittsburg PhD thesis, 1967) deals with Henry VII's attitude towards commercial taxation.   .

Direct taxation in the Yorkist period still needs investigation, but H. L. Gray 'The First Benevolence', in *Facts and factors in Economic History: Essays presented to E. F. Gay*, ed. A. E. Cole, A. L. Dunham and N.S.B. Gras (Cambridge, Mass., 1932) is suggestive. R. S. Schofield, 'Parliamentary Lay Taxation, 1485 – 1547 (unpublished Cambridge PhD thesis, 1964) is most useful. See also J.J. Scarisbrick, 'Clerical Taxation in England, 1485 – 1547', *JEH* II (1960).

7   The Church and Religion

Ecclesiastical organization and the state of the clergy

The most comprehensive account is A. Hamilton Thompson, *The English Clergy and their Organisation in the Later Middle Ages* (Oxford, 1957). It is, however, over-severe in its condemnation of bishops. R. L. Storey, *Diocesan Administration in the Fifteenth Century* (St Anthony's Hall Publications, no. 16, York, 1959) is mainly concerned with the first half of the fifteenth century and its conclusions need some modification for this period. J. T. Rosenthal, 'The Training of an Elite Group: English Bishops in the Fifteenth Century', *Transactions of the American Philosophical Society*, new series LX, part 5 (1970) deals with social origins, education and careers but does not go beyond 1485. See also R. J. Knecht, 'The Episcopate and the Wars of the Roses', *University of Birmingham Historical Journal* VI (1958). The *Dictionary of National Biography* contains useful articles on a number of bishops. The following items also contain useful information: R. Masek, 'The Humanistic Interests of the Early tudor Episcopate', *Church History* XXXIX (1970); A. F. Judd, 'Thomas Bekynton, Bishop of Bath and Wells', *JEH* VIII (1957) and *The Life of Thomas Bekynton* (Chichester, 1961); R. M. Haines, 'Aspects of the Episcopate of John Carpenter, Bishop of Worcester, 1444 – 76', *JEH* XIX (1968); R.B. Dobson, 'Richard Bell, Prior of Durham (1964 – 78) and Bishop of Carlisle (1478 – 95)', *Transactions of the Architectural and Archeological Society of Durham and Northumberland*, new series LXV (1965); M. Creigton, 'The Italian Bishops of Worcester,' in *Historical Essays and Reviews* (London, 1902); R. I. Woodhouse, *The Life of John Morton* (London, 1895); G. Parrish, *The Forgotten Primate: Archbishop Warham* (Historical Association, Hastings and Bexhill Branch, 1971); F. W. Steer, *Robert Sherburne, Bishop of Chichester* (Chicester Papers, no. 16, 1960); R. J. Knecht, 'The Political and Intellectual Activities of Cardinal John Morton and his Episcopal Colleagues' (unpublished MA thesis, London, 1953).

The best modern accounts of parish clergy are now to be found in M. Bowker, 'Non-Residence in the Lincoln Diocese in the Early Sixteenth Century', *JEH* XV (1964) and *The Secular Clergy in the Diocese of Lincoln* (Cambridge, 1968); P. Heath, *The English Parish Clergy on the Eve of the Reformation* (London, 1969); D. M. Owen, *Church and Society in Medieval Lincolnshire*, *History of Lincolnshire* V (Lincoln, 1971). These works are also most valuable for parish life and religious atmosphere. See also R. W. Dunning, 'Rural Deans in England in the Fifteenth Century', *BIHR* XL (1967); K. L. Wood-Legh, *A Small Household of the Fifteenth Century being the Account Book of Munden's Charity, Bridport* (Manchester, 1956); J. R. H. Moorman, 'The Medieval Parsonage and its Occupants, *BJRL* XXVIII (1944); W. Pantin, 'Medieval Priests' Houses in South-West England', *Medieval Archaeology* I (1957).

On endowment, benefactions and finances see K.L. Wood-Legh, *Perpetual Chantries in Britain* (Cambridge, 1965); E. F. Jacob, 'Founders and Foundations in the Later Middle Ages', *BIHR* XXXV (1962); G. H. Cook, *Medieval Chantries and Chantry Chapels* (London, 1947); R. B.

Dobson, 'The Foundation of Perpetual Chantries by the Citizens of Medieval York', *Studies in Church History*, ed. C. J. Cuming, IV (leiden, 1967). J. T. Rosenthal, The Purchase of Paradise: The Social Function of Aristocratic Benevolence, 1307 – 1485 (London, 1972) contains a great deal of useful information, but is unfortunately marred by irrelevant and anachronistic sociological speculation. W. K. Jordan, *Philanthropy in England, 1480 – 1660: A Study in the Changing Pattern of Social Aspirations* (London, 1959) should be read with W. G. Bittle and R. T. Lane 'Inflation and Philanthropy in England: 'A ReAssessment of W.K. Jordan's Data', *EcHR*, 2nd series XXIX (1976), which corrects its very dubious statistics. D. I. Hill, *The Ancient Hospitals and Almshouses of Canterbury* (Canterbury Archeological Society, Occasional Papers, no 6, 1969); J.A.F. Thomson, 'Piety and Charity in Late Medieval London', *JEH* XXI (1965).

Piety

The form and tone of piety can be studied in W. A. Pantin, *The English Church in the Fourteenth Century* (Cambridge, 1955) which contains a good deal of information equally relevant for the fifteenth century; E. M. G. Routh, *Lady Margaret, A Memoir of Lady Margaret Beaufort* (Oxford, 1924); C. A. J. Armstrong, 'The Piety of Cecily, Duchess of York: A Study in Late Medieval Culture', in *For Hilaire Belloc*, ed. D. Woodruff (London, 1942); K. Chesney, 'Notes on Some Treatises of Devotion intended for Margaret of York (MS. Douce 365)', *Medium Aevum* XX (1951); R. Lovett, 'The Imitation of Christ in Late Medieval England', *TRHS*, 5th series XVII (1968); V. M. Lagorio, 'The Evolving Legend of St Joseph of Glastonbury', *Speculum* XLVI (1971); R. W. Pfaff, *New Liturgical Feasts in Later Medieval England* (Oxford, 1970); F. Warren (ed.), *The Dance of Death* (Early English Text Society, old series, no. 181, 1931); E. F. Jacob. 'The Book of St Albans', *BJRL* XXVIII (1944); E. C. Dunn, 'Popular Devotion in the Vernacular Drama of Medieval England', *Medievalia et Humanistica* IV (1973); J. W. Blench, *Preaching in England in the Late Fifteenth and Sixteenth Centuries* (Oxford, 1964); T. H. McDonald 'The Piety of Englishmen under Henry VII' (University of Washington PhD thesis, 1957). See also Bowker, 'Non-Residence in the Lincoln Diocese' and *The Secular Clergy*, and Heath, *The English Parish Clergy*. A. G. Dickens, *The Marian Reaction in the Diocese of York* (St Anthony's Hall Publications, nos. 11 and 12, York, 1957) contains reflections which equally apply to this period. D. J. Hall, *English Medieval Pilgrimage* (London, 1966).

Heresy

K. B. McFarlane, *Lancastrian Kings and Lollard Knights* (Oxford, 1972) brilliantly analyses the development of lay piety and its relationship to Lollardy. J.A.F. Thomson, *The Later Lollards, 1414 – 50* (Oxford, 1965); A.G. Dickens, *Lollards and Protestants in the Diocese of York, 1509 – 1558* (London, 1959). Also M. Aston, 'Lollardy and the Reformation: Survival or Revival?' *History* XLIX (1964) and 'John Wycliffe's Reformation Reputation', *PP* no. 30 (1965); A.G. Dickens, 'Heresy and the Origins of English Protestantism', in *Britain and the Netherlands*, ed. J.S. Bromley and E.H. Kossman (1964); J. Fines, 'Heresy Trials in the Diocese of Coventry and Lichfield, 1511 – 12', *JEH* XIV (1963); E.F. Jacob, 'Reynold Peacock, Bishop of Chicester', *Procedings of the British Academy* (1952). J.F. Davis,

'Lollard Survival and the Textile Industry in the South-East of England', in *Studies in Church History*, ed. C.J. Cuming, III (Leiden, 1966) deals with the later phases of Lollardy. M.D. Lambert *Medieval Heresy: Popular Movements From Bogomil to Hus* (1977), chapters 14 and 15 provide a lively and useful summary.

Relations with the Papacy

Anglo-Papal relations are dealt with by F.R.H. Du Boulay, 'The Fifteenth Century', in *The English Church and the Papacy in the Middle Ages*, ed. C.H. Lawrence (London, 1965); C. Head, 'Aeneas Silvius Piccolomini's Reflections on England, 1436 – 1458', *Catholic Historical Review* LIX (1973); J.J. Scarisbrick, 'Clerical Taxation in England, 1485 – 1547'. *JEH* XI (1960); E.F. Jacob, *Essays in the Conciliar Epoch* (2nd edn, Manchester, 1953); D. Hay, 'The Church of England in the later Middle Ages', *History* LIII (1968).

Taxation and patronage

The following also deal with clerical taxation: F.R.H. Du Boulay, 'Charitable Subsidies granted to the Archbishop of Canterbury', *BIHR* XXIII (1950). For patronage see J.T. Rosenthal, 'Richard, Duke of York: A Fifteenth-Century Layman and the Church', *Catholic Historical Review* L (1964) and R.I. Jack, 'The Ecclesiastical Patronage Exercised by a Baronial Family in the Late Middle Ages', *Journal of Religious History* III (1965).

C. B. Firth, 'Benefit of Clergy in the Time of Edward IV', *EHR* XXXII (1917) and L. C. Gabel, *Benefit of Clergy in England in the Later Middle Ages* (Smith College Studies in History XIV, nos 1 – 4, Northampton, Mass., 1928 – 9) analyse the technicalities of juridical relationships.

Monasticism

Writers on the late middle ages must rely upon Dom David Knowles's magisterial *The Religious Orders in England* II, III (Cambridge, 1955, 1959) which also contains much fascinating information about the church generally. However, it is perhaps a shade too severe in its condemnation of the religious. Some of his conclusions are summarized in 'The English Monasteries in the Later Middle Ages', *History* XXXIX (1954). R. B. Dobson, *Durham Priory, 1400 – 1450* (Cambridge, 1973) and E. Searle, *Lordship and Community: Battle Abbey and its Banlieu, 1066 – 1538* (Toronto, Pontifical Institute of Medieval Studies, 1974) brilliantly analyse the relationships between major monasteries and their local communities and the former also gives a very good analysis of the spiritual and intellectual atmosphere of the house.

P. Cowley, *The Church Houses* (London, 1970) describes an interesting religio-social development.

8 Education and Culture

The development of education

This is best discussed in N. Orme, *English Schools in the Middle Ages* (London, 1973), with an excellent bibliography. J. Simon *Education and Society in Tudor England* (Cambridge, 1966) is excessively anti-clerical in tone. For numbers of schools see J. N. Miner, 'Schools and Literacy in Later Medieval England', *British Journal of Educational Studies* XI (1963) and P. J. Wallis, *Histories of Old Schools: A Revised List for England and Wales* (Department of Education, University of Newcastle upon Tyne, 1966). H. G. Richardson, 'An Oxford Teacher of the Fifteenth Century', *BJRL* XXIII (1939) and 'Business Training in Medieval Oxford', *American Historical Review* XLVI (1940 – 1941) discuss the training of lay officials. See also J. W. Adamson, 'The Extent of Literacy in the XV and XVI Centuries, *The Library*, 4th series X (1929 – 30). R. Weiss, *Humanism in England During the Fifteenth Century*, (2nd edn, Oxford, 1957) and R. J. Mitchell, *John Free, From Bristol to Rome in the Fifteenth Century* (London, 1955) discuss the introduction and development of humanism.

Literature and Drama

E. K. Chambers, *English Literature at the Close of the Middle Ages* (Oxford, 1945), H. S. Bennett, *English Books and Readers 1475 – 1557* (Cambridge, 1952), A. Renoir, *The Poetry of John Lydgate* (London, 1967) and T. D. Kenderick, *British Antiquity* (London, 1960) discuss contemporary taste in historical writing and literature. A. B. Ferguson, *The Indian Summer of English Chivalry* (Durham, N. Carolina, 1960); *The Macro Plays: The Castle of Perseverence, Wisdom, Mankind* (Early English Text Society, 1969). For editions of mystery plays, *The Wakefield Mystery Plays*, ed. M. Rose (New York, 1961). Excellent on the development of drama are R. Southern, *The Medieval Theatre in the Round* (London and Oxford, 1957) and G. Wickham, *The Medieval Theatre* (London, 1974).

W.J.B Crotch, *The Prologues and Epilogues of William Caxton* (Early English Text Society, 1928, reprinted 1956) and N.F. Blake, *Caxton and his World* (London, 1969) provide excellent accounts of England's first printer. K.B. McFarlane illustrates the provincial literary scene in East Anglia in 'William Worcester: A Preliminary Survey', in *Studies Presented to Sir Hilary Jenkinson*, ed. J. Conway Davis (Oxford, 1957). Worcester's own *Itineraries*, ed. J.H. Harvey, (Oxford, 1969) vividly reveal the interest of an intelligent, antiquarian-minded layman. See also J.H. Fisher, 'Chancery and the Emergence of Standard Written English in the Fifteenth Century', *Speculum* LII (1977).

Architecture and the arts

Of recent works the following are stimulating: G. Webb, *Architecture in Britain: The Middle Ages* (Pelican History of Art, 1956); J.A. Wright, *Brick Building in England from the Middle Ages to 1550* (London, 1972) discusses the revival of this material. M. Girouard, *Robert Smythson and the Architecture of the Elizabethan Era* (London, 1966) is of far wider scope than its title indicates; M.W. Barley, *The English Farm House and Cottage* (London, 1961); M. Wood, *The English Medieval House* (London, 1965); M. Rickert, *Painting in Britain: The Middle Ages* (Pelican History of Art, 1954); L. Stone, *Sculpture in Britain: The Middle Ages* (Pelican History of Art, 1955). E. G. Millar, *English Illuminated Manuscripts of the Fourteenth and Fifteenth Centuries* (Paris and Brussels, *1928*) and F. E. Howard and M. Crossley, *English Church Woodwork* (London, 1917) remain standard works. B. Snook, *English Historical Embroidery* (London, 1960) is interesting.

9 Politics

J. R. Lander, *The Wars of the Roses* (London, 1965, paperback edn, New york, 1967), presents a selection of contemporary documents and a narrative. C. D. Ross, *The Wars of the Roses* (London, 1976) is an excellent narrative and analysis with splendid illustrations. S. B. Chrimes, *Lancastrians, Yorkists and Henry VII* (London, 1964) gives a good account of the dynastic conflict. For the events leading up to the Yorkist revolution of 1461, K. B. McFarlane, 'The Wars of the Roses', *Proceedings' of the British Academy* L (1965) stresses the weakness of Henry VI and R. L. Storey, *The End of the House of Lancaster* (London, 1966) also emphasizes the growth of local feuds. See also R. A. Griffiths, 'Richard of York's Intentions in 1450 and the Origins of the Wars of the Roses', *Journal of Medieval History* I (1975). For the most recent interpretation of Henry VI's character and its effects on politics see B. P. Wolffe, 'The Personal Rule of Henry VI', in *Fifteenth-Century England*, ed. Chrimes, Ross and Griffiths. The following also provide interesting information and new interpretations. R. A. Griffiths, 'Gruffydd ap Nicholas and the Rise of the House of Dinefwr', *The National Library of Wales Journal* XIII, no. 3 (1964) and 'Local Rivalries and National Politics: the Percies, the Nevilles and the duke of Exeter', *Speculum* XLIII (1968); R. L. Storey, 'Lincolnshire and the Wars of the Roses', *Nottingham Medieval Studies* XIV (1970); R. Virgoe, 'The Death of William de la Pole, Duke of Suffolk' and 'William Tailboys and Lord Cromwell: Crime and Politics in Lancastrian England', *BJRL* XLVII (1965) and LV (1973); M. I. Peake, 'London and the Wars of the Roses, 1445 – 1465', (unpublished London MA thesis, 1925), summarized in *BIHR* IV (1926 – 7); T. B. Pugh, 'The Marcher Lords of Glamorgan, 1317 – 1485', in *Glamorgan County History* III; J. R. Lander, 'Henry VI and the Duke of York's Second Protectorate, 1455 – 6', *BJRL* XLIII (1960) and 'Marriage and Politics in the Fifteenth Century: The Nevilles and the Wydevilles', *BIHR* XXXVI (1963), both reprinted in *Crown and Nobility*; J. S. Roskell, 'The Problem of the Attendance of the Lords in Medieval Parliaments', *BIHR* XXIX (1956); G. L. Harriss, 'The Struggle for Calais: an Aspect of the Rivalry between Lancaster and York', *EHR* LXXV (1960); C. A. J. Armstrong, 'The Inauguration Ceremonies of the Yorkist Kings and their Titles to the Throne', *TRHS*, 4th series XXX (1948).

On the Yorkist period, C. L. Scofield, *The Life and Reign of Edward IV* (2 vols, London, 1923) provides an immensely detailed and accurate political narrative but its general interpretation is out of date. C. Ross, *Edward IV* (London, 1974) has now provided a very well-written interpretation soundly based on recent scholarship. See also J. R. Lander, 'Edward IV: The Modern Legend and a Revision', *History* XLI (1956). Also the same author's 'Marriage and Politics' and 'The Treason and Death of the Duke of Clarence: A Reinterpretation', *Canadian Journal of History* II (1967). These studies are reprinted in *Crown and Nobility*, together with an Introduction analysing the current trends of late fifteenth-century English scholarship. For Edward IV's personal activities in government see J.G. Bellamy, 'Justice Under the Yorkist Kings', *American Journal of Legal History* IX (1965). The following are also interesting accounts of particular episodes: M.A. Hicks, 'The Case of Sir Thomas Cook, 1468', *EHR* XCIII (1978); C.F. Richmond, 'Fauconberg's Kentish Rising of May, 1471', *EHR* LXXXV (1970); J.A.F. Thomson, 'The Arrival of Edward IV: the Development of the Text', *Speculum* XLVI (1971); E.W. Ives, 'Andrew Dymmock and the papers of Anthony Earl Rivers, 1482 – 3', *BIHR* XLI (1968); N. Baker and R. Birley, 'Jane Shore', *Etoniana*, nos., 125, 126 (1972); A. R. Myers, 'The Household of Queen Elizabeth Wydeville, 1466 – 7', *BJRL* L (1967 – 8); D.H. Thomas, 'The Herberts of Raglan as supporters of the House of York in the Second Half of the Fifteenth Century', (unpublished MA thesis, University of Wales, 1968).

J. Gairdner, *The Life and Reign of Richard III* (revised edn Cambridge, 1898) still provides the best detailed account of the reign though too uncritical of Sir Thomas More's views. A. Hanham, *Richard III and His Early Historians, 1483 – 1535* (Oxford, 1975) is interesting but the author's views on Lord Hasting's death have not found general acceptance. See also: M. Levine, 'Richard III – Usurper of Lawful King', *Speculum* XXXIV (1959); A.R. Myers, 'The Character Richard III' *History Today* IV (1954) and 'Richard III and Historical Tradition', *History* LIII (1968). See also H.G. Hanbury 'The Legislation of Richard III', *American Journal of Legal History* VI (1962). P. Tudor-Craig, *Richard III* (National Portrait Gallery Exhibition Catalogue, 2nd edn, 1977) provides fascinating, unusual information which throws considerable light upon Richard's character. A.J. Pollard, 'The Tyranny of Richard III' *Journal of Medieval History* III (1977) provides a new interpretation of Richard as a 'tyrant' based largely upon opinion in southern England which the king, flying in the face of contemporary opinion, tried to control by grants of estates and offices to northerners.

The standard work on Henry VII is now S.B. Chrimes, *Henry VII* (London, 1972). See also by Chrimes, 'The Reign of Henry VII', in *Fifteenth-Century England*, ed. Chrimes, Ross and Griffiths; R.L. Storey, *The Reign of Henry VII* (London, 1968) is shorter and most readable. Sir Francis Bacon, *The History of the Reign of King Henry the Seventh*, ed. R. Lockyer (London, 1971) remains worth reading for its insights, but see the criticism of it given in Chrimes. See also G.L. Harris and P. Williams, 'A Revolution in Tudor History: Dr Elton's Interpretation of the Age', *PP* no. 25 (1963). Conflicting views on the king's character and the nature of his government are to be found in the following articles: G. R. Elton, 'Henry VII: Rapacity and Remorse', *HJ* I (1958); J. P. Cooper, 'Henry VII's last years reconsidered', *HJ* II (1958), and G. R. Elton, 'Henry VII: A Restatement', *HJ* IV (1961). For Henry's relations with the nobility see J. R. Lander, 'Attainder and Forfeiture, 1453 to 1509', *HJ* IV (1961) and 'Bonds, Coercion and Fear: Henry VII and the Peerage', in *Florilegium Historiale*, ed. Rowe and Stockdale, both reprinted in *Crown and Nobility*. For contemporary revelation of the king's character, 'The Petition of Edmund Dudley', *EHR* LXXXVII (1972). R. Somerville, 'Henry VII's Council Learned in the Law', *EHR* LIV (1939) and *History of the Duchy of Lancaster* I (1953) are useful for Henry's administrative methods.

For both Yorkists and Tudors see also the sections on 'Government and the State' and 'Royal Finance'.

Foreign Policy

Foreign policy is best studied in Scofield, *Edward* IV; J. Calmette and G. Périnelle, *Louis XI et l'Angleterre 1461 – 1483* (Paris, 1930); A. J. Dunlop, *The Life and Times of James Kennedy, Bishop of St Andrews* (Edinburgh and London, 1950); M. R. Thielmans, *Bourgogne et Angleterre, Rélations*

Politiques et Economiques Entre Les Pays-Bas Bourguignons et l'Angleterre, 1435 – 1467 (Brussels, 1966); B. A. Pocquet de Haut-Jussé, *Francois II, duc de Bretagne et l'Angleterre, 1458 – 88* (Paris, 1929); R. Vaughan, *Philip the Good* (London, 1970) and *Charles the Bold* (London, 1973); C.A.J. Armstrong, 'The Burgundian Netherlands', in *The New Cambridge Modern History* I, ed., G.R. Potter (1957). R.B. Wernham, *Before the Armada* (London, 1966) is a brilliant synthesis. See also J.R. Lander, 'The Hundred Years War and Edward IV's 1475 Campaign in France', in *Tudor Men and Institutions: Studies in English Law Government*, ed. A.J. Slavin (Baton Rouge, Louisiana, 1972, reprinted in *Crown and Nobility*).

Additional note

Since this book was written the following very valuable works have appeared: C. Platt, *Medieval England. A Social History and Archaeology from the Conquest to A.D. 1600* (London, 1978) and M. Blatcher, *The Court of King's Bench, 1450 – 1550: A Study in Self-Help* (London, 1978).

Index